Instructional
Software

Instructional
Software

Principles and Perspectives for Design and Use

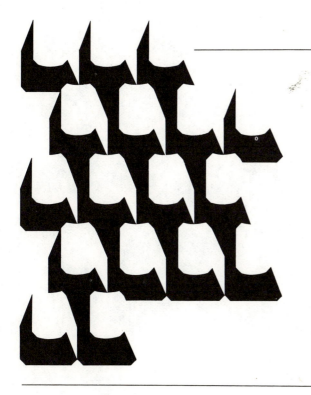

Decker F. Walker
Stanford University

Robert D. Hess
Stanford University

Wadsworth Publishing Company
Belmont, California
A Division of Wadsworth, Inc.

Education Editor: *Bob Podstepny*
Production Editor: *Gary Mcdonald*
Managing Designer: *Detta Penna*
Designer: *Adriane Bosworth*
Copy Editor: *Brenda Griffing*
Technical Illustrator: *Innographics*
Cover: *Adriane Bosworth*
Signing Representative: *Tina Allen*

Printed in the United States of America

1 2 3 4 5 6 7 8 9 10—88 87 86 85 84

ISBN 0-534-01459-3

Library of Congress Cataloging in Publication Data

Main entry under title:

Instructional software.

  Includes bibliographies.
  1. Computer-assisted instruction—Addresses, essays, lectures. 2. Computer-assisted instruction—Computer programs—Addresses, essays, lectures. I. Walker, Decker F. II. Hess, Robert D.
LB1028.5.I54 1984   370′.28′5   83–12531
ISBN 0-534-01459-3

Table of Contents

Part 3
Strategies for
Developing
Educational
Software   95

Preface

We believe that educators can do great things with computers but whether or not they will depends on their ability to create exciting, powerful educational utilities that optimize the computer's potential for engaging students constructively and improving the quality of their education.

It is not obvious whether we will do so, or how rapid our progress will be. The spirit of technology is in the human purpose to which it is addressed. Television is a sobering—some believe depressing—example for the growing cadre of educators who believe in educational uses of technology. The enormous power of TV to act as "a window to the world" to introduce us to inaccessible domains is reality in our everyday and public life. We see men walk on the moon, the Superbowl is watched by millions of viewers throughout the world, the dust and blood of war are brought home daily. But television has scarcely begun to influence formal education. The uses of TV and videotape in the classroom are routine—televising lectures to huge assemblages of students, videotaping those lectures for later viewing. But these uses do not touch the power, excitement, and information packed into a slow motion replay of a winning touchdown.

One reason for this state of affairs, it is said, is expense. If that is a valid excuse (which we doubt), it no longer holds. Video cameras and tapes are available at reasonable prices. It certainly will not hold for the educational technologies of the future if the current estimates of expanded power at lower prices are even roughly on target.

Creating educational programs for computers has been the work of a few brilliant, farsighted pioneers working in large, expensive facilities. Although we expect that high-quality educational software will continue to be produced by teams in technologically sophisticated centers, computers and the programs necessary to use them are within reach of most educators. Machines are available in most schools in the United States (the number of elementary schools with computers increased by more than 50 percent last year). Learning to program is not as difficult as learning to write. The pool of potential developers of educational software will soon be as large as the pool of potential authors of printed materials.

A golden age of educational computing would seem to be at hand, except for one barrier. Learning to program is no more learning to develop good educational software than learning to write is learning to develop good textbooks. The development of effective educational software is partly craft and partly applied science. Much of the necessary competence can be learned. A number of practitioners and researchers have the knowledge and experience to help the newcomer but this knowledge is not readily available. We have created this book to make some of the best published work on software development available to those who want to contribute to the growing list of high-quality educational software.

In preparation for our first seminar in Stanford's Interactive Educational Technology Program in the autumn of 1981, we searched without success for a suitable text. We found several useful books on computers in education but these did not deal in sufficient depth with the problems of designing good courseware. In a search for materials for the program, we combed the libraries at Stanford, conducted on-line searches of all relevant bibliographic data bases, and followed up recommendations of colleagues at Stanford and elsewhere. The number of people active for more than ten years in the development of educational software is not large; the field is relatively young. But they have produced articles in an impressive variety of journals—computer science, psychology, education, and other disciplines—as well as occasional papers in various forms. Our search, which began with that seminar and continued into the last production stage of this book, generated over 300 titles from which we selected the 21 included here.

Developing good educational software requires competence of several kinds. The courseware writer must know some technical aspects of the computer—its capabilities and limitations—and the languages to which it will respond. This volume is primarily for students who already have a knowledge of micros and programming or are gaining such knowledge. Our concern is with the use of the technology: The coursewriter must possess a firm knowledge of design of educational materials and the psychological/educational principles that make the student's exchange with the computer most effective. The writer of high-quality educational software is thus an expert in the applied science of software design. This expertness must cover a variety of fields.

The outline of this cluster of readings shows our view of the major areas in which competence is most essential. First, there should be a view of the role of computer-based education in the society and what the prospects are for the future. We include relevant articles in Part 1. Next, the coursewriter needs to have an understanding of the principles, both educational and psychological (if, indeed, these are not inextricably interwoven) that govern learning and teaching. Matters of attention, motivation, the effects of feedback, the importance of using organizers to guide and prepare the students' thinking, and the cognitive processes involved in problem solving are relevant here. We selected articles in Part 2 to provide some of these theoretical perspectives.

With this understanding, the task of implementing such knowledge through a program that is effective requires knowledge about how to display information on the screen, how to design for interactive learning, how to handle response time, provide knowledge of results, and tailor the program to the characteristics of the student. Part 3 includes some of these principles of design and implementation.

Evaluation, informal and formal, is not only as essential in educational courseware as in other educational forms, but the capabilities of the computer open new areas in evaluation. The machine, with its prodigious memory and speed, can accumulate information about the student and use this information to guide the student's progress. Some programs have built-in evaluations—it is not possible to complete the program without having mastered the concepts or used the information the course offered. This capability has implications for testing. The issues raised will be around for a long time; the articles in Part 4 offer the coursewriter some of the knowledge and concepts that will help keep her in touch with the field.

Part 5 stretches the imagination. The future of educational computing is uncertain in some respects but there is no doubt that it is exciting and challenging. The articles in this part of the book are intended to open possibilities, encourage the students to imagine what can be done in the future, and sense that they are, or can be, part of a new era in education.

Acknowledgments

We have many debts. We thank the authors who agreed to let us share their writings with our readers. A large number of our colleagues at and near Stanford have encouraged us in our efforts to begin a new program and put together a volume that would express our view of some current issues: Pat Suppes, Jamey Friend, Derek Sleeman, Ed Haertel, Mike Genesereth, Tom Malone, Mark Lepper, Bill Clancy, Michael Carter, Wallace Judd, Bobby Goodson, and Ann Lathrop.

The students in our first class supported, nudged, criticized, and inspired us with their commitment to the field. We are grateful for their help in getting a new enterprise underway. Dean Myron Atkin provided support, both administrative and financial, which made the program, and this book, possible. We acknowledge, with more thanks than they realize, the contributions of Ted Kahn, Director of the Institute for Educational Action Research, set up by ATARI, and Gregg Smith and Carolyn Stauffer, both of the Foundation for the Advancement of Computer-aided Education, established by Apple Computer Company, who provided us with computers for our program.

No support was more essential or more efficient than that provided by Dorothy Brink.

Our reviewers gave us the sort of critiques we expect from knowledgeable colleagues. They were Royal Van Horn, University of North Florida; Mary Grace Kantowsky, University of Florida; William H. Sanders, Indiana University; John C. Belland, Ohio State University; Herb Nickles, California State University at San Bernardino; and Charlie Reigeluth, Syracuse University. Phil Cartwright prepared an original article on short notice and under pressure. The staff at Wadsworth was outstanding in its intelligence, tact, and efficiency. The book benefits greatly from their guidance; we benefited personally from the chance to work with them.

DECKER F. WALKER
ROBERT D. HESS
Palo Alto

Introduction: Designing Educational Software

The Potential of a New Medium for Teaching

It is difficult to appreciate the possibilities and limitations of a new medium of instruction. For decades after printing became widespread, printed books imitated manuscript forms. Early movies and television shows imitated plays for the stage. Only gradually did publishers realize the versatility of print and producers learn what film and TV could accomplish by exploring the features that made these media distinctive.

Educators are now presented with a tool, the microcomputer, that adds several dimensions to their repertoire of educational instrumentalities. It enables the educator to collect information about whether the students' responses are right or wrong, to categorize the students' errors, and to note the time delay of the response. These things can be done unobtrusively and can be recorded as part of a file of information that is gathered about the mental characteristics and progress of each student. Such information can be used to tailor subsequent instruction—to adjust the level of difficulty of succeeding problems, to send the student on a branching program to work out a specific aspect of a problem that is creating difficulties, or to practice an aspect of a problem that needs to be learned more thoroughly. These possibilities greatly expand the capacity of the teacher to interact with the students individually. This fast, intelligent medium enables teachers to offer such individualized instruction to a larger number of students than is possible in a classroom setting.

The computer also opens a world of graphics and image processing. Manipulating images is for the first time as simple, in principle, as manipulating symbols. Visual and spatial abilities can be drawn into the educational enterprise much more readily. Combining image processing with interactivity makes it possible to create simulated worlds with which students can interact in an almost unlimited variety of ways. Simulations offer a new tool for combining experiential learning with abstract analysis and symbolic reasoning.

This medium opens a different world for students and their teachers. It presents new opportunities for mastery and for self-expression. For example, in fields such as computer-aided design, it lowers the entry barriers to complex activities by carrying out some of the necessary complex calculations automatically. In other respects, the computer offers a demanding environment. It forgives few errors; it demands that students learn to use its peculiar logic. But it carries no grudges, has no ethnic or gender bias, and forgives mistakes of the past once students have learned its language.

All these powers and others of which we may not yet be aware lie ready to be put to use. The opportunity and, we believe, the responsibility for helping students and teachers use these resources are in the hands of the designer of educational software. The designer of software can help us realize the potential of electronic educational technology.

Educators as Computer Software Designers

Educators cannot depend on programmers or computer specialists to invent educational forms for the new medium. The results of programming that makes sophisticated use of technology but is educationally naive are, unhappily, already evident in computer games that are meant to be educational. Spend a few minutes with the software created by someone knowledgeable about educational practice but naive in programming, and it is evident that technically primitive programs—screenfuls of print, dull computer-assisted instruction (CAI), slow, crude block graphics—are not the answer, either. The field of educational software design needs educational skill and imagination. Educators can provide these resources if they can take the time to study the new medium, acquire technical skill, and learn how to put it to best use. This is not easy. Whether working alone or in a team, the educator will have to learn to program. The educator–designer will need to know what the microcomputer can and cannot do, what is easily done, and what takes weeks or months.

No single book can teach educators the technical skills that underlie competence in designing educational software. Months, perhaps years, of study and consultation are required. The programmer or computer scientist who learns to design educational software faces an equally difficult task. Much of what he or she needs to know—the educational intuition and imagination that go into a high quality curriculum—has not been codified in books and courses. Perhaps this is indeed partly an art, not entirely amenable to statement in formal terms. Our aim in this book is to provide material that will help the student build bridges between education, computer science, and psychology so that people who know part of what they need to design good educational software can begin to learn the rest.

Every designer relies on skill, judgment, intuition, artfulness, and personal experience, mixed with trial and error, to create effective uses of computers for instruction. But any person's resources are limited; designers "borrow" from one another and from any other source to augment their personal efforts. The curriculum designer who works with computers has four resources to draw on: the work of other designers, research, new developments in computer systems, and evaluations of computer-based courseware.

The Readings in This Book

We have tried to include contributions of authors from each of the areas just enumerated. Part 1 begins with a review by Chambers and Sprecher of developments in CAI around the world and of the findings from evaluations of these programs. Malone and Levin report the proceedings of a conference held in 1981 in which more than a dozen active developers of educational software discussed the principles they use in their work.

Parts 2 and 3 are distinguishable components of a single process—the application of sound principles to designing educational courseware. The professional who designs a course or lesson for use with computers builds into the structure of the program many assumptions about the human mind—for example, its ability to grasp symbols, the speed with which it can follow instructions, and its ability to hold information in short- or long-term memory. The programmer also makes assumptions about the effectiveness of different kinds of feedback to the students' errors when selecting the type of feedback to give to an incorrect response or the appropriate reaction to a correct answer. In the training of human teachers, we rely on the judgment and experience of each teacher to decide how to deal with such specific situations. In the design of computer programs, everything in the program is included deliberately; what is included follows an implicit or explicit decision about the properties of the mind or principles of pedagogy.

A rapidly growing body of research about

human learning and mental activities offers a resource for programmers who want to base their decisions on empirical work. Systematic investigations conducted during the past two decades (much of it stimulated by attempts to model human thought with computers) have focused on specific mental operations, rather than on attempts to measure intelligence as a global ability. Studies of memory, in particular, have yielded a great deal of information that will be useful to the educational programmer. For instance, some aspects of memory are affected very little by practice. Short-term memory remains limited to the classic "seven plus or minus two" principle, identified more than twenty years ago. But techniques of chunking a large number of items into fewer groups can increase effective memory. Research on mental processes is a powerful resource for designing educational programs.

The readings in Part 2 describe some of the fundamental ideas from cognitive and motivational psychology and human factors research that can be applied to computer-based educational design. They present ideas of interest to the educational software designer, illustrating what can be done by the programmer who studies the research literature and applies the most relevant findings.

In Part 3 the application of psychological and instructional principles is more explicit. Alfred Bork describes the software production system he uses at the University of California, Irvine, and considers the issues involved in different approaches to software production. Brian Gaines of the Centre for Man–Computer Studies in London offers seventeen rules he and his staff have developed for designing interactive man–computer dialogues. Jamesine Friend and James Milojkovic draw on experience in designing CAI to develop guidelines for handling certain aspects of interactive learning, especially processing students' responses and offering verbal rewards. Neil Rowe discusses rules for good simulations, and Balman describes a strategy in which the computer substitutes for laboratory experiments in teaching science and technology.

These authors are experienced educational software designers talking to their peers, explaining what they have learned in their work. They offer specific examples of working with programming languages and illustrate ways of thinking about problems of software design.

Evaluation as a Means of Improving Educational Software

The final and most direct test of the value of any design is how it performs in practice. Unfortunately, rigorous evaluation of the educational outcomes of new computer programs is not yet an established practice. Evaluation of programs seems to be following the traditional pattern of assessing other educational materials. Few textbooks receive more than a cursory field trial, with impressionistic testimony from the teachers in the field. The same can be said for most educational films and television programs and, indeed, for all but a handful of educational reforms. We now have techniques that permit a flexible, powerful assessment of most outcomes sought in conventional instruction, as demonstrated by the evaluations of federally sponsored reforms devised in the 1970s.

In Part 4, Reeves and Lent take stock of evaluation methods applicable to microcomputer-based educational programs. Evaluations of computer-based educational programs are reviewed by Kulik, Bangert, and Williams. Walker and Hess examine some of the evaluation options open to the developer, ranging from informal assessment by reviewers to full-scale formal evaluations.

The importance of sound field evaluations to the continued development of quality educational software cannot be overemphasized. As the use of computers in schools mushroomed, the demand for software ran ahead of the supply. Teachers and schools have been obliged to buy almost anything that seemed to meet their immediate needs; any usable product has found a market. In such a climate, bad software thrived along with the good. Without evaluation, good software can get lost amid the bad and the mediocre. Not even the most experienced computer-using educator can know for certain the marks of a first-rate educational program. Our judgment in this matter must be informed by careful evaluations of the educational results achieved by various programs.

New Developments in Computer Capabilities

Computers form a dynamic, evolving medium for teaching. Small, inexpensive machines can do today what only large, expensive ones could do just a few years ago. New hardware and software appear almost daily on the market or in the research and development laboratory, offering the designer new tools and new resources. What is difficult or impossible today may become commonplace tomorrow, so the designer needs to follow developments in computer systems. For instance, computer graphics on microcomputers were slow and crude until recently. Now high resolution graphics with multiple shades and color mixing are readily available, along with graphics tablets for "drawing" the images. Just over the horizon are interactive video disks, which promise even more realistic images by the thousands, making computer animation feasible at low cost. Another developing area is the interfacing capability of microcomputers as control devices with mechanical and electrical equipment. This growing field will offer new resources for training a range of skills. David Hon's work in interfacing a microcomputer with a dummy to teach cardiopulmonary resuscitation (CPR) is an example of what can be done with this type of hardware.[1]

The readings in Part 5 explore developments in two areas that are important to educational software design. The first of these is programming. Most educational software for

microcomputers today is written in BASIC. Where speed is important, programs must be written in assembly language. Authoring languages and authoring systems such as Pilot or Tutor have their proponents. Newer languages such as C and Forth are gaining adherents. What will the future hold? What computer language(s) should today's designer learn? What aides and utilities for programming will appear? Wasserman and Gutz identify several powerful trends in the development of programming languages that we may expect to see in the future.

The remaining readings in Part 5 deal with intelligent computer-assisted instruction (ICAI)—the application of techniques from artificial intelligence to educational software. Artificial intelligence programming techniques promise several powerful additions to the designer's tool kit. One of these is natural language communication. A second is comprised of self-modifying programs—programs that can change their own parameters in response to information accumulated over time about a student's learning style or in response to a student's performance on any given session. Also, programs are emerging that respond to student initiative. Within limits, students can query a program as they might a human tutor and stand a reasonable chance of getting a satisfactory answer. Programs can use heuristic strategies to diagnose learning difficulties or to administer tutoring help. ICAI programs require more memory and a higher operating speed than today's personal computers provide, but the rapidity of development in hardware suggests that affordable machines capable of accommodating programs that use these techniques will soon be available.

NOTE

1. D. Hon, Interactive training in cardiopulmonary resuscitation. *Byte* (7), 108–141, June 1982.

Issues in the Educational Use of Computers

Two very different perspectives on computers in education are apparent in the articles selected for an overview of some important issues in developing materials for use with computers. The first is a systematic, historical review of recent developments in CAI; the other takes us to a conference on issues in writing educational software.

Chambers and Sprecher make it clear that, despite the stereotypes about CAI, when you have seen one CAI program you have not seen them all. On close inspection, a remarkable variety of programs can be seen to fit under this broad label. The potential use of computers in education has only recently gained visibility throughout the educational community, and it is easy for beginners to assume that they are stepping into a new field. This chapter helps give some idea of the large, varied, and in many ways excellent selection of educational software that neophytes inherit as they organize code for their first educational programming venture. The computer-based educational community is active and impressive. This article introduces some of the pioneers of the field.

Malone and Levin offer discussions of more recent versions of problems involved in preparing educational materials for computers. They report the proceedings of a conference held in 1981 that brought together more than a dozen active developers of educational software to discuss the principles they actually use in their current work. This group of informal papers gives a brief glimpse of the perspectives that some of the most active professionals have of the task of software development and the interaction between students and the machine. New designers of educational materials will be impressed with how much the field has developed; they may also be impressed with how many problems remain.

Computer-Assisted Instruction: Current Trends and Critical Issues

Jack A. Chambers and
Jerry W. Sprecher

California State University

1. Introduction

The focus of this paper is upon the learning situation and upon the use of the computer to provide course content instruction in the form of simulations, games, tutorials, and drill and practice. In the United States this has come to be known as computer-assisted instruction (CAI), and in the United Kingdom and elsewhere as computer-assisted learning (CAL). Throughout this paper the term CAI should be considered synonymous with CAL.

1.1 Types of CAI

There are several types of CAI, representing distinctions which have been neglected in the CAI literature and in practice. These types are emphasized throughout this paper. The first relates to CAI which supplements the learning situation, as opposed to that which substitutes for other modes of instruction. The former will be referred to as adjunct CAI [35]. It is illustrated by the short (one-half to one hour) CAI programs available through vendor libraries which are used to support or illustrate concepts. These concepts are then usually discussed in the regular classroom.

In contrast, CAI materials which provide instruction of a substitute or stand-alone variety are usually of longer duration and are generally less well known and understood in the educational world. These will be referred to as primary CAI. This approach is represented in the United States by the development of entire credit courses. In the United Kingdom the Open University is experimenting with this type of CAI (as well as with the adjunct type). In many discussions worldwide, primary CAI is being debated as part of distance learning—a term used in many countries to describe efforts to provide education to large groups over broad distances. Distance learning typically encompasses many types of educational technology, including radio, TV, electronic conferencing and mail, and computers, in conjunction with the more traditional methods such as correspondence courses [32].

A second distinction refers to the simplicity–complexity level of CAI. The author approach, employing an easy-to-learn programming language as well as minimal hardware to support the use of the programs, epitomizes the simplistic approach. However, such simplistic CAI produces limited results; i.e., graphics capabilities, large-scale calculations, and the like are not components of such programs. Conversely, complex CAI, which permits extensive use of graphics, large-scale calculations, authoring aids, etc., requires complex author languages (necessitating extensive time for authors to acquire proficiency in use) and large-scale computing capability to support such use.

1.2 Advantages and Disadvantages of CAI

Perhaps the most widely accepted value of CAI is that it involves the individual actively in the learning process. It is impossible for the student to be a totally passive member of the situation, and this very activity and involvement facilitate learning [41]. Another much touted value is the ability of the learner to proceed at his own pace, which has strong implications for both the slow learner and the gifted person.

Reinforcement of learning in such situations is immediate and systematized, which should result in more effective learning, according to established theories of instruction. In addition, the computer in a simulation mode permits students to explore time and space, to mix explosive chemicals together in a simulated laboratory without destroying themselves and the lab, and to investigate complex problems using instruments and methodology which would be excessively costly or not possible at all without the computer.

In addition, the use of computers in this manner frees faculty members or training coordinators to devote more time to the personal, human considerations of their students. Time thus spent with students has been found in a nationwide study of university faculty and students [18] to be *the* most important factor, in students' opinions, in the development of their creative abilities. Thus the use of the computer in these modes should result in an educational environment in which individuals learn more and in which their potential for innovative and creative professional work is more fully developed. Similarly, there should be a greater acceptance of the computer as a helpful tool after the student has used simulations, games, or tutorials.

A final comment regarding the benefits of CAI relates to remedial education. The problems of handling remedial training for students have increased, because the problems of bilingual and disadvantaged students and the inadequate English and mathematics skills of entering university students are being recognized. Computer tutorials, especially in these areas, appear to be both educationally sound and reasonable in cost, if approached in an appropriate manner. Similar cases can be made for the use of CAI to support continuing education and in industrial training programs.

The disadvantages of CAI in the learning process can be divided into three main categories. In order of importance, these are: (1) the need for teachers and training directors to move from accepted methods that work to a new and relatively untried method in which most individuals have little expertise and which arouses considerable fear and antipathy owing to its heavy technological base; (2) the primitive state of the art, in which a diversity of computing hardware and CAI languages compete with little apparent coordination from professionals in the educational world, in which the majority of available CAI course materials are poorly constructed, largely undocumented, and able to be run on only select computers for which they were written, and in which there are relatively few "experts" to whom CAI users can turn for assistance; and (3) the cost of hardware, CAI course materials (courseware), and individuals to help implement the process—especially since computer vendors initially touted CAI as an ultimate cost-saving device. When used as a substitute or replacement method for learning, CAI can be cost saving; however, in actuality CAI is used today mainly as a supplement to enrich learning in the educational scene, and therefore costs should be considered as add-ons.

1.3 Early Developments

CAI usage was initiated in the United States in the late 1950s and early 1960s. Early work was done at Florida State University, Dartmouth, and Stanford.

At Florida State, using an IBM 1500 interactive computer and the newly developed high-level CAI language Coursewriter, several entire university level courses (physics and statistics) were developed and offered for credit. Providing a quite different viewpoint, but occurring in the same general time frame, the Basic language was developed and implemented throughout the campus at Dartmouth. Thus for the first time faculty and students were provided with a simplified programming language which could be learned in a few days and which permitted the development of simplistic CAI programs.

At Stanford in the mid 1960s, Patrick Suppes and Richard Atkinson [as described in Reference 65], applied CAI methodology in a different area. Their work represented the first attempt to increase children's skill levels in basic English and mathematics through computerized drill and practice.

1.4 Scope of the Paper

With this brief orientation to CAI, the authors will first survey current CAI trends and existing centers of activity. This will be followed by a discussion of those studies which have attempted to evaluate the use of CAI in special learning situations. Next, costs will be discussed, and the critical issues in CAI will be highlighted, in order to identify courses of action to alleviate some of these problems. The possible future uses of CAI will then be briefly outlined.[. . .]

2. Current Trends and Existing Centers of Activity

The majority of work in CAI appears to be concentrated in four major areas: the United States, the United Kingdom, Canada, and Japan. Although some discussion of CAI throughout the world will follow, the major thrust will be in identifying activities in these four countries.

2.1 The United States

Dartmouth College served as one of the prime sources for adjunct CAI program de-

velopment for many years. During the early 1970s Dartmouth, in conjunction with the universities of Oregon, North Carolina, Iowa, and Texas, formed a consortium (CONDUIT) to acquire, evaluate, and distribute quality instructional computing materials on a national basis. CONDUIT, supported by the National Science Foundation and the Fund for the Improvement of Post-Secondary Education, is located on the University of Iowa campus, under the direction of James Johnson. It currently offers more than seventy-five computer programs in a variety of fields to support higher education classes [20]. Some CAI programs, mostly in Basic or Fortran, are available both for mini- and larger computers, with a few now available for microcomputers.

A similar effort, but encompassing both pre- and post-secondary education, is ongoing at the Minnesota Educational Computing Consortium at Lauderdale, Minnesota, with Kenneth Brumbough as Director of Instructional Services. One of the major recent accomplishments of this consortium is an extensive comparison of the capabilities and costs of microcomputers and their uses in the educational environment [44]. One result of their study has been the installation of several hundred Apple II microcomputers throughout the state of Minnesota, with an accompanying growth in the development of CAI programs.

Another project emphasizing adjunct CAI programs in Basic that will function on most computers is housed at California State University, Fresno, under the direction of Jack Chambers. This project is concerned with the acquisition, faculty evaluation, restructuring, and sharing of quality CAI materials. Over 135 programs are now available in a diversity of fields for both secondary and higher education. Copies of the library have been requested and distributed to over 125 educational institutions worldwide [1].

Yet another California project is housed at the University of California, Irvine, under the direction of Alfred Bork. This project has been under way for a number of years and has produced a significant amount of courseware of a fairly complex nature supporting instruction in physics at the higher education level.

At Stanford CAI work continues under the direction of Patrick Suppes. Entire CAI courses are now offered in Russian and mathematics.

The PLATO system, funded by the National Science Foundation and housed at the University of Illinois under the direction of Donald Bitzer, is probably the most well-known CAI project in the world and therefore will not be dealt with in any great depth here. This system uses the Tutor language, a much higher level language than Basic, and requires large-scale computing capability, at least for authoring purposes. Despite this, the system has been extensively used as supplemental to the learning situation. Since the system can produce complex CAI programs having graphics capabilities (including animation), voice output, and the like, it is quite possible that the system will be used even more heavily in the future in the primary CAI mode.

A second major PLATO installation, emphasizing support for music education, is located at the University of Delaware. A third is centered at Florida State University at Tallahassee. At this installation support is provided to select Florida high schools for PLATO-based remedial studies in mathematics. Other, smaller PLATO installations are scattered throughout the United States.

A final project of interest, emphasizing the use of primary CAI, is represented by the TICCIT (Time-Shared Interactive Computer-Controlled Information Television) project. Funded by the National Science Foundation through a grant to the MITRE Corporation, TICCIT was developed at the University of Texas and Brigham Young University under the direction of Victor Bunderson. Using minicomputers and modified TV receivers, the system was designed to provide basic undergraduate instruction in English and mathematics. It was initially implemented at Phoenix College (Arizona) and the Alexandria Community College (Virginia). The English portion is still in use at Phoenix [45], and both the English and mathematics courses are still in use at Alexandria [59].

2.2 The United Kingdom

Computer-assisted learning (CAL), as CAI is known in the United Kingdom, began in the late 1960s in scattered but important projects headed by Peter Smith at Queen Mary College, Robert Lewis at Chelsea (both part of the University of London), and James Howe at the Artificial Intelligence Laboratory at the University of Edinburgh. The British government began to be seriously interested in this type of activity at about this time. This interest resulted in funded work at Leeds and, in 1972, in a £2 million, five-year CAI project. With Richard Hooper as director, the program began in 1973 as the National Development Program in Computer Assisted Learning (NDPCAL) [31].

The NDPCAL project was primarily concerned with stimulating CAI through development of new courseware and was essentially based on work already under way. Thus Leeds University became the base for projects in chemistry and statistics, Queen Mary College for the engineering sciences project, while the University College and Chelsea College, both of the University of London, combined with the University of Surrey to develop materials in support of undergraduate education in the sciences. This latter project became known as Computers in the Undergraduate Science Curriculum (CUSC).

The NDPCAL project was completed in 1978, and government funding in the United Kingdom is currently at a minor level. However, the project did result in a number of ongoing centers dedicated to the improvement of instruction (with emphasis on CAI) at a number of universities. The authors of this paper visited several of the United Kingdom campuses in late 1979 and found CAI activities to be flourishing, especially at Chelsea College, University College, and Queen Mary College of the University of London; the University of Surrey; and the University of Edinburgh. A significant number of quality CAI programs developed under this project are now in use—between 75 and 100 units from all NDPCAL projects [32]—and exchange programs are now emerging both within the United Kingdom and between

United Kingdom and United States institutions. A particularly strong exchange program is housed at Imperial College under the direction of Nicholas Rushby [57]. In addition, enthusiasm runs high and initial work appears most promising at a number of other United Kingdom institutions, especially Anthony Hoare and Frank Pettit's laboratory at Oxford [56].

In addition to the NDPCAL project, the British Open University (OU), which opened in 1969 to criticism, is by most accounts now considered highly successful [47]. The OU is now using the computer in a CAI mode. Although the authors of this paper visited the main campus of the Open University, the extent to which CAI is now in use in the OU is not totally clear. It is apparent, however, that current usage is expected to increase both in the CAI adjunct and primary modes.

Another CAI-related activity currently in the research and experimentation stage in the United Kingdom is Viewdata. This is a computer-based information and communications medium under development by the Post Office. The intent is to provide an interactive nationwide service to the general public and professional community. It will operate via terminals based on TV receivers, the regular dial-up telephone network, and a set of interconnecting computers and databases [26].

2.3 Other Activity Worldwide

Canada and Japan both have shown strong interests in CAI and have developed centers of activity. Major Canadian centers include the Ontario Institute for Studies in Education, the National Research Council of Canada, Queen's University, Concordia University, and the Universities of Alberta and Calgary [32].

In Japan, experimentation with CAI is in progress at the university and the secondary school level, as well as in industry. Research studies in CAI have been conducted by the Nippon Telegraph and Telephone Corpora-

tion, the Japanese Society for the Promotion of Machine Industry, and by scholars at such institutions as Osaka University, Hokkaido University of Education, Aschi University of Education, and others. Research on CAI at the secondary school level is proceeding under the auspices of the National Institute for Educational Research [59].

With the exception of Russia, in which minor CAI activities have been reported [58], the authors are unaware, either through personal experience or the literature, of major CAI activities elsewhere in the world [32]. However, the developing nations, especially India and those of South America and Africa, faced with problems of large numbers of persons spread across thousands of miles, limited funds, and the desire to provide a reasonable education for everyone, are experimenting with distance education. Although their initial attempts are concentrating on radio and TV, they have also begun to look to the British Open University as a model. Thus, as the Open University develops CAI materials and uses them both successfully and financially, the widespread use of CAI for distance learning, particularly of the primary CAI type, can be anticipated [8, 17, 21, 27, 48].

3. Evaluations of CAI Effectiveness

The effectiveness of CAI has been defined differently by different investigators. To some, effectiveness means the amount of learning that takes place initially. To others it means the degree of retention of learning, or at the very least, whether or not an individual stays in or drops out of a learning experience. Still others are concerned with the learner's change in attitude toward the computer as an instructional medium or simply as a helpful tool in the culture. Finally, owing to the fact that CAI is in its infancy, some are simply concerned with transportability of materials and/or acceptance of the materials for use by others.

In general, well-designed, tightly controlled evaluative studies of the use of CAI are rare. Some have been conducted by this time, however, and trends are becoming discernible. Several of the more prominent studies will therefore be reviewed, followed by a summary of the bulk of the others.

The CAI physics course developed at Florida State University is in the form of a computer tutorial. Tentative evaluations indicate that instructional time was reduced by 17 percent over the traditional lecture course, and students scored higher on final exams and attained superior conceptual mastery [37].

The medical school of the University of Southern California has used computer-controlled modeling to teach anesthesiology. A lifelike model exhibits a variety of human responses, allowing the student to test his knowledge of anesthesiology. Evaluations using experimental and control groups demonstrated that when the model was used, fewer trials over a shorter period of time were required for students to reach an acceptable level of professional performance [37].

Studies of the CAI Russian course at Stanford, using experimental and control groups, revealed positive results in terms of student performance on examinations, student behavior, and student responses to a questionnaire about the program. Students taking the computer-based course scored "significantly better" on the final exams. In addition, far fewer students dropped out of the computer-based course [37].

Probably the most significant uses of the computer in simulation, game, or tutorial modes are represented by the Chicago City Schools Project (using Suppes and Atkinson's materials), the PLATO project, and the TICCIT project.

The Chicago City Schools Project was begun in 1971 and is continuing today. It affects over 12,000 fourth through eighth grade children in the inner city schools, with 850 terminals providing tutorial lessons in mathematics and reading. Originally designed to improve skills in these areas, the project has had significant results. As an example, the average increase in reading ability in the schools was 5.4 months per pupil for each 10 months of regular classroom instruction. Using the computer tutorial approach, the average rose to 9.0 months improvement for 8 months of instruction [55]. This program is now being formally evaluated by the Educational Testing Service under a grant from the National Institute of Education [64].

Both PLATO and TICCIT have recently been evaluated in a controlled, systematic manner by the Educational Testing Service [2, 46]. Donald Alderman of ETS commented in regard to the outcome of these evaluations as follows.

> The PLATO evaluation covered five fields: accounting, biology, chemistry, English, and mathematics. Computer uses in these fields represented supplemental or replacement instruction for regular classroom work—in no cases were these PLATO programs in lieu of entire courses.
>
> The PLATO materials were used and evaluated at five community colleges; four were a part of the City Colleges of Chicago, the fifth was in Urbana, Illinois.
>
> On the positive side, a large number of students and faculty became involved in the use of these materials, and students' attitudes toward PLATO-type materials did improve. Additionally, a significant positive achievement effect was found for PLATO vs. traditional classroom procedures in the area of mathematics. No further significant achievement effects were found for any other subjects, either in favor of PLATO or in favor of the regular classroom.
>
> The TICCIT evaluation concerned both of the mathematics and English courses in use at Phoenix College and the Alexandria (VA) Community College. These two applications represented entire courses, although *the English TICCIT program included much more personal interaction between students and faculty than did the mathematics course.*
>
> The results of the mathematics evaluation, comparing TICCIT courses to the regular classroom, and adjusting for entrance ability of students, indicated a significant achievement effect of TICCIT over the regular classroom, although fewer TICCIT students completed the course within the semester

than did those in the regular classroom. Additionally, more students had favorable attitudes toward the lecture classes than toward the TICCIT approach, although there did not appear to be any changes in overall attitudes toward additional learning in mathematics.

The results of the English evaluation also indicated a significant achievement effect in favor of the TICCIT approach, and in this situation, the completion rate for TICCIT was the same as for the classroom. Additionally, there were no significant attitude differences in favor of either approach.

ETS' responsibility in this regard was to evaluate the educational aspects of PLATO and TICCIT, and therefore no cost comparisons are available [3].

Does the above mean that such uses of the computer are effective? Certainly those who have become involved with the projects already mentioned would answer that question in the affirmative. Many who have studied the subject from a more objective vantage point also agree.

Overall, a review of the literature revealed the following consistencies:

1. The use of CAI either improved learning or showed no differences when compared to the traditional classroom approach [2, 24, 35, 42, 46, 54, 62, 66].

2. The use of CAI reduced learning time when compared to the regular classroom [15, 24, 35, 42, 60, 62, 66].

3. The use of CAI improved student attitudes toward the use of computers in the learning situation [15, 35, 42, 46, 62, 66].

4. The development of CAI courseware following specified guidelines can result in portability and their acceptance and use by other faculty [1, 20, 36, 41].

There are also some indications that low aptitude students profit more from the use of CAI than either average or high aptitude students [24, 66], and that retention rates may be lower than for traditional means [62].

The studies reviewed thus have shown striking consistencies in results, even though the type of CAI mode used (tutorials, drill and practice, games, simulations) has varied and the learners concerned have ranged from elementary school children through adults in training programs. One factor has remained relatively constant, however. The bulk of the studies have concerned the use of adjunct CAI, in which a classroom teacher is, at the least, available for consultation as needed. In the one major situation of primary CAI in which entire mathematics and English courses were taught through the TICCIT system and evaluated in a controlled manner, completion rates for the mathematics course dropped considerably below the traditional classroom, and student attitudes toward the CAI mathematics course were not positive. The opposite was true for the English course, as indicated earlier. The apparent cause of these discrepant findings was the more significant involvement of the English faculty with the students in the CAI English course, as compared to the limited involvement of the mathematics faculty with students in the mathematics CAI course. Thus, by implication, primary CAI, and distance learning in general, may achieve results similar to those for adjunct CAI as long as there is sufficient human interaction accompanying the use of the CAI materials. The Open University is currently researching this problem to determine the optimum level of human interaction necessary to produce the most effective results for various learning situations [51].

4. Costs

Costs account to a significant extent for the lack of use of CAI in learning situations, especially at the elementary/secondary level. As Kearsley [35] has pointed out, although CAI may be perceived as instructionally effective, educators may be reluctant to utilize it if it is perceived as being prohibitively expensive.

The accepted method for assessing CAI costs is to total all expenses for computing hardware, software, telecommunications, courseware, and implementation, and then divide by the total number of student hours used. However, in actual practice, many so-called hidden costs are seldom entered into the equation [6]. For example, terminals and line costs are frequently considered user costs and are omitted from the calculation. Similarly, space costs, heat, electricity, etc., are often paid by the educational institution directly and thus are not considered. Also, the life span of courseware is seldom considered, and implementation costs (staff to develop teaching guides for use of the programs, etc.) are often ignored. Compounding this situation, educators, who have been the major developers of CAI, are seldom good accountants, and thus data as to actual time taken to develop courseware often is reported inconsistently. Cost estimates for CAI, for example, are highly variable. Only recently have patterns been emerging which permit comparison of costs for complex CAI on very large computers with more simplistic programs running on mini- or microcomputers.

Other than hardware costs (which are rapidly diminishing), the cost of developing CAI courseware appears to be the greatest single factor of concern. Various authorities report courseware development time ranging from 50 to 500 hours of preparation to produce one hour of student CAI contact time at a terminal. One hundred hours appears to be the most widely accepted rule of thumb [7, 42, 49, 64]. The key variables appear to be the complexity of the programs produced and the expertise of the individuals involved. Costs per student hour of programs developed to date range from $0.50 to $28.50 [41, 52, 61, 64, 67].

In addition to development costs, other factors in the equation must be considered. Materials running on microcomputers have been reported to have the lowest costs. Similarly, the greater numbers of students using the materials, the lower the per-student-hour cost reported. Thus the CUSC programs in the United Kingdom show the highest costs (apparently due to low usage). CAI programs running on microcomputers at the Highline

School District in Seattle [61] and those used by large numbers of students in the Philadelphia schools [64] show some of the lowest costs. Thus, in addition to using inexpensive hardware, one major way to lower costs is to share courseware.

Norris [50] has pointed out another appropriate factor quite often overlooked in cost studies of CAI, i.e., that traditional instructional costs have been increasing at the rate of 13 percent per year for the past three years, while CAI costs have been decreasing at 5 percent per year, coupled with a 10 percent improvement in performance. Therefore the cost avoidance aspect of CAI should also be considered.

Finally, as McKenzie [41] has pointed out, if our goals are to improve the learning situation, then costs must be set beside a qualitative assessment of educational change to answer the question: Is it worth the cost?

5. The Critical Issues

The critical issues in CAI today relate to computer hardware, CAI languages, courseware development and sharing, and courseware implementation. Again, the major concern is with the effects of these variables upon improvements in the learning situation in relation to the costs involved.

5.1 Computer Hardware

At the current time the availability of microcomputers with their multisensory capabilities and low costs appears to be the technological breakthrough which may well result in significant increases in CAI usage at all educational levels. Eisele [25] feels that an entire new era of educational application is at hand. Critchfield [22] predicts that within the next ten years all educational institutions will have one or more microcomputers, while Matthews [43] points out that in time microcomputers may become more commonplace in schools than some audiovisual devices.

A major advantage of microcomputers is their low cost. A $3,000 investment is currently sufficient for a configuration capable of providing adequate support for CAI. In addition to providing similar capabilities to minicomputers, however, some microcomputers also permit voice input and output, color displays, high resolution graphics, and text editing. Video disk enhancements at reasonable costs appear imminent [38]. Microcomputers are essentially portable and require minimal maintenance. Their disadvantages are in the areas of file handling techniques, processor capabilities, and disk capacity. Thus their strengths lie in their use for instruction in computer languages such as Basic, applicability for production of novel and innovative CAI materials, etc., while a significant weakness is in their handling of standard administrative data processing applications. In this latter regard, although agreeing that microcomputers will likely be prominent shortly on the high school scene, Blaschke [10] has pointed out that a survey of secondary and elementary principals indicated that financial resources for purchases of microcomputers would be more readily available were the microcomputers able to serve the dual purpose of supporting both instruction and administration.

The advent of the microcomputer has resulted in heated debates concerning the relative merits of CAI systems supported by large-scale, powerful computing configurations as contrasted to the CAI capabilities of the microcomputers. Bitzer has amply championed the cause of the large-scale CAI systems such as PLATO, while Bork has spoken strongly in favor of the microcomputer approach. Both have recently softened their stances, however—Bitzer by developing the means whereby PLATO materials may be downloaded and run on a microcomputer, although still requiring the large computing capability for authoring [9]. Bork, conversely, seeing the need for students to communicate with one another, now envisions the possibility of a distributed environment, especially for development [12].

Returning once more to the topic of ad-

junct CAI and primary CAI, it would appear that microcomputers may well provide both the adequate technology and the low cost which, in a distributed network environment, will permit wide-scale use for both types of CAI worldwide. This seems especially likely if microcomputer cost/performance ratios continue to improve as predicted.

Licklider [38], for example, has estimated that by 1988, owing to technological advances, $500 worth of computing equipment could provide a 1-microsecond, 32-bit machine with 32,000 words of fast memory plus console or secondary memory. This type of equipment, with satellite communication in a distributed environment, and with the central machine used for authoring and communications, might well support the type of distance learning envisioned by the Open University.

5.2 CAI Languages

CAI languages developed specifically for high-level, complex, interactive use include Coursewriter, developed by IBM; Tutor, developed for PLATO and now marketed by Control Data Corporation; ASET (Author System for Education and Training), developed and marketed by UNIVAC; and CAN, developed and marketed by the Ontario Institute for Studies in Education. All systems provide authoring aids, calculation capabilities, and varying levels of graphics commands. However, they are all machine dependent except CAN, which will function on computers from several major vendors and is now being prepared for use on a microcomputer [53].

In a different vein, a number of other languages have been used extensively for CAI, owing to some extent to the ease of learning to use them (although they do not have CAI authoring aids). These languages include Basic, APL, Fortran, and Pascal. Each has unique features which appeal to different authors. It is interesting to note that Kearsley [34] in a study of CAI languages found that the emphasis shifted from the use of Coursewriter and Tutor in 1970, to APL, Tutor, and Basic in

1976. Since Basic is the predominant micro-computer language, it is likely to continue to gain in usage for CAI development.

The critical issue indicated in the above, however, is that there is no standard, high-level, complex CAI language which is machine independent, and which combines authoring aids, calculational mode, and graphics capabilities. This is currently one of the major impediments to the widespread use of CAI to support the learning process. Although the possibility of language independence (i.e., the ability to translate automatically from one language to another and thus to achieve portability) has been discussed for some time, such software is not now available.

5.3 Courseware Development and Sharing

The single most critical issue in CAI today is the development and sharing of quality CAI materials. The majority of CAI courseware currently available is of the adjunct type, developed by individual faculty members for specific purposes. It has largely been written in a machine-dependent language and is undocumented. Thus the available courseware is difficult to share and, in many cases, protected by copyright if of significant value. In *The ABC's of CAI* project [1] over 4,000 CAI programs written in Basic were reviewed, and about 3–4 percent were found acceptable by faculty in the fields concerned. To permit sharing of these programs, restricted Basic standards had to be developed and programs restructured at an average cost of 100 hours per program.

In regard to authoring, the authors are in agreement with Alfred Bork that "The notion that computer-based materials can be produced by anybody, completely by themselves, is an archaic concept" [11, p. 20]. This concept has also been reiterated by Dean [23], who believes the team approach, using at least three faculty members, a programmer, and an instructional designer, has the best chance of developing courseware of high caliber which will be acceptable to the

greatest number of faculty and students. Howe and du Boulay [33], although not arguing for or against teams, do caution that we not repeat our previous mistakes, and they point out that learning principles should be recognized in the development of future CAI programs.

The team approach and specific learning strategies were used in the preparation of TICCIT materials, while a more singular faculty member approach was used with the PLATO system. As indicated earlier, although student attitudes were generally more favorable toward PLATO, the most significant learning gains over the traditional classroom approach occurred with TICCIT.

Perhaps a more basic question than the individual versus team approach to development, however, centers around the question of faculty motivation to develop and share materials. Both Hawkins [29] and Sprecher and Chambers [63], in broad-based studies, found that direct financial reward was not a primary motivator. Rather, the traditional rewards for the scholarly life appeared to be the goals. Thus, recognition and acceptance by one's peers for courseware development and sharing of such materials, release time, and acceptance of courseware development by peers and by administrators as equivalent to research publications for promotion and tenure, appeared important as means to resolve the incentive question.

5.4 Courseware Implementation

Until recently, those concerned with facilitating the use of computers in the curriculum were content to offer seminars on "How to Program," and the like. With the probability of widespread CAI usage at all educational levels, however, a great deal more attention will need to be paid to the question of how best to integrate the CAI materials into the curriculum. Otherwise, as preliminary data indicate, CAI materials will be used as add-ons, with little regard to their effectiveness in the total learning environment.

The CUSC staff at the University of Surrey

identified courseware transfer and implementation as major goals of the British NDPCAL project. To achieve these goals, the programs were developed by teams from two or more educational institutions. The programs were all student-tested a number of times, and written student guides were prepared for use with each CAI package.

Although transfer goals were realized, *the ability* to rewrite student guides effectively had to be transferred since faculty tended to reject the original student guides which accompanied the transfer of the programs. The transfer was achieved by including in the documentation copies of all student guides that had been developed and thoroughly tested. In addition, a teacher's guide was also included which outlined the rationale behind the guides, as well as possible uses of the computer program.

Thus, in regard to both adjunct and primary CAI, some type of personal support and written materials from teacher, advisor, etc., appears necessary in order to achieve maximal benefits. Decisions will be required, especially in regard to primary CAI and distance learning, as to the frequency and amount of personal contact and supporting materials which most facilitate learning in these situations.

6. The Future of CAI

6.1 Early Predictions

In the early 1970s several studies were made of the future educational technology in general, and CAI in particular, with 1980 to 2000 as the target prediction dates. The most well known of these studies was published by the Carnegie Commission [16]. In this study the commission predicted both widespread acceptance of educational technology by 1980 and the availability of a large quantity of quality courseware. Further, they predicted that by that time, new professions for persons engaged in creating and developing instructional materials on the nation's campuses

would have emerged. As indicated throughout this paper, however, widespread acceptance and use of CAI has not yet occurred.

Two other studies also independently predicted significant increases in the use of CAI in higher education. The first used community college representatives and persons from computer-related industries active in CAI [40]. The other study was based on faculty response from the nineteen-campus California State University and Colleges [4]. The Luskin study [40] predicted that the major obstacles to the use of CAI would be resolved by 1987, resulting in general acceptance and use of CAI in higher education by that time. Ames in turn [4] found the CSUC faculty predicting a 270 percent ,increase in CAI usage from 1976 to 1980. Although the accuracy of the Luskin study predictions cannot yet be assessed, personal observations by the authors of the use of CAI within the CSUC system indicates increased usage, but probably not to the extent predicted in the Ames study.

6.2 Predictions, 1980 to 1990

Resulting in part from the failure of current usage to match past predictions, predictions of the future of CAI have become guardedly optimistic. Most writers agree that technological (hardware) barriers are largely resolved or will be in the very near future, and further, that cost reductions due to mass production and consumption for home entertainment and learning will permit cost-effective uses of CAI in both the traditional classroom and in other settings [5, 9, 13, 14, 30, 38, 50]. This cost-effective technology will include large-scale mini- and microcomputers with voice input and output, interactive television, video disk systems, and satellite communication.

There is also general agreement that computers linked with video disks on the one hand, or communication satellites on the other, will play significant roles in nontraditional educational practices resulting in a revolution in courses and learning. Luehrmann [39], for example, sees the use of video disk-based learning materials, purchased or leased outside the usual educational framework and used on the home TV set, as possibly playing a significant role in learning in the future. He sees little change in the United States in the next ten years in regard to the roles played by broadcast or cable TV.

Atkinson [5], Bunderson [14], Hirschbuhl [30], and Norris [50], on the other hand, envision nationally or internationally distributed networks with large, shared databases. The individual could then use video disk materials on stand-alone microcomputers or through the network, access larger databases as needed, communicate with other persons, and the like. Norris spells this out in some detail, envisioning international networks of learning centers with CAI as the main delivery system using video disks, audio input and output, and touch input. He foresees these centers as providing direct learning experiences for individuals or providing sales of developed materials to educational institutions, to industries for training purposes, etc.

Futurists are in most disagreement, however, as to the role CAI will play in traditional educational institutions, especially in situations in which academic credit is granted. As opposed to the views of Luskin [40], Norris [50], Atkinson [5], and others who see CAI as playing major roles in education, both Luehrmann [39] and Charp [19] see matters remaining much the same over the next ten years in the traditional educational setting. Both [groups], however, foresee the increased use of CAI for instruction in the basic skills for areas of reading and mathematics, especially in work not involving academic credit.

Licklider [38] also points out the inherent dangers in the widespread use of technology for education. Chief among these concerns are the possibilities that computers will be used to emphasize facts over concepts and principles, and that they will be used to condition acceptance of political doctrines, dictate personal philosophies, etc. Although most other writers have not dealt with these problems, they are matters of concern if CAI becomes as widespread in its use as predicted.[. . .]

ACKNOWLEDGMENTS

The authors wish to express appreciation to the persons who gave generously of their time in order to review early drafts of this paper: C. Moore, Monterey, California; L. Bertrando, California Polytechnic State University, San Luis Obispo; D. Reiss, Sonoma State University; L. von Gottfried, California State University, Hayward; and N. Harbertson, California State University, Fresno.

REFERENCES

1. *The ABC's of CAI,* Fourth Edition. California State University, Fresno, 1979.

2. Alderman, D. L. *Evaluation of the TICCIT Computer-Assisted Instruction System in the Community College.* Educational Testing Service, Princeton, N.J., 1978.

3. Alderman, D. L. Personal communication. Educational Testing Service, Princeton, N.J., January 1977.

4. Ames, R. G., and Carpino, S. *The Demand for Instructional Computing Resources: 1976–1980. California State University and Colleges.* California State University, Hayward, 1977.

5. Atkinson, R. C. Futures: Where will computer-assisted instruction (CAI) be in 1990? *Educational Technology 18,* 4 (1978), 60.

6. Avner, R. A. Cost-effective applications of computer-based education. *Educational Technology 18,* 4 (1978), 24–26.

7. Baker, J. C. Corporate involvement in CAI. *Educational Technology 18,* 4 (1978), 12–16.

8. Basu, C. K., and Ramachandran, K. Educational technology in India. In *International Yearbook of Educational and Instructional Technology 1978/1979,* A. Howe and A. J. Romiszowski, Eds., Nichols Pub. Co., New York, 1978, pp. 242–250.

9. Bitzer, D. Futures: Where will computer-assisted instruction (CAI) be in 1990? *Educational Technology 18,* 4 (1978), 61.

10. Blaschke, C. L. Microcomputer software development for schools: What, who, how? *Educational Technology 19* (1979), 26–28.

11. Bork, A. Machines for computer-assisted learning. *Educational Technology 18,* 4 (1978), 17–20.

12. Bork, A., and Franklin, S. Personal computers in learning. *Educational Technology 19* (1979), 7–12.

13. Brown, J. S. Fundamental research in technology in science education. In *Technology in Science Education: The Next 10 Years,* National Science Foundation, Washington, D.C., 1979, pp. 11–18.

14. Bunderson, C. V. Futures: Where will computer-assisted instruction (CAI) be in 1990? *Educational Technology 18,* 4 (1978), 62.

15. CAI helping pupils move four grades in three years. *Computerworld 11* (June 13, 1977), 16.

16. Carnegie Commission on Higher Education. *The Fourth Revolution: Instructional Technology in Higher Education.* McGraw-Hill, New York, 1977.

17. Chadwick, C. The multidimensional projects of the OAS in educational technology. In *International Yearbook of Educational and Instructional Technology 1978/1979,* A. Howe and A. J. Romiszowski, Eds., Nichols Pub. Co., New York, 1978, pp. 290–296.

18. Chambers, J. A. College teachers: Their effect on creativity of students. *Journal of Educational Psychology, 65* (1973), 326–334.

19. Charp, S. Futures: Where will computer-assisted instruction (CAI) be in 1990? *Educational Technology 18,* 4 (1978), 62.

20. CONDUIT. Catalog of CONDUIT reviewed and tested materials. *Pipeline* (Summer 1979), 13–36.

21. Costa, J. M. de M. Prospects for distance education in Brazil. In *International Yearbook of Educational and Instructional Technology 1978/1979,* A. Howe and A. J. Romiszowski, Eds., Nichols Pub. Co., New York, 1978, pp. 297–311.

22. Critchfield, M. Beyond CAI: Computers as personal intellectual tools. *Educational Technology 19* (1979), 18–25.

23. Dean, P. M. Computer-assisted instruction authoring systems. *Educational Technology 18,* 4 (1978), 20–23.

24. Deignan, G. M., and Duncan, R. E. CAI in three medical training courses: It was effective! *Behavior Research Methods and Instrumentation 10,* 2 (1978), 228–230.

25. Eisele, J. E. Classroom use of microcomputers. *Educational Technology 19* (1979), 13–15.

26. Fedida, S., and Dew, B. Viewdata in education. In *International Yearbook of Educational and Instructional Technology 1978/1979,* A. Howe and A. J. Romiszowski, Eds., Nichols Pub. Co., New York, 1978, pp. 78–86.

27. Garvey, B. Instructional technology in Zambia. In *International Yearbook of Educational and Instructional Technology 1978/1979,* A. Howe and A. J. Romiszowski, Eds., Nichols Pub. Co., New York, 1978, pp. 239–241.

28. Hansen, D. N., and Johnson, B. *CAI Myths That Need to Be Destroyed and CAI Myths That We Ought to Create.* Florida State University, Tallahassee, 1971.

29. Hawkins, C. A. Computer based learning: Why and where is it alive and well? *Computers and Education 2,* 3 (1978), 187–196.

30. Hirschbuhl, J. J. Futures: Where will computer-assisted instruction (CAI) be in 1990? *Educational Technology 18,* 4 (1978), 62.

31. Hooper, R. The national development programme in computer-assisted learning. In *International Yearbook of Educational and Instructional Technology 1978/1979,* A. Howe and A. J. Romiszowski, Eds., Nichols Pub. Co., New York, 1978, pp. 173–179.

32. Howe, A., and Romiszowski, A. J., Eds. *International Yearbook of Educational and Instructional Technology 1978/1979.* Nichols Pub. Co., New York, 1978.

33. Howe, J. A. M., and du Boulay, B. Microprocessor assisted learning: Turning the clock back? *Programmed Learning and Education Technology 16* (1979), 240–246.

34. Kearsley, G. P. Some "facts" about CAI: Trends 1970–1976. *Journal of Educational Data Processing 13,* 3 (1976), 1–12.

35. Kearsley, G. P. The cost of CAI: A matter of assumption. *AEDS Journal 10,* 3 (1977), 100–110.

36. Laurillard, D. M. The design and development of CAI materials in undergraduate science. *Computer Graphics 2* (1977), 241–247.

37. Levien, R. E. *The Emerging Technology: Instructional Uses of the Computer in Higher Education.* McGraw-Hill, New York, 1972.

38. Licklider, J. C. R. Impact of information technology on education in science and technology. In *Technology in Science Education: The Next 10 Years,* National Science Foundation, Washington, D.C., 1979, pp. 1–10.

39. Luehrmann, A. Technology in science education. In *Technology in Science Education: The Next 10 Years,* National Science Foundation. Washington, D.C., 1979, pp. 11–18.

40. Luskin, B. J., Gripp, T. H., Clark, J. R., and Christianson, D. A. *Everything You Always Wanted to Know About CAI.* Computer Uses in Education, Huntington Beach, Calif., 1972.

41. McKenzie, J., Elton, L., and Lewis, R. *Interactive Computer Graphics in Science Teaching.* Halstead Press, New York, 1978.

42. Magidson, E. M. Issue overview: Trends in computer-assisted instruction. *Educational Technology 18,* 4 (1978), 5–8.

43. Matthews, J. I. Microcomputer vs. minicomputer for educational computing. *Educational Technology 18,* 11 (1978), 19–22.

44. *Microcomputer Report.* Minnesota Educational Compting Consortium, Instructional Services Division, Lauderdale, Minn., July 1979.

45. Morrison, F. Personal communication. Phoenix College, Phoenix, Ariz., February 1980.

46. Murphy, R. T., and Appel, L. R. *Evaluation of the Plato IV Computer-Based Education System in the Community College.* Educational Testing Service, Princeton, N.J., 1977.

47. Neil, M. W. Distance learning in developing countries in relation to the Open University. In *International Yearbook of Educational and Instructional Technology 1978/1979,* A. Howe and A. J. Romiszowski, Eds., Nichols Pub. Co., New York, 1978, pp. 104–115.

48. Neil, M. W. The educational imperative in developing countries. In *International Yearbook of Educational and Instructional Technology 1978/1979,* A. Howe and A. J. Romiszowski, Eds., Nichols Pub. Co., New York, 1978, pp. 87–90.

49. Neuhauser, J. J. A necessary redirection for certain educational technologies. *Computers and Education 1,* 4 (1977), 187–192.

50. Norris, W. C. Via technology to a new era in education. *Phi Delta Kappan 58,* 2 (1977), 451–453.

51. Northedge, A., and Durbridge, N. The use of tutorials in the Open University. In *International Yearbook of Educational and Instructional Technology 1978/1979,* A. Howe and A. J. Romiszowski, Eds., Nichols Pub. Co., New York, 1978, 34–43.

52. Okey, J. R., and Majer, K. Individual and small group learning with computer-assisted instruction. *Audio Visual Communication Review, 24,* 1 (1976), 79–86.

53. Olivier, W. P. Personal communication. The Ontario Institute for Studies in Education, Ontario, Canada, June 1979.

54. Paden, D. W., Dalgaard, B. R., and Barr, M. D. A decade of computer-assisted instruction. *Journal of Economic Education 9,* 4 (1977), 14–20.

55. Passman, B. Personal communication. Sperry Univac Corp., Blue Bell, Pa., January 1979.

56. Pettit, F. R. *Computer Assisted Learning—A Review of the Current Practice in the U.K.* Compting Teaching Centre, Oxford University, Oxford, England, 1978.

57. Rushby, N. J. *The CEDAR Project.* Computer Centre, Imperial College, London, 1978.

58. Rushby, N. J. *Computer Based Learning in the Soviet Union,* Computer Centre, Imperial College, London, 1979.

59. Sassar, M. Personal communication. Alexandria Community College, Alexandria, Va., February 1980.

60. Sakamoto, T. The current state of educational technology in Japan. In *International Yearbook of Educational and Instructional Technology 1978/1979,* A. Howe and A. J. Romiszowski, Eds., Nichols Pub. Co., New York, 1978, pp. 251–271.

61. School shifting teaching aid to micros. *Computerworld 12* (Nov. 6, 1978), 63.

62. Splittgerber, F. L. Computer-based instruction: A revolution in the making? *Educational Technology 19,* 1 (1979), 20–26.

63. Sprecher, J. W., and Chambers, J. A. Computer-assisted instruction: Factors affecting courseware development. *Journal of Computer-Based Instruction 23,* 6 (1980), 332–342.

64. Sugarman, R. A second chance for computer-aided instruction. *ICEE Spectrum* (Aug. 1978), 29–37.

65. Suppes, P., and Macken, E. The historical path from research and development to operational use of CAI. *Educational Technology 18,* 4 (1978), 9–12.

66. Taylor, S., et al. The effectiveness of CAI. Annual Convention, Association for Educational Data Systems, New York, 1974.

67. Time-sharing in education—Going, going, but not gone. *Datamation* (January 1977), 138–140.

Microcomputers in Education: Cognitive and Social Design Principles

Thomas W. Malone

Xerox Palo Alto Research Center

James Levin

University of California, San Diego

Abstract

The successful use of microcomputers in education depends critically on the cognitive and motivational processes in learning and the social structure of the educational setting. A number of different groups concerned with these issues have recently tried to specify explicit design principles for using computers successfully in different educational environments. This report summarizes a workshop that brought together people from some of these groups to describe the current state of their groups' efforts and to work toward integrating these efforts into a larger scale statement.

The first part of this report summarizes the short informal presentations made by the workshop participants in order of presentation; the second part describes some examples of well-designed instructional games and articulates several general themes that ran through the conference.

The primary goal of this conference was to specify principles that are actually useful in designing instructional environments. As such, many of the principles discussed here are rough heuristics or rules of thumb rather than precisely defined scientific laws. Experienced workers in this field may find many of the principles obvious or well known, but, in fact, some of the principles that seem the most obvious are the most often violated. It is our hope that this summary will serve both as an introduction to the important issues for those who are not yet familiar with them, and as a stepping stone from which experienced workers can move toward a more powerful set of design principles.

Thomas W. Malone and James Levin, Eds., "Microcomputers in Education: Cognitive and Social Design Principles," pp. 1–20. This is a report of a conference held March 12–14, 1981, at the University of California, San Diego, sponsored by the Carnegie Corporation. Reprinted by permission of Thomas W. Malone.

List of Participants

ORGANIZERS

James Levin
*Laboratory of Comparative Human
Cognition (D003)
University of California, San Diego
La Jolla, California*

Thomas W. Malone
*Cognitive and Instructional Sciences
Group
Xerox Palo Alto Research Center
3333 Coyote Hill Road
Palo Alto, California*

INVITEES

John Seely Brown
*Cognitive and Instructional Sciences
Group
Xerox Palo Alto Research Center
3333 Coyote Hill Road
Palo Alto, California*

Michael Cole
*Laboratory of Comparative Human
Cognition, D003
University of California, San Diego
La Jolla, California*

Allan Collins
*Bolt Beranek and Newman, Inc.
50 Moulton Street
Cambridge, Massachusetts*

Robert Davis
*PLATO Project
College of Education, Curriculum
Laboratory
University of Illinois at Urbana-
Champaign
1212 West Springfield
Urbana, Illinois*

Andrea diSessa
*LOGO Project
Artificial Intelligence Laboratory
Massachusetts Institute of Technology
Cambridge, Massachusetts*

Sharon Dugdale
*PLATO Project
Computer-based Education Research
Laboratory
252 Engineering Research Laboratory
103 S. Mathews Ave.
University of Illinois at Urbana-
Champaign
Urbana, Illinois*

Gerhard Fischer
*Azenbergstr. 12
University of Stuttgart
Department of Computer Science
Stuttgart, West Germany*

Laura Gould
*Learning Research Group
Xerox Palo Alto Research Center
3333 Coyote Hill Road
Palo Alto, California*

James Hollan
*Naval Personnel Research and
Development Center
(Code 304)
San Diego, California*

Edwin Hutchins
*Naval Personnel Research and
Development Center
(Code 304)
San Diego, California*

Ted Kahn
*Atari, Inc.
1265 Borregas Avenue
Sunnyvale, California*

Marge Kosel
*Minnesota Educational Computing
Consortium
2520 Broadway Drive
Saint Paul, Minnesota*

Mark Lepper
Department of Psychology
Stanford University
Stanford, California

Alan M. Lesgold
Learning Research and Development
* Center*
University of Pittsburgh
Pittsburgh, Pennsylvania

Mark Miller
Central Research Laboratories
Texas Instruments, Inc.
P.O. Box 225936, MS 371
Dallas, Texas

SPONSORS

Frederick Mosher
The Carnegie Corporation
437 Madison Ave.
New York, New York

Dave Robinson
The Carnegie Corporation
437 Madison Ave.
New York, New York

Vivian Stewart
The Carnegie Corporation
437 Madison Ave.
New York, New York

Summary of Presentations

Thomas W. Malone

Cognitive and Instructional Sciences Group
Xerox Palo Alto Research Center

Tom Malone described several studies of what makes computer games fun and suggested a framework for using the same features to make computer-based learning environments interesting and enjoyable (see Malone, 1980, 1981). He first described a survey of computer game preferences and two experiments that started with popular computer games and removed features, one at a time, to see which features made the most difference in the appeal of the game. Games studied in this way included "Breakout" and a game called "Darts" designed to teach children about fractions.

Malone then suggested that there are three primary categories of features that make learning fun.

1. *Challenge.* In order for an activity to be challenging, it should present a *goal* whose *outcome is uncertain.* Ways of making outcomes uncertain for a wide range of players include (a) having variable difficulty levels (either chosen by the player or determined

automatically) and (b) having a number of goals at different levels all embedded in a single environment. These multiple level goals can often be encouraged by score-keeping or speeded responses.

2. *Fantasy.* Fantasies in instructional activities can make the activities emotionally appealing. They can also provide practical examples and vivid images for the use of the skill being learned. *Intrinsic fantasies,* which are intimately related to the skill being learned, are hypothesized to be more interesting and more educational than *extrinsic fantasies,* which depend only on whether the students' answers are right or wrong. Since there are large individual differences in the fantasies people find appealing, instructional designers should either pick fantasies very carefully or let students choose among several fantasies for a given educational goal.

3. *Curiosity.* Educational activities can evoke *sensory curiosity* by including audio and visual effects, such as music and graphics. They can evoke *cognitive curiosity* by leading learners into situations in which they are surprised. To be educational, the surprising situations

should include information that helps the learners understand the misconceptions that led them to be surprised in the first place.

James Levin and Michael Cole
Laboratory of Comparative Human Cognition
University of California at San Diego

Jim Levin described observations of children interacting with computers, both in structured classroom settings and in less structured (by adults) computer clubs (see Levin and Kareev, 1980). In these settings, a critical factor for designing educational uses is the role of social resources, especially peers. People just starting to use computers have many low level problems, such as forgetting to hit the RETURN or ENTER key to terminate a response, typing the lowercase letter l instead of the number one, mistyping, etc. Any one of these problems can prevent further progress, and thus pose major design issues for educational programs. Yet in analyses of video tapes of computer novices, Levin found that few of these problems occurred; largely because several children worked together to use the computer. They interacted cooperatively to detect and correct these low level problems almost immediately.

Having more than one person use a computer for educational purposes also allows novices to divide up the task at higher levels so that each can master part of the required skills before moving on to tackle the rest. The side effect of having joint use is that the amount of cooperative peer interaction is increased through educational computer use, rather than decreased as commonly feared.

Levin described a number of heuristics that the members of LCHC [the Laboratory of Comparative Human Cognition] have found important in designing educational computer activities.

1. *Dynamic computer support.* Educational computer systems should initially take the initiative for large parts of the task to be mastered, but allow the learners to assume responsibility as they progress to expertise.

2. *Dynamic social support.* Educational systems should enable and encourage interaction and helping among peers and between novices and experts.

3. *Active/interactive.* Learners should take an active role in the activity.

4. *Breadth.* Learners should have available a wide variety of educational microworlds (each of which exercises the skills they want to acquire) so that each can find a "world" in which they can become actively involved.

5. *Power.* Educational activities should allow even novices to create interesting results with relatively little e ffort.

Michael Cole described how the flexible use of microcomputers in a rich social environment can lead to the creation of zones of proximal development, optimal regions for learning in which a person cannot perform the task to be mastered [alone] but can with the aid of others. In this state, the individual can then internalize this social support, progressing to expertise.

Alan M. Lesgold
Learning Research and Development Center
University of Pittsburgh

Alan Lesgold emphasized that massive amounts of drill and practice are needed to acquire basic skills, and that the practice opportunities must be motivating, appropriate, and capable of providing immediate feedback. In particular:

1. *Practice tasks should be appropriate to the child's level of progress.* One way to achieve this might be to use communications networks or plug-in modules to transfer diagnostic information and practice exercises between computers at school and at home.

2. *Computer-based practice opportunities should provide understandable, productive, and immediate feedback, which should take every error in performance into account.*

3. *In a complex task, the computer can support one aspect of performance in order to allow higher level practice of a second aspect.* Such "intellectual prostheses" can allow students to exercise advanced subskills (such as planning the structure of a story) before they have mastered all the earlier subskills (such as grammar and punctuation).

4. *Practice environments should be motivating.* When computer-based games and instructional systems are commonplace, children may take for granted the "cute bells and whistles" that are motivating for them now. Perhaps computer-based instructional systems can be designed to increase the mental discipline and self-motivation of students. If success is to be rewarding, students must be able to recognize their own successes. A child cannot be motivated by success in writing essays, for example, unless he or she has an internal cognitive model of what a successful essay is.

Andrea diSessa
LOGO Project
Massachusetts Institute of Technology

Andy diSessa emphasized the importance of creating complete examples of good educational environments rather than just listing separate principles of instructional design. He described the LOGO programming environment at MIT [Massachusetts Institute of Technology] (Papert, 1980; Abelson and diSessa, 1981; Papert et al., 1979) and related several examples of students' educational experiences with it. DiSessa highlighted the importance of creating educational environments where students have a sense of con-

trol, set their own goals, and are able to form deeply personal, long-term links with the material they are learning. He also advocated designing instructional environments in which the concepts to be learned are deeply embedded in the environment itself.

One of the examples diSessa described involved an environment in which students could learn about certain concepts of elementary physics. Instead of the "turtle" used in standard LOGO environments, students in this environment controlled what diSessa called a "dynaturtle." In standard LOGO, students draw lines on the computer screen by telling an imaginary "turtle" to turn in certain directions and move specified distances. In the dynaturtle environment, students control the motion of the turtle by "pushing" it with forces of specified direction and magnitude. The turtle then moves on the screen according to the laws of Newtonian physics as if it were an object on a frictionless surface.

One of the first surprises students have in this environment is that the turtle doesn't always move in the direction they push it. For example, if the turtle is moving upward and the student wants it to change direction and go sideways, he cannot just give it a sideways push. Instead, he must give it a push with a direction and magnitude that completely counteract the upward motion and also impart a sideways motion (see Figure 1a, b).

DiSessa described how this environment could be used to impart an intuitive or phenomenological understanding of elementary mechanics that is very hard to get in traditional learning environments. The difficulty of achieving this kind of understanding from traditional methods is illustrated by the fact that the MIT physics students who played with the dynaturtle did nearly as poorly as the elementary school students tested (diSessa, 1982).

Allan Collins
Bolt Beranek and Newman, Inc.

Alan Collins discussed how computers can be used to create new environments in which

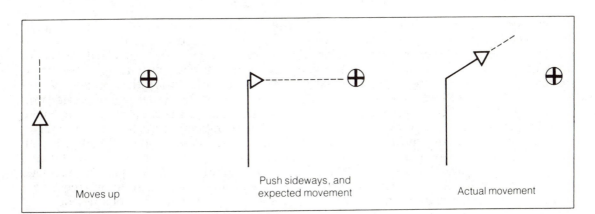

FIGURE 1a: A bug in a student's conceptions about motion

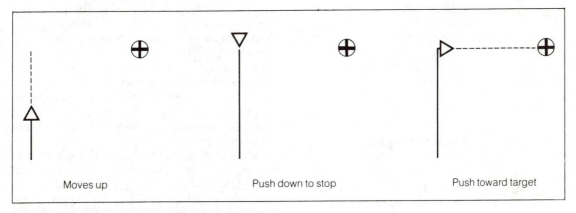

FIGURE 1b: A Newtonian method of negotiating a corner

there is intrinsic motivation to engage in reading and writing. He observed that only some kids get pleasure from reading, and very few get pleasure from writing. So for most children, the only reason to read or write is to satisfy the demands of teachers and schools. Then he listed a number of ways that computers can create environments where kids read and write for their own purposes rather than to satisfy a teacher.

For example, there are *game environments* (like "Adventure") where kids have to read or write to play the game. Not all kids like games, but for those who do, these environments can lead them to want to be able to do the things other kids are doing, to compete with other kids, and to practice on their

own. There are also computer-based *communication environments* like electronic message systems, bulletin boards, and newspapers, where the technology enables kids to communicate with distant friends, with kids they don't know, and with their own classmates. This use of computers is very widespread among adults with message systems and seems to be highly motivating. It provides, in a very natural way, lots of feedback about failures to communicate.

To illustrate the process of creating intrinsically motivating instructional environments, Collins discussed two applications of the principles proposed by Malone. First, he analyzed a motivating arcade game called "Missile Command" in terms of the features

Malone described such as fantasy, audio and visual effects, and adjustable difficulty level. Collins also described several additional features of the game including the *hindsight principle*. This principle says that activities are more motivating when you can see at the end of them how you could have done just a little bit better. Collins then used the same features to analyze an educational game called "Textman" proposed by Andee Rubin. This game is a variation of "Hangman," where players try to select sentences of a particular text (e.g., a paragraph in a suspense story) out of a much larger list of sentences. Describing work he did with Andee Rubin, Collins showed how the Textman game as originally proposed had some—but not very many—of the motivational features of the arcade game. Then he described how the game might be improved by adding motivational features. The plan is to compare the two versions of Textman to see which works best with children.

Robert Davis and Sharon Dugdale
PLATO Project, University of Illinois

Bob Davis suggested three levels for categorizing instructional design principles.

1. *Micro level* involving the minute details of screen layout, control key meanings, and so forth. This level is usually not noticed unless it is done poorly.

2. *Obvious or memorable level* involving the themes and instructional content of the material.

3. *Macro level* involving the structure of the curriculum over the year and its relationship with other aspects of the school and classroom.

Davis also suggested several guidelines for designing meaningful instruction. One technique used in PLATO lessons involved storing examples of students' work for other students to see (Dugdale, 1979). For exam-

ple, in one instance of a "library lesson" children were asked to divide a square into pieces and then color a specified fraction of it. Successful solutions to the problem could be stored in a library that other children could access. The availability of previous solutions inspired many students to try more and more original or artistic solutions including making patterns and spelling words with the colored portion of the square. Since a correct solution had to equal the specified fraction, these original solutions required a thorough understanding of the notion of equivalent fractions.

In lessons [that incorporate] a "hall of fame" (such as the "Green Globs" game described below), the best solutions are stored for others to see. Since the complete games of high scorers are stored, other students can often engage in a kind of "industrial espionage" to learn the secrets of playing the game well (and incidentally of the skill the game is designed to teach). Thus this technique not only takes advantage of a form of competition, it also allows children to learn from their peers.

Sharon Dugdale discussed the use of "intrinsic models" in designing instructional materials. Intrinsic models are instructional activities in which the student explores and manipulates a working model that provides meaningful and constructive feedback. The mathematics to be learned is intrinsic to the model and is treated as inherently interesting, rather than hidden behind irrelevant themes. The activities are designed to be engaged in by students of widely varying backgrounds and abilities, but students find that the more math they apply, the better they do. Dugdale also suggested that:

1. Materials for student use should be designed to engage the student in productive thought and activity rather than to showcase the capabilities of the hardware or the author.

2. [The materials] should draw on the inherently interesting characteristics of the topic rather than trying to hide the

topic under a lot of hoopla (e.g., graphics, animations, and music that are unrelated to the task).

3. [The materials] should keep the student interacting and participating rather than passively watching and listening.

Finally, Dugdale described a new example of an activity that illustrates the use of the "intrinsic models" characteristics, as well as some social aspects of courseware design and usage. This lesson, called Green Globs, is described in the Synthesis section [on page 32].

John Seely Brown
Cognitive and Instructional Sciences Group
Xerox Palo Alto Research Center

John Seely Brown first described an example of how extremely subtle aspects of an instructional environment might have very important effects. The example involved the input format on an early version of the Darts game (described below). Careful observation of a number of students playing this game suggested that they learned to control the position of the arrow by treating the input as a three-argument function (integer, numerator, and denominator) without any understanding at all of the meaning of fractions. For instance, they might have learned that increasing the third number makes the arrow go down without understanding anything about how the denominator specifies the number of equal parts in a whole.

In the version of the game in which this phenomenon was observed, students had to type a carriage return after each of the three parts of the answer. One conjecture is that these explicit delimiters between parts of the answer might have heightened the tendency for students to see the answer as three separate entities rather than as a single mixed number with meaningful parts. This conjecture is supported by the fact that the phenomenon was not observed in a later version of the game that used the conventional im-plicit delimiters as follows: whole number, (space), numerator, (slash mark), denominator.

Next Brown discussed a detailed set of principles for "coaching" students in informal learning environments. These principles are explicitly encoded in a computer-based coaching system for an arithmetic game (see Burton and Brown, 1979). They assume that the student takes turns playing the game against another student or against the computer. The computer constructs a model of the student's skills and weaknesses by observing when the student misses good moves in the game. This student model is based on a set of issues which students can learn about from playing the game. The principles include the following (for a more detailed discussion, see Burton and Brown, 1979).

1. Before giving advice, be sure the Issue used is one in which the student is weak.

2. When illustrating an Issue, only use an Example (an alternative move) in which the result or outcome of that move is dramatically superior to the move made by the student.

3. If a student is about to lose, interrupt and tutor him only with moves that will keep him from losing.

4. Do not tutor on two consecutive moves, no matter what.

5. Do not tutor before the student has a chance to discover the game for himself.

6. Do not provide only criticism when the Tutor breaks in! If the student makes an exceptional move, identify why it is good and congratulate him.

7. After giving advice to the student, offer him a chance to retake his turn, but do not force him to.

8. Always have the Computer Expert play an optimal game.

9. If the student asks for help, provide several levels of hints.

10. If the student is losing consistently, adjust the level of play.

11. If the student makes a potentially careless error, be forgiving. But provide explicit commentary in case it was not just careless.

Laura Gould
Learning Research Group
Xerox Palo Alto Research Center

Laura Gould described a system named TRIP for animating algebra word problems (see Gould and Finzer, 1981). TRIP is intended for students who have mastered the mechanics of algebra but have difficulty translating the English text of the problem into suitable algebraic expressions. TRIP provides an environment where students can develop an intuitive grasp of time–rate–distance problems and their algebraic representations. The system supplies a helpful graphical interface by means of which students construct a diagram of the problem using high-resolution pictures of places, travelers, speedometers, odometers, and clocks (see Figure 2a, b). Once the diagram is judged by the system to be correct, the system asks the student to make a rough guess of the answer. Then the travelers, meters, and clocks all move together, producing an animated representation of the problem. When the state specified by the student's guess is reached, the action stops, and the student gets to see the result of the guess. A record of each successive guess and its consequences is kept in a table from which students induce algebraic expressions and finally an equation for computing the answer.

Gould pointed out some of the successful and unsuccessful aspects of the system in an attempt to discover the underlying design guidelines. The user interface for the system, although apparently quite complicated, was successfully and easily controlled even by students with low confidence levels. This seemed to be due to (1) the extensive help facility (accessed by a large "Help" button always visible on the screen), (2) the fact that students started with a nearly blank screen and built up for themselves a complex representation of the problem, and (3) the consistent use of the same functions in different parts of the system. TRIP was also successfully integrated into an existing classroom curriculum. This was aided by (1) involving teachers in the early design phases, (2) tailoring the computer curriculum to mesh well with what was going on in the class, (3) individualizing the problems by choosing easy or hard numbers based on each student's ability, and (4) collecting feedback from the students using a "gripe" facility.

Students who used the TRIP system learned to make good diagrams of algebra word problems, but they continued to have difficulty actually solving the problems, especially when constructing the "guess table" and forming algebraic expressions. This seemed to be due in part to the fact that the system did too much of the work for them—it automatically constructed table headings and ran the clocks and odometers so that the students were not required to compute these values. The students could presumably have profited from doing more of this work themselves. They could also have been aided by a help system that included substantive coaching in algebra, rather than one that just provided help in how to use the system.

Marge Kosel
Minnesota Educational Computing
Consortium

Marge Kosel suggested that an instructional program designer can be compared to a sculptor working with a piece of stone. Creativity, knowledge of the medium, and consideration of the audience are parts of both processes. Just as it would be difficult to define all the components needed to create a piece of sculpture, there are distinctive qualities in the design of a microcomputer program that are brought out by the designer and the subject. As in sculpting, however, certain subskills of expert performance can be defined.

Kosel then summarized a number of these principles, using the three levels suggested earlier by Davis.

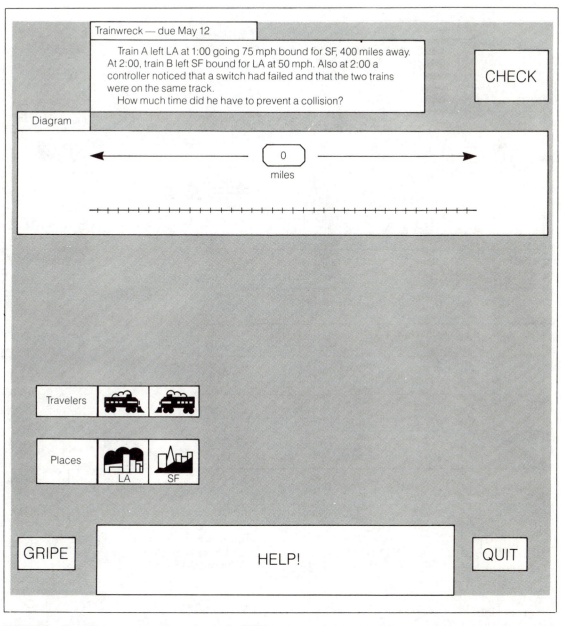

Trainwreck — due May 12

Train A left LA at 1:00 going 75 mph bound for SF, 400 miles away.
At 2:00, train B left SF bound for LA at 50 mph. Also at 2:00 a
controller noticed that a switch had failed and that the two trains
were on the same track.
    How much time did he have to prevent a collision?

CHECK

Diagram

0
miles

Travelers

Places

LA   SF

GRIPE   HELP!   QUIT

FIGURE 2a: An initial screen configuration in the TRIP system

1. The first level can be called the
invisible level, since it is not noticeable
unless poorly designed. This level can be
defined through explicit rules or
checklists such as the following (see
MECC, 1980, for more examples): (a)
avoid crowded displays, (b) vary the way
the text is presented, using boxes and
lines, (c) avoid jumping scrolling of a
screen of text, (d) let users signal when
they are through reading; do not use
standard timing loops.

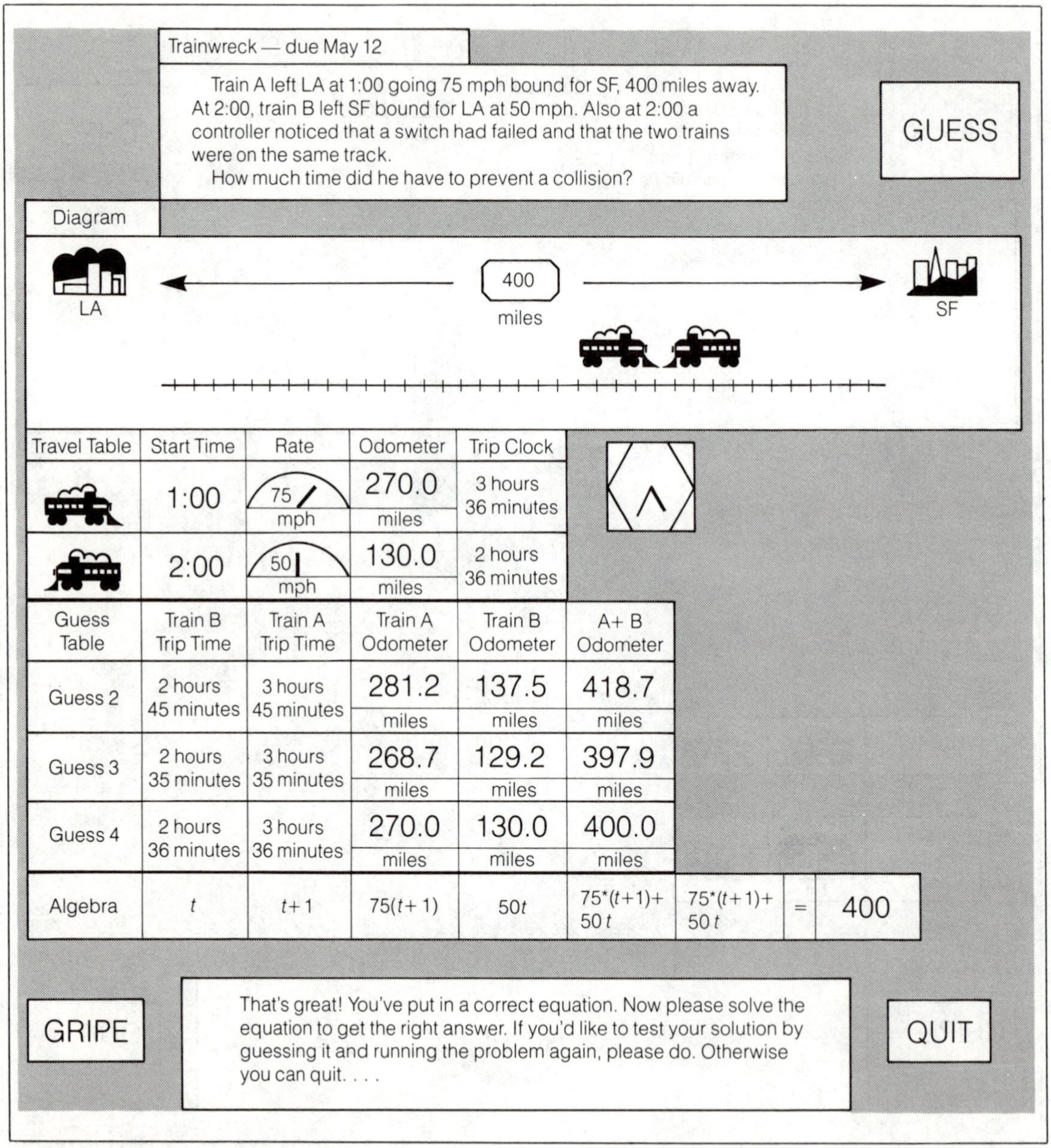

Trainwreck — due May 12

Train A left LA at 1:00 going 75 mph bound for SF, 400 miles away. At 2:00, train B left SF bound for LA at 50 mph. Also at 2:00 a controller noticed that a switch had failed and that the two trains were on the same track.
How much time did he have to prevent a collision?

GUESS

Diagram

LA   ←————— 400 miles —————→   SF

Travel Table	Start Time	Rate	Odometer	Trip Clock
	1:00	75 mph	270.0 miles	3 hours 36 minutes
	2:00	50 mph	130.0 miles	2 hours 36 minutes

Guess Table	Train B Trip Time	Train A Trip Time	Train A Odometer	Train B Odometer	A+ B Odometer			
Guess 2	2 hours 45 minutes	3 hours 45 minutes	281.2 miles	137.5 miles	418.7 miles			
Guess 3	2 hours 35 minutes	3 hours 35 minutes	268.7 miles	129.2 miles	397.9 miles			
Guess 4	2 hours 36 minutes	3 hours 36 minutes	270.0 miles	130.0 miles	400.0 miles			
Algebra	t	$t+1$	$75(t+1)$	$50t$	$75^{*}(t+1)+50t$	$75^{*}(t+1)+50t$	$=$	400

That's great! You've put in a correct equation. Now please solve the equation to get the right answer. If you'd like to test your solution by guessing it and running the problem again, please do. Otherwise you can quit. . . .

GRIPE

QUIT

FIGURE 2b: A final screen configuration in the TRIP system

2. The second level, which can be called the *memory level,* is what the user remembers after completing the program. This level includes concepts or themes used to enhance learning, design of user controls in the program, effective use of graphics, color, and sound, and attention to the use of appropriate reading levels.

3. The third level, which may be called the *educational level,* is concerned with questions such as whether the material is educationally sound, whether the

capabilities of the computer are used in an appropriate way, whether the material will fit in different classroom situations, and what types of support material are necessary. This level also examines whether the system will be used by individuals, by small groups of students, or by an entire class.

Each level is integral to the final product, and although guidelines and principles to be followed can be defined at each level, the success of the final product depends ultimately on the creativity of the individual author and the ways in which the subject matter is interpreted on the screen.

James Hollan and Edwin Hutchins
Navy Personnel Research and Development Center

Jim Hollan and Ed Hutchins presented two examples of microprocessor-based systems they are developing as part of research efforts concerned with the application of microprocessor technology to Navy training needs. One system is based on semantic network databases that represent the information students need to learn. In addition to simply viewing the information in the database, students can play a variety of games (e.g., flashcard and twenty questions) with the information to be learned. The games and exploration facilities are independent of particular databases and thus the system can be used for instruction in a wide variety of domains. Automated facilities are available to assist in the construction of new databases. The system is currently being used to teach a large body of information about the characteristics of various kinds of naval equipment.

The other system provides conceptual instruction and simulationlike practice in the use of an important and conceptually difficult piloting tool called a maneuvering board. In this system, the student can view and control continually updated geographical and relative motion depictions of ships maneuvering in proximity to each other.

Hollan and Hutchins also discussed [two] other issues involved in instructional design.

1. *Instruction begins with elicitation.* It is only when one has a good cognitive task analysis that one can decide how to employ a particular technology to improve instruction.

2. *Is the technology appropriate?* In many domains, the computer is not better than other means of fulfilling educational goals, and in those cases it should not be used. In both of the examples described above, the computer provided instructionally superior facilities that were not available in other media.

Synthesis

One of the issues raised at the workshop involved how best to aid designers of instructional software. On the one hand, analytic design principles run the risk of missing key points altogether and can easily degenerate into being useless platitudes. On the other hand, good examples of actual systems may not help much in designing new systems unless it is clear which elements of the good systems are fundamental to their success and which are incidental and nongeneralizable.

To synthesize the ideas that grew out of this workshop, we have chosen to present both examples and principles. A number of example systems were described in the presentations summarized above. In this section, we will present several of these examples. Then we will summarize some of the most important design principles that are embodied in the examples and that emerged as recurring themes in the discussions at the workshop.

Darts
designed by Sharon Dugdale

The Darts game was mentioned in one form or another in at least four of the presentations

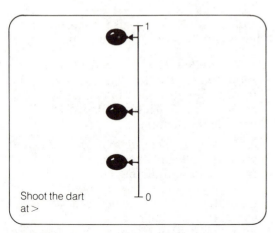

FIGURE 3: Successive screen displays from Darts

at the workshop, so it is described here first. This game was designed to give elementary students practice with estimating fractions (see Dugdale and Kibbey, 1980). In this game, three balloons appear at random places on a number line on the screen and players try to guess the positions of the balloons (see Figure 3).They guess by typing in mixed numbers (whole numbers and/or fractions), and after each guess an arrow shoots across the screen to the position specified. If the guess is right, the arrow pops the balloon. If wrong, the arrow remains on the screen and the player gets to keep shooting until all the balloons are popped. In one microcomputer version of this game, circus music is played at the beginning of the game and if all three balloons in a round are popped in four tries or fewer, a short song is played after the round.

Green Globs
designed by Sharon Dugdale

In Green Globs, which was presented for the first time at this conference, the student is given coordinate axes with thirteen green globs scattered randomly (see Figure 4).The object of the game is to hit all the globs with graphs specified by typing in equations.

When a glob is hit, it explodes and disappears. The scoring algorithm encourages students to try to hit as many globs as possible with each shot.

Student input can be in many forms. For example, $y = x^2 - 3x + 2$, $x = 5 - 2y/3$, $x = (y + 2)(y - 1)^3$, and $y = 3 + x^5 + 5/x - (x - 1)^3/(x^2 - x)$ are all acceptable inputs.

This activity encourages participation of students of widely varying backgrounds and abilities. It is clearly possible to hit all of the globs with linear functions (in fact with constant functions). However, the more mathematical knowledge the student applies, the more globs he or she is likely to hit per shot. Students of different levels are observed to develop various strategies and increase their skill with graphing. Games are often played by two or more students working cooperatively.

When a student's shot misses the expected targets, the graphic feedback (display of the student's graph) gives diagnostic information needed for the student to debug his or her ideas about graphs. Perhaps the graph was too wide, or too steep, or upside down.

The top ten scores are kept in a "hall of fame." Students' names are displayed along with their record-making scores. A very important aspect of the activity is that all of the

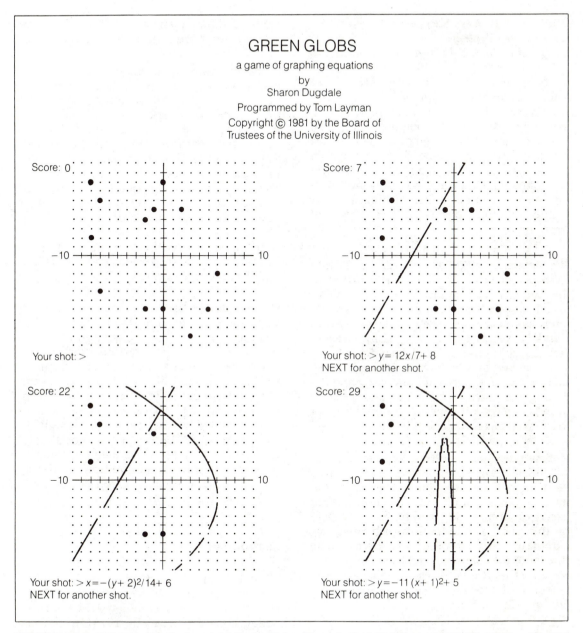

GREEN GLOBS

a game of graphing equations

by

Sharon Dugdale

Programmed by Tom Layman

Copyright © 1981 by the Board of
Trustees of the University of Illinois

Score: 0

Your shot: >

Score: 7

Your shot: > $y = 12x/7 + 8$
NEXT for another shot.

Score: 22

Your shot: > $x = -(y + 2)^2/14 + 6$
NEXT for another shot.

Score: 29

Your shot: > $y = -11(x + 1)^2 + 5$
NEXT for another shot.

FIGURE 4: Successive screen displays from Green Globs. Shown is the initial display of 13 globs, followed by the student's first three shots.

top ten games listed in the hall of fame are stored so that they can be viewed by other students who want to see what shots and strategies the top players have used. Students are frequently observed to "replay" one or more of the record-making games to gather tools that could be useful to them in future games.

Hotline—A Fantasy Microworld for Tutoring Typing
designed by Jim Levin and Allan Collins

An obvious use for microcomputers is to teach typing. Several typing tutor programs already exist, embodying the exercises found in typing textbooks in computer programs. The "Hotline" game attempts to generate a consistent fantasy microworld within which typing can be learned in a highly motivating environment. This game was designed during the workshop as an application of some of the principles discussed. It has not yet been implemented.

The Metaphor: HOTLINE.   You are the White House teletype operator on the Hotline to the Kremlin. You are given encrypted secret messages which you have to type in as accurately as you can (an error could cause World War III), yet as quickly as possible (especially during crises). The metaphor can be strengthened by allowing the learners to use this HOTLINE program for encoding and decoding messages to print out and send to friends, to copy on paper (if no printout), or to save on disk for later reading.

Hotline Teletype Career Path.   You start out as a "Typist," progress to "Master Typist," on to "Pro Typist," then to "Super Typist," and finally to "Hot Shot." Your promotions are based on your typing ability. You get paid on the basis of your level, with bonuses for extra-fast typing and penalties for errors. The threshold for bonuses and the size of penalty for errors increases for each higher level. If you do well enough, you are entered into the Hotline Hall of Fame.

The Underlying Pedagogy.   The same pedagogy embedded in typing courses (and in the Microsoft Typing Tutor) can be used here. Because the Hotline fantasy metaphor makes sensible the presentation of random letters to be typed, the learner can be presented first with home keys, then gradually introduced to nonhome keys. Common bigrams, tri-

grams, and then common words can be given so the learner can acquire these motor units.

Feedback.   After each "message," the learners can be presented with detailed feedback of how well they did, including a graph of time for each keystroke (with a line indicating bonus threshold for that level). Promotion to the next level could depend on getting a fixed percentage of keystrokes faster than the bonus level. Errors that were corrected by the learners would not be penalized except in terms of the necessarily longer time (a corrected error is unlikely to be below bonus threshold). Uncorrected errors would be penalized both by decreasing the learner's "pay" and by counting them as having some fixed long latency.

General Design Issues.   What can we learn from this exercise in designing a motivating environment for teaching typing? The main lesson is that augmentations work better when they are part of an integrated microworld. This is the distinction the workshop was groping toward in discussions of intrinsic vs. extrinsic fantasies, functional vs. nonfunctional exercises, aesthetic design vs. tacked-on frills. There is a need for a simulated world, a fantasy, an integrating concept, to make sensible all the multiple, challenging goals that everyone agreed went toward making motivating environments.

Summary

A number of groups have recently tried to specify detailed principles for designing instructional software (e.g., MECC, 1980; Seiler, 1981; Fischer et al., 1978). In our discussions of this problem, several important issues emerged.

Main Points of Agreement

1. Multiple Levels of Design Concerns.   There exist many different levels at which design issues arise. This point came up in several of the presentations in the workshop and was central to many of the discussions. The levels are ordered along some dimension of generality: there are relatively specific, local concerns like how to arrange text and graphics on the computer display; there are more general issues like how to structure the overall interaction among learners, computers, and human teachers.

2. Integrated Systems/Models/Fantasies. Many of the participants expressed concern about the possible misuse of explicit design principles, as these might lead people to indiscriminately "tack on" features to educational programs, without a concern for the "aesthetics" of design. People agreed that intrinsic fantasies, for example, were generally better than tacked-on extrinsic fantasies. Similarly, "functional" uses of programs, those that served some preexisting goals of the learners, were seen as superior to nonfunctional uses. This concern for the "aesthetics" of design can be partially captured as a need for an "integrated" educational program, one where the user can easily understand what the program is, how it works, and how it is to be used. Integrated systems are easier to understand and use and learn from than unintegrated collections of parts.

3. Active/Interactive Uses. There was a consensus that programs that actively engaged the learners in some activity were better than those which passively presented material and then tested the student. This possibility for active engagement was seen as a major advantage of using computers for education rather than alternate media like books. Even though this point is not new, its importance was reiterated at the conference.

Main Points of Disagreement

1. Educational Games vs. Educational Tools vs. Educational Simulations. There was disagreement about the relative utility of these different kinds of educational program. The prototypical educational game for this workshop was the Darts game, in its various incarnations. For the player, the primary goal is to break all the balloons. The educational goal (to learn about number lines) is secondary to the player. Prototypical educational tools for the workshop were computer languages such as LOGO and Smalltalk and computer text-editing systems, which learners can use for a wide range of possibilities. Educational simulations presented at the workshop included Laura Gould's TRIP system, and Ed Hutchins and Jim Hollan's maneuvering board simulation.

Some participants argued for the motivational value of educational games; others worried that these learning environments were too restrictive. Some participants argued for the value of educational tools, as they allowed learners to transcend the limits of the original design of the program; others raised the issue of how to structure instruction in such unbounded settings. Some participants argued for educational simulations, within which instructional sequences can be defined; others questioned their ability to keep learners motivated for active engagement.

2. Locus of Control (Learner vs. Computer vs. Teacher). This general issue was raised in a discussion of "hints" and how to give them. Although there was some basic philosophical disagreement about where the locus of control in educational settings should reside, the specific discussion of hints led to agreement that there are some specific principles for when to give hints (like those described in John Brown's talk).

3. Evaluation. How to know/show that microcomputer educational uses are "better" than other educational approaches? This critical issue was briefly raised in several discussions, with some participants using conventional measures of achievement (grades or scores on standardized tests) and other participants arguing for evaluation that is not captured in these measures.

REFERENCES

Abelson, H., and diSessa, A. *Turtle geometry: The computer as medium for exploring mathematics.* Cambridge, Mass.: MIT Press, 1981.

Burton, R. R., and Brown, J. S. An investigation of computer coaching for informal learning activities. *International Journal of Man–Machine Studies,* 1979, 11, 5–24.

diSessa, A. Unlearning Aristotelian physics: A study of knowledge-based learning, *Cognitive Science 6,* 1982, 37–75.

Dugdale, S. *Using the computer to foster creative interaction among students.* Urbana, Ill.: Computer-based Education Research Laboratory Report No. E-9, October 1979.

Dugdale, S., and Kibbey, D. *Fractions Curriculum of the PLATO Elementary School Mathematics Project* (second edition). Urbana, Ill.: Computer-based Education Research Laboratory Report No. E-17, July 1980.

Fischer, G., Burton, R. R., and Brown, J. S. Aspects of a theory of simplification, debugging, and coaching. *Proceedings of the Second Annual Conference of the Canadian Society for Computational Studies of Intelligence.* Also available as Bolt Beranek and Newman, Inc. Technical Report No. 3912 (ICAI Report No. 10), Cambridge, Mass., July 1978.

Gould, L., and Finzer, W. A study of TRIP: A computer system for animating time–rate–distance problems. *Proceedings of the IFIP World Conference on Computers in Education,* Lausanne, July 1981.

Levin, J. A., and Kareev, Y. *Personal computers and education: The challenge to schools.* La Jolla, Calif.: Center for Human Information Processing, University of California at San Diego, Technical Report No. CHIP 98, November 1980.

Malone, T. W. *What makes things fun to learn? A study of intrinsically motivating computer games.* Palo Alto, Calif.: Xerox Palo Alto Research Center, Technical Report No. CIS-7 (SSL-80-11), August 1980.

Malone, T. W. Toward a theory of intrinsically motivating instruction. *Cognitive Science 4,* 1981, 333–369.

Minnesota Educational Computing Consortium (MECC). *A guide to developing instructional software for the Apple II microcomputer.* St. Paul, Minn.: MECC Publication No. M(AP) -2, February 1980.

Papert, S. *Mindstorms: Children, computers, and powerful ideas.* New York: Basic Books, 1980.

Papert, S., Watt, D., diSessa, A., and Wier, S. *Final report of the Brookline Logo Project,* vol. II. Cambridge, Mass.: Massachusetts Institute of Technology, Artificial Intelligence Laboratory Memo No. 545, 1979.

Seiler, B. A. *Guidelines for designing PLATO lessons.* Office of Computer-Based Instruction Technical Report, University of Delaware, Newark, 1981.

2 Principles of Software Design for Education

The marriage between technology and education is held together by theories that connect the capabilities of the computer with the needs of the user. Technically elegant programs do not necessarily make effective educational tools. The success of a program hinges on a sophisticated knowledge of the user, on how he or she interacts with the machine, and on the effective instructional features of the software. A miscalculation of the capabilities of the user can be fatal; even good programs can falter or be ignored or ineffective if they disregard the principles that link the machine and the user.

Some of the relevant educational and psychological principles are described in the three articles in this section. The paper by Hartley and Lovell lays out some of the psychological principles that underlie the design of instructional systems. These authors describe the main features in computer-based learning as a context in which to examine educational programs. They argue that ef-

fective designs can best be built on information about the student's level of knowledge and the principles involved in learning. Gagné, Wager, and Rojas complement this view with a discussion of several different types of learning outcome that offer resources to guide the design of educational programs.

For many users, the computer is an appealing instrument; computer games are attractive enough to be seen by some communities as temptations that need to be regulated by law. Malone describes several studies designed to identify the elements of computer games that arouse such powerful motivations. On the basis of his work and of theory in the field, Malone describes the role of challenge, fantasy, and curiosity in motivating students to play computer games and considers whether these elements can be integrated into educational experiences and materials.

3 The Psychological Principles Underlying the Design of Computer-based Instructional Systems

J. Roger Hartley and
Kenneth Lovell

University of Leeds

1.0 Introduction

The last ten years have seen considerable developments in computer-assisted learning (CAL). While most of this activity has taken place in the United States, there have been significant projects in Canada and Western Europe, and in 1972 the British government set aside £2 million for a five-year National Development Program. Many reports of these projects have been published, so there is sufficient data to justify a review of progress, to consider profitable lines of activity, and to debate the difficulties which are, and will be, encountered in present and future work. In general, this paper will take the view that teachers themselves do not make the most efficient use of the CAL materials which have been produced, and that many of these materials do not make the most use of the languages and authoring systems which are available. Of course it is accepted that in the foreseeable future it will not be possible to mimic or replicate the type of instructional dialogue which can take place between the human teacher and student. On the other hand the computer programs can calculate and carry out instructions of data retrieval and processing extremely rapidly; they can also keep detailed records of students' performances and methods. Thus, many facilities and teaching modes become available which can be related to the knowledge which

the system holds of the student, and this level of control and adaptivity cannot be matched by the human teacher faced with a group of students. It is also accepted that teachers will find it difficult to integrate computer-based methods within their normal teaching schemes. The former emphasize individualization and the adaptive nature of teaching, whereas the latter tend to favor minimal variation in the conditions under which individuals are expected to learn.

In providing individualized modes of teaching, efficiency will come from managing those factors which influence learning, and so it might be expected that educational psychology would have a central role in CAL. This is not the case in practice. Much of educational technology has tended to neglect psychology and to concentrate upon techniques of task analysis and the diagnosis of task structure. This analysis has been logical rather than psychological, and the program designs have been simplistic in their methods of individualization. They have often been pragmatically imposed and rarely controlled by valid theories which underpin individual differences.

The purpose of this paper is to redress this balance to a small extent and to indicate some of the psychological work which should be taken into account in designing CAL materials. Before reviewing this evidence, a brief synopsis of the main features of

J. Roger Hartley and Kenneth Lovell, "The Psychological Principles Underlying the Design of Computer-based Instructional Systems," 1977, in A. Jones and H. Weinstock, Eds., *Computer-Based Science Instruction* (Rockville, Md.: Sijthoff & Noordhoff International Publishing Co., 1978), and in James Hartley and Ivor Davies, Eds., *Contributions to an Educational Technology,* Vol. 2 (New York: Nichols Publishing Co., 1979), pp. 73–95. Reprinted by permission of Kogan Page Ltd. (London).

developments in CAL is set out, and this provides a framework for the criticisms of program designs which are made in later sections. The principal arguments are for a more comprehensive representation of the student's knowledge state on which to base decision making, and for a richer form of dialogue between the student and the computer programs. These factors suggest the design of more "knowledgeable" teaching programs, and the paper concludes with some examples and some observations on their potential.

2.0 Summary of Some Styles of Application

2.1 Tutoring

A glance through the catalogs of CAL materials will show a wide variety of program design and subject areas to which they have been applied. However, many of them envisage the computer as a tutoring machine, although there has been a move away from large-scale objectives in which the programs are seen as a complete or major replacement of the teacher. A more typical objective is to provide a framework of support for initial teaching by textbook or lecture. The programs check the student's understanding, provide feedback or supplementary instruction where necessary, and allow him to apply and extend his knowledge in different contexts. For example, a large-scale CAL project in teaching applied statistics has been established at Leeds University (Abbatt and Hartley, 1976). Over a dozen departments in three institutions are cooperating in the work, and approximately one thousand undergraduates per week receive instruction at the terminal. Some of the materials are used for tutoring, and over one hundred small modules deal with topics which occur in a year's course in elementary statistics. The modules have several features. A virtually unlimited number of performance counters are

available for representing the student's knowledge state, and decision rules can be based on these. The learner can have some control also. He can ask for definitions and help if he is unable to answer a problem or a particular question, and he can request a more detailed level of explanation if he is dissatisfied with the feedback. If he were so inclined, the student could go back to earlier sections, explore different routes through the material, and return to his original place in the program when he wished. Calculation and simulation facilities are also available and can be called from the teaching programs.

The tutoring modules act under the command of control programs, which are specified by teachers and macrogenerated. The control programs select sections of the prestored teaching material, link them together with continuity comments, and specify decision rules which refer to the performance data stored by the modules. The rules usually specify minimum performance standards, and when these are met, the student is given choice over the amount and type of any further instruction he wishes to receive. Through their individual control programs, lecturers can place different emphases on the tutoring programs and alter their prominence within the overall statistics teaching.

The student performance data is collected in files specified in size and identifying name by the author. The data is used by the control programs to guide the dialogue and teaching decisions, and by assessment routines which print advice and guidance in further study for the individual student. A third use is by teachers who can process the files to find out which students are having particular difficulties and which topics are proving difficult for the class as a whole. Further teaching or revision can then be given through lectures, textbooks, or remedial teaching at the terminal.

This application has many features which are typical of computer-based tutoring. The teaching initiative and control rests largely with the program. This selects tasks and provides feedback contingent upon completed responses; the learner can only exercise some control through an extremely limited set of commands. The material is designed by experienced teachers who try to specify their objectives, undertake task analyses, sequence the content, [and] set out responses which are anticipated at each point in the program and the routing decisions which are then to be carried out. This detailed and particular teaching specification has to be pre-stored in the computer, and this implies that the student can only have limited control over the teaching dialogue. In general he cannot propose his own methods of solution, or comment on the materials, or ask for explanations, or pose supplementary questions unless they have been anticipated by the course author. Thus the teaching modes, though useful, are limited.

Usually tutoring programs are written using general purpose author languages. These consist of commands and conventions which the writer follows so that, when his material is stored in the computer, the author language processor can retrieve and print labeled portions, accept, process, and evaluate responses, update student histories, and apply routing instructions. The advantages of author languages are that they are easy to learn and can be used with any subject area. However they do have several limitations, a principal one being the ways in which they deal with typed responses. Whereas numbers and symbols can be retrieved from the response, and processed arithmetically and algebraically, words are treated as character strings and are matched or compared with exemplars specified by the author. To make this exercise in anticipation manageable, he must carefully limit the command words which can be used by the student and restrict the size of task, question, or dialogue step put to him.

2.2 Simulation and the Illustration of Concepts

In the sciences many concepts are not only difficult to illustrate, but the relations between them are represented in formal and symbolic terms. Many students find it difficult to link these theoretical terms with the conventional language which describes everyday experience. Thus, to make scientific phenomena accessible to the intellect, the teacher must illustrate the concepts, build up the student's knowledge structures, and allow him to elaborate them in ways which show the nature of the underlying principles. For these reasons, providing "simulation" exercises through computer programs has proved a useful and popular development in science teaching. The idea is that the programs provide a "working model" of the scientific system. In fact it is the formal representation of the system, i.e., a set of equations or a quantitative data base, which can be sampled, which is embodied in the programs. Usually the student cannot edit or amend the program itself, but he can manipulate the input values and observe the effects on the output displays.

An example of such work is an emergency patient simulation program which has been implemented by Taylor and Scott (1975). The patient is represented at any current time as the state values of a set of vital signs such as temperature, pulse rate, respiration, coma, and cyanosis, which are appropriate to the working context. Functions act on these values and so govern their change through time. The student is given a situation, for example, a car accident patient with fractures and airway blockages, and he can ask for investigations and tests to be made and treatments to be carried out. In general the tests do not affect the patient's state directly, but they have a time penalty and during this time his condition could deteriorate. The user can monitor the changes and the rates of change in the values of the vital signs, and the results are shown graphically. To improve the patient's condition, the student can propose treatments. To each of these a time increment simulates its administration, after which functions attached to that treatment alter the patient's counter values. If threshold values are exceeded the patient dies. The treatments can be classified into those which are fatal at any point, and those which have good or bad effects in the short and in the long term. The aim, of course, is to hasten the patient's improvement and achieve a stable condition, and the sole feedback given to the user is the patient's state vector.

The objectives are to ensure that the student realizes the need for comprehensive monitoring and for having several ongoing treatments. (Thus, in the particular example given above, cortisone will resolve the problem of falling blood pressure but unless the airway is cleared in some way, the cyanosis will be fatal.) The student must also learn to evaluate the various effects of the treatments. (For example, although phenobarbitone has a bad effect on respiration, coma, and cyanosis in the long term, it has a good effect on pulse.)

This exercise has many of the features which justify simulation as a teaching device. First, the learner can operate with a simpler system than he would encounter in reality. He has greater control and so it is easier for him to appreciate the relationships, i.e., the patient's requirements and the effects of treatments. Secondly, the student can see the effects of his decisions without detrimental consequences, and the "real" time scale is also compressed so that many exercises can be worked through in a relatively short period of time. However, there are some difficulties. Building simulators to serve as teaching devices is not an easy task and requires careful analysis. The dialogue also is limited. In the example above, the student can merely select the investigation or treatment, he cannot discuss his decisions, nor can he ask why or how the treatments have their various effects. There is no discussion of methods of handling such emergency patient situations, and no general teaching guidance is supplied directly with the program. Further, no records are kept of the learner's protocols and so the program is not able to become adaptive on subsequent runs of the simulation exercise.

2.3 Teaching Problem-solving Skills

These deficiencies become more important in teaching problem-solving[1] skills when experience in developing appropriate heuris-

tics is crucial. By presenting varieties of related tasks, the student can learn to pick out those characteristics which indicate the economical methods of solution. Some workers have attempted to use the computer for teaching such skills either by incorporating extended dialogue facilities within the simulation programs, or by allowing simulation modules to be called from author language programs. For example, Bork and Robson (1972) devised a simulation/teaching program for the study of waves. The computer program simulated an experimental investigation of a pulse in a rope, and the student was provided with a measurement facility by which he could enter time and position and be told the rope displacement. There was a definite aim—he had to discover enough about the disturbance to be able to answer numerical questions about its behavior. On request, the program would summarize the values and plot them graphically. In order to help those students who were working unsystematically and to little effect, Bork and Robson designed the program to retain the student's requests for measurements, make certain checks on them, and print advice based on these evaluations. For example, the program could check if the student had encountered nonzero values; if not, the comments would suggest where they might be found. If data collection was haphazard, the program might advise that time should be fixed and the detailed behavior of the rope studied at a number of different places, or that measurements should be gathered at a particular position for different intervals of time. These hints become progressively stronger, so that if a student was performing poorly, the program almost instructed him how to proceed on a step-by-step basis.

In another example, taken from the applied statistics project at Leeds University, simulation modules are called from dialogue programs written in the author language. The topic area is that of experimental design, and for more experienced students a short background synopsis of an actual experiment is taken from the research literature. The student has to construct a satisfactory experimental plan. He must identify the variables, define hypotheses, [and] set out the methods of measurement, the organization and design of the experiment, and his proposed techniques of data analysis. Populations of data which replicate those reported in the literature have been stored in a simulation program, so the student can try out his decisions, process the data, and draw his own conclusions. After a group of students has undertaken the exercise individually an interesting seminar can result. Some details of this experience have been described elsewhere (Abbatt and Hartley, 1974). Ayscough (1973) has developed other applications which help undergraduates to plan laboratory experiments in physical chemistry.

While simulation programs can provide illustrations which it is difficult to give by any other means, and although teaching dialogue can allow more extended problem-solving types of exercises, the student cannot, in any real sense, place his own construction on the problem and set out his own methods of solution. Practically, the program languages which are used do not permit this. All author language material must be prestored and the student responses anticipated; the author cannot set out the full range of solutions. Again, simulation modules do not permit direct insight into their structure; the student cannot amend the programs, neither is he involved in their designs. Accordingly some workers have attempted to devise programming languages in which students can write their solutions to problems. The exercise of writing and debugging such programs is claimed to be interesting, to provide deeper insights into the subject matter, and to aid general thinking skills. The language itself should be easy to learn, provide immediate and lucid feedback on errors, have a structure which matches that of the subject area, and permit sophisticated programs to be built up from simple procedures.

The most interesting example of this approach is the language LOGO, which can be learned by schoolchildren and which has suggested interesting developments in the curriculum and methods of teaching mathematics (Papert and Solomon, 1972). For ex-

ample, the pupil might devise programs to draw geometric shapes on a crt [cathode ray tube] terminal. The simplest procedure is to instruct the cursor to move forward n steps, rotate through an angle, and repeat these instructions recursively. By labeling the parameters and altering the values, the pupil can study the shapes produced. Simple additions of an extra step length will cause spiraling, putting in tests to control the sequence of commands will allow the shapes to "roll" along, or round themselves. Such programs can be extended and can be generalized as the child develops his notions of the properties of shapes and symmetry.[. . .]

At the university level, Brown and Rubenstein (1973) have used this language with psychology undergraduates, to explore topics in linguistics and grammars. The language APL is also becoming more popular for these problem-solving-type objectives and Berry et al. (1973) have set out some examples for teaching topics in mechanics and in computer science. Again, it should be noted that the dialogue is largely one-sided, with the computer responding to the instructions of the student and providing feedback on syntax errors, or displaying the output of a satisfactory program. The student is strictly limited to the command and syntax structure of the language, and any instruction on formulating the problem or on methods of generalizing or correcting programs has to be supplied by a teacher or by the student himself. At present, experience in using these techniques is largely undeveloped and there has been little evaluation of their effects.

3.0 Factors Influencing Learning

Having summarized some applications in CAL, and considered the advantages and limitations of the techniques, it is appropriate to consider psychological research which shows some of the factors which influence learning. Hopefully this might suggest ways of improving the designs of computer-based teaching programs.

3.1 The Function of Feedback

It is now generally recognized that feedback, i.e., the message or compound statement which follows the response made by the learner, should not be regarded as a reinforcing stimulus, but as information which will locate error and which may inform the student how to correct it. The word "may" is used for two reasons: first the feedback information may not be assimilable to the student's ongoing intellectual structures and secondly, the giving of feedback messages assumes a certain level of attention and motivation. These conclusions must not be considered trite. Although the facilitating effects of feedback are often proposed in psychology, experimental demonstrations of the value of immediate feedback using actual lessons have been rare. Further, it will be argued that few CAL programs take full account of the value of feedback, and are not structured so as to control systematically the amount and type of feedback by managing such variables as task type and difficulty. So there are doubts about the importance of feedback in conventional learning situations which are reflected in the structure of many CAL programs.

The cause of this might well be the influence of initial work in programmed instruction. Following Skinner (1954), it was supposed that the learning task should be analyzed into steps or tasks small enough to ensure that the probability of a successful response was almost unity. Thus the immediate knowledge of correct results (KCR) would reinforce the learner and strengthen the stimulus–response bond. However, when Grundin (1969) reviewed over thirty-five studies, of which thirteen were concerned specifically with feedback, not one showed a significant increase in learning.

Anderson, Kulhavy, and Andre (1971, 1972) have provided some answers to this puzzle. The teaching material they used in their experiments was a linear program on the diagnosis of myocardial infarction from electrocardiograms. This was presented and controlled by computer, and subjects were randomly assigned to several different teaching treatments in which knowledge of correct results was given on several different schedules. These included: (i) no KCR, (ii) 100 percent KCR, (iii) KCR given only after right answers, and (iv) KCR given only after wrong answers. The students were given pencil-and-paper posttests. The results of the experiment showed that all other groups did significantly better than the "no feedback" group. KCR given after wrong responses only was almost as effective as 100 percent KCR, which was the most successful treatment. In a second similar experiment one group was shown the correct response before having to type it at the terminal (i.e., a cheat condition). This time the posttests showed significant differences between the feedback procedures, with the cheat group performing significantly worse than all other groups, even the one which was not given feedback. The interpretation of the results is that the effects of feedback are beneficial, and that whereas in textbooks and programmed texts students can short-circuit the instruction and look ahead to the right answers (i.e., a cheat condition), presentation by computer means that it is possible to ensure that feedback is unavailable until after the student responds. Checks can also be made on his processing of this information. A second conclusion is that the main function of feedback is not to strengthen or reinforce correct responses, but to locate errors and provide information so that the learner can put them right (for KCR following wrong responses only was almost as good as the 100 percent feedback treatment). Guthrie (1971) has also given a persuasive demonstration of this. Thus CAL tutorial programs should not necessarily be small step but have tasks large enough to expose the student's misunderstandings and correct them.

As well as the emphases on activity and control which computer-assisted methods can place on learning, the type of information which is provided by the feedback message is important. Further, these variables are likely to interact with the student's abilities. For example, in one experiment carried out at Leeds University, twenty-nine second-year undergraduates in physical chemistry were randomly allocated to three computer-based teaching treatments. In the first the student was merely told if his responses were correct or not. In the second treatment the program evaluated the student's response, located the error, and provided information by which the student could see how the correct answer had been derived. However, there was no check that the student had attended to or comprehended the feedback message. The third treatment was similar to the previous one except that the student had to demonstrate his understanding by typing in a satisfactory response. The teaching material was to guide students in planning laboratory experiments in physical chemistry. (More specifically, the experiments concerned reaction kinetics and the determination of equilibrium constants.) Students came to the terminal on the three occasions which were necessary to complete the material. Retention tests and other pencil-and-paper posttests on planning experiments were given. The results showed significant gains in performance. Not unexpectedly the first teaching treatment was the least satisfactory for learning but took less time. However, the more able students (as measured by performances in the traditional chemistry examinations) from this group learned almost as much as students of similar ability in the other two groups. Thus the results argue for adaptive teaching decision rules which relate type of feedback to a student's competence.

In general, type of feedback information is also related to the type of task, which is determined by the educational objectives. A discussion of these matters is contained in Pask (1975). He distinguishes between feedback which relates to the answer itself, to the methods of determining the answer, and to techniques of learning. So it should be noted that giving a central role to feedback does not imply that educational objectives should be limited, or that the teaching mode should be tutorial and directive.

3.2 Structure and Organizing Frameworks

Several experiments involving feedback tend to show that for a given set of tasks, the greatest learning gains are made by the less able students. This is understandable for frequency of errors, and therefore feedback is a decreasing function of competence. A first inference then, is that task difficulty (a function which relates the student's working levels of success to task or subject-matter characteristics) will be a determining factor in learning since, as well as affecting motivation, it will control the quantity of feedback the student receives. Also, since educational aims are often concerned with the transfer of learning, it is expected, even required, that the feedback messages given to students will have a wider generality than the particular questions to which they refer. Hopefully the student will be stimulated to make these associations with previous experience. Thus methods of sequencing material and tasks are likely to be important in learning, and providing generalizing frameworks within which new material can be subsumed might be beneficial also. This section will briefly consider these three aspects of organization, namely task difficulty, the sequencing of material, and the provision of organizers.

In some circumstances, for example, in the learning of algorithmic practice tasks, specific models of task difficulty can be set up. The suboperations which make up the algorithm can be identified, error factors associated with each of them, and by making some simplifying assumptions of mathematical independence, the overall probability of obtaining a successful outcome can be calculated. The student is then represented by his proficiency in the suboperations and from this, estimates of his working level of success can be made for any future task which requires their use (Woods and Hartley, 1971). In other circumstances such models cannot be proposed even when the material has repeated applications. In this case certain classes of task are chosen and difficulty estimates of them are made from experimental data with a sample of students. Then computer programs can select and mix tasks together so that a specified working level of success is ensured.

It is now necessary to produce some evidence that task difficulty will influence the improvement of performances, and ask the subsidiary question of which levels of difficulty should be set in various tasks. If they are too easy, the internal search process the student uses to produce the response will become impoverished. If they are too difficult, as well as lowering student motivation, the quantity of feedback might be such that it cannot be assimilated within the ongoing cognitive structures of the student. In an experiment at Leeds, concerned with arithmetic practice with schoolchildren, such a hypothesis was proposed. It was predicted that a curvilinear relationship would be obtained with tasks of intermediate difficulty producing the most improvement. The difficulty of the questions was altered by computer programs so that a pupil worked at a high (95 percent), moderate (75 percent), or low (60 percent) level of success. Subjects were given an arithmetic pretest, stratified and randomly assigned to one of the three treatment groups.

The results were clear. Posttest performances showed that the intermediate group had the advantage in speed and accuracy over the high group, which in turn was significantly better than the low group. A three-way analysis of variance using pretest level, treatment group, and difficulty of items in the posttest showed that those pupils who were low on pretest scores were more sensitive to the differences in the teaching treatments. It was also possible, from the analyses, to propose quantitative models which allowed feedback and time factors to explain these results without needing to consider subsidiary hypotheses about motivational factors.

Controlling task difficulty is one method of sequencing the educational material by means of decision rules which are based on models or hypotheses of student performances. A general, but less well-defined, method is to use the educational objectives and task analyses to subdivide the course into a set of concepts and techniques which have to be learned. These can be partitioned into a series of levels depending on their complexity, and usually checks are made to ensure that the student has reached a satisfactory standard of mastery before he is allowed to continue to higher levels. Some workers, for example Gurbutt (1976), have used graph theory to work out more detailed arrangements within the various levels. Thus devising and managing such material has two components. The first is an analysis and arrangement of the subject-matter skills, and the second the performance standards required of the learner within the different curriculum levels.

Robert Gagné has been most influential in proposing and developing these methods of analysis. For him a hierarchy is the relationship between the behaviors of students as they interact with subject matters. It is a classification of student intellectual skills from making discriminations through the learning of concepts to the assimilation of higher order rules (Gagné, 1968). In 1961 and 1962, Gagné et al. reported studies which showed the value of such an analysis. The experiments were set in mathematics, and the materials were hierarchically arranged with the seemingly simpler behaviors appearing first in the instructional scheme. One result was that the best predictor of performances on the higher level tasks was the degree of mastery shown by the individual learners at the lower levels of the task hierarchy. Thus it might be expected that computer programs would be good decision makers in these situations, for detailed performance data would allow hypotheses to be made about the student which could be used to bias his future instruction.

However, there has been argument about whether such a rigid and, in some respects, logical organization of learning is necessary or even desirable. Merrill (1973) maintains that a Gagné-type analysis is insufficient, and that for developing instructional materials a content analysis of the material is also required. More controversial is his assertion that such an analysis can proceed independently of student behavior or instructional strategy. He organizes subject matter into concepts (a set of symbols, objects, or events which share a common attribute or attributes) and operations (the ways concepts can be described, related, or transformed). The results of this analysis do not imply an instructional sequence directly, and Merrill argues for showing the student the content structure and allowing him to develop his own performance algorithms (Merrill, 1973). Similar ideas for the use of "maps" of objectives and content by learners have been taken up by several workers, including Grubb (1968).

Pask [1976] also acknowledges that there are advantages in providing both the expert and the student with some external representation of the material so that topics can be identified and discussed, and explanations initiated by either teacher or learner. However, the methods of content analysis proposed by Pask are somewhat different from those of Merrill, and reestablish the individuality of the teacher and, indirectly, the influence of teaching strategy on the structuring of educational material. In Pask's view the teacher projects his own arguments and interpretations of the subject matter, so the external content map is obtained by the individual subject-matter expert analyzing the various topics and relations which are involved in his own theses.

The teacher is required to show these are valid by constructing explanations, i.e., by showing how one topic is derived from others. The statements are set out as a network with the nodes representing topics, the arcs for parts of a derivation, and the arc clusters showing the various derivation paths. To give direction and definition to his particular lesson, the teacher chooses a head node, i.e., the main topic, and a pruned, hierarchical topic map is obtained. On the basis of this structure tutorial conversations are planned, and for Pask a crucial point is that understanding is reached when teacher and student agree both on a description and on an explanation of a particular topic. Thus the

conversation explores the nodes, arcs, and arc clusters which make up the network, and the computer is able to control and assist the student in collecting information and in testing his understanding. Examination of the paths students take has led Pask to identify characteristic learning strategies and systematic individual differences to learn and discover (Pask, 1976).

A theory of the role of organization in learning has been developed by Ausubel (e.g., Ausubel, 1968). He states that the degree of meaningful learning of new material is related to its interaction with the student's cognitive structures. If his existing knowledge can be used to provide "ideational scaffolding" or anchorage for the new material, then learning becomes facilitated. To ensure this Ausubel suggests that, prior to the instruction, relevant organizing material of greater generality and inclusiveness should be studied by the learner. Several studies set in the sciences have tried to test these ideas, but the characteristics of "good" organizers have not been thoroughly worked out, and research results of their effects have been equivocal (Hartley and Davies, 1976). However some work has shown that organizers are more beneficial when given before rather than at the end of the instruction, although several studies are in disagreement as to whether most benefit is enjoyed by students of low, intermediate, or high verbal ability.

There are several plausible arguments for incorporating organizers within computer-based teaching programs. For example, the organizer need not only be given prior to instruction but can also serve as a teaching framework for the interactive program. In a preliminary study at Leeds, two teaching programs with differing degrees of organization were used. The objective was to study their effects on students' ability to plan laboratory experiments in chemistry, and a pool of six experiments formed the material of the programs. The organizer was a three-page document which gave general rules and methods for use in planning experiments. The on-line tutorial treatments differed in the level of generality of the questions they asked the student and in the organization of the questions themselves. In one treatment, after the students had studied the organizer, general questions taken from it required the learner to contrast the six experiments before making a response. The organizing themes, e.g., control of variables, cut across all the experiments rather than concentrating on each experiment in turn. The questions were sequenced to follow the order of the organizer. In the second treatment the organizer was not studied; the questions were made specific to each experiment and were essentially unordered. The content of both programs was equivalent. The examination grades of each participating student were taken as a measure of his general ability in chemistry. Eighteen undergraduates participated in the study; these were paired on chemistry grades and then randomly allocated, one to each of the two teaching treatments.

Both groups showed significant learning gains on all the planning posttests, but the first treatment showed significantly better results on the test of detecting flaws in given experimental plans. This result was repeated on the knowledge of planning posttest, but there was little difference between the groups on retention of material. Also there were positive correlations between chemistry grades and most of the posttests, and the values of the rank correlation coefficients were usually higher for those students who followed the second "unorganized" treatment. Thus it appeared that lack of structure penalized the less able students. Examination of the on-line performance data showed that the groups were approximately equivalent in the time they spent on the programs and the quantity of feedback they received. A questionnaire completed by all students clearly distinguished between the treatments. The first group gave significantly higher ratings as they reported on the amount they thought they had learned, their confidence in their ability to plan experiments, the interest of the program, and its continuity.

Pask has provided further evidence that organization of material is an important variable in learning and one which he believes should be matched to a student's cognitive style (Pask and Scott, 1972; Pask, 1976). He distinguishes between "serialists" and "holists." It is maintained that the former habitually learn, remember, and recapitulate a body of information as a series of items related by simple links. Holists, on the other hand, work in more global terms, using higher order relations and grouping material in more complex structures. In an experimental study, using relative small numbers ($N=8$) in each group, and with tasks which require the students to learn taxonomies, Pask showed that teaching was most effective when the sequencing of material was matched to the individual's particular type of cognitive competence.

The importance of the type of organization of material and its effect on assimilation by students has been further reinforced in an interesting paper by Mayer and Greeno (1972), which should be read by anyone wishing to experiment in education. They argue that different teaching materials and feedback comments activate and become assimilated within different cognitive structures. They maintain that although the mix of final performances on posttests may not reveal a significant difference overall, the detailed test profiles of the treatment groups can be very different. Mayer and Greeno divised two teaching treatments for topics in probability theory. The first emphasized the interrelations between the tasks themselves, and concentrated heavily on formulas and quantitative relations. The second tried to relate the structure of the subject matter to the existing cognitive structure of the student. This teaching organization was therefore more thematic; it emphasized meanings and relations and their attachment to common experience. Various criterion posttests were used. One set contained numerical calculations and problems requiring algebraic techniques. A second set included problems which looked plausible but had no solution, and other questions emphasized the noncomputational aspects of probability measures. Overall there were no significant differences between the groups on the combined sets of tests, but the first "formal" treatment produced superior results on the first set of quantitative problems, whereas the second treatment group had the better profiles on the other tests.

3.3 Teaching Mode and Learner Control

In the learning situation the problem of transfer involves the type of feedback which is to be given to the student, and this is related to the type of task he is set, the facilities and help he is allowed, and the freedom he has to direct his own learning. This type of variable will be referred to as "teaching mode" and used to contrast techniques which allow different amounts of initiative by the student. For example, the mode may be highly directed and tutorial in which the computer programs ask all the questions to which the learner must respond. Alternatively, the style might be more open ended and allow the student access to facilities of help, example, and explanation, with some control over the course of his own instruction.

It has been argued that when computer programs closely control the content and sequence of prestored teaching, students have little opportunity for taking responsibility and developing their own learning strategies. To counter this, the American TICCIT [Time-shared Interactive Computer-Controlled Information Television] system (Merrill, 1973) has implemented a type of command language which allows the student to regulate both content and teaching strategy. He will need to decide on his learning goals and the methods of accomplishing them by using the resources and materials which have been provided. So the command language should enable the learner to review material, explore fresh subject matter, and set required performance levels. To help him form his learning strategy, an adviser program should provide feedback and give guidance on content sequence, presentation mode, item difficulty, and remedial instruction. The resources include the teaching material with content maps, practice and test items, exam-

ples, and graphics support. Thus in the TICCIT system there are three levels of discourse dealing with answers to specific questions, the instructional process and the language to control it, and the modification of this control under the adviser program. The subject-matter expert performs a content analysis and divides the material into concepts, operations, and rules, which can be presented at two levels (as generalizations or as instances), and in two modes "asking" and "telling." The quantity of instances determines the amount of practice and examples/nonexamples are classified as hard or easy on an abstract–concrete dimension. The command language allows the student to control the presentation in content, sequence, quantity, and difficulty. For example, in order to help his choice of a particular lesson unit he can ask for a content map of the course to be displayed. Response buttons are then used to ask for rules, examples or further practice. Pressing the "hard" or "easy" key regulates the difficulty of the material. The adviser function operates either on student request or when the student's choices appear nonproductive. However, although the rationale underlying the design of the programs has been thoroughly worked out, there has been no large application of the methods and no independent evaluation of the project.

There are several experiments which suggest that students in such a free learning situation do not make a good appraisal of their abilities, and do not make such effective decisions as a program controller. For example, Pask (1975) reached such conclusions after studies which used a variety of tracking and concept learning tasks. However, he noted that a compromise strategy in which the control programs allowed student decisions where they were judged reasonable, maintained motivation and produced equally good results. A similar experience occurred at Leeds, where three teaching modes varied the controls which they placed on the learner. The subject area was teaching the planning of laboratory experiments in chemistry, and in the directed mode the planning questions were put to the student in a predetermined sequence. Failure to respond correctly resulted in active feedback being given in which further responses had to be made to subquestions which located and corrected his errors. The second teaching treatment had intermediate control and allowed the students to access chemistry facts/definitions and teaching. These facilities were stored in three indexed files named CHECK (for testing the planning decisions), HELP (for giving teaching), and FACTS. Students could use and browse through these files as they wished but they had to enter the CHECK file before leaving the program and, if they made an incorrect response in this file, the program did not give feedback or remedial teaching explicitly but routed them to the HELP or FACTS files. The third teaching mode only allowed access to CHECK and FACTS files. If he made an unsatisfactory response to a CHECK question, the correct information was printed. The chemistry content was equivalent in all the programs.

Some thirty students from the physical chemistry laboratory took part and, after pre-tests, they were randomly assigned to the teaching treatments. The results of posttests showed overall improvements for all the groups, but the posttest scores for the second group were significantly lower than the others. An inspection of the ways in which students used the teaching files suggested an explanation of these findings. In the third treatment students tended to check all parts of the plan in an acceptable sequence and feedback was given to them when their responses were unsatisfactory. In other words, the teaching they received was very similar to that of the first mode except that feedback was printed and required no further response. In the second teaching treatment students generally collected insufficient teaching or facts before entering the CHECK file. When incorrect responses were made, they were routed to the teaching files again, where they had to decide which parts to access. For this treatment there was also a significant correlation between chemistry ability and posttest performances. Thus, in the initial states of learning a complex skill, the teaching treatment which required decision making and information collection was not used efficiently, particularly by the less competent students. However, in a further experiment which used an extended series of laboratory experiments, the performances of the second group improved on subsequent occasions so that eventually the method produced equivalent learning gains and took a shorter time. It was also the method which students seemed to prefer. Similar results were also obtained in teaching the planning of statistical investigations with psychology students (Abbatt, 1972). Again the evidence argues for adaptive decision rules in which more responsibility is given to the student to direct his own learning as he becomes more competent.

Similar difficulties in student learning were observed by Bork (Bork and Robson, 1972) when he used the wave simulation program referred to earlier, with forty undergraduates from the Department of Engineering and Science. Ratings showed that half the students liked the program, half did not. It became clear that, for the weaker students, the program did not sustain interest long enough for them to make sufficient discoveries about the behavior of the wave pulse in the rope. When more advanced students used the program (many of whom understood the basic physics and so had a frame of reference), they became more involved, were more successful with the program, and the ratings of this group were enthusiastic.

4.0 Some Design Problems of CAL Programs

The preceding research suggests some general principles which are important in learning. A central place is given to the informational role of feedback and its control by the computer-based teaching programs. The tasks which are given to the student determine the type of learning activities and the type of feedback he receives. The complexity of the task governs the quantity of feedback.

When the educational objectives involve transfer of learning, the program organization (through task sequencing, and by using previous knowledge or advance organizers to provide conceptual frameworks) is likely to be important. For aims which also require the student to develop learning strategies, the degree of learner control will be influential.

Two general comments should be made about this summary. First, all the experiments show that these variables interact with student knowledge and abilities, hence none of them can be efficiently used in CAL unless the programs have adequate information of the student's knowledge space. This is particularly true for determining the type of feedback, the degree of task difficulty, the use of organizers, and the amount of learner control. Secondly, the educational interaction occurs through the dialogue which is transmitted at the terminal. The differing types of task, levels of feedback, and degree of learner control require a student command language and a dialogue which not only permits answers to questions, but methods and explanations, lines of arguments, and teaching/learning strategies.

An examination of current CAL programs will show that few systematically contain or exploit these principles in their designs. Many are put together in a pragmatic way, sometimes without any systematic statement of objectives or analysis of learning tasks. These comments apply to both tutorial and simulation programs; superficially the latter might appear to have clear underlying models, but incorporating these into learning packages for the student is deceptively difficult. Of course, there are many constraints imposed by the computer languages. Essentially author language programs rely on keyword matching, so that responses of the students have to be anticipated and prestored. So either the program takes the initiative and asks small-scale questions, or arranges a small number of commands to serve as a learner control language. These allow him access to facilities, e.g., HELP or CALCULATE, and to select material which is arranged in labeled files. With author languages other forms of educational dialogue are not practical. In simulation programs the dialogue is also restricted. For example, in the rope-pulse simulation program of Bork and Robson referred to earlier, although the teaching dialogue enhanced the program, the comments were prestored and could not respond to any type of data collection which had not been anticipated. The teaching subprogram had not the capability of directing the simulation routines to discover the wave characteristics, hence it could not evaluate student strategies in any general sense, nor respond to suggestions from him. Again, although the student has control over the input values which he selects, and can see their effects, he is unable to inspect, amend, or discover (because of its complexity) the inner structure of the program by which these results are produced. Thus its function is limited to illustration for the naive student and elaboration of knowledge for the student who understands the underlying principles.

In order to individualize teaching, the programs must retain data of a student's performance so that hypotheses can be held about his knowledge state. Typically author language programs do this by a register of counters which summarizes evaluations made of the student's responses. Since, in many programs, the decision to branch from one teaching element to the next is largely determined by the quality of the last response only, the student records which are retained are meagre, and usually consist of a few broad indices of performance. In simulation programs the data is even more sparse. Generally, no records of the learner's protocols are retained, although some "tag" the facility or type of material which is currently being explored. Hence some advice can be given if the student asks questions, but even this information is unlikely to be retained between occasions, so that no advice can be given individually on subsequent runs of the program.

If the dialogue from the student is restricted so that he can only respond to questions, or use a limited set of commands, he will not be able to set out his methods or lines of reasoning, and data about his information processing cannot be obtained. After answering small-step questions, knowledge of the correct response might be adequate feedback, but to give feedback of method and explanation requires knowledge of the student's working procedures, and advice on learning strategy needs information of students' goals.

Therefore the general argument is that current CAL programs have not given sufficient attention to a design for learning, and that some improvements could be made within present author languages and simulation packages. However, a full exploitation of psychological principles in design requires the programs themselves to have a more general "knowledge" of the teaching tasks, of the student, and of teaching strategy.

5.0 The Design of Knowledgeable Programs

In order to increase the teaching power of CAL materials, it is necessary that the programs have three data structures. The first is a representation of the task, ideally in terms which will allow the programs to generate problems and undertake their solution. The second is a representation of the student. This should include not only counters, i.e., hypotheses which are held about his competence, but computer programs which can replicate to some extent his information processing. A knowledge of teaching is the third data structure. This is probably best represented as control programs which are ordered sets of condition–action statements. The conditions relate to characteristics of the task and to programs which model the student's working methods and performances. The teaching actions can select teaching mode, task complexity, facilities of help, and type of feedback. The conditions which are met determine which of the actions are applied.

The advantages which come from having programs with these data structures are inter-esting, but it must be admitted that, at present, they can only be designed in a limited number of well-structured subject areas, and that the costs of their development are large. A first example is taken from Brown et al. (1974) who have developed a program, SOPHIE, to teach fault-finding in electronic circuitry. The papers also give ideas on how some of the current teaching and simulation programs in science could be redesigned and supplied with sufficient information of the subject area and techniques of problem solving to be able to respond to students' inquiries about working strategies. SOPHIE works with specific prestored circuits, but the routines which control the fault diagnosis and the help which is given to students are designed to operate over a variety of electronic circuits. When the student comes to the terminal, he is presented with a circuit diagram and the program automatically selects and inserts a fault of some specified degree of difficulty. The student can then ask for specific circuit readings, for components to be replaced, for hypotheses to be evaluated, and for help. In this case the system suggests plausible hypotheses which are consistent with the readings the student has taken. When he is ready, the user can specify the nature of the fault. The system is fully operational and is an "intelligent" teacher in the sense that it can generate hypotheses about malfunctioning circuits, evaluate the student's hypotheses during his fault-finding, and allow him to communicate with the system in relatively unconstrained English.

Many of the program's logical and inferencing capabilities are derived from using simulation models of the circuit. For example, in fault evaluation the programs modify the circuit to contain the fault suggested by the student's hypothesis. This model is run to repeat the readings gathered by the student. These values of the faulty circuit are compared with the values of the unmodified circuit, and the program decides if the readings are sufficiently close to be considered equivalent. If the hypothesis is not acceptable, the student is given the reasons for its decision. The system is also capable of generating hypotheses about faults. From output voltage measurements taken by the student, possible hypotheses are generated which are capable of explaining these measurements. Each hypothesis is evaluated in turn by using the simulation programs in the manner outlined above. The interesting feature is that the program answers the student after running an experiment on-line.

Although SOPHIE does not produce or store an adequate representation of student performances, it does provide a framework from which such models can be developed. The student has to use a language to request help and to state his hypotheses and lines of reasoning. An examination of his printout will show the various reasoning operations which he employed and the knowledge which he used. When supplemented with individual interviews, the programs become a research tool for investigating problem solving.

A second example is taken from programs which have been designed for the learning of diagnosis skills of the sort which are encountered in medicine. Typically, information is collected sequentially from a patient by interview, examination, and medical tests, and these symptoms and signs have to be summarized so that a course of treatment can be given. Preparatory to this, a diagnosis is usually made in which the patient is assigned with some probability to a limited disease set. Several simulation and tutorial programs have been written (e.g., Weber and Hagamen, 1972; Harless et al., 1971). A "diagnosis" program has also been developed at Leeds, and the data base includes six diseases and some seventy attributes or symptoms. The data include the relative frequencies of the diseases, and for each disease the probability of occurrence of each symptom state. Provided certain mathematical assumptions of independence are met, probability theorems can be used for "diagnosis." In addition, anticipated questions and the patients' comments which are appropriate for each of the symptoms have to be stored. This is the underlying knowledge base which is used by the teaching programs. There can be arguments about

validity, for it is statistical and not strictly medical, but the educational aim is the limited one of illustrating the underlying relationships between patterns of symptoms and diseases.

Consider the advantages which come from such a task representation. First, random number generators operate on probabilities to select a disease and then generate a "patient," i.e., a set of attribute states. The program can easily restrict or expand the disease set so that suitable and individual curricula can be built up on-line for students. A plausible teaching strategy would be to start with a limited number of well-discriminated diseases and add to them as the student improves his performance. Since material is generated by the program when it is needed by the student at the terminal, it makes economic use of store, and an unlimited number of "patients" are potentially available.

A second advantage is the variety of teaching modes and types of feedback which can be developed. Examples of specific diseases can be generated and printed on request, the student can be asked to diagnose the complete case history, or be required to collect the information sequentially by conducting his "interview" at the terminal. Alternatively, the student can specify a disease set, and symptoms. The computer replies by calculating the disease probabilities for that symptom set. By allowing the student to backtrack, and alter symptoms he had previously typed, their effects on the disease probabilities can be explored. These and other facilities arise because the programs can undertake a statistical diagnosis. Since the data base allows generation of "patients," it is essential for the programs to be able to diagnose or they would give misleading information or be unable to proceed. Since they can solve the tasks, it is straightforward to have them output the stages of solution. Similar routines can monitor the student's work at the terminal and be used to provide feedback and help. For example, the programs can calculate how the current diagnosis would be altered by further attribute states. These calculations allow the programs to advise the student on the sequence of his information collection. The computer can withhold such help if the learner is competent, and other controls can be used to prevent him making a premature diagnosis. Finally, if the programs disagree with a student's conclusions, he is asked to list the symptoms which support his decision. For comparison, the computer calculates the support level of each symptom for his diagnosis, and then recalculates their support for the correct diagnosis.

Of course these programs have their limitations. They are specialized, can only be used in classification tasks, which have probabilistic data bases, and the effort which is needed to provide such data is considerable. There are also educational difficulties. Although the programs can use the different facilities of teaching mode, help, and feedback to maximize learning, such decision rules are pragmatically stated. Also the representation of the student is extremely limited. It consists of a record of the facilities which he uses and his overall performance levels of correct diagnosis. This lack of knowledge is being remedied by studying the methods and strategies individual students use in selecting the patient information and processing it. Models, i.e., programs which distinguish between groups of students on the basis of these skills and which give significant predictions, have been developed and are described in an introductory paper (Hartley, 1976). This knowledge of the student can be stored as procedures and run on the teaching tasks to test hypotheses about the likely ways he would perform. This information can then be used to decide on the task and type of feedback which should be given.

A more serious criticism is that the program uses mathematical methods for diagnosis which the student or physician does not replicate and perhaps does not understand. Thus the dialogue is limited, for the computer program cannot explain its decisions or recommendations; the student must accept or reject the mathematical conclusions. However an interactive program, MYCIN, has been designed which uses the clinical decision rules and methods of experts. It advises

physicians in selecting appropriate antimicrobial therapy for hospital patients with bacterial infections (Shortliffe et al., 1975). The aim of the program is not to teach students but, since the system has to explain its recommendations when queried and in terms which the physician can understand, the dialogue itself is educational. The knowledge base is a set of approximately 200 decision rules (if–then statements) which permit an action to be taken (e.g., a drug treatment) or a conclusion drawn if the set of preconditions of characteristics or organisms taken from the patient is met.

After being given some patient data, the MYCIN consultation program has to select those decision rules which apply to the patient. If, during the search, a condition (i.e., a clinical parameter) is not known, a subprogram attempts to find it. If it is not in the records, the user is asked to supply this data. In order to discuss the decisions which are made by the consultation program, an interactive explanation program has been developed. The initiative is taken by the physician, who can ask various types of question. For example, if, during the consultation, the program asks the user for certain data, he can ask WHY it is necessary to obtain this. In reply, the MYCIN explanation program has to state its goals, and show how the current decision rule set is to be used to establish that conclusion. Thus statements are printed which show how the data will satisfy the preconditions of those rules and so enable the conclusion to be drawn. The question WHY can be repeated during this line of reasoning so that inquiries can be made further into the subgoals. If the physician wishes to examine other ways by which the goals can be achieved, he asks the question HOW. The program replies by giving alternative connections of rules through any part of the reasoning network. In these ways the user can question both goals and methods. The program also keeps a trace of its consultation so that any element which contributes to the final treatment decision can be examined or reexamined. Although the language of the program is stilted and largely composed of If/Since

<conditions> Then <conclusion> statements, the decision-making processes are clearly shown.

6.0 Some Conclusions

The teaching potential of MYCIN would be increased if a similar language were devised so that the student could set out his own goals, lines of reasoning, and conclusions. The computer programs would need to evaluate this information, ask questions if the steps were too large or incomplete, and provide feedback. The implementation of mixed initiative teaching dialogues will be difficult to achieve, but some attempts have been described (Carbonell, 1970; Collins et al., 1975).

Providing and using student models which can manage these dialogues is another distant but necessary objective, and Self (1974) has provided a small but useful illustration. Furthermore, even in so-called adaptive programs, the decision rules have been followed in a fixed way. Although the estimates of students' performances can be improved as more learners work through the material, this only enables decision rules to be applied more accurately. The programs must operate in the same way and continue to apply the same rules for a student even if they are not proving satisfactory. In other words, the programs are not self-critical and cannot alter their teaching strategies at run time. To accomplish this, programs need to be able to make assertions which relate student performances to teaching variables in order that larger-scale goals will be attained. These might be to maximize performance objectives or to minimize time at the terminal. The programs then need to be capable of running experiments which test these assertions. This work is still in its infancy, but such a system has been implemented for teaching the solution of quadratic equations by the "discovery" method (O'Shea and Sleeman, 1973).

The researches of learning theorists and the techniques of artificial intelligence might appear somewhat remote from practical problems of writing CAL programs which are to be used regularly by students. In these circumstances the work of the program designer is shaped by practical considerations of computing facilities and development costs. However, the suggestions which have been made could be profitably taken into account and at least partially implemented within present designs of CAL materials. Hopefully the progress in research will be maintained and its ideas more readily assimilated so that the teaching roles of the computer will continue to be extended, particularly in the teaching of problem-solving skills.

ACKNOWLEDGMENTS

Many of the experiments referred to in this paper were designed and carried out by the staff of the Computer Based Learning Project at Leeds University. In particular, acknowledgements should be made to F. Abbatt, A. Cole, J. Green, C. Macrae, M. Rawson, D. Sleeman, and K. Tait. Much of this work has been supported by grants from the Social Science Research Council, and the National Development Programme in Computer Assisted Learning.

NOTE

1. "Problem solving" is a term which is even more loosely defined and ill used than "simulation." This paper will not attempt a technical definition of either term, but their meanings should be clear from the specific contexts. Problem solving implies a novel situation for the student; he has the requisite knowledge and subskills to solve the problem, but he has to sequence his reasoning and/or develop heuristics which take him from the initial to the goal state.

REFERENCES

Abbatt, F. R. (1972) Preliminary experience in using a computer to teach the planning of experiments in the social sciences. Internal Report *P1,* Computer Based Learning Project, University of Leeds.

Abbatt, F. R. and Hartley, J. R. (1974) Teaching planning skills by computer, *International Journal of Mathematical Education in Science and Technology* 5: 665.

Abbatt, F. R., and Hartley, J. R. (1976) Teaching applied statistics by computer, *Aspects of Educational Technology X.* London: Kogan Page.

Anderson, R. C., Kulhavy, R. W., and Andre, T. (1971) Feedback procedures in programmed instruction, *Journal of Educational Psychology* 62: 148.

Anderson, R. C., Kulhavy, R. W., and Andre, T. (1972) Conditions under which feedback facilitates learning from programmed lessons, *Journal of Educational Psychology* 63: 186.

Ausubel, D. P. (1968) *Educational Psychology— A Cognitive View.* New York: Holt, Rinehart & Winston.

Ayscough, P. B. (1973) Computer-based learning in the teaching laboratory, *Chemistry in Britain* 9 2: 61.

Berry, P. C., Bartoli, G., Del'Aquila, C., and Spadavecchia, V. (1973) *APL and Insight: The Use of Programs to Represent Concepts in Teaching.* IBM Bari Scientific Centre Technical Report Number CRB 002/513-5302, Italy.

Bork, A. M., and Robson, J. (1972) A computer simulation for the study of waves, *American Journal of Physics* 40: 1288.

Brown, J. S., and Rubenstein, R. (1973) *Recursive Functional Programming for Students in the Humanities and Social Sciences,* Technical Report 27. Irvine: Dept. of Information and Computer Science, University of California.

Brown, J. S., Burton, R. R., and Bell, A. G. (1974) *A Sophisticated Instructional Environment for Teaching Electronic Trouble-shooting,* Report 2790. Cambridge, Mass.: Bolt Beranek & Newman, Inc.

Brown, J. S., and Burton, R. R. (1975) Multiple representations of knowledge for tutorial reasoning. In D. G. Bobrow and A. Collins (eds.) *Representation and Understanding.* New York: Academic Press, p. 351.

Carbonell, J. R. (1970) Mixed initiative man-computer instructional dialogues (Ph.D. thesis, MIT), Report No 1971. Cambridge, Mass.: Bolt Beranek & Newman, Inc.

Collins, A., Warnock, E. H., Aiello, N., and Miller, M. L. (1975) Reasoning from incomplete knowledge. In D. G. Bobrow and A. Collins (eds.) *Representation and Understanding.* New York: Academic Press, p. 383.

Gagné, R. M. (1968) Learning hierarchies, *Educational Psychologist* 6: 1.

Gagné, R. M., and Paradise, N. E. (1961) Abilities and learning sets in knowledge acquisition, *Psychological Monographs* no. 518.

Gagné, R. M., Mayor, J. R., Garstens, Helen L., and Paradise, N. E. (1962) Factors in acquiring knowledge of a mathematical task, *Psychological Monographs* no. 526.

Grubb, R. F. (1968) Learner controlled statistics, *Journal of Programed Learning* 5: 38.

Grundin, H. U. (1969) Response mode and information about correct answers in programmed instruction. In A. P. Mann and C. K. Brunstrom (eds.) *Aspects of Educational Technology III.* London: Pitman, p. 65.

Gurbutt, P. A. (1976) *Thoughts on graphs in physics,* UCODI Working Paper 14. Belgium: IMAGO Centre, Batiment Sc 16-B, 1348 Louvain-la-Neuve.

Guthrie, J. T. (1971) Feedback and sentence learning, *Journal of Verbal Learning and Verbal Behavior* 10: 23.

Harless, W. G., Drennon, G. G., Marxer, J. J., Root, G. A., and Mill, G. E. (1971) CASE: A computer aided simulation of the clinical encounter, *Journal of Medical Education* 46: 443.

Hartley, J., and Davies, I. K. (1976) Pre-instructional strategies: the role of pretests, behavioral objectives, overviews and advance organisers, *Review of Educational Research* 46: 239–65.

Mayer, R. E., and Greeno, J. G. (1972) Structural differences between learning outcomes produced by different instructional methods, *Journal of Educational Psychology* 63: 165.

Merrill, D. M. (1973) Premises, propositions and research underlying the design of a learner controlled computer assisted instruction system: A summary for the TICCIT system, *Working Paper No 44.* Provo, Utah: Division of Instructional Sciences, Brigham Young University.

Merrill, D. M., and Gibbons, A. S. (1974) Heterarchies and their relationship to behavioral hierarchies for sequencing content in instruction. In J. M. Scandura et al., *Proceedings of 5th Conference on Structural Learning.* Pennsylvania: MERGE Research Institute, Pennsylvania 19072, p. 140.

O'Shea, T., and Sleeman, D. H. (1973) A design for an adaptive self-improving teaching system. In J. Rose (ed.) *Advances in Cybernetics and Systems.* London: Gordon & Breach.

Papert, S., and Solomon, C. (1972) Twenty things to do with a computer, *Educational Technology* 12: 9.

Pask, G. (1975) *The Cybernetics of Human Learning and Performance.* London: Hutchinson.

Pask, G. (1976) Styles and strategies of learning, *British Journal of Educational Psychology* 46: 128.

Pask, G., and Scott, B. C. E. (1972) Learning strategies and individual competence, *International Journal of Man–Machine Studies* 4: 217.

Self, J. A. (1974) Student models in computer-aided instruction, *International Journal of Man–Machine Studies* 6 2: 261.

Shortliffe, E. H., Davis, R., Axline, S. G., Buchanan, B. G., Green, C. C., and Cohen, S. N. (1975) Computer-based consultations in clinical therapeutics: Explanation and rule acquisition capabilities of the MYCIN system, *Computers and Biomedical Research* 8: 303.

Skinner, B. F. (1954) The science of learning and the art of teaching, *Harvard Educational Review* 24: 86.

Taylor, T. R., and Scott, B. (1975) Emergency patient simulation program. Internal report, Department of Computing Science, University of Glasgow.

Weber, J. C., and Hagamen, W. D. (1972) ATS—A new system for computer mediated tutorials in medical education, *Journal of Medical Education* 47: 637.

Woods, Pat, and Hartley, J. R. (1971) Some learning models for arithmetic tasks and their use in computer-based learning, *British Journal of Educational Psychology* 41 1: 35.

Woods, Pat, Hartley, J. R., and Sleeman, D. H. (1972) Controlling the learning of diagnostic tasks, *International Journal of Man–Machine Studies* 4: 319.

4

Planning and Authoring Computer-Assisted Instruction Lessons

Robert M. Gagné, Walter Wager, and Alicia Rojas

Florida State University

In this article, we propose a system for planning and authoring lessons in computer-assisted instruction (CAI). Such a system might be used with the new generation of microcomputers and associated hardware that has recently become available. We consider it likely that an author would need to engage in a considerable amount of advance planning before addressing the computer console. Alternatively, such planning procedures themselves could be incorporated in a computer program.

In designing instruction, existing author languages generally follow the procedure of traditional programmed instruction of the branching type (Eisele, 1978; Lower, 1980; Rudnick, 1979). The student views some information and is then asked a question. Positive reinforcement or corrective feedback is given to the student's response. If the response is incorrect, the student is told why and given another opportunity to respond to the same question. Authors can provide for branching the student to a remedial sequence before returning to the main program or for skipping frames when the student can demonstrate prior knowledge.

This procedure typically begins with "TEXT," a statement of what the student is to learn. Provisions follow for branching, replies to correct and wrong answers, and remediation. In this article, we make no suggestions for improvement of the "feedback-remedial" portion of this traditional authoring system. What we propose is a more thoroughly planned "TEXT," designed differentially in accordance with the type of learning outcome expected.

Designing CAI Lessons

Learning has a different form depending on what is being learned. Learning tasks can be categorized into several different types, and these different types require different teaching strategies. In planning CAI, these strategies can be cast in the form of "prescriptions", or directions for the programmer to follow in designing instruction.

Types of Learning Outcomes

One of the first steps in designing CAI, so as to take advantage of principles of learning derived from theory and research, is to categorize the type of *learning outcome.* Typically, this is done by examining the target objective of a lesson, and identifying what type of performance is expected of the learner after he or she has learned.

Categories of learning outcomes have been described by Gagné (1977). These are as follows: (1) verbal information; (2) intellectual skills, having five subordinate types called discrimination, concrete concept, defined concept, rule, and problem solving; (3) cognitive strategies; (4) motor skills; and (5) attitudes. Each of these categories has at least one critical attribute that distinguishes it

Robert M. Gagné, Walter Wager, and Alicia Rojas, "Planning and Authoring Computer-Assisted Instruction Lessons," *Educational Technology,* 21 (September 1981), 17–26. Reprinted by permission of Educational Technology Publications.

from the others, and that makes it possible for the designer of instruction to determine into which category a given learning task fits.

Although it would be possible to deal with each of these categories and their subordinate types, we intend here to consider only those learning outcomes which are most likely to be aimed for in CAI instruction. Definitions of these outcomes are in the following paragraphs.

Verbal Information. Meaningful knowledge which may be recalled as words and sentences, including names, labels, sentences, and organized bodies of semantically related propositions, such as are found in connected discourse (oral or printed). The most common performance is implied by the word *state,* as in "states what the first amendment says about freedom of the press." The verb *recall* is also commonly used, as in "recalls the names of three major Texas cities."

Concrete Concept. Learners have acquired a concrete concept when they have learned to identify instances of an object property ("round"), of an object ("ceiling"), of an event ("turning"), or of a spatial direction ("up"). The instances identified as members of the concept class must be "previously unencountered," which means they have not been used for the instruction itself—they are "new" to the learner. Concepts of this sort are *identified* by pointing to them or marking them in some manner; they do not have to be identified by means of a definition. Example: Identifying the shape of a solid object as a "cone."

Defined Concept. Many concepts cannot simply be "pointed at" to identify them; instead, they must be identified by showing (or "telling") the rule which defines them. For example, the concept "family" must be identified by a definition, as is true of many other concepts such as "electrical resistance" and "weaving." When a learner has acquired a defined concept, he or she is able to show (demonstrate, or "tell") the concept by identifying the "thing concepts" it contains, and to indicate how they are related. For example, in a bar balanced on a fulcrum, the clockwise *torque* is defined as the force times its distance from the fulcrum. To show the meaning of this defined concept, the learner must be able to identify (1) the force, (2) the distance from the fulcrum, and (3) the relation between them, which is "times." As in the case of concrete concepts, the learning of defined concepts would be exhibited by the learner in applying this definition to one or more "new" instances.

Rule. Learners have acquired a rule when they can demonstrate its application to one or more previously unencountered instances. A rule is a "relation"; that is, it relates two or more concepts. (Note that the rule is a stored capability of the learner; it is not a statement that represents the rule, which is called a "rule statement.") Continuing the example of the previous section, a physical principle is reflected in the rule statement: "In a bar balanced on a fulcrum, the clockwise torque equals the counterclockwise torque." To demonstrate the possession of this rule, a learner would need to demonstrate, given a value for an instance of a counterclockwise torque, that the value of the clockwise torque was equal to it. In other words, the learner would be demonstrating an application of the rule to a "new" instance.

Problem Solving. When learners encounter an unfamiliar situation posing a question to be answered, they are expected to engage in *problem solving.* Of course, problem solving requires the application of known (previously learned) rules. In addition, since the situation is itself unfamiliar, learners must search out and choose what rules to use. For example, rules of trigonometry may have been learned and exhibited in situations containing questions like this: "In triangle ABC, if side A is 20 feet and side B is 36 feet, what is the value of angle p?" This is simply a rule-application situation. In contrast, the learner may be presented with this sort of question:

"A tree 40 feet in height casts a shadow which has a length of 52 feet. What is the angular distance of the sun from the horizon?" (In using this example, we assume that this is not a situation familiar to the learner.) The capability of problem solving is developed in learners by providing them with practice in a variety of situations, preferably those which resemble the "real-life" or "joblike" problems they will encounter in the future.

In general, a learning objective may be classified by identifying the category in which it fits. In doing this, it is usually helpful to think, "How would the learning outcome of this objective be tested?" This is the specific answer to the question, "How would I know if the learner has learned this objective?" Thus, if the learning objective is, "produces an example of elapsed time," this defined concept might be tested by asking the learner to show that he or she can apply the definition of elapsed time by producing an example (e.g., 8:27–8:42), or that he or she can apply the definition to "categorize" an instance when given instances and noninstances. By thinking of such a test item or items, the designer can readily recognize that the learning outcome is one of "showing by definition that a particular instance belongs to a particular category," and that the objective, therefore, represents a defined concept.

Events of Instruction

Once the learning outcome, or outcomes, of a lesson have been classified, the CAI designer is ready to proceed with a sequence of steps that "teach." By teaching is meant the presentation of a series of displays that stimulate the learner so as to make learning readily occur. There are several stages to learning, and so there must be several stages to the series of displays that support or enhance learning (Gagné, 1977). The support for learning occurs by means of several steps called *events of instruction*. The relation of these events to internal learning processes is described in Table 1.

TABLE 1: Internal Processes of Learning and the External Instructional Events Which May Be Used to Support Them

Internal Learning Process	External Instructional Event
1. Alertness	1. Gaining attention
2. Expectancy	2. Informing learner of lesson objective
3. Retrieval to working memory	3. Stimulating recall of prior learning
4. Selective perception	4. Presenting stimuli with distinctive features
5. Semantic encoding	5. Guiding learning
6. Retrieval and responding	6. Eliciting performance
7. Reinforcement	7. Providing informative feedback
8. Cueing retrieval	8. Assessing performance
9. Generalizing	9. Enhancing retention and learning transfer

Learning theory and the research arising from it tell us that the nine processes listed in the first column are all part of what is meant by "the learning process" (Estes, 1978; Klatzky, 1980). More extensive accounts of these relationships are contained in books by Gagné (1977) and Gagné and Briggs (1979). In any complete act of learning, there must be nine *events of instruction,* as shown in the second column of Table 1.

Depending on the learning objective and the intended learners, the planning of specific displays to represent each of the nine events is subject to variation. For example, if the learners are new to CAI, Event 1 of gaining attention may not need to concern itself with general alertness, but may need to assure that learners watch the screen, rather than looking at the keyboard. The second event, informing learners of lesson objective, needs also to be assured; but the requirement of a specific display depends on an estimate (by the designer) as to whether the learners are already highly aware of the lesson's objective. Event 3, stimulating recall of prior learning, is surely an essential step. Yet, *what* prior learning is to be recalled depends not only on what the intended learners have previously learned, but also very importantly on the category of learning outcome being taught.

Summing up this point, nine different events of instruction *always* need to be considered as potential ways of providing external support to learning. However, the different events are not always presented in different displays. Sometimes one or another of the events is not included, because it is evident to the designer that the learning audience, or the learning task, or both, make its inclusion unnecessary. The decision to exclude should, however, be a deliberate one, and not a matter of inadvertent omission.

The nine events of instruction require different specific forms depending on the category of learning outcome being taught. Accordingly, while the preceding list applies to any lesson in general, the specific form to be taken by the instructional events differs with the learning outcome. These differences are more apparent for some of the events than for others. For instance, Event 5, guiding learning, requires quite different forms of "organizing" for the learning of verbal information and for the learning of a defined concept or rule.

The planning of CAI instruction needs to make potential provisions for the display of frames containing print and diagrams to reflect all of the nine events of instruction. The sequential order of these events is roughly from one to nine, although reversals within this sequence may sometimes be desirable. Obviously, Event 7, providing informative feedback, would not be scheduled to occur before Event 6, eliciting performance. In contrast, Events 3, 4, and 5 are less rigidly sequenced, since they all pertain to presenting to the learner "stimuli to be used in learning."

Authoring CAI

There are a number of types of CAI, each of which has different characteristics with regard to the events of instruction usually included. The three most common types are *drill and practice, simulations,* and *tutorial.*

Drill and practice, probably the most common type of CAI, contains only two events of instruction. It elicits a response from the learner (by asking a question), and provides feedback, generally in the form of knowledge of results. The purpose of this type of CAI is to provide practice for skills already learned. It is possible to teach new skills by this technique, but such learning would partake more of "trial and error" than of directed learning, and would probably not constitute an efficient use of the learner's time.

Simulations used in instruction may also be analyzed in terms of the events of instruction they contain. Like the lessons of drill and practice, they contain the events, "elicit performance" and "provide informative feedback." In addition, the simulation usually includes a presentation of the objective and the presentation of a stimulus in the form of information about the present status of a system. A simulation usually has the purpose of teaching a learner to identify the relationships between components of a system, and how to control these relationships. After eliciting a response from the learner, the simulation typically provides feedback in the form of a new stimulus situation. Simulations are most appropriate for presenting problem-solving tasks, in which the learner is to determine the relationships among variables through manipulating them.

A more comprehensive form of instruction is exemplified by the tutorial program, which could conceivably contain all nine events of instruction. As an instructional form, it is usually considered to be "primary" instruction, as opposed to "supplementary" instruction. That is, a good tutorial program ought to be able to stand alone. The tutorial lesson can probably benefit most through the application of principles of instructional design.

Tutorial programs come in two general forms, linear and branched. The linear form is the most common, and is represented in Figure 1.

In this form of instruction, the learner is presented with an instructional sequence

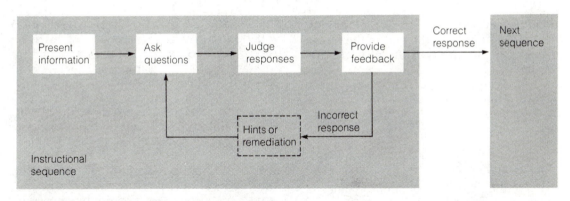

FIGURE 1: Typical procedure for tutorial programs

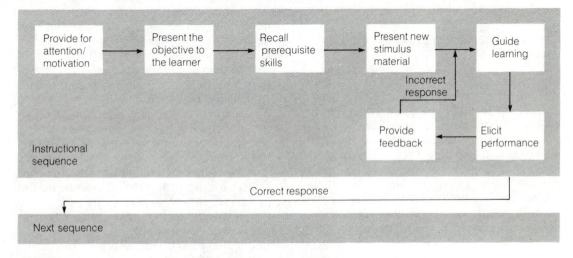

FIGURE 2: Procedure incorporating additional events of instruction

consisting of text presentations, questions, and feedback. There may be a large number of instructional sequences in a single lesson, but they all follow the same format. This format has been incorporated into computer-based authoring programs, so that relatively naive computer users can create their own lessons. When prompted by the computer, the user of one of these authoring programs provides the text that the learner will receive, the question that the learner will be asked, and the feedback that will be given. An example of such an authoring program is Bell and Howell's GENIS 1.

In using this type of program, what does the author put into the "text" display? Typical users of these programs start with the event "present stimulus." They then ask the

learner a question (which is what the program guides them to do), followed by providing feedback. This sequence is then repeated with more information, questions, and feedback. In most cases, the author is employing only three events of instruction.

It is possible, however, using the same authoring package, to provide additional instructional events, since these events may be viewed as elaborations of the presentation of "text." Figure 2 represents the "events of instruction" paradigm for a tutorial program in which these events perform different functions within the text displays of a lesson. One or more displays may be used for any particular event presented, but in general the sequence follows that shown in Figure 2. The last two events, assessing performance, and enhancing retention and learning transfer, may be grouped at the end of the lesson or provided off the computer in another medium.

Most CAI authoring guides concentrate on giving the prospective CAI author practical tips for a good lesson. These suggestions include:

a. Leaving the pace of the lesson under the control of the user

b. Avoiding the placement of too much text on a screen display

c. Providing the learner with instructions on what to do next

d. Other practical arrangements of this sort

Guidelines of this kind provide for "human engineering" concerns, and if followed, should help produce a program that is easy to use, and "comfortable" for the learner. However, it is possible to follow all these guidelines and still produce ineffective instruction. The suggestion of this article is that a different set of guidelines, those based on the events of instruction, can best serve the CAI author in designing effective instruction. These are described in the following section.

Guidelines for CAI Authors

Tables 2 through 6 present guidelines for authors of CAI programs, based on the nine events of instruction previously described. These events are considered to be deliberately arranged communications having the purpose of supporting internal learning processes. As has been pointed out, the nine events can be related specifically to cognitive processes which are assumed by most theorists favoring the "information-processing" view of learning.

The major point made by these guidelines is that designers of CAI instruction need to attend to all nine of these events, rather than simply to two or three (such as questions and feedback). The nine events are described in relation to five different kinds of learning outcomes, chosen for their high frequency of occurrence in CAI instruction: concrete concept, defined concept, rule, problem solving, and verbal information. The events of instruction are listed for each of these outcomes, followed by an indication of the procedure to be used by the author in designing them.

Are the nine events always included in an instructional module? The answer is no, because any given event may not be necessary, or may be supplied by the learner. For example, if the learner has just previously completed a lesson on adding decimal numbers, the objective of a lesson titled "subtracting decimal numbers" may be obvious. Decisions to omit any of the nine events, however, should be deliberate and rational; omission should not result from oversight. Making sure that all events are adequately represented is the key to effective instruction.

In each table, the nine events of instruction are successively listed in the first column. The second column then describes procedures for the author to follow in designing the lesson. It may be noted that each procedure is described in general terms. The description does not supply the author with exact content entries; rather it tells the author what he or she must do to develop such entries.

REFERENCES

Eisele, J. Lesson Design for Computer-Based Instructional Systems. *Educational Technology*, 1978, *18*, 14–21.

Estes, W. K. The Information Processing Approach to Cognition: A Confluence of Metaphors and Methods. In W. K. Estes (Ed.), *Handbook of Learning and Cognitive Processes*, Vol. 5, *Human Information Processing*. Hillsdale, N.J.: Erlbaum, 1978.

Gagné, R. M. *The Conditions of Learning*, 3rd edition. New York: Holt, Rinehart & Winston, 1977.

TABLE 2: Outcome Category: Concrete Concept

Event of Instruction	Procedure
1. Gaining Attention	Present initial operating instructions on screen, including some displays which show geometric figures and rapid changes in them. Call attention to screen presentations.
2. Informing Learner of Lesson Objective	These three figures are very much alike:
	Only one of them is a triangle. Do you know which one? This lesson teaches you to identify figures that are triangles.
3. Stimulating Recall of Prior Learning	Ask questions designed to recall prerequisite concepts (and discriminations, if necessary) involved in the concept to be learned. Prerequisites to be recalled include: 1. Concept: straight line 2. Concept: closed curve 3. Concept: three Example: What is there about the top figure that makes it different from all the others?
One side of the upper figure is different from all other sides of all the figures. Which is it?	
4. Presenting Stimuli with Distinctive Features	Present one or two triangles, with the statement: "Each of these is a triangle":
5. Guiding Learning	Present a series of screen displays generating the outlines of triangles, one at a time. Example: These are triangles:

Event of Instruction	Procedure
	This is a triangle: This is not: (side not straight)
	This is a triangle: This is not: (figure not closed)
	This is a triangle: This is not: (four sides)
6. Eliciting Performance Example: Type each letter which labels a triangle:	Present three lines of figures, within which the triangles are to be identified.
7. Providing Informative Feedback	Make it possible for the student to check his or her answers, by displaying correct responses. If all three are wrong, send student through remedial frames beginning with guiding learning, containing new examples. This time around, the display might be made to "flash" distinctive features.
8. Assessing Performance	Present three sets of five figures, randomly selected from a pool. Ask for identification of triangles, by typing letters corresponding to labels on display screen. Provide feedback by telling student he or she has mastered this objective (identifying triangles). If he or she has not, tell him or her what to do next.
9. Enhancing Retention and Learning Transfer Use light pen, if available; otherwise, ask for letter typing. Example:	Present drawings of three different objects which contain the concept (triangle) as components, and ask for identification of the concept.

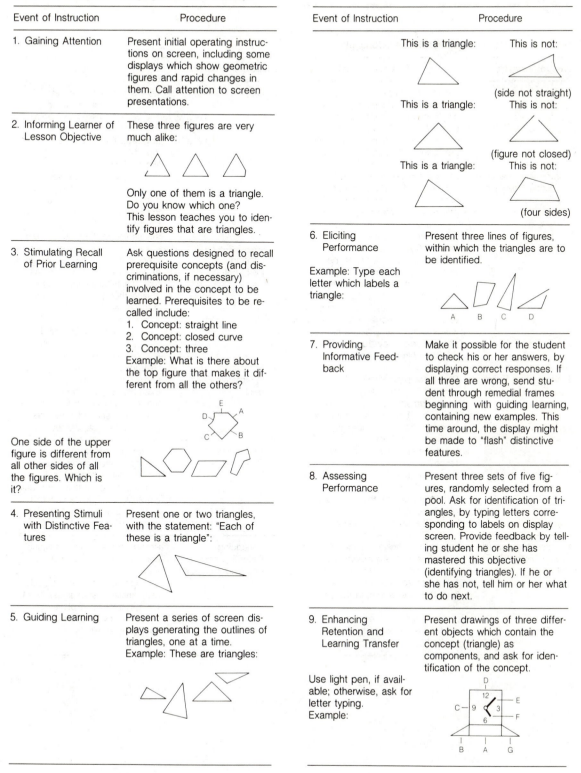

TABLE 3: Outcome Category: Defined Concept

Event of Instruction	Procedure	Event of Instruction	Procedure
1. Gaining Attention	Present initial operating instructions on screen, including some displays which change second by second. Call attention to screen presentation, using words like "Look!", "Watch!", etc.	5. Guiding Learning	Take a sentence like this: Peter milked the cow. The verb is "milked." What did Peter milk? The answer is *the cow*, and that is the *object* of the verb. Notice, though, that some sentences do not have objects. The rain fell slowly down. In this sentence, the action of the verb ("fell") is not stated to be directed at something. So, in this sentence, there is *no object*.
2. Informing Learner of Lesson Objective	State in simple terms what the student will have accomplished once he or she has learned. Example: Two sentences, such as: Joe chased the ball. The sun shines brightly. One of these sentences contains a word that is an *object*, the other does not. Can you pick out the object? In the first sentence, *ball* is the *object* of the verb "chased". In the second sentence, none of the words is an object. You are about to learn how to identify the *object* in a sentence.	6. Eliciting Performance	Present three to five examples of sentences, one by one. Ask, type 0 if this sentence has an object, then type the word that is the object. Examples: Sally closed the book. The kite rose steadily.
		7. Providing Informative Feedback	Give information about correct and incorrect responses. Example: *Book* is the object of the verb "closed" in the first sentence. The second sentence does not have an object.
3. Stimulating Recall of Prior Learning	Recall concepts previously learned. Example: Any sentence has a *subject* and a *predicate*. The subject is usually a noun, or a noun phrase. The predicate begins with a verb. What is the *subject* of this sentence? The play began at eight o'clock. What verb begins the predicate of this sentence? The child upset the cart.	8. Assessing Performance	Present a new set of concept instances and noninstances, in three to five additional pairs of sentences. Ask questions requiring answers. Tell the learner if mastery is achieved, and what to do next if it is not.
4. Presenting Stimuli with Distinctive Features	Present a definition of the concept. Example: An *object* is a noun in the predicate to which the action (of the verb) is directed. For example, in the sentence The rain pelted the roof, *roof* is the *object* of the verb "pelted."	9. Enhancing Retention and Learning Transfer	Present three to five additional concept instances, varied in form. Example: Use sentences such as: Neoclassical expressions often supplant mere platitudes. Introduce review questions at spaced intervals.

TABLE 4: Outcome Category: Rule

Event of Instruction	Procedure
1. Gaining Attention	Present initial operating instructions on screen, including some displays which change second by second. Call attention to screen presentations using words like "Look!", "Watch!", etc.
2. Informing Learner of Lesson Objective	State in simple terms what the student will be able to do after he or she has learned. Example: When we convert to the metric system, you may have to change Fahrenheit temperature to Celsius. Thus, if someone tells you the Fahrenheit temperature is 77°, you may need to be able to know that the Celsius temperature is 25°. This program tells you how to do this, in the simplest way. Optionally, in addition, relate what is to be learned to the situation later to be presented in event 9, enhancing retention and learning transfer. Example: Australia converted to the metric system about 10 years ago. If you were in Australia with your Fahrenheit thermometer, you would need to convert a reading like 23° F to 5° below 0 Celsius.
3. Stimulating Recall of Prior Learning	Example: An expression like $2/3 \times (13 - 4)$ may be simplified by *first:* a. Multiplying 13 by 2 b. Subtracting 4 from 13 c. Dividing 13 by 3 d. Subtracting 2 from 13 Yes! Subtracting 4 from 13.
4. Presenting Stimuli with Distinctive Features	Present the stimulus material to which the learner is to respond, emphasizing distinctive features. Example: Suppose you are told that the Fahrenheit temperature is 41 degrees, or F = 41°. Notice that what you are given is a numerical value, 41, which can be substituted for F in the formula $C = 5/9 (F - 32)$.

Event of Instruction	Procedure
5. Guiding Learning	Present guidance about the procedure of applying the rule to a particular instance. Example: You are told that the Fahrenheit temperature is 41 degrees. First, confirm that F = 41°. Second, recall the equation $C = 5/9 (F - 32)$. Do the subtraction, $41 - 32 = 9$. Multiply $5/9 \times 9$. $C = 5°$.
6. Eliciting Performance	Present three questions, each calling for a different application of the rule. Example: What is the Celsius temperature if the Fahrenheit is 105? To the nearest whole number?
7. Providing Informative Feedback	Make it possible for the student to check his or her answers. If all three are wrong, send student back to a frame beginning with guiding learning, using a different approach.
8. Assessing Performance	Present three questions, differing from those previously given, each calling for an application of the rule. Example: You are told that Fahrenheit temperature is 5 degrees. What is the Celsius temperature?
9. Enhancing Retention and Learning Transfer	Present three to five additional questions requiring application of the rule. Elaborate by describing different concrete contexts. Example: If you were to visit Australia in December, the Fahrenheit temperature might be as high as 90 degrees. But Australian thermometers show Celsius degrees. What would they read?

Gagné, R. M., and Briggs, L. J. *Principles of Instructional Design,* 2nd edition. New York: Holt, Rinehart & Winston, 1979.

Klatzky, R. L. *Human Memory: Structures and Processes,* 2nd edition. San Francisco: W. H. Freeman, 1980.

Lower, S. K. IPS: A New Authoring Language for Computer-Assisted Instruction. *Journal of Computer Based Instruction,* 1980, *6,* 119–124.

Rudnick, M. F. Now You Can Program the Computer in English. *Audiovisual Instruction,* 1979, *24,* 36–37.

TABLE 5: Outcome Category: Problem Solving

Event of Instruction	Procedure
1. Gaining Attention	Raise the learner's curiosity. Present a hypothetical situation; ask a rhetorical question.
2. Informing Learner of Lesson Objective	State in simple terms what the student is to accomplish once he or she has learned. Example: At the end of this lesson, you should be able to generate hypotheses about the probability of occurrence of any particular trait or combination of traits in the fruit fly.
3. Stimulating Recall of Prior Learning	Have the learner recall the rules that are applicable. The learner will have to synthesize these rules himself or herself. In this example, tell the learner to recall rules about binomial distributions, Mendelian genetic principles, and sex-linked traits. State that these rules will have to be applied to solve the problem.
4. Presenting Stimuli with Distinctive Features	The stimulus, in the case of most problem-solving materials, is information about an existing state of affairs. The learner is not given any direct learning guidance, unless he or she specifically requests it. Guidance may be given in the form of telling the learner of available options.

Event of Instruction	Procedure
5. Guiding Learning 6. Eliciting Performance	The computer is best used to simulate responses to action choices supplied by the learner. That is, the learner will input information into the computer, and the computer will present a changed stimulus display. (In the case of the fruit fly, a sample of 16 of the offspring of any particular breeding may be presented after the learner has specified a cross.)
7. Providing Informative Feedback	Feedback is generally provided by changing the stimulus situation in response to the learner's action. However, it may be appropriate to give verbal feedback as well. (For instance, "No, you cannot cross two female flies.") The feedback cues the learner for his or her next response.
8. Assessing Performance	Provide the learner with a different situation that calls for another synthesis of the applicable rules. Judge his or her ability to generalize his or her new problem-solving skill.
9. Enhancing Retention and Learning Transfer	Have the learner generate other strategies for solving similar problems using other rules.

TABLE 6: Outcome Category: Verbal Information

Event of Instruction	Procedure	Event of Instruction	Procedure
1. Gaining Attention	Present initial operating instructions on screen, including some displays which change second by second. Call attention to screen presentations using words like "Look!", "Watch!", etc.	6. Eliciting Performance	Ask five to ten questions. Example: How many countries make up the Common Market? When did the United Kingdom join the Common Market?
2. Informing Learner of Lesson Objective	State in simple terms what the student will be able to do after he or she has learned. Example: Would you be able to tell someone what the European Common Market is, what countries make it up, how it operates, and how long it has existed?	7. Providing Informative Feedback	Give answers to questions, and feedback about correctness or partial correctness of learner's answers. Use encouraging statements.
3. Stimulating Recall of Prior Learning	Present a map of Europe. Show east-west division. Label the countries one by one. Show one or two major exports of each country, one by one.	8. Assessing Performance	Present a series of five to ten questions as a test. Multiple-choice or true-false format is convenient. When the learner has completed the test, report the score. If the score is satisfactory, say so; otherwise, tell the learner what to do next.
4. Presenting Stimuli with Distinctive Features	Present the information to be learned in an organized, systematic fashion. Give suitable emphasis to distinctive features by using bold-letter words, "flashing", or other techniques.	9. Enhancing Retention and Learning Transfer	Give additional linking information, relating the subject to additional familiar knowledge. For example, present speculative information about an American Common Market. Conduct an additional exercise. Example: Show a newspaper headline (could be fictitious) about ECM, such as *Market to Impose License Fees*, and ask the learner to interpret it, responding to true-false questions. In addition, conduct a review by asking questions at later intervals.
5. Guiding Learning	Inform the learner of linkages between new information and what he or she already knows. Relate abstract ideas to concrete examples, either directly or through analogies. Where possible, provide pictures to give concrete illustrations.		

5 Toward a Theory of Intrinsically Motivating Instruction

Thomas W. Malone

Xerox Palo Alto Research Center

Abstract

First, a number of previous theories of intrinsic motivation are reviewed. Then, several studies of highly motivating computer games are described. These studies focus on what makes the games fun, not on what makes them educational. Finally, with this background, a rudimentary theory of intrinsically motivating instruction is developed based on three categories: *challenge, fantasy,* and *curiosity.*

Challenge is hypothesized to depend on goals with uncertain outcomes. Several ways of making outcomes uncertain are discussed, including *variable difficulty level, multiple-level goals, hidden information,* and *randomness.* Fantasy is claimed to have both cognitive and emotional advantages in designing instructional environments. A distinction is made between *extrinsic fantasies* that depend only weakly on the skill used in a game and *intrinsic fantasies* that are intimately related to the use of the skill. Curiosity is separated into sensory and cognitive components, and it is suggested that cognitive curiosity can be aroused by making learners believe their knowledge structures are *incomplete, inconsistent,* or *unparsimonious.*

"No compulsory learning can remain in the soul. . . . In teaching children, train them by a kind of game, and you will be able to see more clearly the natural bent of each." (Plato, *The Republic,* Book VII)

What makes things fun to learn? How can instruction be designed in a way that captivates and intrigues learners as well as educates them? As the above quotation from Plato illustrates, these are not new questions. But there will be two new aspects in my treatment of them. First, I will be primarily concerned with a new kind of instructional environment—one involving interactive computers. Second, as a source of insight into the problem, I will analyze a new kind of intrinsically motivating activity—computer games. In other words, I will try to answer two questions:

1. Why are computer games so captivating?

2. How can the features that make computer games captivating be used to make learning—especially learning with computers—interesting and enjoyable?

To help answer these questions, I will first review a number of previous theories of intrinsic motivation and learning. Then I will describe a series of empirical studies of what people like about computer games. Since these studies are a first step in addressing the complex question of what makes things fun to learn, they focus only on what makes the games fun, not on what makes them educational. Finally, using these empirical studies as a base, I will outline a rudimentary theory of how to design environments that are both interesting and educational.

Much recent research on instructional design has involved detailed hypotheses about the changes in cognitive structures and processes that occur in learning academic skills

Thomas W. Malone, "Toward a Theory of Intrinsically Motivating Instruction," *Cognitive Science* 4 (1981), 333–369. Reprinted by permission of Ablex Publishing Corporation.

like arithmetic and geometry (e.g., Resnick, 1976; Greeno, 1976; Brown and VanLehn, 1980). The assumption behind much of this work is that more detailed and formal descriptions of what is to be learned will help in deciding how it should be taught. In a few cases (e.g., Resnick, 1976) alternative teaching strategies suggested by these representations are actually tested. In a similar vein, the most impressive recent work in intelligent computer-assisted instruction has involved programming elaborate cognitive models of the learners so the program can make real-time instructional decisions based on inferred knowledge states of the learners (Brown and Burton, 1978; Burton and Brown, 1979; Atkinson, 1976; Stevens, Collins, and Goldin, 1979; Goldstein, 1979).

One potentially overpowering factor that has been largely neglected in most of this recent work is the role of motivation in learning. There already exists an extensive psychological literature about the motivational effects of various kinds of reinforcement—material reinforcement, social reinforcement, and self-reinforcement—and of various kinds of modeling (e.g., Skinner, 1953; Bandura, 1969). But externally administered reinforcement is not a motivational panacea for instructional designers. Another growing body of research has begun to explore the conditions under which external reinforcement destroys the intrinsic motivation a person has to engage in an activity and degrades the quality of certain kinds of task performance (Condry, 1977; Lepper and Greene, 1979). For example, Lepper, Greene, and Nisbett (1973) found that when nursery school children who liked to play with marking pens received a promised reward for doing so, they later played with the marking pens less than children in a control group who received no reward. Another reason for hesitation in the indiscriminate use of external reinforcement as a motivation comes from the work of cognitively oriented learning theorists (Piaget, 1951; Bruner, 1962) who argue the importance of intrinsically motivated playlike activities for many kinds of deep learning. If students are intrinsically

motivated to learn something, they may spend more time and effort learning, feel better about what they learn, and use it more in the future. Some theorists would also argue that they may learn "better" in the sense that more fundamental cognitive structures are modified, including the development of such skills as "learning how to learn" (Shulman and Keislar, 1966).

1. Characteristics of Intrinsically Motivating Instructional Environments

An activity is said to be intrinsically motivated if people engage in it "for its own sake," that is, if they do not engage in the activity in order to receive some external reward such as money or status. I will use the words "fun," "interesting," "captivating," "appealing," and "intrinsically motivating," all more or less interchangeably, to describe such activities. In this section, I will review a number of theories about what makes environments intrinsically motivating. The theories are loosely organized under the three major categories to be used in Section 5: *challenge, fantasy,* and *curiosity.*

Challenge

A number of theorists have emphasized the importance of challenge in intrinsic motivation. White (1959) argues that motivational theories based only on the reduction of primary drives are inadequate to account for much of human and animal exploration, manipulation, and general activity. He postulates a new "effectance" motivation that leads an organism to develop competence and feelings of efficacy in dealing with its environment. This new motivation can be used to explain both exploratory striving toward new skills and also what Piaget (1951) calls "practice games," the repetitive, pleasureful exercise of recently acquired skills.

Neither White nor Piaget, however, has

much to say about exactly what features of an environment or activity make it challenging. Csikszentmihalyi (1975, 1979) extends their analysis by describing what he feels are the most important structural features of in' nsi- cally motivating activities. Based on inter- views with rock climbers, chess players, and other people who seemed to be highly intrin- sically motivated, Csikszentmihalyi describes intrinsically motivating activities as follows:

1. The activity should be structured so that the actor can increase or decrease the level of challenges he is facing, in order to match exactly his skills with the requirements for action.

2. It should be easy to isolate the activity, at least at the perceptual level, from other stimuli, external or internal, which might interfere with involvement in it.

3. There should be clear criteria for performance; one should be able to evaluate how well or how poorly one is doing at any time.

4. The activity should provide concrete feedback to the actor, so that he can tell how well he is meeting the criteria of performance.

5. The activity ought to have a broad range of challenges, and possibly several qualitatively different ranges of challenge, so that the actor may obtain increasingly complex information about different aspects of himself. (1979, p. 213)

All of these features, except 2, involve ways of making an activity challenging. While Csikszentmihalyi's analysis is useful, it gives us little idea of why these features are impor- tant or how they relate to each other. In Sec- tion 5 below, I will show how these ways of structuring a challenging activity all follow from the need for a challenging environment to have a goal with uncertain outcome.

Eifferman (1974) illustrates the impor- tance of the notion of "challenge" by using it to explain the different patterns of popularity in children's playground games. According to her insightful analysis, a game is a steady game (i.e., played steadily throughout the year, like tag) if each participant can adjust the level of challenge to his or her abilities while still leaving the outcome of each round of the game undetermined. (In tag this ad- justment of challenge occurs by the "It's" choice of whom to chase and the other play- ers' choice of distance to stay from the "It.") A game is a recurrent game (i.e., played in intermittent but intense "waves," like jump- rope and marbles) if, after the hierarchy of players is established, the outcome of each round becomes predictable. A game is spo- radic if there is little variation in the degree of challenge and little challenge to begin with. And finally, a one-shot game (like Hula-Hoop) has considerable initial chal- lenge, but little hope of improvement be- yond an early mastery level even after several years.

Fantasy

Another motivational aspect of environments has to do with the themes or fantasies which they embody or encourage. Disneyland is perhaps an archetypical example of an intrin- sically motivating environment that derives much of its appeal from the fantasies it evokes. Many children's games also include essential fantasy elements (e.g., "cowboys and Indians," "playing house").

Piaget (1951) explains fantasy in chil- dren's play primarily as an attempt to "assimi- late" experience into existing structures in the child's mind with minimal needs to "ac- commodate" to the demands of external real- ity. In a somewhat similar vein, Freud's (1950) explanation of symbolic games that children invent for themselves emphasizes an attempt by the ego to actively repeat trau- matic events that have been experienced pas- sively. This repetition allows a kind of be- lated emotional mastery over the event. In addition to this symbolic conflict resolution, Freud sees much of fantasy, especially dreams, as the fulfillment of (often uncon- scious) wishes. For example, Sears (1950) describes a study of the aggressive doll play of preschool children that is consistent with both these aspects of Freudian theory. The children who received the most punishment for aggressive behavior at home showed less interpersonal aggression than moderately punished children, but they were more aggressive in their fantasy play with dolls. The presumption is that the highly punished children had acquired strong aggressive motivation through frustration at their parents' punishment, and that this frustrated aggression was expressed primarily in fantasy. Even though these theories of fantasy deal primarily with the fantasies people *produce* (as in dreams or imaginary play), their proponents would presumably argue that similar processes are involved in determining the fantasies people find *appealing* in external environments.

Curiosity

One of the most important features of intrinsically motivating environments is the degree to which they can continue to arouse and then satisfy our curiosity. Berlyne (1960, 1965, 1968) has studied these processes extensively with humans and other animals and proposed the rudiments of a theory emphasizing concepts like *novelty, complexity, surprisingness,* and *incongruity.* He reports, for example, that rats are more likely, other things being equal, to enter a maze arm that differs from the one they entered on the preceding trial (Berlyne, 1960), and that people spend more time looking at the more complex or incongruous stimuli in a pair of similar pictures or patterns (Berlyne and Lawrence, 1964).

Ellis and Scholtz (1978) used similar concepts to explain their studies of toy preferences in children. While attributes like color made little difference in choice of play object, novelty was very important in determining which toys a child began playing with, and complexity—either of construction or of possible uses—was crucial in determining how long a child played with a given toy.

The kind of complexity or incongruity that is motivating is not simply a matter of increased information in the technical sense used in information theory. Rather it involves surprisingness with respect to the knowledge and expectations a learner has. Berlyne, as well as others (e.g., Hunt, 1965; Piaget, 1952) point out, however, that there are limits to the amount of complexity people find interesting. They postulate that there is some *optimal level of informational complexity* for a given person at a given time.

So far this is all very hard to argue with. But in his last major work on the topic, Berlyne (1965) goes further and claims that the principal factor producing curiosity is what he calls *conceptual conflict.* By this he means conflict between incompatible attitudes or ideas evoked by a stimulus situation. For example, imagine someone who believes that fish cannot survive outside of water and then hears about a fish (the mudskipper) that walks on dry land. Conceptual conflict, and thus curiosity, will be induced. It is clear that conceptual conflict is an important factor in curiosity, but a theory based primarily on this factor seems to be unduly limited. In Section 5, I will suggest an alternative theory based on a cognitive motivation to bring the three qualities of *completeness, consistency,* and *parsimony* to all knowledge structures. In essence, Berlyne's "conceptual conflict" would be called a "lack of consistency" in the new theory. But the new theory hypothesizes two other kinds of curiosity-evoking situations and some of Berlyne's own examples seem to fit more naturally into these other categories.

Structural Features. Moore and Anderson (1969) discuss several other kinds of informational complexity that are particularly relevant to structuring educational environments. In particular, they enunciate four principles of instructional design: the perspectives principle, the autotelic principle, the productive principle, and the personalization principle.

The perspectives principle suggests that learning is more rapid and deeper if the learner can approach the subject matter from as many as possible of the following perspectives: agent, patient, reciprocator, and referee. For example, learning to read may be facilitated by concurrently learning to write messages, both to yourself and to others, and to read similar messages.

The autotelic principle requires that, in general, the initial learning of complex skills be protected from serious consequences (such as prizes or physical dangers) so that it can be enjoyed for its own sake. Once the learning of a skill is well underway, however, it may be appropriate to test it in serious competition. (This view is consistent with Zajonc's (1965) principle that the presence of other people hinders the performance and learning of new skills but enhances the performance of well-learned skills.)

The productive principle suggests that learning is more efficient in environments that are structured in such a way that students can make inferences about parts of the environment that they have not yet observed. For example, in a mathematical system, once a student learns the axioms and transformation rules, he or she can in principle deduce all sorts of theorems independently.

The personalization principle includes the ideas that an environment should be both responsive to the learners' activities and helpful in letting them take a reflexive view of themselves. A responsive environment permits the learners to explore freely and make full use of their capacities for discovering relations of various kinds. It is self-pacing and informs the learners immediately about the consequences of their actions. As an example of a responsive environment, Moore and Anderson describe the "talking typewriter" (Moore and Kobler, 1963; Kobler and Moore, 1966), a typewriter that says the names of the letters as their keys are pressed. The reflexive condition requires an environment structured so learners can learn not only about the subject matter, but also about themselves as learners. For example, the use of motion pictures of athletic contests to help players spot their weaknesses and strengths encourages a reflexive view of learning.

Other Structural Features. In a brief but very useful article specifically devoted to computer games, Banet (1979) lists thirteen structural features that, based on his informal observations, make for successful computer games. These features include:

> Skilled performance is made instrumental to attaining an objective posed by the rules of the game.
>
> The game increases in its ability to challenge the player; it does not become boringly simple.
>
> The game incorporates fantasy elements (piloting a space ship, finding treasure, etc.).
>
> The computer can time the players' responses and calculate scores based in part on quickness of response.

Choice. As Zimbardo (1969) and others have shown, giving people a choice, or even just the illusion of choice, often increases their motivation to do a task. While freedom of choice seems to be important in making environments appealing, it is not clear how to structure educational environments in which free choice leads to productive learning. Groen (1978) nicely summarizes Piaget's (1971) view on this point as follows: "Free activity is important, and so is the structure of the environment. . . . Ignoring the second can lead to aimless play. Ignoring the first can lead to a sophisticated curriculum that most students fail to assimilate or understand" (pp. 290, 293).

Summary

I have just described a number of features of intrinsically motivating environments—things like informational complexity, responsiveness, challenge, and fantasy. In a sense, this list suggests a set of competing theories for what makes learning fun. One purpose of the three studies I will describe next is to distinguish between these competing theories—to give some insight into which factors are most important in making computer games fun and to see how the importance of these factors varies for different people and different games.

It is certainly not the case that all intrinsically motivating instructional environments are games or that all educational problems can be solved using games. But games often provide particularly striking examples of highly motivating activities. Furthermore, computer games are especially clear illustrations of how the unique capabilities of computers can be used to create motivating environments. For these reasons, I chose to study gamelike activities on computers as a source of insight for designing intrinsically motivating instructional environments.

2. Survey of Computer Game Preferences

While games are perhaps as old as civilization, games played on computers are a new phenomenon in our culture. It is only in the past two or three years that computer games have become widely available outside the restricted world of scientific and business computing centers. There have been numerous scholarly studies of games in general (e.g., Avedon and Sutton-Smith, 1971), but there is almost no systematic knowledge about the new phenomenon of computer games. As a preliminary approach to understanding this phenomenon, I interviewed sixty-five elementary students about their computer game preferences.

Method

Subjects. The subjects for this study were all students in the computer classes at a private elementary school near Palo Alto, California. There were forty-two boys and twenty-three girls, ranging from kindergarten through eighth grade with a concentration in the early elementary grades.

All the children had been playing with computer games in a weekly class for at least two months and some for over two years. In addition to the approximately 45 minutes per week in the computer classes, many of the students had also played computer games during free time at school or at home. There were classes in beginning computer programming as well as games, so a few of the students had some experience programming the computers they played with.

The children to be interviewed were selected randomly from those present. The sixty-five children surveyed constituted about 75 percent of the children enrolled in computer classes and about 25 percent of the children enrolled in the school. Since it was very easy for all the children in the school to participate in the computer classes if they wanted to, this sample is in some ways less biased than groups of children who have to make a special effort to go to a science museum or other public access computer center.

Procedure. The teachers of the computer classes provided a list of the twenty-five games they thought were the most popular among the students. Then each child was asked to rate each game on a four-point scale: 0, never played; 1, didn't like; 2, liked; and 3, liked a lot. To test for any possible effect of the order in which the games were mentioned, the order of the list was randomized and half the subjects saw one order, the other half saw the reverse order.

To get a rough measure of how reliable the children's ratings were, the questionnaire was administered two times, one week apart, to four children. There were no scheduled classes during this week, but some of the children may have played with the games outside of class. The children rated 71 percent of the games identically both times. Their ratings for 18 percent of the games changed by 1 point, and on 11 percent of the games they changed their mind about whether they remembered playing the game.

Results

Two possible sources of error need to be discussed before considering the main results of this survey. First, to test for a possible effect of the order in which the games were presented, an analysis of variance was performed with order of presentation, sex of child, and game as factors. There was no significant influence on ratings of the order of presentation, either as a main effect (F $(1,779) = .50, p > .4$) or as an interaction effect with games ($F (24,779) = .99, p > .4$). The only significant effects in this analysis of variance were the sex of the child ($F (1,779) = 11.52, p < .001$) and the sex by game interaction ($F (24,779) = 1.63, p < .03$). A detailed examination of these sex differences is presented below.

Popularity of Different Games. Table 1 lists all the games in order of their average rating by children who had played the game. As a rough indication of the precision of these overall ratings, the correlation between the average ratings of the children who saw the games in one order and those who saw the games in the opposite order was .64.

Personal Differences In Game Preferences. One might have expected to find that there was a strong consensus among children about which games were best, but as it turned out, this was definitely not the case. For example, no single game received more than 17 percent of the first place rankings. We can understand these differences better by looking at the games for which there were significant relationships between the ratings of the game and the personal characteristics I recorded about the children interviewed. Table 2 shows the games for which an analysis of covariance of game ratings showed a significant effect of the sex, grade in school, or amount of computer experience of the child. (Game rating was the dependent variable, sex was the independent variable, and grade and experience were covariates.) Since there was a significant tendency for older children and children with more computer experience to rate games less favorably, the ratings on which Table 2 is based were first adjusted to be deviations from each subject's average rating.

Game Features That Affect Popularity. One of the most interesting questions we can ask about these results is what features the popular games share that the unpopular games don't have. To answer this question, I rated each game on a number of dimensions that

APPENDIX: Descriptions of Games Mentioned in Text (See Also Table 1)

Game	Description
Adventure	The player explores a vast underground system of caves with dragons, etc., trying to find treasures. The cave is populated with knife-throwing dwarfs and other dangers.
Chase	Two players chase each other across an obstacle course.
Hangman	The player tries to guess a word, letter by letter. After each incorrect letter guessed, one more body part of a man being hanged is drawn. The player loses if the whole body is drawn.
Hammurabi	Player acts as king of ancient Babylonia and decides each year how much wheat to plant, how much to store, and how much to save. There are occasional plagues, rat infestations, etc. The number of people who are born, starve, etc., each year is reported.
Hurkle	The player tries to guess where an animal called a "Hurkle" is hiding in a Cartesian coordinate grid. After each guess, the player is told in which direction the Hurkle is from the guess.
Lemonade	The player runs a lemonade stand buying supplies, advertising, etc., and tries to make a profit.
Snoopy	Snoopy and the Red Baron appear at different positions on a signed number line. Player says how far Snoopy should shoot to hit the Red Baron (as a signed integer).
Star Wars	Player tries to shoot down enemy space ships as they appear in a graphic display.

TABLE 1: Computer Games in Order of Preference[a]

Game	Average Rating	Description
Petball	2.8	Simulated pinball with sound
Snake2	2.6	Two players control motion and shooting of snakes
Breakout	2.6	Player controls paddle to hit ball that breaks through a wall piece by piece
Dungeon	2.6	Player explores a cave like "Dungeons and Dragons"
Chase S.	2.6	Two players chase each other across an obstacle course with sound effects
Star Trek	2.5	Navigate through space and shoot Klingon ships
Don't Fall	2.5	Guess words like Hangman but instead of a person being hanged, a person or robot advances to a cliff
Panther	2.4	Guess who committed a murder by questioning witnesses who may lie
Mission	2.4	Bomb submarines without getting your ship sunk
Chaser	2.4	Capture a moving square with perpendicular lines
Chase	2.4	Like Chase S. but without sound
Horses	2.4	Bet on horses that race along track
Sink Ship	2.3	Bomb a ship from an airplane
Snake	2.3	Like Snake2 but snakes can't shoot
Lemonade	2.3	Run a lemonade stand: buy supplies, advertise, etc.
Escape Robots	2.2	Escape from moving robots
Star Wars	2.2	Shoot Darth Vader's ship on screen
Maze Craze	2.2	Escape from randomly generated maze
Hangman	2.1	Guess letters of a word before man is hanged
Adventure	2.0	Explore cave with dragons, etc.
Draw	2.0	Make any design on the screen
Stars	2.0	Guess a number; clues given by number of stars
Snoopy	1.9	Shoot Red Baron by subtracting Snoopy's position on number line from Red Baron's position
Eliza	1.8	Converse with simulated psychiatrist
Gold	1.5	Fill in blanks in story about Goldilocks

[a] Average ratings are on the scale: 1 = don't like, 2 = like, 3 = like a lot.

seemed likely to affect their motivational value (see, e.g., Banet, 1979). Most of the dimensions (like whether there were audio or visual effects) were fairly easy to rate as either present or absent. One dimension—randomness—was rated on a scale from 0 (not present) to 5 (present and very important in the game).

Table 3 shows the correlations between these game features and the average ratings the games received from the children. The

most important feature determining game popularity in this sample was whether the game had a goal. For example, the top three games all had obvious goals (getting a high score in Petball, trapping the other person's snake in Snake2, and destroying all the bricks in the Breakout game), while the bottom two games had no clear goals (conversing with a simulated psychiatrist in Eliza or filling in blanks in a story in Gold). Other features that had high correlations with game popularity

TABLE 2: Individual Differences in Computer Game Preferences

Games with significant effect of grade
Petball   (+)*

Games with significant effect of computer experience
Star Wars   (+)*
Star Trek   (+)*
Escape Robots   (−)*

Games with significant effect of sex, controlling for grade and computer experience
Gold   (F)**
Star Trek   (M)**
Petball   (M)*

Key:
(+) Older or more experienced like the game more.
(−) Older or more experienced like the game less.
(M) Boys liked the game better than girls.
(F) Girls liked the game better than boys.

*$p<.05$
**$p<.01$

TABLE 3: Importance of Game Features in Determining Game Preferences

Feature	Correlation with average preference
Goal	.65 **
Computer keeps a score	.56 **
Audio effects	.51 **
Randomness involved in game	.48 **
Speed of answers counts	.36 *
Visual effects	.34
Competition	.31
Variable difficulty level	.17
Cooperation	.02
Fantasy	.06
Kind of game	
Graphic game	.38 *
Math game	−.20
Word game	−.38 *

*$p<.05$
**$p<.01$

included scoring, audio effects, and randomness. Graphic games were liked and word games were significantly disliked.

Discussion

This study begins to answer questions that any instructional game designer must deal with. First of all, it is clear that there are big differences between people in the kinds of games they like. No single instructional game can be expected to appeal to everyone. There are, however, some tantalizing indications of the kinds of feature that are important in general. Most surprising, in a way, is the importance of having a goal. This theme will reappear several times in the studies and discussions below.

There are, of course, large problems with trying to draw strong conclusions from the kind of correlational study I have described here. It is impossible to know whether the factors I measured actually caused the effects I attributed to them. Among other things, the results depend entirely on the sample of games used. For example, if I had included a number of totally uninteresting nongames in the survey, there might have been a much stronger consensus about which games were the most fun. In order to make stronger infer-

ences, the two studies I will describe next each focus on a single game and systematically vary the features of the game by having different versions of the same game.

3. Breakout: A Sensorimotor Skill Game

Figure 1 shows a typical screen display in the Breakout[1] computer game. The player uses a knob to control the position of the paddle on the left side of the screen. The paddle is used to bounce the ball against the wall of bricks on the right side of the screen. Each time the ball bounces off the wall, it knocks one brick out of the wall and adds to the score. The ultimate goal of the game is to knock out all the bricks. The survey above and other casual observations indicate that this is one of the most popular contemporary computer games. Why is it so popular? What is the "secret" of the success of the Breakout game?

Many devotees of the Breakout game and similar games mention their score—usually their highest one—when talking about the game. Is the challenge of getting a higher score than your own or someone else's rec-

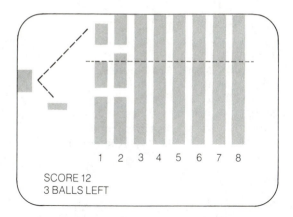

FIGURE 1: **Display format for the Breakout game**

ord the principal attraction of the Breakout game? Is it something about the visual stimulation of watching the bricks break out? Or is it simply the enjoyment of the sensorimotor skill involved in putting the paddle in front of the ball? There are, of course, many other features of the Breakout game, but these three—the score, the breaking out of the bricks, and the ball bouncing off the pad-

dle—seem to capture the essence of the game.

Method

To see which of these three features was most important in the appeal of the game, I constructed six different versions of the game varying the three features in all sensible combinations (see Figure 2). Version 1 is the original Breakout game. Each ball keeps going until the player misses it. There are five balls in a game. Each brick scores the number of points at the bottom of its column on the screen. In Version 2, the ball bounces back and forth between the paddle and the wall without ever breaking out any bricks. One point is scored for each bounce. In Version 3, the ball does not bounce off the paddle; it is simply "caught" when the paddle is placed in front of it. One point is scored for each "catch." Versions 4, 5, and 6 are just like Versions 1, 2, and 3, respectively, except that the scores are omitted. In all versions, if the

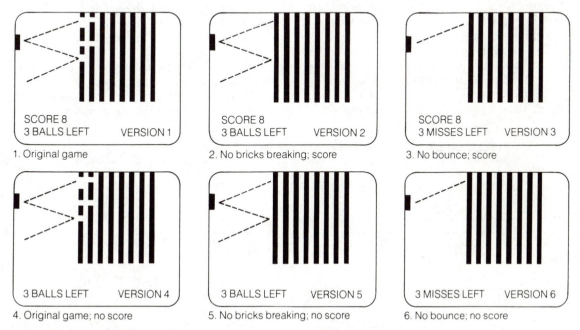

1. Original game

2. No bricks breaking; score

3. No bounce; score

4. Original game; no score

5. No bricks breaking; no score

6. No bounce; no score

FIGURE 2: **Different versions of the Breakout game**

ball is hit (or "caught") correctly five times in a row, it automatically speeds up. To make all the versions seem equally difficult, the distance from the paddle to the wall in the "catch" versions (3 and 6) was increased. This adjustment was apparently successful, since five of the ten subjects thought the versions were equally difficult and the other five had no consensus about which versions were more difficult.

Subjects. The subjects for this experiment were Stanford [University] undergraduates who volunteered to participate in the experiment in their dormitories. There were ten subjects, eight men and two women. All the subjects had played with computer video games before the experiment, but only five of them had played the Breakout game before.

Procedure. Each subject played with each of the six versions of the game for about 3 minutes. Half the subjects saw the versions in one random order, the other half saw the versions in the reverse order. At the end of the session, the subjects were asked to rate each version on a scale from 1 to 5, with their least liked version(s) being 1 and their most liked version(s) being 5.

The subjects who had never played the Breakout game before were told that it takes a long time to get used to the paddle so they shouldn't worry if they had trouble at first. When they played the first version of the

game in which the bricks broke out, they were told that the object of the version was to destroy all the bricks in the wall. These instructions were added after the first three subjects who had not played the Breakout game had difficulty learning to play the game. These three subjects were discarded from the analysis and were not included in the total of ten subjects in the experiment.

Results

Table 4 shows the average rating for each version. A four-way analysis of variance predicting rating from order of presentation, sex, amount of computer game experience, and version, found a significant effect only of version ($F(5,24) = 25.84$, $p < .001$). Not surprisingly, the original version of the game was shown by a priori contrasts of the ratings to be significantly more fun than all the other versions. Using Tukey's HSD a posteriori contrasts at the .05 level, the questionnaire ratings for Versions 3, 5, and 6 were found to be significantly worse than the others. In other words, when there is no breaking out of bricks and no scoring, the game is much less fun. It is also less fun when there is no bouncing off the paddle even if there is scoring.

Table 5 shows the results of a multiple regression predicting ratings from the features in the versions. The most important feature in determining whether the game is liked is

TABLE 4: Appeal of Different Versions of the Breakout Game

Version	Features			Average rating	A posteriori contrasts[a]
	Break bricks	Bounce from paddle	Score		
1	×	×	×	4.8	ı
4	×	×		4.1	ı ı
2		×	×	3.3	ı
3			×	2.1	ı
5		×		2.0	ı
6				1.4	ı

[a] The versions that have vertical lines in the same column were not significantly different from each other using *a posteriori* contrasts.

TABLE 5: Importance of Game Features in
Preference for the Breakout Game

Feature	Beta in multiple regression
Breaking out bricks	.77
Score	.32
Bounce from paddle	.30
Multiple *r*	.87

the breaking out of bricks. According to the regression, the bouncing from the paddle and the score are approximately equal in importance, and both are much less important than breaking out the bricks.

Discussion

It is not clear from this study what aspects of the bricks breaking out are most important, but the list of features in Table 3 suggests a number of important possibilities. A partially destroyed wall of bricks presents a visually compelling fantasy goal and at the same time is a graphic scorekeeping device telling how close the player is to attaining that goal. It thus provides a goal, a visual effect, fantasy, and scoring all at the same time. In fact, the structure of the wall suggests all sorts of goals at different levels: knocking out a brick in the third row, destroying the first row completely, etc.

The results also showed that the versions that had neither a score nor bricks breaking out were significantly less appealing (using a posteriori contrasts) than the other versions. In other words, the versions in which there was no clear goal, other than a vague "keep the ball going as long as you can," were significantly less fun than the others. Without a clear goal, the game was not really a game at all.

Certainly the results of this short experiment with a relatively small number of subjects do not definitively reveal the "secret" of the Breakout game. The results do, however, illuminate the importance of a clever combination of challenge and visual effects in the design of the Breakout game. I believe a sim-

ilar combination is important in the success of other popular games like Space Invaders.[2]

4. Darts: A Cognitive Skill Game

The second game I studied in detail was a game called Darts that was designed to teach elementary students about fractions (Dugdale and Kibbey, 1975). In the version of the game used, three balloons appear at random places on a number line on the screen and players try to guess the positions of the balloons (see Figure 3). They guess by typing in mixed numbers (whole numbers and/or fractions), and after each guess an arrow shoots across the screen to the position specified. If the guess is right, the arrow pops the balloon. If wrong, the arrow remains on the screen and the player gets to keep shooting until all the balloons are popped. Circus music is played at the beginning of the game, and if all three balloons in a round are popped in four tries or fewer, a short song is played after the round.

Darts is a good example of what may be called an *intrinsic fantasy* where the fantasy (the positions of arrows and balloons on the number line) is intimately related to the skill being used (estimating fractions). By contrast, an *extrinsic fantasy* (like Hangman) is only weakly related to the skill being used

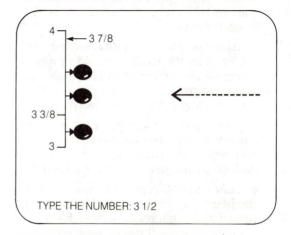

FIGURE 3: Display format for the Darts game

(spelling and vocabulary). In extrinsic fantasies, the fantasy usually depends only on
whether the answers are right or wrong, so
the same fantasy may be used for many different subject matters. For example, the Hangman fantasy could be used just as well for
arithmetic problems as for spelling problems. This distinction is discussed in greater
detail in Section 5 below. Besides the intrinsic fantasy, Darts has a number of other potentially motivational features such as feedback, music, and graphics.

To find out which of these features contribute most to the appeal of the game, I constructed a sequence of eight different versions of the game, each of which had one
more presumably motivational feature than
the last. As illustrated in Figure 4, the following versions were used.

1. *Noninteractive drill.* The student
guesses the location of rectangles on a
number line, but there is no feedback
about whether the guesses are right or
wrong. This version is a rough analog of
paper-and-pencil worksheets.

2. *Add performance feedback.* After each
guess the student is told whether the
guess was right or wrong. This version is
a rough analog of traditional drill-and-
practice computer programs.

3. *Add scoring.* A scoreboard at the
bottom of the screen tells the number of
tries and the number of correct answers
in each round.

4. *Add constructive feedback.* After each
incorrect try the student is told in which
direction and by approximately how
much the answer was wrong (e.g., "A
little too high," "Way too low").

5. *Add extrinsic fantasy.* Each time the
student guesses the position of a
rectangle correctly, an arrow pops a
balloon in another part of the screen.

6. *Add music.* Circus music is played at
the beginning of the game, and a song is
played after each round in which the
student guesses all three numbers in four
tries or fewer.

7. *Add graphic representation.* All
correct and incorrect answers are marked
by short lines on the number line.

8. *Add intrinsic fantasy.* The original
Darts game is used with arrows popping
balloons on the number line.

The sizes of the rectangles in each version
were adjusted to try to make the probability
of success (number of correct answers/num-
ber of tries) approximately the same for all
versions. Also when the introduction of a
new feature in a version made the information of an old feature redundant, the old feature was dropped.

To eliminate the possibility of "contami-
nation" between versions, each subject saw
only one version of the game. If each subject
were to see several versions of the game,
then subjects who saw balloons popping in
one version, say, might imagine balloons
popping in later versions that did not actually
show the balloons. Furthermore, it would be
difficult to control for other effects of the order of presentation such as boredom with later versions or heightened contrasts between
similar versions. By comparing averages between groups of subjects who each see only
one version, all these problems are eliminated. This design thus tests how important different features would be in natural situations
where there is only one version of each
game.

Method

Subjects. There were eighty subjects in this
experiment, ten assigned randomly to each
of the eight conditions. There were thirty-six
boys and forty-four girls. All were fifth grade
students at public schools in the Palo Alto
area. Half were from a school in a predominantly low-income minority neighborhood;
the other half from a school in a
predominantly middle or upper-middle class
neighborhood. To as great an extent as
possible, the number of subjects of each sex
from each school was kept constant over
conditions.

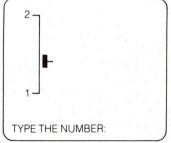

1. Noninteractive drill

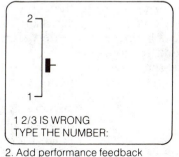

2. Add performance feedback

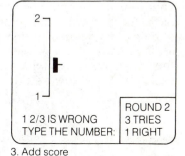

3. Add score

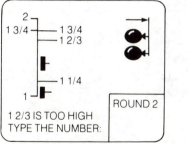

4. Add constructive feedback

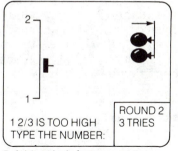

5. Add extrinsic fantasy

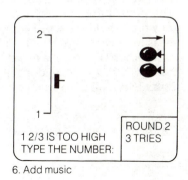

6. Add music

7. Add graphic representation

8. Add intrinsic fantasy

FIGURE 4: Different versions of the Darts game

Procedure. Each student was assigned to one condition and was allowed to choose freely between the version of Darts in that condition and a version of the Hangman computer game that was the same in all conditions. Students were able to change back and forth between the two games as often as they wanted during two 20-minute sessions. At the end of the second session, they were asked to say which game they liked best and to rate how well they liked the two games.

Results

There were three measures of how interesting subjects found the Darts game: how long they played with Darts in preference to Hangman (up to a maximum of 40 minutes), how well they said they liked Darts (on a scale from 1 to 5), and which game they said they preferred (Darts or Hangman). All three measures were significantly correlated with each other ($r_{12} = .30$, $r_{13} = .45$, $r_{23} = .69$; each $p < .01$). The amount of time spent on Darts had a higher variance in proportion to its mean and was the most sensitive of the three measures.

A separate three-way analysis of variance (using condition, school, and sex as independent variables) was performed for each of the three measures of interest. Both time spent on Darts and preference for Darts revealed significant effects of condition ($F(7,48) = 4.90$, $p < .001$; and ($F(7,48) = 2.21$, $p < .05$). There was also, surprisingly, a highly significant interaction between condition and sex in determining time spent on Darts ($F(7,48) = 4.84$, $p < .001$). No other main effects or interactions were significant. Since there were no significant effects of school, students from the two schools were pooled for the remainder of the analyses, giving cell sizes of four to six.

Because each pair of adjacent conditions differs by only one feature, a priori comparisons were planned between each adjacent pair of conditions. Table 6 shows the average values and the significant differences between conditions for the three interest measures. Because of the significant interaction between sex and condition, these comparisons are shown separately for boys and girls.

TABLE 6: Interest in Different Versions of the Darts Game

Condition	Interest Measures					
	Time playing Darts (0–40 min)		"Like Darts" (scale from 1 to 5)		"Prefer Darts to Hangman" (percent of subjects)	
	Boys	Girls	Boys	Girls	Boys	Girls
1. Noninteractive drill	20.5	15.5	3.3	3.2	0	20
2. Add performance feedback	18.8	20.2	3.8	3.2	50	0
3. Add scoring	24.2	19.8	3.0	3.4	0	40
4. Add constructive feedback	16.2*	22.2	3.6	2.6	40	20
5. Add extrinsic fantasy	25.8*	20.8	5.0*	4.2	80	30
6. Add music	21.8	30.0*	4.0	4.0	30	80
7. Add graphic representation	28.3	29.8	4.3	3.8	80	50
8. Add intrinsic fantasy	34.5	19.8**	4.5	3.5	100	50
Average	23.4	22.0	3.9	3.5	48	36

*$p < .05$, for comparison with previous condition.
**$p < .01$, for comparison with previous condition.

Though it is not shown in the table, the only significant difference when boys and girls were analyzed together was a significant increase ($p < .05$) in "liking Darts" when the extrinsic fantasy of arrows and balloons was introduced (Condition 4 vs. 5).

The most surprising result in Table 6 is that the original version of Darts (Condition 8) is significantly *less* interesting for girls than the version in which the intrinsic arrows and balloons fantasy is replaced by an extrinsic version of the same fantasy (Condition 7). The table also shows that boys like the arrows and balloons when introduced as an extrinsic fantasy (Condition 4 vs. 5) and dislike being told in words that their guess is too high or too low (Condition 3 vs. 4), and that girls like the music (Condition 5 vs. 6). Finally, and somewhat surprisingly, the version with no performance feedback (Condition 1) was not significantly less interesting than the version with simple performance feedback (Condition 2) for either boys or girls.

As described in more detail elsewhere (Malone, 1980a, 1981), the boys' apparent dislike of verbal constructive feedback is not significant when a multiple regression model is used to analyze the contribution of each feature in all versions where it is present. Furthermore, when the times spent playing the game are transformed to utilities according to a plausible model of choice behavior, neither the boys' dislike of verbal constructive feedback nor the girls' liking of music are significant (see Malone, 1981). Therefore, these latter two results seem less reliable than the sex differences in fantasy preference.

Discussion

Why should the original game (Condition 8) be significantly less appealing for girls than the version with an extrinsic fantasy (Condition 7)? In Condition 7, the player's guess is marked immediately on the number line, and an arrow goes across the screen only if the guess is right. In Condition 8, an arrow goes across the screen after every guess, and there

is a moment of suspense before the player can tell whether the guess is right or wrong. These subtle differences suggest at least two possible explanations for the girls' preference of Condition 7. The girls might have preferred Condition 7 because they were more impulsive or achievement oriented than the boys and did not like having to wait for the arrow to travel across the screen to find out if their guesses were right or wrong. Or the girls might have preferred Condition 7 because they disliked the fantasy of arrows and balloons in the first place and the fantasy was more salient in Condition 8.

I prefer the latter explanation for several reasons. First of all, the girls in Condition 7 made slightly fewer guesses per minute than the girls in Condition 8. If they had preferred Condition 7 because it allowed them to guess faster, one would have expected them to make more guesses per minute. More importantly, there are no good a priori reasons to expect a difference between boys and girls in their impatience to work more problems or to find out whether their guesses were right or wrong. After an extensive review of psychological studies of sex differences, Maccoby and Jacklin (1974) found no consistent differences between boys and girls in either impulsivity or achievement motivation.

There are several reasons, however, for thinking that girls did not like the arrows and balloons fantasy. When the arrows and balloons fantasy was first introduced in Condition 5, the girls liked it less than the previous condition though this difference was not statistically significant. Rosenberg and Sutton-Smith (1960) in a study of sex differences in children's game preferences found that boys (ages 9–11) liked games that involved propelling objects through space (including darts) and girls did not. Also Maccoby and Jacklin (1974) found convincing evidence that boys are more aggressive than girls. Thus to the extent that the fantasy of destroying balloons with weaponlike objects is aggressive, this may explain the sex difference in preference. Finally there is anecdotal evidence that the girls did not like the Darts fantasy. One girl, in the postexperimental interview, said, "Darts is more like a boys' game." When I went back to the classes where I had done the experiment to tell them about the results, I first explained the conditions, said that there were differences between boys and girls in what they liked, and then asked them to guess what the differences were. Most of the classes guessed that girls would have liked music and boys would have liked exploding the balloons.

For all these reasons, I think that the girls disliked the intrinsic fantasy (Condition 8) because the arrows and balloons fantasy— which they disliked in the first place—was more salient in that version.

Conclusions

The primary result of this experiment was that the boys seemed to like the fantasy of arrows popping balloons and the girls seemed to dislike this fantasy. I do not think the implication of this result is that boys should be given one kind of fantasy and girls should be given another. Instead, I think it would be better to let each person choose whichever fantasy seems most appealing at the time. These choices will presumably depend on many factors besides gender. But even if gender is only one of many determinants of what children find interesting, an understanding of these differences may help prevent unintentionally designing instructional environments in a way that appeals more, say, to boys than to girls.

I think the most important implication of this experiment is that fantasies can be very important in creating motivating instructional environments but that, unless the fantasies are carefully chosen to appeal to the target audience, they may actually make the environment less interesting rather than more (as indeed the arrows and balloons fantasy did for girls here).

The technique developed here of varying specific features in a set of nearly isomorphic games seems to be a useful way of empirically studying intrinsic motivation. In both of the experiments described here, I removed

features from already popular games, but clearly the same technique could be used to study the enhancement of games by adding new features. In the next section, I will outline a set of features that can often be added to games or other educational activities to make them more interesting.

5. Framework for a Theory of Intrinsically Motivating Instruction

Several of the theorists discussed in Section 1 (e.g., Piaget, 1951; Bruner, 1966; Berlyne, 1965; Moore and Anderson, 1969) deal with intrinsically motivated learning, and several others (e.g., Csikszentmihalyi, 1975, 1979; Eifferman, 1974) deal with intrinsic motivation in general. But none of the theories deals satisfactorily with all three of the major kinds of motivation discussed above: challenge, fantasy, and curiosity. Csikszentmihalyi, for example, presents a detailed analysis of the role of challenge in intrinsic motivation, but since he is not dealing specifically with learning he does not mention curiosity, the most obvious intrinsic motive for learning. Similarly, Berlyne analyzes curiosity in some detail, but neglects challenge and fantasy altogether. Bruner perhaps comes closest to the taxonomy presented here by giving prominent roles to challenge and curiosity, but he does not develop the implications of either in much detail, and he does not mention fantasy. Piaget does a very admirable job of synthesizing all three elements into a coherent theory. To greatly oversimplify his theory for the purpose of comparison, he claims that people are driven by a will to mastery (challenge) to seek optimally informative environments (curiosity), which they assimilate, in part, using schemas from other contexts (fantasy). But though a number of people have applied Piaget's ideas to educational practice (e.g., Furth, 1970; Kamii and DeVries, 1977), the implications of his theory for instruction are often ambiguous or extremely general (Groen, 1978).

In short, none of the theories is satisfactory as a basis for instructional design that captures what seem to be the most important aspects of the computer games studied above and other well-known computer games (e.g., Ahl, 1973, People's Computer Company, 1977). Using these computer games as inspiration, I will suggest in this section how a more comprehensive theory of instructional design might be developed based on three categories: *challenge, fantasy,* and *curiosity.* The framework for this theory is outlined in Table 7.

Challenge

A number of writers have noted that in order for an environment to be challenging, it must provide *goals* whose attainment is *uncertain*

TABLE 7: Framework for a Theory of Intrinsically Motivating Instruction

I. Challenge
  A. Goal
    1. Personally meaningful goals
    2. Obvious or easily generated goals
    3. Performance feedback
  B. Uncertain outcome
    1. Variable difficulty level
      a. Determined automatically
      b. Chosen by learner
      c. Determined by opponent's skill
    2. Multiple-level goals
      a. Scorekeeping
      b. Speeded responses
    3. Hidden information
    4. Randomness
  C. Toys vs. tools
  D. Self-esteem

II. Fantasy
  A. Intrinsic and extrinsic fantasies
  B. Cognitive aspects of fantasies
  C. Emotional aspects of fantasies

III. Curiosity
  Optimal level of informational complexity
  A. Sensory curiosity: audio and visual effects
  B. Cognitive curiosity
    1. "Good form" in knowledge structures
      a. Complete
      b. Consistent
      c. Parsimonious
    2. Informative feedback
      a. Surprising
      b. Constructive

(e.g., Kagan, 1978, p. 157; Eifferman, 1974). A number of important consequences follow from this simple principle.

Goals. There are several reasons for believing that goals are important to intrinsically motivating environments. In the survey described above, the single feature of the computer games that correlated most strongly with preference was whether the game had a goal. In a sense, the very notion of "game" implies that there is an "object of the game." In order for a goal to be motivating it should have several characteristics.

First, a good goal is *personally meaningful.* A study by Morozova (1955) has some tantalizing implications for making goals personally meaningful. In this study, children read several variants of a text passage about latitude and longitude. The version in which a child hero was faced with the practical problem of finding his location was much more interesting (and understandable) to the children than the other versions. The goal in this version had several intriguing qualities.

1. Using the skill being taught was a means to achieving the goal, but it was not the goal in itself.

2. The goal was part of an intrinsic fantasy as discussed below.

3. Because of the child hero, the goal was presumably one with which the child readers could identify.

This is related to what Papert (1980) calls the "power principle," that the knowledge being learned should ". . . empower the learner to perform personally meaningful projects that could not be done without it" (p. 54).

Most games have what Csikszentmihalyi (1975) calls a *fixed goal,* that is, a goal that is predetermined by cultural convention. Fixed goals can be made obvious and compelling by the use of visual effects (Breakout) or fantasy (Hangman). In contrast to games, other kinds of activity, like drawing pictures or writing stories, may have what Csikszentmihalyi (1975) calls *emergent goals,* that is, goals that arise out of the interaction between a person and the environment. In order to be motivating, environments like this should be structured so that users can easily generate goals of appropriate difficulty. For example, Papert (1980) describes a computer-based environment in which a moving "turtle" draws designs on a computer screen or on the floor in response to the learner's commands. One of the strengths of this environment is that it is easy for children to think of things they would like a moving "turtle" to do. But unless beginners have some help evaluating the difficulty of possible projects, they might easily pick tasks that are discouragingly difficult. Finally, in order to be motivated by a goal, learners usually need some kind of *performance feedback* to tell whether they are achieving their goal.

Uncertain Outcome. An environment is not challenging if the person is either certain to reach the goal or certain not to reach the goal. A careful analysis of the computer games studied above shows that there are at least four general ways that the attainment of a goal can be made uncertain for a wide range of people or for the same person at different times: *variable difficulty level, multiple-level goals, hidden information,* and *randomness.*

Variable difficulty level. Most good computer games are playable at different difficulty levels. In computer games, as well as in other educational activities, the choice of difficulty level can be either determined automatically according to how well the player does (e.g., Breakout, drill-and-practice), chosen by the learner (perhaps with ego-involving labels like "Cadet," "Captain," "Commander" in Star Wars), or determined by the opponent's skill (chess, Chase, etc.). I think one of the important reasons why competition is motivating is simply because it provides a challenge at an appropriate difficulty level.

Multiple-level goals. Good computer games often have several different levels of goals. With this feature, players whose outcome is certain at one level of goal may still

be challenged by another level of goal. There are at least two kinds of multiple-level goals.

In the first kind, all the goals are of the same type, but they vary in difficulty. For example, in Breakout, the goal of destroying all the bricks in the first row, is different in difficulty but not different in kind from the final goal of destroying all the bricks. The chief advantage of this type of multiple-level goal seems to be simply that it provides a variable difficulty level within a fixed problem environment.

In the second kind of multiple-level goal, the higher level goals involve accomplishing the lower level goals "better." In the Darts game, for example, the high level goal is not just to pop all the balloons, but to pop them in as few tries as possible. High level goals, in other words, often deal with solving problems faster or with fewer steps. In terms of a problem-solving model (Newell and Simon, 1972; Newell, 1979), this implies that the search control knowledge is becoming more efficient based on experience (see Anzai and Simon, 1979), or that the execution of the transformations is becoming faster (e.g., "automatized," see LaBerge, 1975; Shiffrin and Schneider, 1977).

The implication here is that well-designed instructional environments, by providing high level goals, can take advantage of a "natural" cognitive motivation to optimize existing mental procedures. Environments that include *scorekeeping* or *speeded responses* often emphasize this sort of high level goal, and therefore these features seem especially appropriate for instructional situations (like drill-and-practice) where the purpose is to optimize previously learned procedures.

Hidden information. Many games, especially guessing games, make the outcome of a game uncertain by hiding information from the player or players and selectively revealing it. This feature seems to provoke curiosity as well as contributing to the challenge of an activity.

Randomness. A final way of making the outcome of a game uncertain is to introduce randomness. Many gambling games seem to succeed almost entirely on the basis of this principle, and randomness can be used to heighten interest in many other kinds of game or activity (e.g., Hammurabi, Adventure).

Toys vs. Tools. This analysis of challenge illuminates an important distinction between toys and tools. Toys can be defined as systems used for their own sake with no external goal (e.g., computer games, puzzles). Tools can be defined as systems used as a means to achieve an external goal (e.g., text editors, programming languages). The requirements for good toys and tools with respect to challenge are mostly opposite. Since a good tool is designed to achieve goals that are already present in the external task, it need not provide a goal. Furthermore, since the outcome of the external goal (e.g., writing a good letter, getting a program to work) is already uncertain, the tool itself should be reliable, efficient, and usually "invisible." In a sense, a good game is intentionally made difficult to play to increase its challenge, but a tool should be made as easy as possible to use. This distinction helps explain why some users of complex computer systems may take a perverse pleasure in mastering tools that are extremely difficult to use. To the extent that these users are treating the systems as toys rather than tools, the difficulty increases the challenge and therefore the pleasure of using the systems.

Self-esteem. Challenge is captivating because it engages a person's self-esteem. Success in an instructional environment, like success in any challenging activity, can make people feel better about themselves. The opposite side of this principle is, however, that failure in a challenging activity can lower a person's self-esteem and, if it is severe enough, decrease the person's interest in the instructional activity. The complexities of this relationship between self-esteem and achievement have been extensively studied by attribution theorists and others (see Weiner, 1980, for a comprehensive review). One simple implication of this relationship is that instructional activities should have a variable

difficulty level so learners can work at an appropriate level for their ability. Another implication might be that performance feedback should be presented in a way that minimizes the possibility of self-esteem damage. Note that there is a tension here between the need to provide clear performance feedback to enhance challenge and learning, and the need not to reduce self-esteem to the point where the challenge becomes discouraging rather than inviting.

Fantasy

Fantasies can make instructional environments more interesting and more educational. I define a fantasy-inducing environment as one that evokes "mental images of things not present to the senses or within the actual experience of the person involved" (*American Heritage Dictionary*). These mental images can be either of physical objects (e.g., darts and balloons) or of social situations (e.g., being the ruler of a kingdom), and they may or may not be likely to occur in the learner's environment (e.g., balloons vs. dragons).

Intrinsic and Extrinsic Fantasies. One relatively easy way to try to increase the fun of learning is to take an existing curriculum and overlay it with a game in which the player progresses toward some fantasy goal (Baseball), or avoids some fantasy catastrophe (Hangman), depending only on whether the player's answers are right or wrong. These are examples of *extrinsic fantasies*, where the fantasy depends on the use of the skill, but not vice versa. Other factors such as speed of answering can also affect extrinsic fantasies. For example, the Speedway game in which students' race cars move along a race track depending on how fast they answer arithmetic problems is an extrinsic fantasy. Since the exercise of the skill does not depend in any way on the fantasy, the same fantasy could be used with completely different kinds of problems. For example, Baseball and Hangman fantasies could just as well be used for arithmetic problems as for spelling problems, with people being hung or advancing around a baseball diamond depending on whether the arithmetic problems are worked correctly.[3]

In *intrinsic fantasies*, on the other hand, not only does the fantasy depend on the skill, but the skill also depends on the fantasy. This usually means that problems are presented in terms of the elements of the fantasy world, and players receive a natural kind of constructive feedback. For example, in Darts, the skill of estimating distances is applied to the fantasy world of balloons on a number line, and players can see graphically whether their answers are too high or too low and if so by how much. Other intrinsic fantasies in math games include the search for a hidden animal on a Cartesian grid in the Hurkle game and Snoopy shooting at the Red Baron on a number line in the Snoopy game. The Adventure game in which a vast underground cavern system is explored in response to the players' commands can be considered an intrinsic fantasy for the skills of reading (the cave descriptions) and writing (the commands).

I would like to claim that: *in general, intrinsic fantasies are both more interesting and more instructional than extrinsic fantasies*. The Darts experiment described above was intended, in part, to test the first part of this hypothesis, but the apparent unappealingness of the basic fantasy for girls prevented a strong test. One advantage of intrinsic fantasies is that they often indicate how the skill could be used to accomplish some real world goal. Simulations, like the Lemonade stand simulation, are obvious examples of this. More importantly, the cognitive advantages of fantasies discussed in the next section apply only to intrinsic fantasies, not to extrinsic ones.

Cognitive Aspects of Fantasy. Metaphors or analogies of the kind provided by intrinsic fantasies can often help a learner apply old knowledge in understanding new things. For

example, players in the Darts game already know about physical objects (like arrows and balloons) being higher or lower than other objects. If they make the crucial connection between number size and position on the number line, then they are able to use this old knowledge in the new domain to make inferences about the relative sizes of unfamiliar fractions.

Another cognitive advantage of intrinsic fantasies is simply that by provoking vivid images related to the material being learned, they can improve memory of the material (Bower, 1972; Paivio, 1971).

Emotional Aspects of Fantasy. Fantasies in computer games almost certainly derive some of their appeal from the emotional needs they help to satisfy in the people who play them. It is very difficult to know what emotional needs people have and how these needs might be partially met by computer games. It seems fair to say, however, that computer games that embody emotionally involving fantasies like war, destruction, and competition are likely to be more popular than those with less emotional fantasies.

One obvious consequence of the importance of emotional aspects of fantasies is that different people will find different fantasies appealing. If instructional designers can create many different kinds of fantasy for different kinds of people, their activities are likely to have much broader appeal. For example, one can easily envision a math game, where different students see the same problems, but can choose which fantasy they want to see. Instructional designers might also create environments into which students can project their own fantasies in a relatively unconstrained way. For instance, one could let students name imaginary participants in a computer game.

Clearly these things are much easier said than done. The unexpected difference between boys and girls in the Darts experiment illustrates the difficulty of predicting what kinds of fantasy will be appealing to different people. There are also difficult questions about whether it is sometimes bad to encourage certain fantasies. For example, if a computer game provides an outlet for aggressive fantasies (which seem to be very popular in computer games), will players become more aggressive in real life? (See Liebert and Poulos, 1976, for a related view of empirical studies on the effects of television violence.)

Curiosity

As discussed in Section 1, environments can evoke a learner's curiosity by providing an *optimal level of informational complexity* (Berlyne, 1965; Piaget, 1952). In other words, the environments should be neither too complicated nor too simple with respect to the learner's existing knowledge. They should be *novel* and *surprising*, but not completely incomprehensible. In general, an optimally complex environment will be one where the learner knows enough to have expectations about what will happen, but where these expectations are sometimes unmet.

There are a number of parallels between challenge and curiosity. Since both require an optimal level (of difficulty in one case and complexity in the other), both often depend on adjusting the environment to the learner's ability or understanding. Both also depend on feedback to reduce uncertainty (about one's own ability in the case of challenge and about the state of the world in the case of curiosity). In fact, challenge could be explained as curiosity about one's own ability, or curiosity could be explained as a challenge to one's understanding. In spite of these similarities between challenge and curiosity, however, I think it is useful to separate the two concepts. While the notion of self-esteem is central to the idea of challenge, self-esteem is not involved in most curiosity. Similarly, the cognitive models of curiosity I will sketch below have little to contribute to an understanding of challenge. It is also useful, in the following discussion, to

distinguish between two kinds of curiosity—*sensory curiosity* and *cognitive curiosity*—depending on the level of processing involved.

Sensory Curiosity. Sensory curiosity involves the attention-attracting value of changes in the light, sound, or other sensory stimuli of an environment. There is no reason why educational environments have to be impoverished sensory environments. Colorfully illustrated textbooks, television programs like *Sesame Street*, and tactile teaching devices (e.g., Montessori, 1912) demonstrate this point. Computers provide even more possibilities for graphics, animation, music, and other captivating *audio and visual effects*. These effects can be used: (1) *as decoration* (e.g., circus music at the beginning of Darts), (2) *to enhance fantasy*, (3) *as a reward*, and perhaps most importantly, [or] (4) *as a representation system* that may be more effective than words or numbers (e.g., graphic representation of fractions in Darts, and different tones in Breakout to signal bounces and misses of the ball).

Cognitive Curiosity. In contrast to the perceptual changes that evoke sensory curiosity, cognitive curiosity is evoked by the prospect of modifying higher level cognitive structures. Cognitive curiosity can be thought of as a desire to bring better "form" to one's knowledge structures. In particular, I claim that people are motivated to bring to all their cognitive structures three of the characteristics of well-formed scientific theories: *completeness, consistency,* and *parsimony.* According to this theory, the way to engage learners' curiosity is to present just enough information to make their existing knowledge seem incomplete, inconsistent, or unparsimonious. The learners are then motivated to learn more in order to make their cognitive structures better formed.

For example, if you have just read all but the last chapter of a murder mystery, you have a strong cognitive motivation to bring completeness to your knowledge structure by finding out who the murderer was (i.e., filling in the murderer "slot" in the murder "frame"; see Minsky, 1975). Or, as Morozova 1955) suggests, curiosity can be stimulated by pointing out inconsistencies or paradoxes in a learner's knowledge. For instance, students may be told that plants require sunlight for the photochemical processes on which they depend, but that some plants, namely fungi, can live in the dark. Finally, one might evoke curiosity by giving a number of examples of a general rule before showing how (or letting students discover that) all the examples can be explained more parsimoniously by the single new rule.

The "Socratic method" and the tutorial strategies of master teachers (Collins and Stevens, 1981) can be seen as ways of systematically exposing incompletenesses, inconsistencies, and unparsimoniousness in the learner's knowledge structures. One extremely powerful tool for tailoring feedback in this way for specific learners in computer-based learning environments is to maintain on-line cognitive models of the learners (e.g., Burton and Brown, 1979).

Informative feedback. Several more specific principles for designing instructional environments follow from these general ideas. One way of making environments interestingly complex is to make them responsive (see Moore and Anderson, 1969). In particular:

a. *To engage a learner's curiosity, feedback should be surprising.* The "easy" way to do this is by using randomness. A deeper way to do this is to have environments whose underlying consistency is revealed by things that seem surprising at first. For instance, players of the Hammurabi simulation may be surprised at how many people starve at first. But the underlying relationships between amount of grain and number of people are consistent and can be discovered by the players.

b. *To be educational, feedback should be*

constructive. In other words, the feedback should not just reveal to learners that their knowledge is incomplete, inconsistent, or unparsimonious, but should help them see how to change their knowledge to become more complete, consistent, or parsimonious.

6. Conclusion

In this article, I have suggested a coherent framework for a theory of intrinsically motivating instruction. As described in more detail elsewhere (Malone, 1980a, 1980b), one use of this framework is as a checklist of heuristics to be used in designing instructional environments. Few instructional environments include all the features mentioned above, and it is usually possible to think of ways that any given activity could incorporate more of these features. For example, at least one fifth of the computer games in the survey described above do not have any way of varying their difficulty level and could probably be improved by adding this.

I have focused in this article on features that can be present in all intrinsically motivating learning environments. In so doing, I have neglected two important kinds of features. First, I have assumed as part of the definition of intrinsic motivation that learners are free to choose their activities without external pressures. As mentioned briefly above, however, this freedom of choice can itself be an important motivator.

Second, I have neglected phenomena, like cooperation and competition, that emerge only in situations involving more than one person. It seems clear, however, that interpersonal motivations are often very important in learning. A number of sources suggest how a theory including these motivations could be developed. For example, Bruner (1966) points out the importance in instruction of social processes like *reciprocity* (by which he means cooperation) and *identifica-*

tion (or modeling one's self after some respected person). DeVries and Slavin (1978) and Allen and Ross (1977) describe how competitive academic games can be used to stimulate both interest and learning. Finally, Cole (1979) and Levin and Kareev (1980) have begun to perform detailed cognitive analyses of how children cooperate in learning to solve new problems. Clearly a complete theory of intrinsically motivating instruction should suggest ways that learning can be fostered by interpersonal—as well as individual—motivations.

ACKNOWLEDGMENTS

This article is based on the author's Ph.D. dissertation submitted to the Department of Psychology, Stanford University. Parts of the article were also presented at the Cognitive Science Society Conference, New Haven, Connecticut, June 19, 1980. The research was supported by the Xerox Corporation Palo Alto Research Center and by a National Science Foundation Graduate Fellowship.

The author would especially like to thank Patrick Suppes, his dissertation advisor, and Mark Lepper and John Seely Brown, the other members of his reading committee, for their extremely helpful suggestions and continued encouragement.

The author would also like to thank Robert Calfee, Bill Clancey, Allan Collins, Jamey Friend, George Furnas, Laura Gould, David Klahr, Tom Moran, Brian Ross, John Sheehan, Ed Smith, and Mike Williams for helpful suggestions at various stages of this project, Chris Rodriguez for help in performing the experiment in Section 3, and the teachers and administrators who gave permission to interview and observe students in their schools.

NOTES

1. Breakout is a trademark of Atari, Inc.

2. Space Invaders is roughly analogous to the Breakout game. Instead of a stationary wall of bricks, there is an advancing squadron of alien invaders, and instead of knocking bricks out with a ball, one destroys invaders by shooting them.

3. For those readers who are not familiar with the computer games I use as examples, Table 1 and the Appendix contain brief descriptions of all the games mentioned but not described elsewhere in the text.

REFERENCES

Ahl, D. *101 BASIC computer games.* Morristown, N.J.: Creative Computing, 1973.

Allen, L. E., and Ross, J. Improving skill in applying mathematical ideas: A preliminary report on the instructional gaming program at Pelham Middle School in Detroit. *Alberta Journal of Educational Research*, 1977, *23*, 257–267.

Anzai, Y., and Simon, H. A. The theory of learning by doing. *Psychological Review*, 1979, 86, 124–140.

Atkinson, R. C. Adaptive instructional systems: Some attempts to optimize the learning process. In D. Klahr (Ed.), *Cognition and instruction.* Hillsdale, N.J.: Erlbaum, 1976.

Avedon, E. M., and Sutton-Smith, B. *The study of games.* New York: John Wiley, 1971.

Bandura, A. *Principles of Behavior Modification.* New York: Holt, Rinehart & Winston, 1969.

Banet, B. Computers and early learning: A new direction for High/Scope Foundation. *Calculators/Computers*, 1979, *3*, 17.

Berlyne, D. E. *Conflict, arousal and curiosity.* New York: McGraw-Hill, 1960.

Berlyne, D. E. *Structure and direction in thinking.* New York: John Wiley, 1965.

Berlyne, D. E. Curiosity and exploration. *Science*, 1968, *153*, 25–33.

Berlyne, D. E., and Lawrence, G. H. *Journal of General Psychology*, 1964, *71*, 21.

Bower, G. H. Mental imagery and associative learning. In L. W. Gregg (Ed.), *Cognition in learning and memory.* New York: John Wiley, 1972.

Brown, J. S., and Burton, R. R. Diagnostic models for procedural bugs in basic mathematical skills. *Cognitive Science*, 1978, *2*, 155–192.

Brown, J. S., and VanLehn, K. Repair theory: A generative theory of bugs in procedural skills. *Cognitive Science*, 1980, *4*, 379–426.

Bruner, J. S. *On knowing: Essays for the left hand*. Cambridge, Mass.: Belknap Press of Harvard University Press, 1962.

Bruner, J. S. *Toward a theory of instruction*. Cambridge, Mass.: Belknap Press of Harvard University Press, 1966.

Burton, R. R., and Brown, J. S. An investigation of computer coaching for informal learning activities. *International Journal of Man–Machine Studies*, 1979, *11*, 5–24.

Collins, A., and Stevens, A. L. Goals and strategies of inquiry teachers. In R. Glaser (Ed.), *Advances in instructional technology*, vol. 2, Hillsdale, N.J.: Erlbaum, 1981.

Cole, M. Untitled session summary. In M. Cole, E. Hutchins, J. Levin, and N. Miyake (Eds.), *Naturalistic problem solving and microcomputers*. Unpublished report of a conference held at the Center for Human Information Processing, University of California at San Diego, March 29–30, 1979.

Condry, J. Enemies of exploration: Self-initiated versus other-initiated learning. *Journal of Personality and Social Psychology*, 1977, 35, 459–477.

Csikszentmihalyi, M. *Beyond boredom and anxiety*. San Francisco: Jossey-Bass, 1975.

Csikszentmihalyi, M. Intrinsic rewards and emergent motivation. In M. R. Lepper and D. Greene (Eds.), *The hidden costs of reward*. Hillsdale, N.J.: Erlbaum, 1979.

DeVries, D. L., and Slavin, R. E. Teams-Games-Tournament (TGT): Review of ten classroom experiments. *Journal of Research and Development in Education*, 1978, *12*, 28–38.

Dugdale, S., and Kibbey, D. *Fractions curriculum of the PLATO Elementary School Mathematics Project*. Computer-based Education Research Laboratory. October 1975. University of Illinois, Urbana.

Eifferman, R. R. It's child's play. In L. M. Shears and E. M. Bower (Eds.), *Games in education and development*, Springfield, Ill.: Charles C. Thomas, 1974.

Ellis, M. J., and Scholtz, G. J. L. *Activity and play of children*. Englewoods Cliffs, N.J.: Prentice-Hall, 1978.

Freud, S. *Beyond the pleasure principle*. New York: Liveright, 1950.

Furth, H. G. *Piaget for teachers*. Englewood Cliffs, N.J.: Prentice-Hall, 1970.

Goldstein, I. P. The genetic graph: A representation for the evolution of procedural knowledge. *International Journal of Man–Machine Studies*, 1979, *11*, 51–77.

Greeno, J. G. Cognitive objectives of instruction: Theory of knowledge for solving problems and answering questions. In D. Klahr (Ed.), *Cognition and instruction*. Hillsdale, N.J.: Erlbaum, 1976.

Groen, G. The theoretical ideas of Piaget and educational practice. In P. Suppes (Ed.), *Impact of research on education: Some case studies*. Washington, D.C.: National Academy of Education, 1978.

Hunt, J. McV. Intrinsic motivation and its role in psychological development. In D. Levine (Ed.), *Nebraska Symposium on Motivation*, vol. 13. Lincoln: University of Nebraska Press, 1965.

Kagan, J. *The growth of the child*. New York: W. W. Norton, 1978.

Kamii, C., and DeVries, R. Piaget for early education. In M. C. Day and R. K. Parker (Eds.), *Preschool in action*, 2nd ed. Boston: Allyn & Bacon, 1977.

Klahr, D. (Ed.) *Cognition and instruction*. Hillsdale, N.J.: Erlbaum, 1976.

Kobler, R., and Moore, O. K. *Educational system and apparatus*. U.S. Patent No. 3,281,959, 1966. 27 figures, 51 claims granted, 12 references. Also granted in many foreign countries.

LaBerge, D. Acquisition of automatic processing in perceptual and associative learning. In P. M. A. Rabbit and S. Dornic (Eds.), *Attention and performance*, vol. 5. New York: Academic Press, 1975.

Lepper, M. R., and Greene, D. *The hidden costs of reward*. Hillsdale, N.J.: Erlbaum, 1979.

Lepper, M. R., Greene, D., and Nisbett, R. E. Undermining children's intrinsic interest with extrinsic rewards: A test of the overjustification hypothesis. *Journal of Personality and Social Psychology,* 1973, *28,* 129–137.

Levin, J. A., and Kareev, Y. *Problem solving in everyday situations,* Unpublished technical report, Laboratory of Comparative Human Cognition, University of California, San Diego, 1980.

Liebert, R. M., and Poulos, R. W. Television as a moral teacher. In T. Lickona (Ed.), *Moral development and behavior.* New York: Holt, Rinehart & Winston, 1976.

Maccoby, E. E., and Jacklin, C. N. *The psychology of sex differences.* Stanford, Calif.: Stanford University Press, 1974.

Malone, T. W. *What makes things fun to learn? A study of intrinsically motivating computer games,* Technical Report No. CIS-7 (SSL-80-11), Palo Alto, Calif.: Xerox Palo Alto Research Center, 1980a.

Malone, T. W. *What makes things fun to learn? Heuristics for designing instructional computer games.* Proceedings of the Association for Computing Machinery Symposium on Small and Personal Computer Systems, Palo Alto, California, September 19, 1980b.

Malone, T. W. *What makes things fun to learn? A study of an intrinsically motivating computer game.* American Education Research Association Annual Meeting, Los Angeles, April 17, 1981.

Minsky, M. A framework for representing knowledge. In P. H. Winston (Ed.), *The psychology of computer vision.* New York: McGraw-Hill, 1975.

Montessori, M. *The Montessori method.* New York: Frederick A. Stokes, 1912.

Moore, O. K., and Anderson, A. R. Some principles for the design of clarifying educational environments. In Goslin, D. (Ed.), *Handbook of socialization theory and research.* Skokie, Ill: Rand McNally, 1969.

Moore, O. K., and Kobler, R. *Educational apparatus for children.* U.S. Patent No. 3,112,569, 1963. 6 figures, 13 claims granted, 6 references. Also granted in many foreign countries.

Morozova, N. G. [The psychological conditions for the arousal and modification of interest in children in the process of reading popular scientific literature.] *Izv. Akad. Pedag. Nauk,* 1955, *73,* 100–149 (cited and summarized by Berlyne, 1965).

Newell, A. Reasoning, problem solving and decision processes: The problem space as a fundamental category. Technical Report, Department of Computer Science, Carnegie-Mellon University, Pittsburgh, June 1979. In R. Nickerson (Ed.) *Attention and Performance,* vol. 8. Hillsdale, N.J.: Erlbaum, 1980.

Newell, A. and Simon, H. A. *Human problem solving.* Englewood Cliffs, N.J.: Prentice-Hall, 1972.

Paivio, A. *Imagery and verbal processes.* New York: Holt, Rinehart & Winston, 1971.

Papert, S. *Mindstorms: Children, computers, and powerful ideas.* New York: Basic Books, 1980.

People's Computer Company. *What to do after you hit return.* Menlo Park, Calif.: People's Computer Co., 1977.

Piaget, J. *Play, dreams, and imitation in childhood.* New York: W. W. Norton, 1951.

Piaget, J. *The origins of intelligence in children.* New York: International University Press, 1952.

Piaget, J. *Science of education and the psychology of the child.* New York: Viking Press, 1971.

Resnick, L. B. Task analysis in instructional design: Some cases from mathematics. In D. Klahr (Ed.), *Cognition and instruction.* Hillsdale, N.J.: Erlbaum, 1976.

Rosenberg, B. G., and Sutton-Smith, B. A revised conception of masculine–feminine differences in play activities. *Journal of Genetic Psychology,* 1960, *96,* 165–170.

Sears, R. R. Relation of fantasy aggression to interpersonal aggression. *Child Development,* 1950, *21,* 5–6 (cited and summarized by D. Berlyne, Laughter, humor, and play. In G. Lindzey and E. Aronson (Eds.), *Handbook of social psychology,* Reading, Mass.: Addison-Wesley, 1969).

Shiffrin, R. R., and Schneider, W. Controlled and automatic human information processing: II. Perceptual learning, automatic attending, and a general theory. *Psychological Review,* 1977, *84,* 127–190.

Shulman, L. S., and Keislar, E. R. (Eds.),
  Learning by discovery: A critical appraisal.
  Skokie, Ill.: Rand McNally, 1966.

Skinner, B. F. *Science and human behavior.*
  New York: Macmillan, 1953.

Stevens, A. L., Collins, A., and Goldin, S.
  Misconceptions in student's understanding.
  *International Journal of Man–Machine
  Studies,* 1979, *11,* 145–156.

Weiner, B. *Human motivation.* New York: Holt,
  Rinehart & Winston, 1980.

White, R. W. Motivation reconsidered: The
  concept of competence. *Psychological Review,*
  1959, 66, 297–333.

Zajonc, R. Social facilitation. *Science,* 1965, 149,
  269–274.

Zimbardo, P. G. *Cognitive Control of Motivation.*
  Chicago: Scott, Foresman, 1969.

3 Strategies for Developing Educational Software

The engineer who contracts to design a bridge can rely on many established handbooks and textbooks that supply information about the detailed procedures that are needed to handle each of the decisions that he will encounter. The physical features of the ravine or river and the properties of the materials the engineer must use will set harsh limits on his designs. In other fields, the designer of clothing, theater sets, or book jackets is less constrained by the materials and can follow taste and judgment with considerable flexibility. But every form of design has a factual foundation that the designer-as-artist may struggle against, but cannot ignore.

There are not yet any widely accepted handbooks of educational software design. Nor are there minimum industry standards that must be met, although we occasionally hear discussions about the need for such standards. Recently some authors of educational software have begun to write about their work. The readings in this section are the recommendations of software designers who have tried to distill from years of personal experience some guidelines, approaches, and perspectives. These readings touch a variety of types of design decisions and represent many points of view. The reader may find some pieces inspiring and others infuriating, but careful reading reveals a remarkable unanimity on many issues. These may be the first steps toward a loosely defined set of standards for educational software design.

Bork discusses methods and procedures for producing educational software. Most interesting software projects are too large for any single person to complete, so forms of collaboration are necessary, whether we think them desirable or not. His "production system" approach is worthy of careful consideration.

The main group of readings addresses issues of the design of interactions between students and computers—the central problems of educational software design. Although Simpson, Balman, Gaines, and Friend and Milojkovic address many of the same points, they approach them from distinctive viewpoints. Tenneyson and Buttrey raise questions about the function of student control in computer-based instruction. Although it is clearly desirable for students to take initiative about their own learning, there is still a great deal to be learned about how to use student control in CBE.

Information technology offers a versatile and useful resource for students with various handicaps. Many of the principles of instruction and design apply, but educational programs must be adapted with the specific characteristics of the audience in mind. Cartwright's article, prepared for this volume, gives an overview of some special education applications that are possible through technology.

Neil Rowe's article deals with simulation. His detailed, succinct rules may be difficult to absorb on a first reading. We suggest a quick reading for orientation, followed by more extended reflection on individual rules that did not come across the first time through. It may be useful, also, to review a piece of simulation software with these rules in mind.

6 Production Systems for Computer-Based Learning

Alfred Bork

University of California, Irvine

Introduction

This paper is concerned with the variety of possible production systems for generating computer-based and related learning material. A production system is the set of activities beginning with vague ideas about the concepts to be taught and ending with finished materials in the hands of users. These materials may include computer programs of various types, written material, visual material, and other pedagogical aids. They may also involve a variety of machinery for delivery—computers, videodisk players, slide projectors, [and] print material.

The need to seriously consider production systems for computer-based learning development is a result of many initial "cottage industry" efforts. In the early days of developing computer-based learning material, little was known about how such material worked with students, and little was known about the production process. Not too surprisingly beginners in this new experimental medium began to produce material with a variety of strategies. At this early stage projects did not produce sizable amounts of material, because we still had much to learn about the capabilities of the new medium.

As we have moved toward the era of very inexpensive, personal computers, the possibility of large-scale production and distribution has become more and more viable. Little large-scale production and distribution is currently going on, but the prospects look very promising for the immediate future. Many companies are now considering the marketing of computer-based learning material.

Hence, it is important at this stage to explore possible production systems. Without this step, sizable sums of money may be devoted to inappropriate approaches generating poor material.

The production ideas which form the basis of this discussion were developed over a 13-year period at the Educational Technology Center. Thus, it is rooted in the experience of producing a sizable body of curriculum material. I begin by formulating criteria for production systems and by reviewing some of the strategies that have been commonly used.

Criteria for Production Systems

It is reasonable, before discussing particular ways of organizing the production process for computer-based learning material or intelligent videodisk learning material, to develop a set of criteria and emphases for such systems. That is, we need to ask what *should* be the properties of such systems before we begin to develop the systems directly. This section outlines such criteria.

1. *Major focus on pedagogical issues.* As the material developed is to be learning material, the focus must be on the learning or pedagogical issues. This would seem to be almost a truism. Yet it can be argued that many of the production systems in existence dilute this focus and, in fact, tend to place the major emphasis on the technology itself. The overriding considerations should be pedagogical, and these factors should drive the development.

Alfred Bork, "Production Systems for Computer-Based Learning," pp. 1–52. Used by permission of Alfred Bork. This paper was commissioned and funded by the National Institute of Education.

2. *The best possible material.* The system should produce the best possible material for aiding learners. Systems which can produce material of limited capability should be avoided.

3. *Reasonable costs.* The costs associated with the full production process should be reasonable. The implication is that the material developed is to be marketed, either commercially or noncommercially, and that the costs must be in the range that can attract users.

4. *Estimatable costs.* In addition to having a reasonable cost, it is important that a developer be able to estimate costs in advance, within reasonable accuracy. A product will be usable in the market only if this is possible; an extensive product will be developed only if costs can be estimated. In early days of working in an area, it was often difficult to estimate costs. One must work toward systems that produce reliable cost estimates.

5. *Involve a wide range of good teachers.* The development of learning materials is still partially a science and partially an art. There is no substitute at the present time for very experienced, good teachers, familiar with the way students will react and learn. This is particularly important in computer-based learning, as the materials are usually designed to work with a wide variety of students. Hence, strategies which allow many excellent teachers to participate in ways that the *teachers* find congenial are highly desirable. One cannot expect to work with only a few teachers, if one is to produce sizable amounts of material, just because of the volume of material involved.

6. *Easily revisable units.* One of the advantages of computer-based learning material is that it can gather very detailed feedback on a moment-by-moment basis of the responses given by users. Hence, it is potentially very easy to revise, to make the material better and better. This means that whatever is written must be constructed to facilitate easy revision, often many times. Revisions may stretch over a period of years, and so many different people may be involved. Thought must be given in the production process to

how revision is to take place and how it can be as simple and as economical as possible. Maintenance of instructional materials, regardless of the media involved, is an important component of their life cycle.

7. *Encourage interaction.* A major advantage of computer-based learning material is that it can create an *active* learning environment for each student. This is unattainable with most of the mass learning techniques currently in use, primarily "spectator" techniques. The computer allows us to achieve some of the aspects, although not all, of a Socratic dialog.

As our capabilities for developing more and more intelligent computer materials improve, we may be able to approach closer to the Socratic tutor. But even at the present time, we can develop highly interactive units for large groups of students, and we can compete extremely well with books and lectures in this regard. Nevertheless, not all computer material achieves this goal of interaction. In some cases this is the result of the production systems employed; some systems tend to cut down on the amount and level of interaction that takes place.

8. *Encourage individualization.* A computer dialog can offer specific aid to a wide range of students. The notion that different students learn in different ways is widely believed. But many learning strategies find it difficult to provide for this range. We can do so with the computer. But again, computer material does not *necessarily* do this. Rather, individualization and adaptability must be encouraged within the production system.

9. *Maximize motivation.* Computer material should be attractive to the users. That is, it should explicitly consider motivational issues. An important goal of instruction and instructional materials is to increase student time on task, and thus to increase learning. One important way to accomplish this is by making the material more interesting.

There are many facets to motivation. For example, one important set of motivational factors is screen design—how the material is arranged on the screen both temporally and spatially. An issue that needs more consideration is that of which factors should be turned over to the "reader." The reader can potentially control many aspects of the screen which are fixed in book or lecture environments.

10. *Minimize transferability problems.* In the foreseeable future we can expect a continual procession of new, small, personal computers. These machines will reflect some combination of increased capability and reduced cost, depending on the marketing choices of the vendors. Hence, material developed in an effective production process must be economically transferable to these new student delivery machines as they become available.

Many issues are associated with transferability. The first consideration is what might be called technical transferability, the taking of materials written for one machine in one programming language and moving them to another machine with different hardware capabilities and possibly with different programming languages. This is often the *only* aspect considered. The production system can ease this process or can make it very difficult.

Another consideration is the scale of the entire project. Transferability becomes more practical when there will be sizable use of the material on the new machine, because the unit cost is less.

Another issue in transportability is that of visual appearance on the screen. When one moves from a display with 80 characters on a line to one with 40 characters, material must be rearranged, usually both text and visuals, on the screen. Different graphic facilities also may be available—such factors as resolution and intensity control may be different on the systems considered. The production approach must be set up in such a way as to ease the rearrangement of such screen factors during the transfer process.

A final issue in transferability is the use of extensive new capabilities not available on the original delivery machines. It must be possible to redesign the material relatively easily to allow for new capabilities as they become available.

In all these issues of transferability, it should be kept in mind that we will be talking about an increasingly large body of computer-based learning material as we move more and more into the future. Hence, the transferability process must be applicable to many different units of learning material, developed over a wide span of time.

11. *Adaptability to large-scale production.* While currently computer-based learning materials are being produced on a small scale, we need to look forward to the time in the not very distant future when sizable amounts of material will be produced. Strategies which may work for small amounts of production may be quite inadequate for large-scale production.

Components of a Production System

Various production systems may all have the same fundamental components. These components may be arranged in different ways; some may be omitted. Furthermore, the choice of who carries out each activity and how the developers of the components interface with each other will differ from system to system. In some systems a particular component may be repeated at several stages. We will give further details later.

Although we are grouping the components roughly in the order in which they would normally follow, there are many exceptions to this. As indicated, some might be omitted. Some might be repeated in different ways at various stages in the process. A few refer to activities that are typically carried on through much of the process.

The present section should not be taken as a description of any particular production system, but rather only as an overview, delineating components common to *all* production systems.

I assume that the computer learning material may be part of a larger activity, which may involve some print material and possibly other kinds of visual aid. Thus, with the process described, we might be producing intelligent videodisk material, combining the computer and the videodisk.

1. *Preplanning activities.* As with any sizable project, a number of activities must take place before the project begins. For example, it will be necessary to secure the initial funding, arrange for personnel, establish the production mechanism, and generally oversee the beginning of the operation. Development of the proposal, either to a governmental agency or to a company, will be necessary in this stage of the operation. Preliminary consideration of objectives may also take place at this stage.

2. *Production management.* The production process may in some systems be a complex activity. So it is necessary to consider how this activity is to be managed. While we list this second, because it must be set up at an early stage of the process, it is an activity that will continue for the entire project.

3. *Objectives and specifications.* For detailed work to proceed, a detailed overview must be available of what is to be produced. This overview can be developed in a variety of ways. As a minimum it would describe the modules to be produced in terms of the objectives each is trying to attain. It might provide fairly detailed outlines also as to how these objectives are to be attained.

4. *Training activities.* Training activities for the personnel involved might be important in a number of the following stages. Hence, this might be not a single activity but a series of different activities. The people involved in the different stages of producing materials may not know initially how to do the assigned tasks. Even if they are trained in some aspects, they may need special assistance. So several training programs, formal or informal, may be required.

5. *Pedagogical design.* This critical stage in the process involves the full pedagogical specification of the material. It goes far beyond the third step, the statement of objectives and specifications. The "script" which is the product of this stage contains *all* the decisions of an instructional nature, at least in their initial form.

6. *Visual design.* Another component is designing the material—placement of graphical information and textual information on the screen both spatially and temporally. Temporal considerations would also include delays. There might also be some user control as to how the material is to be displayed on the screen. Decisions must be made concerning the details of such user control.

7. *Technical development.* This is the stage in which the actual materials are initially produced. These materials may include computer programs, videodisks, print material (typeset and printed), and other associated materials.

8. *Editing.* Editing is another process which is likely to occur at several stages. For example, it might well occur between Stage 5 (pedagogical design) and Stage 6 (visual design), as well as after technical development.

9. *Evaluation.* Evaluation of computer-based learning materials is important in improving their capability (formative evaluation) and in demonstrating their effectiveness (summative evaluation). Hence, because of these different roles, evaluation will probably occur at several stages in the production process.

10. *Revision.* Formative evaluation implies that there will be a revision cycle or cycles. Revisions can lead to significant improvement of computer-based learning material. Several evaluation–revision loops may take place.

11. *Marketing.* After material is in release form, the issue then becomes how to market it. Marketing includes awareness, making potential users aware that the product is there, and includes providing opportunities for them to "see" and try the materials.

12. *Distribution.* The aim of the production process is to place the material in the hands of users, teachers or students. Distribution may be through commercial or noncommercial channels.

I stress again that this outline of production components does not attempt to describe any *particular* production system. A particular system may leave out some of these components, may combine some, may alter the order, and will have its own particular strategies for executing them. Different systems make different choices in determining what person or persons carry out one component and how the products of the different stages or components interface with each other.

The reader may have noticed that these components are *not* peculiar to computer-based learning material. Rather, they are stages that one might see in a process for producing any type of learning material—print, film, videodisk, or intelligent videodisk. A corollary to this is that the production process is not necessarily different for computer material than for other material. In many multimedia developments, a range of material, computer and others, may be produced.

Production Systems
without Computers

In looking at specific production systems for generating computer-based learning material, it is reasonable to view systems for producing high quality educational material that have already been developed. Thus, we can hope to profit from the types of strategy already in existence. Development of learning materials has many common factors regardless of the media and the subject area, particularly if these materials are to be of the highest quality.

Books

The production of textbooks is an interesting example for us because it represents a mature production system also based on technological development. The printing press invented in about 1450 is the basis for the modern book industry. Later developments, such as the invention of efficient typesetting machines, also played a critical role. So we may learn something about how to use a new technological development, the computer, to aid in the educational process by looking at this older process, printing.

It is worth noting that several hundred years elapsed between the invention of the printing press and the widespread use of textbooks in schools and universities. It is no accident that such a time span is necessary. Initially people do not understand how to use a newer medium for learning, and so much experimental trial work is necessary. Practically everything that has gone on so far with using the computer in education should be viewed as fitting into this early experimental period. We are now beginning to see a variety of modes in which the computer is effective, so we are approaching the end of this experimental stage.

Many variant systems have been employed for producing books. But a typical process might go something like this. Let us consider, for example, a new calculus book to be produced by one of the major publishers. In the preplanning stage the company may decide first that it needs such a book to supplement its product line. Or the idea may have come from an author or group of authors. In modern publishing this decision is likely to be followed by extensive market survey activities, going out to current teachers of calculus courses. This market research, and discussions with possible authors, including eventually those for whom a contract is signed to write the book, determine the objectives and specifications for the book. The specifications may be reviewed by sending them out to outside consultants for suggested modifications.

The book industry has moved from a loose structure, where almost all the decisions about objectives were made by the individual authors, to one in which the publishers, following market research, now play a considerable role in the process. Often detailed outlines, including how much material is to go into each section, are specified before any actual writing is done.

The pedagogical component in writing the book is a well-known activity. Several authors may be involved. They produce a manuscript, one that will typically go through a number of editorial stages, with again outside reviewers playing a role in the process. Some publishers work now with authors putting the "manuscript" directly into a word processor, so it is available in computer-readable form for later stages of the process. But this is still rare. Mostly, manuscripts are done on local typewriters and are not in machine-storable form, but this situation is likely to change.

When the manuscript of the book goes to the publisher several activities take place. First, artists will be employed to create necessary illustrations. The author has sketched these in the manuscript, and the artist may talk to the author in the process of doing the design of these pictures. Graphic designers are employed to determine an overall structure to the book. This includes many decisions, such as typefaces, use of blank space, the size of the type, the placement of the diagrams, the size of the page, the page layout, the paper to be used, and other factors of this kind. The publisher may bring in outside graphic designers for this process or may work in house.

The typesetting activities may or may not occur within the company. Many publishers will "farm out" such technical tasks as setting the type. If the manuscript is developed on a word processor, typesetting is done directly from the floppy disks. After the type is set, many publishers go through a two-stage process of looking for errors in typesetting, first in galleys and then in pages. Both the authors and internal proofreaders may be involved. Publishers strive to keep changes at a minimum in page proofs, because [changes] become increasingly expensive. However, as printers have moved to more automated equipment, perhaps coming out of word-processed manuscripts, the changes at this stage become less expensive.

Printing with most contemporary publishers is not done within the publisher's own organization but in a specialty house. Marketing and distribution are well-known activities, so they will not be described further.

We can see a number of important points in book production. First, it took hundreds of years for the production system to become established. Second, it involves many different people. Third, each person is involved in an activity that that person does effectively.

That is, the teachers teach and the printers print. Finally, the production system is still evolving, under the impact of technological changes.

Although we have described this process for books, it is not too different if one looks, for example, at the production of films for instructional use. The technical development aspects vary because the medium is different, but many of the other details are quite similar.

The Open University

As a second example of production of course materials, I describe briefly the system used at the Open University in England.[1] This system is producing perhaps more curriculum material than any other group in the world. The computer so far has played a minor role in the activity, although some courses developed at the Open University have computer components.

First, it should be emphasized that the Open University offers far more than a production system. In a new and interesting way it combines both the production and delivery of learning materials in an overall process that is economical. Great attention is given to production issues. The Open University represents a financial balance different from the typical conventional university system anywhere in the world. Far more money is spent on the production of learning material and far less money on delivery. The overall results are encouraging both in terms of the effectiveness of the learning process and in terms of the relatively low cost per student involved.

The Open University system begins with putting together a course team. This will be a group of individuals who, typically for an 18-month period, will be concerned with the planning, pedagogical design, and some phases of the production of the overall materials. Technical production will still take place elsewhere. The course team will have a variety of individuals on it, since an Open University course will involve a number of media. Thus, it will have television specialists who will advise on how television could be used, and then later will be involved in designing the actual television material.

The team may begin by reviewing existing similar courses, including the common textbooks. Occasionally the material from existing sources will be found to be useful in the new course, but this is seldom the case. The members of the course team may not all be Open University faculty members. Some people are brought in for a particular development, even from abroad, some for the entire length of the project and some for shorter times.

To some extent the strategies used in the Open University are also employed in commercial and military development of training material, particularly by the various commercial concerns that seek participation in that market. The details will not be discussed. An interesting thing to note is that in all these cases a team effort is involved.

Production Systems for Computer Material

Single-Individual Systems

In looking at production systems for computer material, I make a major distinction. First, I will look at systems which were designed for single individuals, usually [individual teachers], to be concerned with all the stages of the production process. I will argue that these systems, although widely developed and widely advertised, are quite inadequate for the problem at hand.

These systems date from the earliest times of development of computer-based learning material. In their most simple form they combine pedagogical design (Component 5) and technical development (Component 7) into a single process. They then either downplay or ignore most of the other components associated with production.

The fundamental notions of these single-person systems are appealing, but naive.

They are appealing in the sense that it is nice to think of a single individual having complete control of the process and being able to produce a wide range of flexible material. But severe limitations exist, enough to rule out this method from serious consideration for large-scale effective production.

We can distinguish several variants in approaches. One of these might be described as the "CAI language" approach, although [computer-assisted instruction] (CAI) languages, as we will see, can also be used in other ways. In some cases the language involved is a general purpose language. The second approach is the interactive user approach.

The first approach involving one person began with the development of the Coursewriter system within IBM. Its strategy was to develop a computer-based instructional language that would be taught to the prospective user, the writer of materials. The writer would then proceed to write materials using this language. The languages developed for this purpose have always been advertised as easy to use.

In the interactive approach, the second variant of the single-person approach, the developer of the materials sits down directly at a computer display and furnishes information, sometimes in the form of queries from the program, sometimes in other ways more determined by the user. Fixed logic structures, templates, are built into the program by the designers of the program. Both these types of single-person system may have some type of training phase to acquaint authors with the capabilities.

Both approaches are represented by many different reincarnations. Thus, if one looks at "CAI languages," one might estimate that there have been as many as fifty of these developed. Most, indeed almost all, of the CAI languages and interactive systems have had very little material written in them. Examples of the first approach are Coursewriter and Pilot (widely touted on small machines), and examples of the second approach are Ditran, IDF, and the Utah system. New systems of both types continue to be developed.

What are the difficulties with the single individual approaches to production? First, and perhaps foremost, they assume that many good teachers either are or can become good programmers. But this is seldom the case. [Figure 1] indicates a more realistic situation:

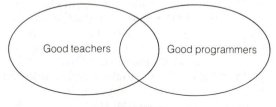

Good teachers　　　Good programmers

FIGURE 1

It might be better to label the right-hand side of this diagram as *potentially* good programmers. If someone can teach, it is not necessarily the case that that person can become a competent programmer or, perhaps even more important, will want to become a competent programmer. The notion that one should persuade teachers to program, even in "simplified" languages, is similar to saying that someone who is going to publish a book must learn how to typeset and how to operate a printing press.

A second problem is that these systems restrict what the user can do. Even the most complex CAI languages around still provide limited capabilities, not the full range of what is possible with the computer. So the creativity of the good teacher is restricted. Furthermore, good teachers may resent these restrictions, as they cannot do what they think is pedagogically best. This violates Criterion 5 above for a production system.

Furthermore, judged as programming languages according to current standards, almost all the CAI languages are quite primitive. They do not provide the features which encourage good structured programming. Perhaps the only exception to this is a programming language developed particularly for this application, Natal74. Thus, they do not conform to the best present practice for modern programming.

Even if the language has a full set of capabilities, the typical *strategy*—involving people without programming experience and pushing them quickly to writing material—is almost bound to lead to a limited use of the language, and therefore simple material. They write limited material because they only know a small subset of the possible capabilities.

The great bulk of the material done with single-individual strategies is pedagogically uninteresting, reflecting the limitations of the strategy. This is not to say that some very shining exceptions to this rule cannot be found. In a number of cases individuals worked for years in this format and became very experienced programmers. Furthermore, extremely good pedagogical ideas will serve to overcome a variety of difficulties. But the evidence indicates that this family of approaches has not been a useful way to produce materials. There are simply too few Renaissance men and women available. In many cases little exists beyond the CAI language itself; it has been employed relatively little for any actual development of material.

The two problems with single-individual systems are closely tied together in an unfortunate fashion. If the "CAI language" is extremely simple, then it can be, as advertised, quickly learned by some teachers. But it can only write very simple-minded material. As the language becomes more complex, increasing the range of computer-based learning material possible, it becomes less and less usable by naive individuals.

Another difficulty with production strategies of this type comes in connection with revision activities. As programs are revised a number of times and become more complex, they become more difficult to revise. The authoring languages, as indicated, do not satisfy the best modern standards of structured languages, and therefore the programs produced are not easy to modify. With some approaches modification becomes almost an impossibility, done only by essentially redoing an entire segment of the material. So the many detailed revisions necessary after evaluation stages become very impractical.

Finally it should be clear from the arguments already stated that the single-individual strategies will not lead to large-scale production. Any one individual can produce only a small amount, because that individual must do a variety of tasks. Strategies which allow the individual to concentrate on particular tasks, such as the pedagogical design task, are likely to lead to increased production. Furthermore, as indicated by the fact that most good teachers will not become good programmers, the supply of people who can write decent material with such systems will always be small.

Team Systems

The other set of possibilities for production activities is that a *group* of individuals will be involved in the process, not a single individual. Sizable production in the future must be done in this vein for the reasons just stated. But saying that the production system should be a team system still leaves many choices to be determined.

Perhaps the first category of team production systems that occurs are those which represent the extensions of the single-individual systems when serious production is considered. The single-individual systems begin to get into difficulty for the reasons described. Then the developers of these systems begin to see that it is *not* necessary to have things done entirely by one individual. So they begin to split the tasks, but maintaining essentially the *same framework*—languages and facilities—indicated above. The major change is to split the pedagogical design stage and the technical development stage; but for each the developers follow similar strategies as they did in single-user systems. Thus, the "CAI language," or interactive capability, becomes used by a person other than the teacher. The teacher is then constrained to Step 5 in the process.

An example of this modification of a single-user system was the development of the Control Data Plato authoring system after Control Data became itself heavily involved in Plato. While the system was at the University of Illinois, at least in the early stages, it was typically a single-individual system, with

one person doing everything. But when Control Data took it over, it became a team system. The strategies for [Step] 7, technical development, were essentially the same strategies that had been developed initially. In this case the Tutor language, initially developed with a single-individual strategy in mind, was extended to a more elaborate production system which in most cases separated off the pedagogical design from the technical development. The programmers in Step 7 used Tutor, although it had initially been developed with teachers as the prospective users.

As the single-individual strategies have begun to move toward larger scale production, they often attempt to preserve some features of their older system, such as the languages, but try at the same time to move toward a team involved in the developmental process. But the difficulty with this approach has already been mentioned. The languages developed were really developed with the novice coder in mind, *not* the professional coder or other special individual who is likely to be involved when the stages are separated. All the problems mentioned above that deal with languages are still problems in the present strategy. In particular, few of the CAI languages satisfy minimum criteria for good programming languages.

A few such groups were willing to recognize this problem with CAI languages, and so completely discarded older software when they moved away from the single-individual strategy. But this is a difficult thing to do, given the emotional involvement in the previous software.

Beyond this extension of the one-user system, many variants are possible in a team production system. Each of the components already discussed allows a number of possibilities. The criteria stated earlier in this paper give a way of looking at any one such system that has been developed.

Much of the remainder of this paper will be devoted to explicating one particular production system, that developed in the Educational Technology Center at the University of California, Irvine. In the course of this exposition I will discuss some of the design considerations that led to the choice of strategies with each component of the production system.

The Irvine Production System

The Irvine production system has been under development in the Educational Technology Center during the past 13 years. It has produced a very sizable amount of material, ranging from elementary school through university material and in a variety of modes. This approach has been well described in the literature, as have the resulting modules.[2]

We will discuss the system in terms of the way we work at Irvine with regard to each of the components of production mentioned. Like the production of books and like the Open University process, a variety of people are involved, so it is a team process. I will describe the system in terms of how it typically operates and how we would like it to operate if the resources were sufficient.

1. Preplanning.   There is little to say [that is] unique about preplanning. In our case, since we are primarily dependent on grant support, the preplanning consists primarily of negotiations with the granting agency, either a federal granting agency or a commercial source interested in producing materials.

Preliminary planning of other stages must go on here. As these may not be funded as yet, this activity can present problems.

2. Production Management.   The process is complex, so management is an important issue. Each of the projects in the Educational Technology Center has a program manager associated with it, a person who is responsible for managing the entire operation.

The management procedure we have followed is one based on the structured analysis and design technique, commonly referred to as SADT.[3] This technique (developed by SofTech), coming out of modern software engineering, is both a way of describing our activities (to be indicated later) and a mechanism for managing the projects. Since it shows the

stages of activity, we can identify the status of each module in a project, within the developmental cycle, at a given time.

3. Objectives and Specifications.   A principal mechanism for developing objectives and specifications is a preliminary meeting. At the beginning of this meeting brainstorming is the principal technique. We bring a variety of people, including many teachers who typically deal with the students we are attempting to reach. The purpose of such a meeting is to develop the objectives and outline each of the sequences of modules contributing to these objectives. Overall decisions about the modular structure are also made at this time. The attempt is to produce a specification for each of the pedagogical writing groups to be formed in Stage 5.

In some cases it is not possible to proceed this way because of budgetary limitations. [Then] the objectives and specifications are done primarily by the internal staff at the Educational Technology Center, perhaps working with outside consultants.

In this stage, as in all the components of our production system, we often bring in outside aid. We do not believe that it is either desirable or necessary to work entirely with people at a particular location. Rather, we seek specialists from everywhere who can contribute to our activities. So it is necessary to budget expenses and honoraria for such specialists from outside our campus.

4. Training Activities.   We conduct, at least for some projects, three types of training, corresponding to each of the next three components of the production process.

In connection with pedagogical design, Component 5, we want to acquaint the teachers and others who write with us with the learning capabilities of the computer. In one-half-day training sessions we put particular stress on how these capabilities differ from more familiar educational media such as lectures and textbooks. A major technique followed is to sit down with the relatively small group involved and show them many examples of different types of material, pointing out in each case the pedagogical factors involved. An important issue is pointing out possible pitfalls for the novice developer, pitfalls often [identified] from previous experience with other media.

Along the same line, we have also been responsible for running many workshops at university campuses and elsewhere that are particularly concerned with training novice faculty in the preparation of materials. These workshops are more formalized than the half-day sessions we typically run for our own work and usually involve groups of about twenty or twenty-five faculty members. The center of these activities is the group production of the pedagogical design of some computer-based learning material, usually followed by supervised small group design experience.

A second type of training, one that we still understand poorly, concerns the training of artists for the development of the visual design material in Stage 6. The artists must learn to use the interactive design facilities, to be described later. We also convey to the artists at this time our general design standards for the visual and temporal appearance of material.

Finally, since we work with student coders and since students graduate, we are constantly in the position of training new student coders. Such training would also be necessary in a commercial environment. We do this training primarily by examples, starting with simple material, a pedagogical design, and tracing through all the coding procedures necessary to get this material running. We have written material to support this activity. After the initial activity we assign a programming task, usually in groups of three beginning programmers, giving the coders a simple bit of flowchart (see Stage 5). An important component of this training is the emphasis on the need for adequate documentation.

At the present time the training activities we are undertaking are restricted to the Irvine campus or to specially run workshops in other locations. These activities are dependent on the individuals who have the experi-

ence. But it would be possible to make the training materials transportable, so that authors in a wide variety of locations could be taught to use them without individuals from the Educational Technology Center presenting the materials. Much of the training could be done using on-line computer materials particularly developed for this application.

5. Pedagogical Design.   We regard the pedagogical design stage, the stage in which the instructional materials are fully specified from an instructional point of view, to be the most critical of all the stages in the production process. Material that is to work well with students must depend heavily on the experiences of extremely good teachers and specialists in the areas involved.

One important issue is whether the pedagogical design is to be done by a single individual or by a group of individuals. Most materials in most of the computer-based production systems followed so far have been developed by single individuals, ignoring the experience of such group design of curriculum material in such institutions as the Open University. But we have long argued, based on experience at the Educational Technology Center, that one obtains much superior material if a *group* works together in the instructional development of learning material.[4] The implication is that the group stays together during the entire developmental stage. We have found that groups of from three to five are the most effective in this process. Smaller groups often do not do a competent job of accounting for all the variants of student input. Larger groups engage in endless pedagogical debates and get little done.

The composition of the groups is very important. We try to pick people because of their experiences, particularly in interactive teaching. At least some of the people must be familiar with the intended target audience. Others may bring in special backgrounds, perhaps from learning theory or instructional design, visual design, or various media. At least one person in the group should already have had experience in developing computer-based learning materials. But it is not at all necessary for the other people in the group to have had previous computer experience. Indeed, our feeling is that usually it is better *not* to have had such experience. What is needed is an understanding of the medium as a learning medium, rather than any view of how to program. People with some programming experience often have a very limited view of the capabilities of the computer in aiding learning.

Another important issue is the environment. We believe that since the task is a difficult one, requiring concentration, it should be done in an environment where there are no interruptions, except those planned by the group itself. Thus, we do not find it conducive to work in the typical office. Rather we tend to work in pleasant environments away from the office. In our case, California provides many such environments.

The question of how long the group should work does not have a clear answer. Many of our recent materials have been developed by groups that stayed together for a week or two. Often in a particular week we will have two or three groups working at the same time, and they may interact over lunch or dinner. In some projects it is desirable to have the group together for longer periods. But because of the exacting nature of the tasks, it may be tiring for the same group to work together for very long periods of time. Our typical experience is that, for average material, a group working for a week will produce between 1½ and 2 hours of material, as viewed in terms of usage by the average student.

The group, working together, must produce a complete pedagogical specification, one that moves into the other stages of the production process and gives all the necessary information for those stages. Hence, it must show the text to be displayed, the pictures to be displayed, the analyses of student inputs, and all the logic decisions.

Since we want the members of the pedagogical design team to have the greatest possible freedom, the method of displaying this information should not restrict them to any fashion. Thus, we do not employ any templated (fixed) logic structures, limited structures

in which it is assumed that everybody will work. Rather, groups are encouraged to make their choices entirely on pedagogical grounds and to be as free as possible about these choices. The training session which preceded this work emphasizes the capabilities of the media and tries to tell of common pitfalls by those first beginning to write materials.

The form we have found most convenient for authors is one that might be described as an informal or loose flowchart. We make no attempt whatsoever to teach formal flowcharting techniques. Indeed, the procedure, mostly learned by watching one member of the group who is already experienced, is presented as a way of specifying the pedagogical situation. The pictures are sketched. Additional information about pictures or other details may be offered to the programmer, as notes on the flowchart. The group may make sketches of the screen as to how material is to be displayed and may indicate delays or other timing considerations. The tests to be made on student input are shown sequentially, indicating (by lines flowing out of the boxes) what to do with success on a particular test, either the first time through that box or at some later time.

The exact form of the structure is not too important, provided the conventions that the individual groups use are made clear in the material. We have usually found it convenient to work on large sheets of paper, since there is less referencing of other sheets. We also encourage developers to make copious comments, notes to the programmer or designer, about what is to happen and for future reference when new media capabilities are available.

6. Visual Design. It is in visual design that actual practice at the Educational Technology Center often departs from what I view as the most desirable strategy. This departure is because of limited resources, and because we have not yet completed all the software to make the most desirable approach feasible.

Ideally visual design should be done by a competent graphic designer who does magazine layout or develops brochures advertising products. The person needs some special training, as indicated, mostly in understanding how appearance on the screen may impact learning capabilities. The person also needs to be trained in the use of special online capabilities that allow the design to take place directly on the screen. Thus, we do not regard it desirable for the screen to be designed on paper, although in the pedagogical stage the authors may offer many suggestions in this direction. Rather, the visual designer should be working directly at the screen. This strategy is not unique with our project, although we have worked in this direction for many years. For example, the Canadian Telidon system has put considerable energy into developing screen design capabilities.

In practice, the visual design aspects at Irvine are often handled by a combination of the pedagogical authors and the coders involved in the technical development stage. In the time-sharing environment we had developed software to work with graphic designers, and this proved to be useful. But the software and the environment we have developed so far on the small machines are not yet fully capable of performing all the necessary tasks. Furthermore, our resources for employing artists are often limited.

7. Technical Development. The next stage is coding computer-based learning materials. The coders work from the dialogs produced in the pedagogical design stage, a loose flowchart arrangement, and from the products of the visual design stage.

The question of how the coders should work is the most important issue. That is, what is the programming environment in which the activities are to be carried out? This not only includes the programming language itself [and] the various auxiliary software for supporting it, but also involves issues of supervision, working conditions, and quality control.

In structuring our approach to the coding task, modern software engineering practices are of considerable aid. Following the practices there, for example, we insist on structure charts before any actual coding takes place. The program manager or supervising programmer will inspect these charts. We also have very high standards for code, insisting that it be "good" code with the highest standards of modern structured programming. It is only by maintaining such high standards for code that we will be able to satisfy several of the criteria mentioned at the beginning of this paper: the material should be easy to revise, and we should minimize transferability problems.

A critical factor is the choice of a language, to satisfy the two criteria mentioned and to make the coding process efficient. We believe that the only reasonable choices are the best languages that have come out of contemporary language design, the languages that allow all the features of structured programming. Our own choice has been to work within Pascal. In particular, we use [University of California, San Diego] Pascal. The fact that the UCSD Pascal *system,* including the compiler as well as all the other features of the system, is easily transferable onto a new small machine means that we have assisted out transferability problems. Pascal at this stage is also more standardized than many other languages that could be used, although the Pascal standards committee in the United States has not yet finished its deliberations. Ada presents interesting possibilities for the future.

Various auxiliary software is also necessary to ease the programming task. Since our coders are typically undergraduate students (or in some cases professional coders), this software is designed with them in mind. An extremely important component of this additional software is a completely new input–output package, including both text and graphic capabilities. The graphic details follow those in the core graphics SIGGRAPH recommendations. The textual details have a similar philosophy in that they too put text on the screen through individual viewports. This software allows much more flexible control over input and output than is possible within the relatively crude capabilities native to the language. This approach is also designed in such a way that the details of differences in screen capabilities can easily be taken care of when one is transferring from one machine to another. The text itself may be part of the program, or it may be kept in separate files called by the program. Full information is available.[5]

In addition, a library of procedures for the commonly carried out functions is also necessary and useful. This library, however, is difficult to maintain in a personal computer environment in which each programmer is using his or her own floppy disks. We hope to move soon to a local network, with a storage machine that will keep all the common library capabilities of this kind. This will assure that all programs have the latest version available at the time they are developed.

Other specialized tools may be developed for particular purposes. Thus, at Irvine we have developed an elaborate quiz driver to assist in giving on-line quizzes. The point of this quiz driver is to allow the individual teacher to make many individual changes in the way the quiz is presented to students.[6] In other situations similar tools might prove useful.

An important issue is that of the hardware, the computer system including associated devices, to be used in this phase of production. The naive assumption is that one would use the same hardware that is intended for delivery. But we have come to believe that this is seldom the correct choice. Because the delivery hardware is evolving rapidly, one needs to develop not for a single delivery machine but for a whole range of delivery machines, many of which do not exist at the time the development is going forward.

The hardware requirements and capabilities needed for development far surpass those needed for delivery of material. Much of the materials we have developed at Irvine recently could not have been developed on some of the delivery systems that these same materials now run on.

The specification of full developmental hardware needs additional attention. In most cases the hardware used for the developmental activities for computer-based learning has been inadequate for aspects of the task.

8. Editing. Editing can and should take place at several stages. The first stage for editing at Irvine is directly after pedagogical design, between Steps 5 and 6. A second stage of editing takes place after initial coding, as indicated by the ordering in our listing of the components.

After the pedagogical design stage, the editor is playing a role similar to that the book manuscript editor plays. Nothing has been cast in concrete at this point, everything can still be changed. We have experimented with a variety of styles.

The typical approach is to give the flowchart, produced in the pedagogical design stage, to someone who is already experienced in reading such charts. This individual makes recommendations for changes, and then the original authors decide which changes should be carried out. Some of the changes may be editorial, changing the vocabulary, while others may reflect pedagogical issues.

But we are worried that this process may be very dependent on who the individual is who does it. Unlike book editing, relatively little experience in the process exists, and so different individuals may look for quite different things. We have also experimented lately with some strategies which have involved "dry runs" with actual students before any coding is done. The person doing this works with predesigned sheets of paper, playing the role of the computer. But it is not yet clear whether this tactic is useful.

The second stage of editing comes after the material is first coded. Then the authors, the visual designers, and the technical developers, or some subset of these, sit down and run the program many times. We find that at this stage many changes are suggested, and so extensive rewriting will typically take place. Material is different in the interactive environment, not like the paper version. This stage of revision emphasizes the need for a system which allows easy revision.

In a sense this process is like editing a

book after all the typesetting has taken place, and the book is in page proofs. With books this is an expensive process, at least with most modern production methods. But with computers, particularly if an effective language has been used in Stage 7, such editing is not only feasible but relatively easy to do. It is, however, somewhat boring for the competent programmer, particularly when he or she goes through many cycles of such changes.

Stages 9 to 12.   Stages 9 to 12, evaluating, revising, marketing, and distributing, the last stages in development, will be considered as a group. The activities do not differ too widely from those involved in any good development of educational material, and so follow the general principles of instructional design.

It does need to be said, however, that the computer is capable of gathering very detailed feedback as to what happens when it is used with students. So formative evaluation is much more easily carried out; we can make many more significant changes in the material than is typical in instructional development, employing other media. Again, the choice of an effective programming language will ease this stage. We believe that one of the real strengths of the computer material is that it can be revised many times, based on evaluations. But unfortunately not too many materials currently in existence have gone through many cycles. Expense becomes an issue, because each evaluation and revision adds cost.

I do not discuss in this paper issues of how the material is to be marketed and distributed. Extremely little marketing experience is available for computer-based learning material. There are clearly problems which need to be overcome, such as the problem of possible pirating of material. Technical solutions are available for some of these problems.

Overview of the Irvine Production System

In the preceding section of this paper, I described the choices made at Irvine as they have evolved over the past 13 years in producing computer-based learning material. The present section is designed to give a visual summary of the approach. The approach used, already mentioned, is the structured analysis and design technique (SADT).

The SADT description of the Irvine production system was developed by Barry Kurtz. A number of diagrams are involved. First, as with other SADT charts, the top level diagram shows the overall details of the process, but without specifics. The charts that we are drawing are concerned with the processes, not the data. Lines coming into the side of a box indicate products entering that process, while lines coming out to the side indicate things produced at that stage. Lines coming into the top represent controls on the process. [. . .] The overall chart [is presented in Figure 2].

The reader will have no difficulty picking out the various features of the production system as we have outlined them already. This chart provides simply an outline, but it does show how the major stages are related to each other.

The next two charts presented [Figures 3 and 4] show the expansion of the first box on the left, "write dialogs," and the second box on the left, graphic and structural design. It is as if we are looking inside each of these boxes and seeing the details of the process. Again, these details can be related to the discussions that we have already had. We will not present SADT charts corresponding to the other components of the main box; they are available on request.

Research Needed

The production system just described, which developed at Irvine, is only one of many possibilities that involve many people.

At the present time developers of computer-based learning material have extremely limited experience with full-scale production systems. We do *not* have the vast amount of experience that has gone into books, and even there many different variants of strategies

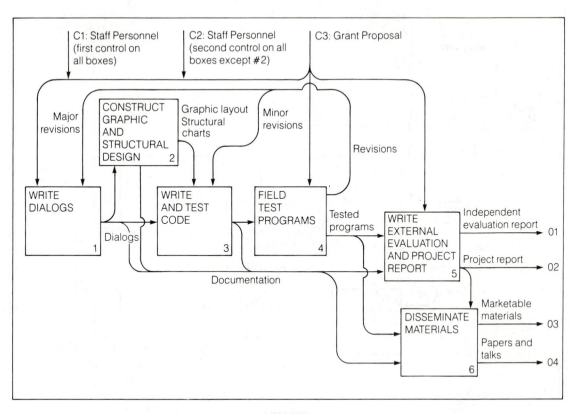

C1: Staff Personnel
(first control on
all boxes)

C2: Staff Personnel
(second control on all
boxes except #2)

C3: Grant Proposal

Major
revisions

CONSTRUCT
GRAPHIC
AND
STRUCTURAL
DESIGN   2

Graphic layout
Structural
charts

Minor
revisions

Revisions

WRITE
DIALOGS   1

Dialogs

WRITE
AND TEST
CODE   3

FIELD
TEST
PROGRAMS   4

Tested
programs

WRITE
EXTERNAL
EVALUATION
AND PROJECT
REPORT   5

Independent
evaluation report   01

Project report   02

Documentation

DISSEMINATE
MATERIALS   6

Marketable
materials   03

Papers and
talks   04

FIGURE 2

have evolved. Hence, it is not too surprising that we have much to learn in this area and that research is badly needed about many of the details. Careful research in this area is critical for future progress in developing computer-based learning material. I mention a few of the areas particularly in need of additional research aid.

1. *Underlying learning capabilities.* In development of learning material we need to understand the process of learning better than we now do. The computer introduces many new variants into this process, ones that were not present in older media, so it is particularly in need of study. For example, at this stage we do not really have a detailed view of what goes on in students' minds when they run computer-based learning materials. We are beginning to get some appreciation of motivational issues in game materials,[7] but even in this area information is limited.

To give one example where additional information is certainly needed, I discuss an interest of the Irvine group, the use of the materials by groups. We have always urged that two or three people work together at a computer display, except in situations in which the student is taking an on-line test. Our casual observations have been that the student interactions in such groups are an important component of the learning process. But we have little empirical information, because we have not made careful studies of the situation. Nor have we particularly tried to design material with groups in mind. Hence, much additional research is needed in understanding the learning process when groups are involved. We remain convinced that students do an excellent job of teaching each other. But it would be desirable to have some evidence for this, particularly in the computer-based learning environment. Furthermore, we need to understand how the materials can

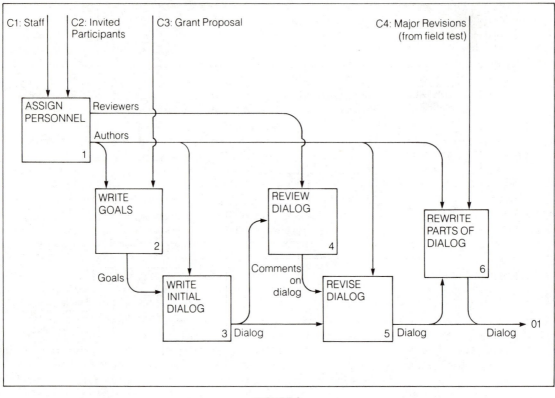

FIGURE 3

encourage group cooperation. This is by no means the only type of learning theory research that would be useful, but is given merely as an example. This example is one of applied research, but fundamental research is also necessary.

2. *Graphic design.* We have already stressed the importance of the spatial and temporal design of the material on the screen. Such design can have a considerable effect on how the material works with students. We find that much computer-based learning material does not allow for this component. In fact, much of the material seen on the screen is very much like material in books, in spite of the very different parameters in the computer situation.

One would like to run experimental studies of the various features of graphic design and experimental studies on several different types of capability provided to those who are

designing the screen. We suspect that these capabilities might be sensitive to the users. Thus, a capability that might be satisfactory for a coder might be very poor for a graphic designer or a novice user.

3. *Editorial control.* We have mentioned several possible stages for an editorial role in the process. In recent book production the commercial companies have moved toward greater and greater editorial control. While it is not clear whether this is desirable in all cases, it probably will be an important factor in commercial production of computer material, simply because the book publishers becoming involved with computer material are already familiar with the process.

One approach would be to design training material for people who are going to be involved in editorial control at several stages. As mentioned, we feel that at the present time the editorial comments that we receive

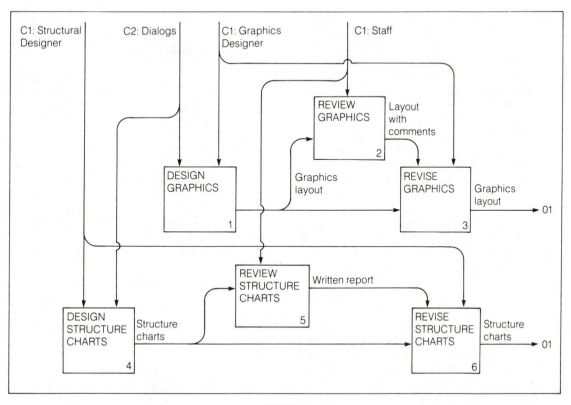

FIGURE 4

on computer-based material tend to be very subjective, different for each individual. While this is true to some extent in dealing with books, there seems to be somewhat more consensus there, perhaps because of greater experience. Training sequences might furnish an answer. But again experimental work is needed to compare different ways of training editors for computer-based learning materials. Research can help us to a better understanding of the editorial process.

4. *Pretesting before coding.* Modern programming environment studies have often recommended a process called "rapid prototyping" of complex programs in the early stages of development. The notion is to bring up a quick "mock" version of the full program. Such a program does not do what the full one does, but it does give some experience with actual users.

It has puzzled us for some time that rapid prototyping seems to be possible only in limited ways with most computer-based learning materials, because of the way such materials are typically organized. Some of the goals accomplished by rapid prototyping would be extremely important in developing computer dialogs.

One possibility is that already suggested, pretesting paper and pencil materials with actual students before the coding activity. Although we have begun to carry out some preliminary efforts in this direction, far more work is necessary. The aim of this new activity is to avoid a long series of very expensive design and coding activities for material that does not turn out to be usable in the form considered by the original designers.

5. *Variants of production system.* As yet, we have little experimental evidence about how varying the production system affects the materials produced, the costs, or other

parameters involved. Experimental studies which produce material with a variety of strategies would be extremely useful. Although many of the components of the production system can be argued on rational, pedagogical, or economical grounds, it will be desirable to have more than arguments available.

6. *Intelligent videodisk production.* As we have stressed, many of the techniques discussed apply to developing curriculum materials involving a full range of media, even though we have emphasized primarily the computer material. A new and very interesting possibility is the development of material that uses one intelligent videodisk, a full combination of the computer and optical videodisk using the capabilities of both media.

Although there have been a number of projects, very limited experience exists in developing intelligent videodisk materials, far more limited than our meager background with the production of computer-based learning material. Since this technology looks as if it may be very important for the future, it seems extremely important to gather such experience and to study variants in the production system. Furthermore, we have almost zero experience in using such material with students.

7. *Rapid coding techniques.* One of the most expensive and time-consuming of the stages we have examined is that of technical development, Stage 7. The development of ways to speed up this stage would, therefore, be an important contribution to the overall production system.

Although we have already commented that development of computer-based learning languages in interactive systems has so far not proved to be a viable approach, there are still possibilities in this direction. We have developed in the Educational Technology Center an interactive code-writing program, one that queries the user and then writes Pascal code. The program is then modifiable easily, just as with any good structured program. This technique still has limited applicability, however, because it allows only a

limited range of capabilities, similar to those in many of the interactive systems developed. But this approach could be explored further. Another approach, tried elsewhere on a small scale, is to develop an interactive capability where one places on the screen essentially the same flowchart that was developed by the authors, by a series of interactive techniques. A third possibility is the use of intelligent editors such as that developed by Teitelbaum and Reps[8] at Cornell for students learning PL/CS and more recently Pascal. Techniques could be developed with modern programming approaches in mind, taking into account the criteria mentioned at the beginning of this paper.

8. *Readability aids.* Students are notoriously poor readers. They tend to read in a careless fashion, stimulated (and often approved) by everyday reading experiences. So a student's reading capabilities are often inadequate for the careful reading needed in most study. Since textual material is in most cases to be part of what is displayed on the computer screen, it is important to consider the questions of readability on the screen.

As indicated, computer learning material has many aspects that differ from print material. Some of these differences, such as very poor type quality on the screen, may be hindrances to reading. But others, such as the fact that blank space is free and that we can use timing as a positive aid to reading, if used wisely, are likely to lead to increased comprehension and retention capabilities.

Until recently, very little study of screen readability has taken place. There is literature of variable quality on print readability. But it is not clear which of these print readability factors can be easily extended to the screen. Furthermore, print readability studies do not take into account things which are possible only on the screen, such as control by the reader.[9]

9. *Visual design.* The process of designing the screen is one that still needs additional attention. As indicated, our work at Irvine has assumed an interactive design process, one in which the designer is working directly at one or several screens for the creation of the

pictorial and textual information. Just what capabilities should be provided to the designer and just how the designer should work are considerations which need to be explored further with detailed empirical research. Furthermore, the question of how to train the designer is one that needs additional consideration.

This examination of needed areas of research is not complete. But it does give some flavor of some of the problems which need to be examined.

NOTES

1. Walter Perry, *The Open University* (Jossey-Bass, San Francisco, 1977).

2. Alfred Bork, *Learning with Computers* (Digital Press, Bedford, Mass., 1981), Chapter 6.

3. Barry L. Kurtz and Alfred Bork, An SADT™ Model for the Production of Computer Based

Learning Material. In *Computers in Education,* R. Lewis and D. Tagg, Editors (North-Holland Publishing Co., New York, 1981).

4. Alfred Bork, *Learning with Computers* (Digital Press, Bedford, Mass., 1981), Chapter 6.

5. Description available from the Educational Technology Center, University of California, Irvine.

6. Description available from the Educational Technology Center, University of California, Irvine.

7. Thomas W. Malone, *What Makes Things Fun to Learn?* (Xerox Palo Alto Research Center, 1980).

8. Tim Teitelbaum and Thomas Reps, "The Cornell Program Synthesizer: A Syntax-Directed Programming Environment," *Communications of the ACM,* vol. 24, September 1981, pp. 563–573.

9. Alfred Bork, "Textual Taxonomy," Technical paper, Educational Technology Center, University of California, Irvine, January 1981.

7 The Technology of Interaction—Dialogue Programming Rules

Brian R. Gaines

Centre for Man–Computer Studies, London

1. Introduction

Thirty years ago a technological revolution took shape as the first stored-program computers stumbled through their early calculations. Fifteen years later computer systems had become sufficiently reliable for a second revolution to take place as the first time-shared *interactive* systems began to offer their services. The MIT MAC system (Fano,

This paper is dedicated to Chris Evans whose own work was closely related and complementary to it. His tragic death has cost this field of research one of its major contributors.
Brian R. Gaines, "The Technology of Interaction—Dialogue Programming Rules," *International Journal of Man–Machine Studies,* 14 (1981), 133–150. Copyright © 1981 Academic Press Inc. (London) Limited. Reprinted by permission of Academic Press Inc. (London) Limited and the author.

1965) in 1963, the RAND JOSS system in 1963–1964 (Shaw, 1968), and the Dartmouth College BASIC system in 1964 (Danver and Nevison, 1969), pioneered a new style of computing in which users at remote teleprinter terminals were in direct communication with the computer. No longer did the user have to prepare all his programs and data meticulously in every detail in advance for submission to a queue of jobs eagerly awaiting the magic moments when the computer was actually working. Titles of books in the mid-1960s give some indication of the dramatic impact of this *Transition to On-Line Computing* (Gruenberger, 1967) through *The Challenge of the Computer Utility* (Parkhill, 1966) using *Conversational Computers* (Orr, 1968) to offer *Computer Augmentation of Human Reasoning* (Sass and Wilkinson, 1965). Now, another 15 years on, the continuing decline in computer costs and increase in reliability have made hands-on, interactive use of computers a commercial reality for end users (Gaines, 1978a) and this will become increasingly the normal mode of operation for the majority of computer users.

Despite the recognized importance of this transition to "conversational" computing, the study of the design of man–machine dialogues has only recently gained recognition as a field for the development of computer science and technology. The first book on the topic was Martin's *Design of Man–Computer Dialogues* in 1973, followed in 1977 by Gilb and Weinberg's *Humanized Input*. Both books give a wealth of anecdotal experience and a variety of recommended techniques, but neither is in a position to give a systematic account of what constitutes good dialogue programming. We are in the position today in *programming man–computer interaction* that we were with hardware design 30 years ago and software design 10 years ago—we are reliant on unsystematized "craft" skills passed on erratically through fortunate "apprenticeships." Through evolution many systems have become reasonably satisfactory in their basic dialogues and these may be copied in similar situations, but we have no production techniques for *dialogue engineering* on

a specified, scheduled, quality-controlled, reliable basis.

In reviewing the next stages of development in man–computer communication (Gaines, 1978d), I stressed the need to consider both the internal models of the "world" within man and computer when setting up and analyzing communication, and also the mutual models that the computer and man have of one another. I have also emphasized the short-term practical role that developing a *technology of interaction* has for developing business applications of minicomputers in the next decade, and placed a "dialogue processing module" on par with other fundamental modules for "database control," "document production," and so on (Gaines, 1978a). This paper may be seen as a more specific attempt to take that framework of mutual modeling and generate within it detailed characteristics for dialogue engineering.

It would be rash to pretend any work at this stage can approach a complete formulation of the techniques for "dialogue engineering." However, it does represent some further steps in the direction taken by the books noted above in beginning to systematize the rules for programming man–machine interaction through formal dialogues.

2. Programming Interaction

First let me make it clear what kinds of conversation and dialogue are under consideration in this paper. Natural language dialogue with computers has been the goal of much "artificial intelligence" research, and Weizenbaum's (1967) ELIZA with its "cocktail party" capability to maintain a conversation without "understanding," followed by Winograd's (1972) SHRDLU that used its "understanding" of a narrow domain to allow facile manipulation of language, both gave hope that the goal was achievable. Petrick's (1976) survey of work on natural language based systems demonstrates the increasing capabilities of such systems, and database query systems such as Hendrix's (1977) LIFER and Harris's (1977) ROBOT are very impressive in their abilities to maintain meaningful and useful dialogues with a wide range of "real" users.

However, there are a number of reasons why such truly "natural language" systems will probably not play major commercial roles for some years yet.

1. They still require large programs in powerful machines for their operation.

2. The typing required by the user to generate complete English sentences is too great—one day speech recognition (Cox and Martin, 1975; Woods et al., 1976) may change this, but for the moment "unnatural" dialogues minimizing user typing activities are essential.

3. In many applications where the computer replaces or mimics the clerk in an office the "natural" dialogue is already highly formalized because it has evolved to carry information clearly and concisely—we have a formal "battle language" that is purely functional, resistant to noise and corruption, and readily assimilated by newcomers.

It is these more formal dialogues with which I am concerned in this paper—they form the major requirement in current commercial systems, but their programming is still too much a hit-and-miss affair. However, most of the points made are basic structural and psychological requirements that carry over to the free form natural language dialogue that may one day become possible and desired. Figure 1 gives a sample of the type of dialogue under consideration—in this case a data entry sequence in a securities dealing system. The line numbers are for reference only—user input follows last colon on each line—lines 4, 7, and 8 offer default options—line 12 is validation before entry.

Some 5 years ago we wrote a paper (Gaines and Facey, 1975) attempting to analyze lessons learned in a wide range of expe-

1	GDR:E
2	Item:S
3	Stock number:85
4	Full name: Treasury:Exchequer
5	Issue date:6/7
6	Type (SMLTN):S
7	Dividends/year: 2:
8	Final div date:1/1:5/8
9	Redemption year(s):81
10	Coupon:3 1/4
11	Number of calls:0:
12	85:Exchequer 3 1/4 1981 5/8 S 6-Jul-77 OK?:Y
13	GDR:

FIGURE 1: Typical dialogue sequence

rience of "Interactive System Development and Application" in a variety of medical, industrial, and commercial projects. One section of this paper was entitled *The Programming of Interaction,* and at the second draft we decided to make it rather more pointed by phrasing the lessons learned as a set of eleven "Rules." While tightly formulated "rules of dialogue" are undoubtedly at this stage of the game still pseudoscience, it has been invaluable in further development of dialogue programming techniques to have a set of well-defined and precise guidelines with which to work. Having a defined set of rules has already led to suggestions for further "rules" and amendments to the first ones in the light of others' experience and these were published in Gaines (1978b). In the next section further developments of these rules are reiterated and expanded with a brief comment on each, and later sections use them as a basis for formalizing dialogue programming, and refine them further. To complete this section I wish to establish some very basic guidelines for the objectives of actually having man–computer interaction to start with, and for the relative roles of man and computer in such systems.

There are two remarks that for me epitomize our objectives in designing interactive systems. Walter Doherty, manager of the in-house systems at IBM's Thomas J. Watson Research Laboratories, remarked in a seminar at Essex University in September 1977: "The computer is a tool to extend man's memory and reasoning power—these are the key bases on which technical advances should be evaluated," and John Cleary at EUROCOMP 74 in discussing the role of such new system concepts as the "virtual machine" said: "The only virtual machine of interest to a user . . . one that has abolished all lower levels of system and presents an *understandable* and *sympathetic* face to its user." Doherty's remark brings out the role of the computer as a *tool* aiding a person in coping with their mental workload—in an interactive system the machine should do all possible to minimize unnecessary activity on the part of the user—it has an emancipatory role (Gaines, 1978d). Cleary's remark emphasizes that the interactive interface seen by the user is actually to a "virtual machine"—too often dialogue programming is treated in an ad hoc fashion that takes no account of the fact that what the user is seeing is the highest level in a hierarchy of virtual machines (Gaines, 1975, 1976c) and that the rigor with which we treat the definition of the lower levels (in terms of procedures, languages, instruction sets, microprograms, etc.) can, and should, be applied at the dialogue level—that is one objective of this paper. Cleary then goes on to say that the virtual machine should have an "understandable" and "sympathetic" face, two apparently nontechnical terms which may however be given quite definite meaning in terms of the comprehensibility of the virtual machine to the user and the availability of helpful aids to the user—much of what follows is concerned precisely with these two requirements.

3. The Basic Rules

This section gives an extended set of dialogue programming rules based on those in Gaines and Facey (1975). The rules are classified into three categories: those concerned with system analysis and development, those

concerned with the user's adaptation to the system, and those concerned with minimizing the mental load on the user.

Systems Analysis and Development

The first rule previously proposed is concerned with the initial design of the dialogue. In performing the systems analysis that precedes dialogue design it is easy to forget how little conception potential users have of the interactive use of computers if they have never experienced it.

> *Rule 1. Introduce Through Experience*: Interactive systems should be experienced not talked about. Get prospective users onto a terminal on a related, or model, system before discussing their expected relationship to their own system.

The phenomenon of assuming that what we personally know and have experienced is "obvious" is a common one for all human behavior. We cannot understand the output of a speech synthesizer and cannot understand how others can do so. Suddenly it becomes clear and we are able to comprehend each word. Thereafter we are surprised when others have the same problem in understanding initially what is for us now transparently clear material. We have to remember always the need for experience and learning on the part of others before we can have a meaningful discussion with them about topics they have never previously encountered.

Another rule is really a warning to the system analyst who attempts to impose a new framework on an already existent and satisfactory situation.

> *Rule 2. Use the User's Model:* Use a model of the activity being undertaken which corresponds to that of the user, and program the interactive dialogue as if it were a conversation between two users mutually accepting this model.

This second rule may be seen as asking the

system analyst to listen and learn the user's vocabulary—not to impose a new language unnecessarily in an existing situation. I use the word "model" deliberately, however, to emphasize that there is rather more than a vocabulary involved. We have to consider the way in which the words are being *used* to achieve some desired change in the world. It is an action-orientated, Gricean view of language (Bennett, 1976) that we have to take in order to make all aspects of the dialogue, its vocabulary, its sequence, its consequences, appear natural to the user.

In this respect, the axiomatic, conventionalist psychology developed by George Kelly (1955) in terms of "personal constructs" has a significant role to play in formalizing the processes of systems analysis for dialogue engineering. As he notes (Kelly, 1955, p. 8): "Man looks at his world through transparent patterns or templets which he creates then attempts to fit over the realities of which the world is composed." And (p. 49) "A person's processes, psychologically speaking, slip into the grooves which are cut out by the mechanisms he adopts for realizing his objectives." It is the "grooves" created by the construct structure of the users that drives their vocabulary in communicating with one another that we have to reproduce. Kelly himself developed a means for eliciting such construct structures through his "repertory grid," and in recent years his technique has been automated and substantially extended by Shaw (1980) in her *Pegasus* and *Focus* systems. These tools for the interactive elicitation of personal construct structures may now be seen as essential tools for the dialogue engineer in his preliminary analysis of the activities and requirements of a new user community. There are fascinating possibilities also, not yet exploited, of building such construct-elicitation processes permanently into a system to expedite some of the continuing system development called for in Rule 3.

The first two rules can also be given more context by noting that, in some sense, "the computer is itself in the situation of a new person coming into the office and adjusting to its procedures" (Gaines, Facey, and Sams,

1976). Rule 1 then says that before you decide how to deploy someone with new ways and skills, take the opportunity to become familiar with [that person], or someone similar. Rule 2 says that if you are a newcomer in an office then try and slip into the familiar ways and jargon expected in that office—the new colleague who tries to impose new ways of performing existent tasks and new vocabularies for old conversations will not be welcome!

This animistic view of the computer is a very useful one if not overdone—at times of doubt the question, "Well, what would I do?" is a good one. Indeed, one early qualm about computer systems, that they would depersonalize tasks through their lack of personality, is very rapidly dispelled as soon as one notes that interactive programs *do* have personality—usually some partial replica of that of their designer! This is unfortunate if the designer has hidden sadistic tendencies that surface in his programs. More usually it is the erratic human nature of the designer that comes over, being ever so helpful at one moment and then forgetting the obvious the next. We have suggested (Gaines, Facey, and Sams, 1974) that the personality one should attempt to project is that of a *servant*—a very Dickensian one with wit and intelligence rather than servility, but a servant dedicated to his master's ends. This role may be an unfamiliar one for the modern technologist, but it provides a sure logical foundation for many of the essential features of a good interactive system.

The model of the interactive computer as a newcomer in an office also suggests the next rule, since one vital characteristic of a person is his *adaptability*. If you as a newcomer have behavior patterns which do not fit well into those of the office then social pressures soon lead you to conform (or leave!). The natural mechanism for such pressures to have effect is ready adaptability to criticism, overt or covert. If what you do is not liked then you adjust rapidly until you gain approval, often through mimicry. At the current state of the art it is clearly the system designer who has to provide the interactive system with its adaptability. Fortunately, an interactive system can, and should, also be interactively pro-grammable at the same location, probably at the same terminal, as the user. This enables the designer to set up a three-part dialogue between himself, computer, and user in which the effects of changes in programming the interaction can be made immediately apparent to the user and his evaluation received.

Rule 3. Design Never Ceases: Use the interactive capabilities of the system for programming also so as to close directly the adaptive loop between system and user through yourself as designer.

This is not intended to say that interactive dialogue *design* should take place at a terminal. Like any programming activity there is a need for thoughtful preparation away from the machine, and the best mode of working depends on the programmer. It is certainly to say, however, that the skill of rapid system modification at an interactive terminal is a very valuable one that should be developed, particularly in the current context.

Clearly the designer cannot remain an integral part of the system forever—even if an attractive role, with the declining costs of hardware relative to liveware, it is too expensive an option for most customers! However, Rule 3 does really mean "never" and provision has to be made both for the designer to play a continuing, but decreasing, role in the adaptation of the system to changing circumstances and changing users, and also for the reversal of roles that will take place once the computer is the "old hand" rather than the "newcomer." When the computer system is established and accepted we do then have to make provision for it to evaluate its users' behavior patterns and inform them of reasons for their difficulties. Fortunately, one of the easiest things to program an interactive system to do is to keep records of its own activities.

Rule 4. Log Activities: Use the computer to maintain selective records of system and user activities and provide programs to analyze these in terms of, for example, errors, broken down by user and by dialogue sequence.

One golden rule is that logging without purpose is useless—the analysis programs must be designed as part of the logging procedure and their applications defined as well as any other on the system. Unnecessary actions on the parts of users are one obvious activity to trace—deletions, line cancellations, transaction aborts, and so on. If one user is producing excessive quantities of these, he clearly needs guidance. If one section of the dialogue is producing excessive quantities, it clearly needs redesign. Proper long-term quality control of this nature is rarely found in current systems and yet the benefits are obvious, both for short-term system improvement and for long-term development of improved design techniques. I suspect the lack of proper dialogue instrumentation is not due nearly so much to the commercial pressures commonly adduced as to the lack of appropriate dialogue "technology."

It seems probable that the logging recommended here will be subject to legislative constraints under pressure from labor organizations. Insomuch as it generates information about individuals, it would seem simplest to deal with by analogy with other records of personal information, i.e., generally to allow free access to the individual concerned. In many ways it is tragic that it should be necessary to take legislation that far, and it is symptomatic of the (proper) fear of the use of computers in what Habermas (1972) calls a "technical cognitive" mode. In practice, if we wish to shape the behavior of cooperative users (and if we wish to make all users cooperative ones!), the most effective technique is to use the computer in an "emancipatory cognitive" mode to portray to a user the structure and consequences of his own behavior [as done by Mulhall (1977) in his clinical studies of personal relationships]. Again one can envision that advanced dialogue processing systems will provide facilities for interactive access by users themselves to analyses of their own behavior. In human terms it is the ability to look up and ask "How am I doing?" that an effective logging system can provide.

User Adaptation to the System

One of the advantages of close man–computer interaction is that one may program the system to minimize the mental workload on the man. In so doing one concentrates upon the weaknesses of the human mind, taking into account limited short-term memory capacity, inaccuracy of calculation, etc., and it is easy to begin to think of the computer as the senior partner which must somehow compensate for the inadequacies of its weaker partners. A natural development of this "senior" role is to attempt to program the system to identify the weaknesses of particular users and to call up compensating facilities to cope with them, e.g., more guidance in the dialogue, closer error checking, tutorial messages, and so on. This was, for example, part of the philosophy of many of the early computer-aided instruction systems, where "individualized" instruction was intended to be generated dynamically by the computer through the infinite wisdom of its programmer. In later developments there has been a swing toward "learner-controlled instruction" (Bunderson, 1974) because the on-line identification of human characteristics required for computer-controlled individualization proved unrealistic to implement.

Part of the problem is that in concentrating on the weaknesses of the person we forget their strengths, one of which is the modeling of the environment. There is a general phenomenon at work there which is summed up in Rule 5.

Rule 5. The User Will Model the System.
Do not assume that the user is a passive static system to be controlled, modeled, and directed by the computer—evaluate all actions of the system in terms of their effect on an actively changing user who is attempting to comprehend the system.

People automatically form internal models of their environment regardless of their naivety or intelligence. The mind is all the time searching out patterns of cause and effect—

Michotte (1963) has shown that much of this activity takes place at a fairly low level and, like the perception of optical illusions, it is not under conscious control. The models formed by users may vary widely and have many connotations that arise from their previous background experience and bear no direct relation to the system. Referring back to Cleary's remark quoted in Section 2, we may say that to make the system "understandable" is to maximize the possibility of the user forming with the minimum of effort a model of the system which aids his effective use of it.

Another phenomenon which makes attempts to program adaption to the user within the system dangerous is that the user is not only coming to comprehend the system but also himself adapting to it. We have a control-theoretic situation in which two coupled systems are each attempting to adapt to one another and instability may result.

Rule 6. User Should Dominate Computer. Either computer or user should dominate interaction or there will be instability—if computer is to dominate it must be programmed to, and have sufficient information to, model user—if user is to dominate then computer system must be simple to understand—at present state of the art user should dominate system.

It is worth emphasizing the grounds for this rule which are not "soft" ones relating to the proper role of computers in society. The channel of communication from person to computer just does not provide a sufficient flow of information for on-line identification of the characteristics of the person. As mentioned previously in Rule 4, it is possible to gather specific useful information about individual users if this is designed into the original system, but the time constant of doing this will be too long for immediate action within the interactive dialogue. A similar phenomenon has been noted in investigations of adaptive process control—the normal channels of control only rarely provide a sufficient information rate about the plant characteristics for on-line adaption to be feasible.

One key rule that we proposed previously that arises out of the requirement to make the computer system understandable to the user is:

Rule 7. Avoid Acausality. Make the activity of the system a clear consequence of the user's actions.

This rule sums up a variety of phenomena in interactive dialogue. The basis for it is one that I have developed in system theoretic terms in a number of publications (Gaines, 1976a, b, 1977): the identification of an acausal system (involving nondeterministic behavior) is very much more difficult than that of a deterministic system; people seem to presuppose determinism in the world, but one may show (Gaines, 1976a) that if this supposition is false they will generate highly elaborate, "superstitious" models. We have suggested this as an explanation of the relative difficulty of using a time-shared computer rather than a dedicated single-user system. The hesitancies of the shared system due to activities that are deliberately hidden from the user have no apparent cause, but this does not mean that the user will not continue, both at conscious and unconscious levels, to invent one. The importance of hesitancy patterns in the perception of speech (Goldman-Eisler, 1961) suggests that use of such information is, like the Michotte illusions, "wired-in" to the person and unavoidable.

All this emphasis on the system being static suggests that one must underutilize the capabilities of the computer to offer different dialogues under different circumstances, e.g., a highly tutorial dialogue to the naive user but a rapid, terse dialogue for the experienced user. This is not the case—just that such changes should be under user control. The next section contains some consideration of minimizing the effort by the user in exerting such control, but there is one sim-ple technique that has proved very effective in practice that we have previously noted.

Rule 8. Parallel–Sequential Tradeoff. Allow the user maximum flexibility to make his responses holistically (in parallel) or serially (in sequence) according to his wishes.

Figure 2 shows the same sequence as that in Figure 1 but with the user grouping his responses into clusters rather than making one at a time in sequence.

```
1'   GDR:ES85
4'   Full name: Treasury :Exchequer
5'   Issue date:6/7S2
8'   Final div date: 1/1 :5/8 81 3 1/4 0
12'  85:Exchequer 3 1/4  1981  5/8  S  6-Jul-77 OK?:Y
13'  GDR:
```

FIGURE 2: Dialogue sequence with grouped responses

At line 1' the user puts in what were previously three separate inputs, E, S, and 85. The system finds it has the responses to what were previously prompts 2 and 3 as well as that to 1 (in Figure 1), and goes straight on to prompt 4'. Similar groupings occur in response to 5' and 8', and the overall dialogue is much terser. As far as the user is concerned, the advantage is not just in reducing the verbosity of the system, but also in that he comes to *think* in terms of the clustered responses so that the dialogue really is mentally shortened i.e., ES85 is the unitary *sentence* "Enter Stock 85." Such groupings of basic actions together to form single unitary sequences is a major characteristic of the formation of any skill, and it is very natural for the user to adapt his actions in this way. Note, as emphasized previously, that the change in the way the system is being used is entirely under user control— the dialogue is adapting to the user's increasing skill and the system is programmed to allow such adaption, but it is still the user who dominates the interaction by deciding when to group his inputs.

There are clearly some syntactic constraints upon responses that may be grouped in this way but they are rarely severe in practice.

Minimizing the Mental Load on the User

It is common to find systems in which much effort has been put into user aids but where this has not been enforced so that every now and again the aids are not available. Similarly one finds that dialogue terminologies or command structure are similar throughout a system except for a few particular modules. In both cases the user becomes familiar with certain features of the system and then occasionally finds that what he has learned does not always apply. This not only puts an additional memory load on the user but can also be devastating psychologically when a naive user has at last gained confidence in his familiarity with a system and then suddenly finds that his trust in himself (and system and its designer) is misplaced. This leads to Rule 9:

> *Rule 9. Uniformity and Consistency.* Ensure that all terminology and operational procedures are uniformly available and consistently applied throughout all system activities.

This is clearly a particularly important rule for the naive user becoming familiar with the system. However, we have also found it important to skilled users *transferring* to a new system—a good standard dialogue technology has the same impact as a good standard programming language—users can transfer experience from one situation to another.

One of the most important facilities to make consistently and uniformly available is a good "help" command that enables a user to obtain selective advice from the system at any point in the dialogue. There is nothing more daunting to a naive user (or any of us!) than a thick user manual with masses of fine detail about the nuances of every transaction. Yet such documentation clearly should exist and there are times when particular details in

it are required. In practice there is a close connection between the state of a transaction and the information that may be relevant from the user manual, and the system itself may be used to make the relevant parts of the manual available as the user requires them. This basically corresponds to the "help" facility available on many systems whereby the user can request information and advice as he goes through a transaction. The difficulty with this is to know what advice would be most valuable to the user at any point: sometimes a list of possibilities; sometimes an example; sometimes an explanation of what will result from an input; and so on. We have developed a technique that enables a simple user command structure to control a multi-level help facility.

> *Rule 10. Query-in-Depth.* Distribute information and tutorial material appropriately throughout the dialogue system to be accessed by the user through a simple uniform mechanism— organize the material so that the user accesses brief memory aids first at any point but has further access to more detailed expansions.

We use a question mark, ?, as the command which is always available to the user to obtain help. It may be typed as a reply at any point of a dialogue and immediately elicits a short note of the main actions available at that point, or an example of data that could be entered. Typing question mark again drives the help system to greater depth so that it gives a full range of options and their effects. Typing a further question mark may lead to further expansion or, more probably, to a manual reference. Figure 3 shows query-in-depth in action during the dialogue sequence of Figures 1 and 2.

The successive question marks at lines 1, 3, 10, and 27 show questioning in depth, as do those at lines 38 and 40.

The extensive use of query-in-depth may be seen as a way of embedding a *manual* interactively within the system such that is al-

```
 1   GDR:?
 2       B (buy), S (sell), I (invest), L (list)
 3   GDR:?
 4       E (enter), R (remove), L (list)
 5       B (buy), S (sell), I (invest), M (modify)
 6       D (vary dates), C (vary commission rates)
 7       V (vary VAT rate)
 8       SUM (summarize deals), SYS (system status)
 9       INIT (initialize GDR)
10   GDR:?
11       E enter a stock, client, dealer or jobber
12       R remove a stock, client, dealer or jobber
13       L list stocks, clients, dealers, jobbers,
14       total files, records, or free closing
15       B buy a stock
16       S sell a stock
17       I invest an amount in a stock
18       M Modify an incorrect record of a deal
19       D vary date to update back records
20       C commission rate entry and listing
21       V VAT rate change
22       SUM summarize all deals for day
23       SYS give system status
24       INIT reinitialize this system as if just starting
25       :   abort GDR
26       ½ exit to GDR: command level
27   GDR:?
28       See Gilt Dealing Records User Manual p. 12
29   GDR:E
30   Item:?
31   Item to be entered: S (stock), D (dealer),
32   J (jobber), C (client)
33   Item:S
34   Stock number:?
35       Number of stock in range 10–99
36   Stock number:85
37   Full name: Treasury :Exchequer
38   Issue date:?
39       e.g. 7/5/87 or 6-MAY-77
40   Issue date:?
41       Date at which stock issued
42       e.g. 30/8/64 or 30-AUG-64
43   Issue date:
```

FIGURE 3: Examples of query-in-depth in dialogue

ways "open" at the right page when required by the local context. This may be viewed as a means of avoiding the need to write user manuals altogether and indeed we have found that users readily transfer to new systems without using manuals. However, when a manual is written, it is certainly a rationale for linking the text back to the query-in-depth and not creating yet another level of discourse with which to confuse the user. This leads to Rule 11.

Rule 11. User Manuals Should Be Based on Actual User Dialogue. Illustrate the use of the system in action by showing actual dialogue sequences that achieve specific objectives. Illustrate the structure of the system through dialogue sequences where question marks are typed to elicit information about the system.

Thus in practice, rather than distributing a manual through the system using query-in-depth, one inserts the appropriate material and then creates a manual from an existing system by using query-in-depth to generate the text.

The availability of query-in-depth is a very great aid to on-system training and we have found that new users can most rapidly acquire knowledge of the system through actual experience of it rather than formal training. This leads to Rule 12.

Rule 12. Train Through Experience. Get users interacting with an actual system as their initial training and introduce them to the system facilities such as query-in-depth.

The dialogue examples have all shown the user inputting short codes. Many of the rules so far may be seen as techniques for avoiding the need for explicit training. Through Rule 2 we are "using the user's model" so that the activity and terminology itself is natural to the user. Through Rule 9 we are ensuring "uniformity and consistency" to aid the transfer of experience from one part of the system to another. Through Rule 15 [below] we are enabling the user to make errors freely knowing he can avoid the consequences using a clean "reset" facility. *Training* is something that we have to put great effort into when we have a poorly designed system that is unnatural to the user. We can measure our success in system design by the degree to which explicit user training is unnecessary. In cases where we have installed a number of systems in succession over a period of years it has been gratifying to note that users who have learned to operate one system have been completely happy to transfer to a new one having very different functions without explicit training, relying on the query-in-depth and reset facilities to allow them to learn about the new system through their own unguided efforts.

The dialogue examples have all shown the user inputting short codes for commands rather than full English words. This is desirable to minimize typing effort since most users are not trained typists nor ever will be. However, the use of short codes increases the possibility of error in command sequences and it is important to give the user feedback as soon as possible as what action he has actually requested. In particular, dialogue sequences for different activities which go through the same initial dialogue may reinforce the user's opinion that he used the right command, and the effect of finding the error later when the sequences diverge is much more devastating since it is unexpected and the user has to look back for the source of error. Hence we formulated Rule 13.

Rule 13. Make the State of the Dialogue Observable. Give the user feedback as to the state of the dialogue by making an immediate unambiguous response to any of his inputs which may cause the dialogue to branch—the response should be sufficient to identify the type of activity taking place.

For example, if the prompt, "Item:", could follow a command other than E, then it would be better to qualify it appropriately, e.g., "Item to be entered:". Note how this requirement interacts, however, with Rule 9 since the dialogue of Figure 2 bypasses the prompt, "Item:". In this case the dialogue programmer may either decide that it does not matter since the user is skilled (or, what amounts to the same thing at this level of discourse, is pretending to be skilled—we should not be too paternalistic toward us-

ers!), or, if the possibility of error at this step is very significant (e.g., a little-used command), the observability prompt may be made an output in response to the initial command [as illustrated in Figure 4],

```
1   GDR:E
2   Stock Entry Sequence
3   Item:
```

FIGURE 4: Immediate feedback of state of dialogue

which will not be bypassed by a grouped initial command like ES85. However, such messages should not be used too freely or the dialogue will become annoyingly pedantic—it is like the listener who repeats each sentence back at you.

Error Detection and Correction

One of the significant reasons for using interactive data entry systems is to have on-line validation at source. In the light of the preceding discussion, validation of data entered may be seen as part of the process of informing the user about errors in the transaction. We have found that absolute validation involving complete rejection of data is a dangerous procedure—it is rare that sooner or later some data do not come up that lie outside the prescribed "norms" and yet must legitimately be entered. It is far better to *query* suspect data, asking the user if that is really what he meant, rather than reject [the suspect data]. However, too frequent queries also disrupt the dialogue and it is best to set norms reasonably wide so that queries are infrequent but have a final validation just before the transaction is accepted. This happens at line 12 of Figure 1, and the clarity of the procedure is very apparent. The user knows that he is coming to a natural checkpoint where action will be taken when such validation is requested. Up to that point he is assured of being able to abort the transaction with no side effects. He also sees the overall transaction in a global fashion that was not apparent before and, since the printout can be a standard one used for normal documents from the system, it can be a familiar form of output where errors will be most obvious. The rule is:

> *Rule 14. Validate Data on Entry.* [Check] syntax and values, but beware of rejecting data or querying too much as being outside norms. Have the user himself revalidate major updates before acting upon them.

Errors in dialogue are not essentially key problems to be avoided at all costs. The naive user should feel free to make errors as part of his exploration of the system—even highly skilled users will make errors because they will only devote to the dialogue that part of their channel capacity necessary to maintain the error rate to an acceptably low level for them. In both cases the users need the "sympathetic" system noted by Cleary—they should be able to make most errors with absolute confidence that they can readily escape the consequences—or at least all but the administrative chore of going back and doing it correctly. This led us to Rule 15.

> *Rule 15. Provide a Reset Command.* [There must be a command] that cleanly aborts the current activity back to a convenient checkpoint: the user should be able at any stage in a transaction to abort it cleanly with a system command that takes him back to a well-defined checkpoint as if the transaction had never been initiated.

We used the colon, :, as a uniformly available command to abort a transaction—it is easy for users to remember, "If you don't want to continue, type back to the computer the last character of its prompt to you, i.e., the colon." Thus one might get the sequence [shown in Figure 5]. This rule is a very important one for the user, but often the most difficult to implement for the system programmer. There may well be transactions involving many resources on a time-shared system where the "rollback" required to allow such

```
1   GDR:ES85
2   Full name: Treasury ::
3   GDR:
```
FIGURE 5: Use of reset command

free aborting is almost impossible to implement. This is a very good example where making the system simple and understandable to the user may involve great complexity in the programs—however, this is clearly the right division of labor.

The user may realize that he has made errors part way through a transaction, or at the final validation, and wish to go back to correct them. This is not an easy operation to offer to an unskilled user and, if such action is rarely required, it may be better to recommend that they use the abort facility of Rule 15 and go through the transaction again. Another alternative is to provide a good record update and correction facility as discussed in the next paragraph and advise users to complete the incorrect entry and then correct it as a separate activity. We have found it useful to provide a backtrack facility that allows users to unwind the dialogue in reverse order on the assumption that the error will be in the immediately preceding sequence.

> *Rule 16. Provide a Backtrack Facility.* [There should be a facility] that allows a user to return through the dialogue sequence in reverse.

We use the "up-arrow" character as a backtrack request, where [for example], at line 4 [in Figure 6] the user backtracks once to change the stock number entered and then at lines 8, 9, and 10 does so three times to change the number again.

The updating and correction of records is just as important as their original entry. We have learned to assume that any field whatsoever in a record may require updating—people seem to change their name, sex, and age far more frequently than one might reasonably expect! To avoid the user having to master another dialogue sequence for record correction, it is possible to use exactly the same

1   GDR:E

2   Item:S

3   Stock number:85

4   Full name: Treasury :ˆ

5   Stock number:58

6   Full name: Treasury :

7   Issue date:6/7

8   Type (SMLTN) :ˆ

9   Issue date:ˆ

10 Full name: Treasury :ˆ

11 Stock number:57

12 Full name: Treasury :

13 Issue date:6/7

14 Type (SMLTN):

FIGURE 6: Correction by backtracking

sequence as for data entry but print out field values after the prompt and take a RETURN input alone as meaning that the value has not changed. This is a particularly rapid way of modifying even a single field at a visual display terminal. The rule is:

Rule 17. Make Corrections Through Reentry. Use the entry dialogue with default field printouts from a record as a means of correcting the record.

For example, in terms of Figure 1, if we reenter stock 85 [we will get the sequence shown in Figure 7].

1   GDR:E

2   Item:S

3   Stock number:85

4   Full name: Exchequer :

5   Issue date: 6-Jul-77 :

6   Type (SMLTN): S :

7   Dividends/year: 2 :

8   Final div date : 5/8 :6/8

9   Redemption year(s): 81 :

10 Coupon: 3 1/4 :

11 Number of calls: 0 :

12   85:Exchequer 3 1/4 1981 6/8 S 6-Jul-77 OK?:Y

13 GDR:

FIGURE 7: Correction of record through entry sequence

At lines 4–7 and 9–11 the user just presses the RETURN key to indicate field unchanged. At line 8 he types in a correction input. Note how the stored record in this sequence appears exactly as do the default values in Figure 1.

4. Implementing the Dialogue Programming Rules

Enforcing the dialogue programming rules detailed in the preceding section is best done through a standard dialogue procedure which is written once and used thereafter as the only means of interacting with the user. The systems described in this paper were written in the interactive systems programming language BASYS II (Gaines, 1976d, 1978c; Gaines and Facey, 1977) which provides special facilities for string processing. The standard BASYS II operating system has a dialogue processing procedure embedded in it and all dialogue, including that of the operating system job control language, goes through this procedure.

The procedure is called with parameters giving the prompt string, query-in-depth replies, and branches for reset and backtrack. Its operation is most readily understood by considering how each rule is implemented in turn:

Rules 1, 2, and 3 do not require any special features in the procedure. Rule 2, *Use the User's Model*, implies ease of decoding strings returned by the procedure in an arbitrary format natural to the user, and this is particularly simple in BASYS II. Rule 3, *Design Never Ceases*, implies some form of interactive programming language with a modular structure, and again BASYS II satisfies this requirement. However, other languages offer equally good string handling or can be provided with suitable procedures.

Rule 4, *Log Activities*, is the first where the dialogue procedure itself should provide facilities. One of the parameters that can be passed to it is the name of a logfileprocedure.

This may default either to no action or to logging the complete dialogue. However, it is also possible by this mechanism to provide selective logging of the dialogue at points which require study or are dependent on other parameters such as the identity of the user.

Rules 5, 6, and 7, in the context of the dialogue procedure are warnings not to make it too "clever" in its actions.

Rule 8, *Parallel–Sequential Tradeoff*, is readily implemented. The string returned by the dialogue procedure is in a global variable and the calling routine extracts what items it wants from it. When the dialogue procedure is next called it checks the global variable and only if it is null does it refer to the user for input. Thus the user may input several items at the same time and they will be passed to the appropriate callers of the dialogue procedure.

Rule 9, *Uniformity and Consistency*, is primarily ensured by requiring all dialogue to go through the standard procedure.

Rule 10, *Query-in-Depth*, is implemented by passing to the procedure a table of strings which are used to reply to each successive question mark.

Rules 11, 12, 13, and 14 depend on how the procedure is used rather than its own characteristics.

Rule 15, *Provide a Reset Command*, is implemented through the procedure returning not to its normal address but to the branch passed as the reset parameter. This branch can usually be set up as a default for a dialogue sequence and should be to code which cleans up any actions taken during the course of the dialogue before returning to the top level program.

Rule 16, *Provide a Backtrack Facility*, is implemented in a similar way to Rule 15 except that the abnormal branch is to the parameter passed which will usually be the previous call on the dialogue procedure or any parameter calculations immediately preceding it.

Rule 17, *Make Corrections Through Reentry*, is implemented by passing to the dialogue procedure a computed prompt string which contains the previous value of the item requested.

Thus most of the key rules may be implemented simply and automatically through a dialogue procedure. It is useful also to incorporate in the procedure facilities for diagnostic purposes and for taking the input from a command file rather than a terminal.

5. Conclusions

This paper has proposed an approach to *dialogue engineering* which has been used in a wide range of interactive systems in the past 12 years. It has proved very successful in allowing naive users to cope rapidly and adequately with complex interactions while not frustrating highly skilled users. The rules proposed are intended as guidelines rather than absolutes and each is substantiated by arguments based on both theory and practice. Some of the rules are specific to the particular style of dialogue discussed whereas others are general to all forms of interaction. I hope that this presentation will act not only as a guide to those attempting to create effective interactive systems but also as a stimulus to others to improve, vary, and generally develop both the rules and the entire domain of dialogue engineering.

ACKNOWLEDGMENTS

I am grateful to Peter Facey, John Gedye, and John Sams for their collaboration in the work reported in this paper.

REFERENCES

Bennett, J. (1976). *Linguistic Behaviour*. Cambridge University Press.

Bunderson, C. V. (1974). The design and production of learner-controlled courseware for the TICCIT system: A progress report. *International Journal of Man–Machine Studies*, 6(4), 479–491.

Cox, R. B., and Martin, T. B. (1975). Speak and the machines obey. *Industrial Research* (November), 1–6.

Danver, J. H., and Nevison, J. M. (1969). Secondary school use of the time-shared computer at Dartmouth College. *AFIPS Spring Joint Computer Conference*, **34**, 681–689. New Jersey: AFIPS Press.

Fano, R. M. (1965). The MAC system: A progress report. In Sass, M. A., and Wilkinson, W. D., Eds., *Computer Augmentation of Human Reasoning*, pp. 131–150. Washington, D.C.: Spartan Books.

Gaines, B. R. (1975). Analogy categories, virtual machines and structured programming. In Goos, G., and Hartmanis, J., Eds., *GI—5. Jahrestagung, Lecture Notes in Computer Science*, 34, pp. 691–699. Berlin: Springer-Verlag.

Gaines, B. R. (1976a). On the complexity of causal models. *IEEE Transactions on Systems, Man and Cybernetics*, **SMC**-6(1), 56–59.

Gaines, B. R. (1976b). Behaviour–structure transformations under uncertainty. *International Journal of Man–Machine Studies*, **8**(3), 337–365.

Gaines, B. R. (1976c). Human factors in virtual machine hierarchies. *Proceedings Colloquium on the Influence of High Level Languages on Computer System Design*, March, IEE, London.

Gaines, B. R. (1976d). Interpretive kernels for microcomputer software. *Proceedings Symposium Microprocessors at Work*, September, Society of Electronic and Radio Technicians, University of Sussex, pp. 56–69.

Gaines, B. R. (1977). System identification, approximation and complexity. *International Journal of General Systems*, **3**, 145–174.

Gaines, B. R. (1978a). Minicomputers in business applications in the next decade. *Infotech State of Art Report on "Minis Versus Mainframes,"* pp. 51–81. Infotech International, Berkshire, U.K.

Gaines, B. R. (1978b). Programming interactive dialogue. *Pragmatic Programming and Sensible Software, Online Conferences,* Uxbridge, Middlesex, U.K., pp. 305–320.

Gaines, B. R. (1978c). A mixed-code approach to commercial microcomputer applications. *Microprocessors in Automation and Communications IERE Conference Proceedings No. 41*, pp. 291–301.

Gaines, B. R. (1978d). Man-computer communication: What next? *International Journal of Man-Machine Studies*, **10**, 225–232.

Gaines, B. R., and Facey, P. V. (1975). Some experience in interactive system development and application. *Proceedings IEEE*, **63**, 155–169.

Gaines, B. R., and Facey, P. V. (1977). BASYS—A language for processing interaction. *Proceedings Conference Computer Systems and Technology (IERE No. 36)*, March, University of Sussex, pp. 251–262.

Gaines, B. R., Facey, P. V., and Sams, J. B. S. (1974). An on-line fixed-interest investment analysis and dealing system. *Proceedings European Computing Congress, EUROCOMP 74*, May, pp. 155–169.

Gaines, B. R., Facey, P. V., and Sams, J. B. S. (1976). Minicomputers in security dealing. *Computer*, **9**(9), 6–15.

Gilb, T., and Weinberg, G. M. (1977). *Humanized Input*. Cambridge, Mass.: Winthrop.

Goldman-Eisler, F. (1961). Hesitation and information in speech. In Cherry, C., Ed., *Information Theory*, pp. 162–174. London: Butterworths.

Gruenberger, F., Ed. (1967). *The Transition to On-Line Computing*. Washington, D.C.: Thompson Book Co.

Habermas, J. (1972). *Knowledge and Human Interests*. London: Heinemann.

Harris, L. R. (1977). User oriented data base query with the robot natural language query system. *International Journal of Man–Machine Studies*, **9**(6), 697–713.

Hendrix, G. G. (1977). Lifer: A natural language interface facility. *Proceedings Second Berkeley Workshop on Distributed Data Management and Computer Networks TID-4500-R65*, May, pp. 196–201.

Kelly, G. A. (1955). *The Psychology of Personal Constructs*. New York: W. W. Norton.

Martin, J. (1973). *Design of Man–Computer Dialogues.* Englewood Cliffs, N. J.: Prentice-Hall.

Michotte, A. (1963). *The Perception of Causality.* London: Methuen.

Mulhall, D. (1977). The representation of personal relationships: An automated system. *International Journal of Man-Machine Studies, 9,* 315–335.

Orr, W. D., Ed. (1968). *Conversational Computers.* New York: John Wiley.

Parkhill, D. F., Ed. (1966). *The Challenge of the Computer Utility.* Reading, Mass.: Addison-Wesley.

Petrick, S. R. (1976). On natural language based computer systems. *IBM Journal of Research and Development,* 20, 314–325.

Sass, M. A., and Wilkinson, W. D., Eds. (1965). *Computer Augmentation of Human Reasoning.* Washington, D.C.: Spartan Books.

Shaw, J. C. (1968). JOSS: Experience with an experimental computing service for users at remote consoles. In Orr, W. D., Ed., *Conversational Computers,* pp. 15–22. New York: John Wiley.

Shaw, M. L. G. (1980). *On Becoming a Personal Scientist.* London: Academic Press.

Weizenbaum, J. (1967). Contextual understanding by computers. *Communications ACM, 10*(8), 474–480.

Winograd, T. (1972). *Understanding Natural Language.* Edinburgh: Edinburgh University Press.

Woods, W., Bates, M., Brown, G., Bruce, B., Cook, C., Klovstad, J., Makhoul, J., Nash-Webber, B., Schwartz, R., Wolf, J., and Zue, V. (1976). Speech understanding systems. *BBN Report Number 3438,* December. Cambridge, Mass.: Bolt, Beranek and Newman.

8   A Human-Factors Style Guide for Program Design

Henry Simpson

Anacapa Sciences, Inc.

Human factors is a small but growing discipline which seeks to provide a method for taking into account human strengths and limitations during the design of computer hardware and software. In this article, I'll present a brief introduction to human factors and discuss its application to program design. I'll define six human-factors design principles and show how they can be applied to three areas of program design: data entry, display-screen design, and sequence control.

Human factors can be applied to any area in which a human being interacts with a machine. The discipline applies, or at least can and should be applied, to many aspects of man's interaction with computers. The most obvious area, and the one most people think of when considering human factors, is hard-

Henry Simpson, "A Human-Factors Style Guide for Program Design," *BYTE* (April 1982), pp. 108, 110, 114, 116, 118, 122, 124, 126, 130, 132. Copyright © 1982 Byte Publications, Inc. Reprinted by permission of Byte Publications, Inc.

ware design. Human-factors specialists often design video displays and controls.

More recently, human factors has been applied to software design. Research has led to the development of human-factors guidelines that programmers can use to make their programs easier to use and less prone to error. Human factors is also important to the design of computer operating systems, programming languages, and documentation, although the discipline has received less attention in those areas.

Human factors matter because people must operate machines. If you fail to take people into account during design, then your machine (or system or program) may be difficult or impossible for people to operate. As obvious as it seems, this point is often overlooked. Consider some recent examples. No brand names are mentioned in what follows, but you may recognize some of the players:

The microcomputer whose nonstandard keyboard made it awkward for touch-typists—all keys were there, but they were the wrong kind of keys and in the wrong locations. (The keyboard has since been redesigned.)

The minicomputer whose operating system identifies program errors with numeric codes that are contained in three separate manuals. (This machine was recently discontinued.)

The computer program whose screen displays are cluttered and confusing, whose data-entry sequences permit input errors that cause the program to interrupt, whose menus can lead the operator down blind alleys and into stable program states from which he or she cannot escape. The documentation for this program consists of three smudged photocopies of an original that displays creative spelling and grammar and omits many important details.

We often blame human error for disasters and near disasters, from nuclear near-meltdowns to bank errors in checking account balances. Equally often, we blame "the com-

puter" for some ill fate that befalls us. Seldom do we recognize that neither man nor machine alone is completely responsible. In today's complex world, man and machine work together interactively. The "system" is the combination of both.

When we design things, it is usually fairly easy for us technically oriented people to take into account the limitations of our hardware. However, we are likely to forget that the operator or maintainer of our system has limitations. We can design much better systems—more workable and more maintainable—if we accurately take human limitations into account.

What are human limitations? First and most obvious, no two human beings are alike. They vary in size, strength, acuity, intelligence, education, and level of motivation. The general requirement for considering human factors in the design of your system, whether hardware or software, is to *recognize the needs of the users*. The type of user varies with the application. If you are designing an arcade game with a coin slot and two push buttons, you are aiming at a different sector of the population than if you are developing a computer-based econometric model to predict the gross national product in 1985. Either of those programs can be written for specific, definable, homogeneous groups of users.

More often than not, however, the hardware or software we design will be used by a varied group that ranges widely in sophistication. Knowing your system users and recognizing their needs are the first two steps in taking human factors into consideration during system design.

In general, the rules for designing a system with the user in mind parallel those for good writing: define your system users, know their limitations, and find the simplest way to get your message across.

That which separates good programs from bad cannot always be described in terms of simple, obvious things such as bad keyboard designs or cumbersome error-handling procedures. I can name some general qualities to look for, however. First, programs that consider human factors are generally easier to learn and use than those that do not. They usually have simpler displays, are less likely to "bomb," and are supported by good user documentation; they appear to be written for less specialized users and not for computer experts. These programs also refrain from trying to make the machine behave as if it were a human being. Poorly designed programs lack some or all of these features.

To illustrate when human factors matter I'll limit my discussion to software design and, more specifically, to microcomputer software in which the operator controls the computer and interacts continuously with it. This scope includes such applications as games, business and scientific programs, computer graphics, and computer music but excludes most control, robotics, and other minimally interactive applications.

A human-factors purist might say that serious consideration of human factors *always* matters, but this simply isn't true. You can decide in each case how important human factors are by looking at four different aspects of your program: (1) number of people who will operate the program, (2) diversity of the operators' backgrounds, (3) complexity of the program, and (4) consequences of operator error.

Obviously, the more people who will operate your program, the more time and energy you will invest in its development. If you are running a business, you want to assure that your A/R (accounts receivable) program works efficiently and effectively because it will cost you money and perhaps your credit rating if it doesn't.

If that same program must serve a wide group—ranging, say, from clerk to company president—then you must assure that the program serves all levels well. This takes special effort during program design.

The more complex the program, the greater the chance of error, and the more you must strive to reduce the likelihood of error by carefully considering human factors.

Last, and probably most important, are error consequences. The more serious these

are, the more important the human element becomes. If the reactor core will melt down, the navigator will get lost, or the names and addresses of all the people who owe you money will disappear, then the consequences of error are very serious indeed. If the worst that can happen is that the bouncing ball in your game program may disappear from the screen, then the consequences are not quite so serious (unless you depend upon the program for your livelihood).

In sum, if you are writing programs purely for your own use and are not tracking important data, then you have probably spent too much time on this article already. On the other hand, if you are writing programs for a wide and varied group of users to track things that matter to them, then human-factors considerations *are* important.

Design Principles

If you decide to apply human factors to your program design, where do you begin? Probably the best way is to familiarize yourself with some general human-factors design principles. Six such principles are presented below. These principles grow out of behavioral research conducted over the last several decades, although their application to program design is recent. Later in this article I'll give specific examples of how these principles may be applied.

Provide Feedback

People need to know that an action they have taken has had an effect. When you turn the wheel of your automobile, you receive feedback in the form of resistance from the wheel, centrifugal force on your body, and movement of your visual field. In turn, you adjust the rate at which you turn the wheel to conform to the feedback you are receiving. Without this feedback, you would find it much more difficult to control your automobile.

The user of your program also needs feedback. If he makes a keyboard entry and nothing appears on the screen, then he has no way of knowing that his action has had an effect. In consequence, he may repeat his action or try another, possibly causing something unintended to happen.

Feedback should be immediate and obvious. Show it on the screen in a place where it is expected.

Be Consistent

Mention "consistency" in a group and someone will probably quote Emerson to the effect that it is the "hobgoblin of little minds." Emerson may have been able to get along without it in certain trivial matters, but computer programmers cannot. The tools and programming languages with which they work are based on rigid adherence to rules of syntax, the order of programming operations, and the laws of mathematics. Rigid adherence to these "laws of the machine," which are internally consistent, reduces uncertainties and makes it possible to program the machine exactly. Human beings can tolerate more ambiguity than machines, but ambiguity reduces people's effectiveness. If we paid half as much attention to consistency in our programs' interactions with human beings as we do in the interactions between programs and machines, most of our programs would be improved.

What, exactly, do we mean by "consistency"? One way of defining it is as a set of rules that you, the programmer, establish for yourself and follow compulsively. These rules permit the operator to learn one part of your program's operation and then to apply the new knowledge to other parts of the program. For example, you might make a rule that all of your error messages will appear on the bottom line of the display screen. When the operator sees one error message displayed on the bottom line, he expects all others to be displayed there, too. If they are, then the rule is adhered to, and the operator will not have to learn a new rule for each new

display. If not, then the operator's learning task is that much more difficult.

Minimize Human Memory Demands

Psychologists have determined that human beings possess two types of memory—short term and long term. A vast amount of research has been conducted on the subject, most of which will interest only the specialist. About human memory, the computer programmer needs to recognize two things. The first of these is obvious, the second less so.

First, computers have better memories than people. (We said it was obvious.) Data stored on magnetic media are never forgotten.

Second, computers always remember things exactly as they were stored. People usually do, but sometimes they get things mixed up.

What follows from these two points is that when designing programs, you should rely on computer memory as much as possible. Suppose, for example, that your program has many subprograms. How should the operator select a subprogram—from a displayed menu or by entering a memorized mnemonic? Although selection with memorized mnemonics (used in "programlike languages") has advantages in some situations, the displayed menu depends much less on operator memory and is generally preferable. (Some players of "Star Trek" games may recall the frustration with which they attempted to master the game in the absence of displayed menu options.)

Keep the Program Simple

Simplicity in programming, as in writing, does not come easily or painlessly. You must work to achieve even the appearance of simplicity. Simplicity usually results from paring down or editing. In programming, as in writing, simplicity is an ideal that one strives to achieve by conscious design, by trial and modification, by cutting away the unnecessary, and by reorganizing and rearranging.

Match the Program to the Operator's Skill Level

You must determine the operator's skill level before you write your program. Determine also if operators of differing skill levels will use the same program. Human-factors specialists do these two things systematically by conducting a task analysis. There are several ways to do this, but usually it involves defining what *mission* a system must perform, what *functions* are involved in this mission, and what *tasks* are required to accomplish the functions. Conducting task analyses is time-consuming, technical, expensive, and probably beyond your needs or interests. Still, you do need to think about operator tasks as you write your program and ask questions like the following:

What will operators be expected to do?

What decisions must they make?

What must they know to make the decisions?

What skill levels will be required?

Consider these questions before you write your program. Then design your program so that it matches the skill level of your system users.

Sustain Operator Orientation

If you have ever been lost then you know what *not* being oriented is. Anyone who has ever used a computer has had the experience of getting into some new program and not being able to find the way out. This often happens when you try the program without first reading the manual (as all of us are prone to do).

You have an obligation as a programmer to minimize the possibility of disorientation. Provide your operator with signposts that tell him where he is and how to get back to where he came from. Menu-driven programs often do this by providing a main menu which serves as a home base. The program

begins with this menu from which the operator can select various subprograms, perform them, and then return.

Some game programs are intentional mazes, consciously designed to disorient the operator. If that's your intention, all well and good. But if it's not, remember that an unwanted maze is about as much fun as an inaccurate road map on a dark and rainy night.

The six principles described above reduce to one idea: know the needs of your system users. Recognize that they need feedback to avoid confusion, consistency to ease the learning process, minimal strain on memory capacity, simplicity rather than complexity, demands gauged to their skill levels, and constant, clear orientation.

The remainder of this article will focus on three areas of computer programming: data entry, display-screen design, and sequence control. Data entry concerns how you get data into a database; display-screen design concerns layout of video-terminal-display screens; and sequence control concerns how you interact with your program to get it to do something.

I'll show how the six human-factors principles apply in each of these areas. In most cases, recommendations made are based on research that has shown that the suggested feature permits more effective man–machine interaction. In a few cases, recommendations are based on prevailing practice. None of these guidelines should be applied blindly, and all of us will find it necessary to ignore them from time to time. But most of these are simple things to do, and if you follow them, you will write a better program.

Data Entry

The following guidelines apply mainly to programs in which data are entered through the keyboard to build a database which the program accesses later. Typically, the data-entry process consists of the following sequence of steps.

Presentation of a prompt

Data entry by the operator

Display of entered data on the screen

Error test

Presentation of an error message if entered data fail error test

Editing of data

Acceptance of data into database

Prompting

If data are to be entered into the computer from a standardized data-entry form, then the data-entry screen should resemble that form as closely as possible. The cursor should move from field to field as the operator fills in the form. It is easier to write a program consisting of a series of INPUT statements that cause the screen to scroll. However, the operator can more readily orient himself to a screen that looks like a data-entry form. Figure 1 shows a data-collection form and a data-entry screen designed to elicit the necessary data. The screen presents prompts, states acceptable ranges, and delimits fields.

The program should provide a prompt for every data input. The prompt should be brief and specific, and [should] show the range limits and entry format of data to be entered. Range limits or entry format can be shown parenthetically after the prompt. For example, a date entered in the form of month-day-year could be prompted as follows: "Enter Date (Month/Day/Year)". If there is a length limit, then this length should be shown on the screen using an underline, pair of brackets, or other visual cue. If certain data entries have *default* values (i.e., values that the computer will assign unless the operator enters others), then display the default values—do not rely on operator memory. If there are similar or identical data-entry requirements in different parts of the program, prompt consistently. One way to do this is to put data-entry statements into subroutines that can be called from various parts of the program.

Entering Data

You do not always control the length of the data to be entered, but when you do, keep length to a minimum. This saves keystrokes and time and reduces errors. Provide feed-

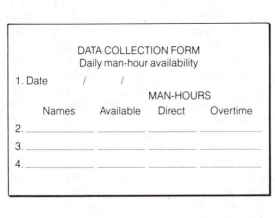

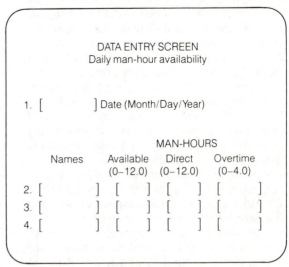

FIGURE 1: A data-collection form and the data-entry screen that goes with it. The data-entry screen resembles the form. Prompts shown in parentheses on the screen make clear the expected data formats and give range limits. The brackets serve as field delimiters, showing the maximum length allowed for each entry.

back by displaying entered data on the screen. If data being entered consist of logically related groups, then permit the user to enter several fields together, rather than requiring him to enter each item separately.

Error Check

Check all entered data for errors. The types of checks you must make depend upon the data and what will be done with them. Anticipate possible errors, check for them, and protect against them. For example, if the entry is supposed to be a number, anticipate what will happen when (not if) the operator enters a letter. Many programmers protect against this by taking all inputs as character strings and then converting them to equivalent numeric values.

Analyze the situation and be ready for errors. Are there range or length limits to what is acceptable? Is it possible for the operator to enter something that will cause an illegal program action to take place—for example, dividing by zero or attempting to take a substring of illegal length?

When an entry error is detected, alert the operator, identify the error, and tell him how to recover. In other words: *alert, identify, direct.* Alerting signals must differ from the customary background. An audio tone—a beep—is alerting but meaningless if the program is already emitting a continuous stream of beeps. Similarly, a flashing message can effectively alert, provided that the screen is not filled with other flashing messages. Many programmers reserve the use of both sound and flashing messages for those conditions that truly require an alert.

The error message itself should be placed consistently from screen to screen. Ideally, it should appear near the erroneous entry. The content of the message must tell what is wrong—for example, that the entered value is too long. If error identification will permit the operator to figure out what to do next, then that is all the message needs to contain. However, if many possible actions may be taken, then the message must also tell the op-

erator which to take. If prompts to the user are adequate, then it should be possible in most cases for the operator to figure out what corrective action to take based solely on definition of the error. Figure 2 shows a helpful error message.

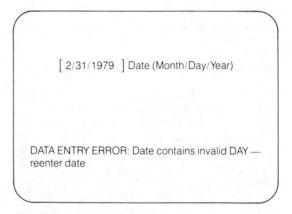

[2/31/1979] Date (Month/Day/Year)

DATA ENTRY ERROR: Date contains invalid DAY — reenter date

FIGURE 2: A sample error message. The message is specific and helps the operator correct the error identified.

Editing

Editing is an important part of the data-entry process, and no data-entry program is complete without editing capability. Being human, operators will make data-entry errors that they may not recognize until later. You should therefore permit them to edit entries before the program accepts data into a database. Many programs permit data to be edited at three stages: during initial data entry (while being typed in), after a block of related entries has been made, and after the data have become part of the database.

The first editing capability is routine and in fact most people probably do not think of this as editing. If you make a typing error, you can usually back up the cursor before data are stored. The last capability, editing the actual database, varies in importance, but in many programs with large databases it is considered as necessary as utility programs for copying files, purging files, or the main menu itself.

Less routine, often ignored, yet very important is the block editing capability mentioned above. Often the program user will not recognize an error until after he has made several data entries. If he cannot go back and correct the error at that point, it may be uncorrectable, or he may have to use a separate database editing program to make the correction. The way block editing typically works is that after the operator has made a set of related entries, the screen presents a prompt asking if he wants to edit any earlier entries. If he indicates that he does, the program asks him to define the entry he wants to correct, usually by line number. Then the cursor moves to the appropriate data-input field to permit reentry of data, and the edit prompt reappears to permit corrections. When the operator indicates that he has no more changes to make, the program moves on to the next step.

Certain data entries have far-reaching effects. A "profound, irreversible data entry" is one that will significantly affect the database or a phase of program operation. How profound the data entry is depends, of course, on the situation. Consequences of data-entry errors in these cases vary from inconvenience (you are delayed because you must print a report) to disaster (you just purged 6 months' worth of data).

Clearly, it is important to protect the operator from such traps by providing "fail-safe" devices. The general idea is to make the operator action more complex than for usual data entry. One way is to make data entry require two stages. For example, when the operator selects the "FIRE ICBM" program from the menu, firing does not occur immediately but causes a message to appear on the screen that tells what will happen next. This is accompanied by a prompt that permits the operator either to continue or to back out.

Protect your operator against himself. The programmer who writes a program that will purge all files at the stroke of a single key deserves no mercy and will receive none from program users. Figure 3 shows a message that provides sufficient warning to the operator before beginning to purge data.

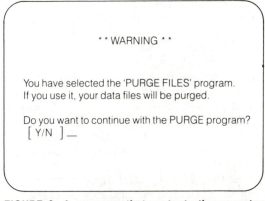

** WARNING **

You have selected the 'PURGE FILES' program. If you use it, your data files will be purged.

Do you want to continue with the PURGE program? [Y/N] —

FIGURE 3: A message that protects the operator against a serious error. The operator must confirm the decision to purge the data files before the program will proceed.

Display-Screen Design

Screen layout design is partly art and partly science, but all programmers can profit by observing the guidelines in this section.

Designing a good screen requires planning. Many experienced programmers find that a screen design aid, consisting of a paper matrix that identifies all possible character locations on the screen, is useful. This permits design of the screen with paper and pencil. The design can be perfected before it is committed to code. (It is much faster to make pencil erasures than to change a series of tab settings.)

As a general rule, access screens by paging, not by scrolling. Keep in mind that people find it easier to read stationary pages than moving pages. The only people who like to read scrolling information are those at the end of hot news wires. Unless your program has that sort of application, clear the screen before you put up a new display.

Most displays need a title to tell the operator what he is looking at. The title should be centered at the top of the screen.

Display-screen designers center displayed information primarily for aesthetic considerations, although centering assumes more practical importance with large screen displays. With large screens, if information is not centered, the operator will spend his time turned to the left side of the screen instead of along a more natural line of sight—straight ahead.

Your screens will probably contain a variety of different types of information: title block, numerical information, prompt line, error-message line, operating-mode indicator, etc. Analyze your needs and determine how many different categories apply. Then allocate a screen area for each information category.

Assure that information on screens does not stray from its assigned area. This is an application of the consistency principle discussed earlier. The more complex your screen displays, the more important it is to allocate areas. If you have complex screens and do not design them consistently, you will confuse the operator.

If possible, separate each area of the screen from the next by at least three rows or columns of blank spaces. Different blocks can also be separated by lines, which will make the separation more distinct. More effective still is to color-code different screen areas.

"Keep it simple" has become a cliché but is valuable and important advice. Unfortunately, keeping it simple is, to use another cliché, easier said than done. What, after all, is "simple"? And when is something "not simple enough"?

Finding the answers to these questions requires you to take a close look at the information needs of your program users at each point in your program. Present no more information than necessary.

Some programmers use the "one logically connected thought or step per screen" rule. Where much information must be conveyed, these programmers break it up into logical thoughts or steps and present each one on a separate screen. This is like the rule of presenting one idea in each paragraph of prose.

Programmers in the "densely packed display" school of thought hold the view that if they can get everything onto one screen they are saving something. What, exactly, they are saving is unclear, although they must gain a

certain satisfaction by rising to the challenge of making everything fit. This satisfaction resembles the exultation of the first guy who engraved the Declaration of Independence on the head of a pin. Judge for yourself how useful that was.

In designing screen displays, it is important to follow prevailing conventions. Because of experience with written language, people have certain built-in expectations for the way information will be presented to them. If you don't follow convention in displaying information, you make things more difficult for the operator.

Think of your display screen as the page of a book. In a book, information is normally presented in lines that are read from left to right and from top to bottom. Numeric information is usually presented in tabular format, i.e., beneath column headings from top to bottom. Certain obvious things you should avoid are printing numeric information from left to right or presenting very wide columns of text. If in doubt, recall how you have seen such information portrayed in books.

You should display information in a recognizable order. Some screens present directories or lists through which the operator must search. A menu is one such list, although it is usually short, with the most frequently called options listed at the top and the least frequently at the bottom (more on this later). Long directories or lists should be presented in an order that the operator will recognize, for example, alphabetic, numeric, or chronological order. This simplifies the search and saves time. Figure 4 shows the same information presented in random order and again in alphabetical order. Judge for yourself which ordering makes it easier to find the name "Grogono".

Long strings should be broken up. A "long" string is one that has more than about five independent characters. By "independent" we mean characters that do not unite to form a recognizable whole such as a person's name. A telephone number without the separating hyphen would be such a string. People have difficulty recognizing and separating the individual characters of long

NOT THIS

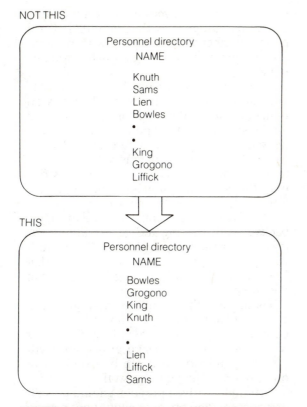

Personnel directory
NAME

Knuth
Sams
Lien
Bowles
•
•
King
Grogono
Liffick

THIS

Personnel directory
NAME

Bowles
Grogono
King
Knuth
•
•
Lien
Liffick
Sams

FIGURE 4: The same list presented in random order and in alphabetical order. Recognizable orderings— e.g., alphabetical, numerical, and chronological— make data easier for the operator to comprehend.

cated formatting statements makes alignment easy. Justifying numbers to the right and aligning decimal points are more difficult with most microcomputer BASICs, although subroutines for performing these functions have appeared in publications, and most moderately skilled programmers can write their own. Figure 5 illustrates conventional alignment of information on the display screen.

Sequence Control

Sequence control is the manner in which the operator controls the sequence of program operations. In menu-driven programs, the

ACCOUNT REPORT

DESCRIPTION
      Account #: 3181
      Name: Budget

STATUS
This account is not currently up to date.
Last payment was made 12 months ago.

ACCOUNT INFORMATION
      Balance: $31,000.00
      Payment: 292.89
      Amt last pmt: 3.69

FIGURE 5: Standard methods of presenting text and numbers on the screen. Text is easier to read if left justified. Numbers are easier to read if right justified and aligned on the decimal point (if any).

strings. If you have ever tried to count over to, say, the fifteenth character of a forty-character string, you know the problem.

Elements of the string can be more readily located if you display the string as several short strings (i.e., consisting of five or fewer characters) separated by spaces. (Better yet, find an explicit, uncoded method to present your information.)

According to standard practice, text is normally justified to the left side of the screen or to a defined tab value. Numerical information is normally justified to the right. Where the number of decimal places may vary on successive lines, decimal points on all lines should align at a particular tab value. These conventions are carryovers from mainframe practice, where the availability of sophisti-

operator exercises sequence control through menu choices. These let the operator select the subprograms he needs to do his job.

An operator can exercise sequence control in many other ways. Control simply requires an interaction or "dialogue" with the program. The menu-driven program permits a particular type of dialogue. Other common dialogue types are question and answer, query, programlike language, and action code.

In *question-and-answer* dialogue the program displays a question and the operator responds with an answer. The expected answer is one of a limited set of alternatives, such as "yes" or "no." Example: Program asks whether output should be displayed on video terminal or printer.

Query dialogue is an extension of question and answer: a question is posed but the number of alternatives is large. Example: Program requests the number of the file it should display.

Programlike language dialogue uses a defined set of commands to control the program. Valid commands are usually brief mnemonic abbreviations of action words. Example: Command words used to control the Star Wars game.

Action code dialogue usually involves the use of specially defined and labeled function keys for calling up displays or programs. User-defined function keys are not widely available on microcomputers, but we will see more of them in the future. The new IBM Personal Computer has fifteen or more user-defined function keys.

Beside these methods, sequence control can be exercised in a number of other ways—in fact, via any channels that permit the operator to enter data into the computer and receive feedback. Possibilities include trackball, joystick, optical device, human voice, and whatever else creative minds can invent and implement.

The Old Standby—The Menu-Driven Program

In this article I cannot cover sequence-control design principles that apply to all dialogue types. For one thing, there isn't room. But more important, the research with many of these methods is limited, and I can offer few definitive recommendations. For these reasons, I will focus on that old standby, the menu-driven program. Though its origin is traceable to the earliest days of computing machinery, the menu-driven program remains the principal means by which people carry on dialogues with computers. Until people perfect ways of talking with computers, the menu-driven program will probably remain the mainstay.

There are good reasons for its popularity and success. First, it makes no demands on human memory. Menu options are displayed on the screen and the operator picks the one he wants. This makes a menu-driven program easy to learn. Second, menus help the operator orient himself because they explicitly display the available "roads" (subprograms) from each "crossroad" (menu).

Menu-driven programs have certain drawbacks as well. Storing and generating menus cost memory and time overhead. Once familiar with a program, operators may find that layers of menus impede progress more than they help.

For all that, the menu-driven program is a good vehicle for our discussion of sequence control because most people are familiar with it. Many of the design principles I will discuss in relation to it can be extended to other types of dialogues as well.

Your menu-driven program should be self-explanatory. The operator should not have to refer constantly to a manual to figure out how to make something happen. Obviously, you cannot explain everything within the program, but you should provide screens that describe special sequence-control features. For example, suppose that your program has several subprograms, each containing sub-subprograms, and so on, and that different program levels are accessed through layers of menus. Suppose further that you have designed certain sequence-control features to shortcut some menus so that the experienced operator can move quickly around to different parts of the program. Special features such as these should be explained within the program, either on separate screens which precede menus or, if the explanation is brief enough, on menus themselves.

Your program will function, of course, without built-in screen documentation. However, the operator will learn the intricacies of your program much more quickly if you do your explaining when and where he needs it—within the program itself.

If the operators using your program will vary in skill level, attempt to build in features that will accommodate skill growth. For example, let the operator select the level of prompting—full, partial, or none. This will help the inexperienced operator gain skill and confidence and [will] save the experienced operator a lot of time. Make the choice of the prompting-level convenient, as shown in Figure 6.

Your program may have one menu or several, depending on complexity. If it is a complex program with many options, analyze

PROMPTING LEVEL SELECTION MENU

Please select desired level of prompting:

1. Full
2. Partial
3. None

Enter choice # __

FIGURE 6: Menu which allows the operator to choose the prompting level. Features like this accommodate operators who differ in skill.

how each subprogram will be used. Determine which subprograms are functionally related. Estimate how often each menu choice will be made. You may be able to make a very long menu into a number of short ones.

Functional relationships and *frequency of use* of the subprograms are the two most important criteria to consider in designing a menu. List functionally related subprograms on the same menu. If possible, list frequently called subprograms on the same menu. If these requirements conflict, let functional relationships rule menu design. Avoid designing very long menus that contain a grab-

bag of unrelated options. This only makes sense if all programs are equally likely to be called under all conditions. That is seldom the case.

Make menu choices brief, explicit, and distinct from one another. To make up the label, consider exactly what each subprogram does and then label it accordingly.

Use terminology consistently. For example, don't call subprograms that do essentially the same thing by different names in the same program—don't call a program "edit" in one place and "modify/delete" in another.

The menu itself has three essential parts: title, list of menu choices, and prompt line. Some menus also contain a statement that directs the operator to "select one of the menu choices." This feature is useful to operators unfamiliar with computers and can be considered optional.

Center the menu title at top of the display and put the word "menu" at the end of the title. If you are providing the (optional) directive line, print this next, offset to the left, so that it is recognized as an instruction and not a title. Center the prompt and the data-input field at the bottom of the screen. The prompt should be brief and explicit, for example, "ENTER CHOICE #", as shown in Figure 7.

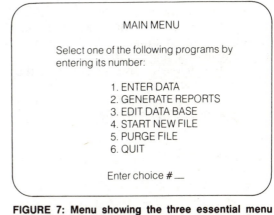

MAIN MENU

Select one of the following programs by entering its number:

1. ENTER DATA
2. GENERATE REPORTS
3. EDIT DATA BASE
4. START NEW FILE
5. PURGE FILE
6. QUIT

Enter choice # __

FIGURE 7: Menu showing the three essential menu parts: title, list of choices, and prompt line. Some menus also have a directive to prompt operators unfamiliar with the system.

Menu selection can be done in several different ways: by entering the number of a menu option, by entering a letter, by typing in the menu choice, and by moving a cursor to the choice. Typing in the menu choice label usually requires several keystrokes and should be avoided. Most microcomputer software is not set up to permit cursor selection of menu choices.

The most common selection method is to type in a number or letter. In general, short menus should permit selection by letter—preferably the first letter of the choice label. (This can present problems if different menu choices start with the same letter.) On longer menus, numbered menu choices are more convenient.

If you do use numbers, then any list of numbered items appearing on one of your display screens will resemble a menu. This may cause confusion. Minimize confusion by titling menus as menus and titling other displays appropriately. Avoid numbered items on nonmenu displays, if possible. If you are presenting a list of instructions, for example, precede each instruction by a bullet instead of a number.

Conclusion

This brief excursion into the world of human factors covered areas of interest to the average microcomputer programmer. Much more is written on the subject, and those interested should consult the references listed at the end of this article.

Note that application of human-factors considerations to software design is imma-ture as a technology and that much research still needs to be done. At present there is no single source to which the reader can refer to find all the important answers. (Martin's book is comprehensive but aimed primarily at the mainframe user.) Much of what is now available comes as technical reports that present recommendations cautiously labeled as "preliminary" or "tentative" findings.

In this article, I have attempted to congeal this somewhat indefinite material into a form that is useful to the average reader. Much has been left out because of inapplicability to microcomputers or because the material was of a specialized nature and would probably not be of interest. In general, what was presented is based on the references, although at some points I have condensed and simplified things. I hope that I have not distorted any author's intentions in the process.

REFERENCES

Anacapa Sciences Inc. "Fundamentals of Human Factors for Engineering and Design—Session 22: Human-Computer Interface Design" (classroom notes from seminar). Santa Barbara, Calif.: 1981.

Engel, S. E., and Granda, R. E. *Guidelines for Man/Display Interfaces,* Technical Report TR 00.2720. Poughkeepsie, N.Y.: IBM, Dec. 19, 1975.

Martin, J. *Design of Man–Computer Dialogues.* Englewood Cliffs, N.J.: Prentice-Hall, 1976.

Smith, S. L. *Man–Machine Interface: Requirements Definition and Design Guidelines—A Progress Report,* Project No. 572R. Bedford, Mass.: Mitre Corp., February 1981.

9 Designing Interactions Between Students and Computers

Jamesine Friend and
James D. Milojkovic

An educational computer program consists of a series of exercises in which the student interacts with the computer. The quality of the program is dependent on the content of the exercises, the order in which the exercises are given, and the nature of each interaction between the student and the computer. The first two of these (content and sequence) are the heart of the instructional design problem and are closely related to traditional curriculum design, while the third (interaction) is unique to computerized instruction and includes a number of programming as well as pedagogical considerations. This article focuses on this third consideration, presenting a number of guidelines for designing effective student–computer interactions.

Each exchange in an interactive educational program contains four fundamental parts:

1. The computer presents an exercise to the student.

2. The student responds.

3. The computer checks the student's response.

4. The computer provides feedback to the student.

Each of these components will be discussed in turn.

Presentation of the Exercise

Conciseness

The statement of exercises should be as short as possible while conveying all necessary information. Verbosity, while merely an annoyance to adults, is a real deterrent to young children who cannot read well. As a rule of thumb, there should ordinarily be no more than 100 words per exercise for adults and no more than 20 words for children in elementary school.

Reading Level

The reading level should be appropriate. Professional courseware designers often employ readability formulas to ensure that the reading level is correct. Another way to check reading levels is to field test the exercises with students, perhaps asking them to read exercises aloud and quizzing them on the meaning of what they have read. This kind of field testing can be done even before the program is completely operational.

Response Mode

It must be clear to students how they are to respond. Are they to type their answers, touch the screen with a light pen, or draw on a graphics tablet? (We once observed a third-grader answering orally, unable to understand why the computer didn't respond.) To avoid confusion, it is best to use the same

Jamesine Friend and James D. Milojkovic, "Designing Interactions Between Students and Computers," *Journal of Courseware Review*. Reprinted by permission of Jamesine Friend.

kind of responses throughout a program. If changing modes is really necessary, the instructions must be very clear, and such changes should be kept to a minimum.

Terminators

If responses are to be typed, it may be desirable to have the students signal the end of their answers by typing a "terminator" such as the ENTER key or the RETURN key. If all the responses are to be single letters (as with multiple-choice exercises), it is not necessary to impose a terminator, since it is more natural for the student to simply type the one letter. The use of a terminator should be consistent. The students should not use the space bar in one exercise and the ENTER key in the next. Consistency within a single program, however, is often not sufficient. If the student will use a number of programs coming from many sources, find out what terminator, if any, is most commonly required by those other programs before making a decision. When a terminator is required, students must ordinarily be given explicit instructions regarding its use. Some programs include this instruction within a set of general instructions at the beginning of the program; however, students may not remember this important instruction, especially if the initial directions contain a lot of information. While there is no need to repeat the terminator instructions with every exercise, it is advisable to include a reminder with the first few exercises.

Asking Questions

Questions must not mislead students into giving inappropriate responses. Do not, for example, ask a student "Do you know how to multiply 12 times 5?" If you expect him to type "60". Some young children will take the question quite literally and answer "Yes" to mean "Yes, I do know how to multiply those numbers." It is better to ask directly "How much is 12 times 5?" Often, if the question is phrased straightforwardly, the students will understand how to answer without explicit

instructions. For instance, almost everyone—including young children—would understand that they were to answer either yes or no to the question "Is Georgia one of the New England states?" There is no need to include the specific instruction "Type 'yes' or 'no' to answer this question." Some programs allow abbreviations of commonly used answers ("Y" for "yes," "T" for "true," and so on). If most of the exercises are yes/no or true/false questions, this can be quite a time saver, especially for children who cannot type well. However, if very few of the questions are of one of these standard forms, the time saved may be lost by the child who has to read and puzzle over an instruction like "Type 'Y' for 'yes' or 'N' for 'no.'"

Multiple-choice exercises, like simple yes/no questions, do not ordinarily need specific instructions, since all but the very youngest children are accustomed to this type of exercise. Indexed multiple-choice exercises are overused in educational programs, undoubtedly because the answers are easy to check. It is often the case, however, that little learning takes place with multiple-choice exercises in comparison with what can be gained from more freely constructed responses. Consider, for example, the following exercise:

Which of the following is the major export of Costa Rica?

1. Wheat
2. Automobiles
3. Coffee
4. Electric appliances

With only minimal knowledge of the economy and geography of Central America, a student could correctly guess that coffee is the most likely export. Contrast this with the more open-ended question:

What is the major export of Costa Rica?

Checking the student's answer for such open-ended questions is more of a programming problem—some aspects of which will be discussed below—but the extra programming effort can result in much greater learning gains.

There are two cases when multiple-choice exercises are clearly indicated. One of these is [found] when the question would require a longer response than an inexperienced typist could comfortably produce. The other is [found] when the nature of the task is a discrimination, as in the following exercise, which could not be rephrased to require a constructed response without basically altering the nature of the exercise.

Which is the greatest number?

A. 5.712

B. 23.1

C. 7.99

Screen Layout

Text. The layout of an exercise on the screen can often affect the ease with which a student can comprehend what is expected of him, as well as his attitude toward the program and the computer. The display should be pleasing aesthetically and should be arranged to make the student's task of determining how to solve the exercise as easy as possible. For greatest readability, text should be displayed in both upper- and lowercase letters, and should be double spaced. It should not be crowded at the top or at the left of the screen. It is essential that all words be spelled correctly, that sentences be grammatically correct, and that text be properly punctuated. (One would think this obvious except for the large number of violations in programs that the programmers apparently considered to be finished.)

Graphics. Graphics should be used sparingly, since good pictures are difficult to design and are usually time-consuming to display. Graphics should be used only if they convey some important information that is not included in the text. If graphics are used, the same information should not be repeated in the text; for instance, if the student is to determine whether there are more dogs or more cats in a picture shown at the top of the screen, there is no need to say "Here is a picture of some dogs and some cats." The "readability" of graphics should be field tested to ensure that the students can tell what they are supposed to represent. Again, this field testing can (and should) be done before the program is completed. Select perhaps a dozen of the least able of the students for whom the program is designed, show them the graphics, and ask them to identify the object or action pictured. If any of the students cannot name the object or hesitate unduly, the graphic should be redesigned or discarded.

The Student Response

As mentioned above, the student response may be of several kinds: via the keyboard, by use of a light pen, by means of a graphics tablet, or even by use of a voice recognition device. Typed responses are by far the most common, and we restrict our discussion to them.

Standard Input Routines

Usually, a system subroutine is used for typed input. These routines are a great convenience for the programmer, since they ordinarily take care of a number of details automatically. For example, they will display a cursor in the position the student's answer will appear. As the student types, each character appears in place of the cursor and the cursor moves to the right. The student may erase by using a DELETE or BACKSPACE or back arrow key, and the erasure is performed immediately. Most of these system subroutines require the use of some fixed terminator such as ENTER although some allow any of several terminators (RETURN and ESC, for example).

For some kinds of exercise the standard keyboard input routines are not applicable. For example, the programmer may sometimes want the student to type characters from right to left, as in the following arithmetic exercise.

$$\begin{array}{r} 456 \\ -\ 108 \end{array}$$

In order to allow the student to work from right to left, the programmer must handle the input character by character, rather than using standard system subroutines for keyboard input.

Echoing

Whenever the programmer is coding the input routine instead of using built-in subroutines, he must consider whether to "echo" the characters the student types, that is, [whether to] display the typed character on the screen. In some programs, it may not be desirable to echo the character typed. For instance, if certain keys are to be used to move a picture or the cursor around the screen, the character itself should not be shown, since the effect of typing the character will be immediately obvious to the student because of the movement of the graphic on the video screen. In some programs, only certain characters are echoed; for instance, in an exercise that requires a numeric response, the programmer may "disable" the letter keys and keys for other symbols by not displaying them on the screen if they are typed. The assumption is that these keys would be typed only by accident. One disadvantage of this is that the student may not have made a simple typographical error but may have typed the key on purpose; for instance, some experienced typists will type the letter "l" for the number "1" and will not understand why [a "1"] is not displayed.

The Cursor

If characters are not to be echoed, the programmer will probably not show a cursor on the screen. If characters are to be echoed, it is usual to display a cursor that will show the

student where his response will appear. However, if the position is obvious, as in an exercise that requires the student to fill in a missing word in a sentence, a cursor may not be needed. With some computers, the programmer can control the characteristics of the cursor. Cursors may be any shape and may or may not blink. A blinking underline is commonly used, but for elementary school children a small (empty) box may be more understandable, since they are accustomed to filling in boxes.

Erasures

Another consideration when programming character-by-character input is whether to allow for erasures. If erasures are allowed (by means of a DELETE or BACKSPACE key), the erasure may be character by character, in reverse order, or there may be an erasure of the entire response. For young children who are typing only one or two letters, it is less confusing for them if the entire response is erased, but for older students who are typing longer responses, character-by-character erasures are best. In either case, the erasure should be shown by actually erasing the characters from the screen and moving the cursor (if one is used) back.

Timing Responses

Many programs set a time limit for student responses. There are both advantages and disadvantages to time limits so they should be used with some care. Unless the time allowed is appropriate for the individual student, it can cause great frustration. One alternative to imposing a time limit is simply to record the time taken and use that number in future decisions about how much more practice the student needs for mastery of the topic. Time limits are generally appropriate only when the material being presented must be learned to a very high level of skill, or when an artificial means of enhancing the interest of the program is desired. If a high skill level is the objective, then elapsed time should be measured to the first character the student types instead of the last character. The reason for this is that the time a student takes to complete a response is composed of two segments. The first segment is taken up with the mental processing the student does to arrive at the answer, and the second segment is the time needed to find and type the right keys. For skills such as memorizing the multiplication table, it is the mental processing time that is important, not the student's ability to type the answer. This mental processing time can best be estimated by measuring the time up to the point at which the first character is typed.

Checking the Student Response

Response Classification

The usual purpose of checking a student response is to determine whether or not it is correct. (In some cases, the concept of correct/incorrect is not appropriate, as when the program asks a student whether he wants more specific instructions; in those cases, the purpose of checking the student response is to determine the student's preference rather than whether the response was "correct.") One simple procedure that is used in many programs is to compare the student's response to a precoded correct answer and to classify the response as correct if it is an exact match and incorrect otherwise. In general, this is poor educational programming since it can never be certain that a mismatch is really incorrect. For one thing, the student may have the correct answer in principle but have entered it in an inappropriate form; for example, in a multiple-choice exercise (like the Costa Rica example above), if the program is expecting an answer "3" and the student types "coffee", he will be told his answer is incorrect. It would be better in cases like this to classify student responses as:

1. Correct (an exact match with the precoded correct answer, 3)

2. Incorrect (any of the numbers 1, 2, or 4)

3. Unrecognizable (any other response)

The student who types an unrecognizable response could then be given a message such as:

You must answer by typing one of the numbers 1, 2, 3, or 4.

Please try again.

Even better for the above example (and with most multiple-choice exercises) would be to precode two correct answers, the literal answer (coffee) and the label of the correct choice (3). This is especially important when the literal answer is short, since the tendency to type the literal answer is greater when not much typing is involved.

Exercises that require numeric responses might use a classification scheme like this:

1. Correct (an exact match with the precoded numeric answer)

2. Incorrect (any other response that contains only digits and possibly a decimal point and plus or minus sign)

3. Unrecognizable (any response that contains characters that are not digits)

With a scheme like this, if a student struck the letter "t" when he intended to type the nearby number "6," he could simply be informed that his response was not a number and that he could try again.

Response Editing

The above solution would not work well, however, if the program were expecting an answer of "2780" and the student typed "2,780"—using a comma as the classroom teacher had taught. In this case, a more elaborate procedure is needed for recognizing a correctly formed number. Rules for this procedure include allowing commas (if correctly placed), allowing the letter "l" in place of the number "1," allowing the letter "O" in place of the number "0," and possibly allowing other characters such as decimal points, minus and plus signs, dollar signs, and percentage signs, provided they are properly placed. If the program is to be used by people accustomed to bookkeeping notation, negative numbers might also be allowed in forms like <3,400> or ($45,000.00). Although students will very rarely type number words ("twelve" for "12"), they may do so if some other exercises in the program require them to type such words; if this is the case, an elegant program would allow number words as correct answers.

An error that is sometimes made in programs is to make a distinction between upper- and lowercase characters when such a distinction is not educationally meaningful. For instance, a program that allows "YES" and "Y" as responses to a yes/no question should also allow "yes" and "Yes". An easy way to avoid problems with case is simply to convert all letters in both the student response and the precoded answers to uppercase (or lowercase) before comparing them.

Students occasionally type unexpected punctuation marks. For example, the following dialogue between one little girl and a computer was observed in a classroom in California.

COMPUTER: The crops were very dry. Every day the farmer looked at the sky and hoped for. . . .
  1. sunshine
  2. the moon
  3. rain

STUDENT: 3.

COMPUTER: Wrong. Try again.

STUDENT: 3.

COMPUTER: Wrong. The correct answer is 3.

From the student's point of view the computer was telling her that the answer she typed was wrong but was also the correct answer! A more common error of the same kind occurs when students put periods at the end of every

response because their classroom teachers have emphasized that all sentences must end with a punctuation mark. In exercises in which punctuation is not important to the meaning of the response, it is best to eliminate all such characters from the response before it is compared with the correct answer.

An even more mysterious treatment—from the student's point of view—occurs when the student inadvertently types a space before or after the response. If exact matching is done to determine a correct response, a response like "car " will not match "car" since one string of characters contains a space that the other does not. However, the display on the video screen usually looks just the same, so the student is unable to discern the difference between his response and the word the computer insists is the correct answer. Since the space bar is so easily struck by accident, this kind of error is not really as rare as one might expect. The rule to follow here is to never penalize a student for an error he cannot see. Before comparing the student response to the correct answer, all leading and trailing spaces should be removed as well as any other "invisible" characters that might inadvertently occur in the response.

Misspellings

When students are required to type words rather than just numbers or labels of choices given in multiple-choice exercises, a good program would allow reasonable misspellings as correct answers unless one purpose of the instruction was to improve spelling. Some comment might be made about the correct spelling, without penalizing the student by classifying the response as incorrect, for example:

COMPUTER: What is the capital of France?

STUDENT: Parris

COMPUTER: Correct. (Be careful! You misspelled Paris.)

A completely effective algorithm for processing answers that contain misspellings and typographical errors is quite complex, and beyond the scope of this article, but a few simple rules will make programs considerably more flexible.

1. The most common misspelling is the substitution of double consonants for single and vice versa. (Example: apealling)

2. Another common error is the substitution of one vowel for another. (Example: inadvertant)

3. Transposition of letters may be either misspellings or typographical errors. (Example: infromation, beleive)

4. Young children, especially, sometimes substitute phonetically equivalent consonant clusters. (Example: reseive, telefone)

Providing Feedback to the Student

Feedback vs. Reinforcement

After the student's response is classified, the program will usually inform the student about the result of this classification, telling him that his response was correct or that it was wrong, perhaps with some specific information about the way in which it was wrong. This kind of information is called "feedback." Although feedback is also commonly called "reinforcement," these two words are not entirely synonymous. "Feedback" means simply "information" and does not carry the connotation of psychological reinforcement (praise or censure). "Reinforcement" is also sometimes used in the sense of information, but also often carries the idea of reward or punishment. While informative feedback is a great aid to learning, especially when it is immediate in both space and time, the use of the computer as a device for meting out re-

wards and punishments is very questionable and is rarely used by the best instructional designers.

Extrinsic and Intrinsic Feedback

Informational feedback may be either extrinsic or intrinsic. As an example of the former, consider the case of a student response that is incorrectly formed or that contains typographical errors preventing the program from determining the intended meaning. A well-written program would provide explicit feedback in the form of message-containing specific instructions on the desired form of the answer:

You must type one of the letters A, B, C, or D.

or

Please type a number to answer this question.

Whereas extrinsic feedback is artificially mediated and thus external to the student, intrinsic feedback is a direct result of the student's actions. In consequence, intrinsic feedback is usually more effective than extrinsic feedback, and some of the best educational programs have such feedback built directly into the display. For example, consider a game of sea rescue where a lifeline has to be projected with a certain student-determined angle and force to a sailor adrift in a small boat. If the lifeline fails to reach the stranded sailor, then the graphics display will communicate this to the student instantly without the need for superfluous messages like "missed" or "try harder." Intrinsic feedback is more characteristic of simulation programs than of programs that provide instruction in the form of a directed dialog.

Feedback Messages

Feedback should be succinct and unambiguous. Neither graphics nor sound is advised as a means for communicating success or failure—unless it is part of a simulation program such as the sea rescue mentioned above. Graphics and sound are frequently distracting both to the student and to his neighbors, and take time that would be better spent in more directly educational activities.

"Correct" is ordinarily sufficient for correct responses. This may be varied by using words like "right" or "good," but excessively enthusiastic messages like "super" or "fantastic" are more often than not inappropriate. In fact, it is often not necessary to provide explicit feedback for correct answers. Some very good programs simply present the next exercise as soon as a student gives a correct response, and provide explicit feedback only for incorrect answers; students soon learn that the presentation of another exercise is a signal that their previous response was correct.

For incorrect responses, "incorrect" may be sufficient to convey the desired information especially for questions that have a small number of choices such as yes/no questions, multiple-choice exercises, and true/false questions. If there is a greater variety of possible answers, it is usually more educational to inform the student of the nature of the error. Many programs offer students a second chance to respond before giving detailed information about an error, and whenever there is a good possibility that the student made a simple error that he can correct without extra help, this is a good idea. However, more than two chances are rarely beneficial. If the student cannot answer correctly, even when given a second chance, he should be told the correct answer; for young children, an overt correction (that is, typing the correct answer after it is shown) should be required, since this will focus their attention on a cor-

rect answer that they might otherwise ignore in their eagerness to get on with the next task. However, if the correct answer is very long and the student is likely to be a poor typist, the program should not ask for an overt correction.

Self-reinforcement

For many students, the very act of producing an answer seems to generate a small but positive self-reinforcement, independent of the feedback from the program. Negative feedback needs to be more forceful than positive feedback simply to overcome this natural self-reinforcement. This greater elaboration should not, however, result in the negative feedback being more attractive or more interesting than the positive feedback. If the attempts of our student rescuer prove fruitless, the sailor's demise should not be depicted in a spectacular shark attack that holds greater fascination than the goal of lifesaving.

Conclusion

There are many component decisions and features that contribute to the educational value of an interactive educational program. We have attempted to present some of the more basic considerations in the design of the interactions between the student and the computer. Ultimately, the only way to gauge the quality of the program is to field test it with students. Observing their performance, testing them to find what they have learned, and listening to their comments and suggestions are essential activities for modifying and improving the program.

10 Implementation Techniques for Interactive Computer-Assisted Learning Programs

T. Balman

University of London

Introduction

Computer-assisted learning (CAL) includes a wide range of computer-based educational activities involving various techniques of programming. One possible approach to CAL entails the use of preprogrammed mathematical models of engineering problems. The engineering student can interact with the program and manipulate the parameters of the problem in order to investigate the relationship between the parameters and their effects on the response and performance of the model. This is the teaching strategy adopted by the Computer Assisted Teaching Unit (CATU) of Queen Mary College [1].

In this context, the student–computer interaction can be viewed as a "laboratory experiment" with the programmed model serving as the apparatus. In some cases, this service can be a substitute for expensive, dangerous, or time-consuming experiments which would be impossible to set up in a conventional laboratory; in others, the computer model can be used to consolidate lecture material by providing access to parameters relevant to the underlying physics of the processes being modeled.

To a great extent the educational value of the computer experiment will depend on the choice of the mathematical model, the parameters exposed to student manipulation, and the responses displayed to the student. However, these factors will only create a skeleton for the experiment. The programming techniques employed in the computer implementation will determine the impact of the program on the student. Unnecessary or elaborate interaction will waste valuable on-line time and hence diminish the educational benefits: too many choices may confuse the student. The display methods used in presenting the results can accentuate the important features of the model; repetitive or clumsy displays might obscure important features and distract student attention.

The operating system and hardware configuration hosting the computer experiments also affect their educational value. As the teaching of computer science is not the main objective, the experiment should be easy to set up, requiring minimal knowledge of computer operating procedures. There should be a rapid response time in order to sustain student interest, and the student should be able to dictate the pace of the experiment. The hosting system and the implementation must be reliable, and the student needs to have confidence in the validity of the model.

Design Characteristics

The initial design specification involves the selection of the model, the calculation methods to be used, the parameters to be manipulated by the student, and the output parameters to be displayed.

With most experiments the model will go through several adjustments during implementation in order to improve performance

T. Balman, "Implementation Techniques for Interactive CAL Programs," *Computers and Education,* 5 (1981), 19–29. Copyright © 1981 Pergamon Press, Ltd. Reprinted by permission of Pergamon Press, Inc. (New York) and the author. Figures and some text omitted.

and educational value. Further modifications might become desirable after observing student reactions to the experiment when it goes into service. If adequate measures are not taken during the implementation phase the extent of the required modifications can be prohibitively large, affecting the overall harmony of the model.

Another factor to consider in designing and implementing an experiment is its long-term prospect as an educational tool. Any normal selection of academics will have differing views about the way a model should be used in teaching. For this reason the implementation should be as general and uncontroversial as possible. Ideally, the teaching philosophy should be embodied in a "laboratory procedure sheet" which can be changed with relative ease to suit the needs of each individual academic.

However, it is difficult in practice to preserve complete generality. Quite often the student will find that some parameter values of a model have been selected for him. These might be computational constraints such as the maximum number of iterations, or data values reflecting the characteristics of a particular instance of the generalized model (a submodel). In some cases the student might be provided with a facility to select from a list of predefined submodels rather than being required to specify all the constituent values [2]. [. . .] Restrictions might be imposed on the acceptable ranges of values for input parameters than can be manipulated by the student.

All these cases are departures from generality and result in code that is potentially prone to modification both during and after implementation. Apart from academically controversial issues like the choice of submodel(s) and choice of parameters than can be manipulated, there can be more fundamental objections: for example it may be considered important to promote student familiarity with the characteristics of the submodels under investigation by forcing the input of *all* constituent parameters.

Although the restrictions placed on the generalized model inevitably become an in-

tegral part of the eventual program, it is possible to isolate them during implementation and to keep the mathematical model in its most general form. This gives the program a certain degree of flexibility and enables easy modeling of related subsystems. Experience has shown that there is rarely any doubt about the validity and educational value of the generalized mathematical model itself. However, the restrictions implemented inevitably go through several modifications before they can be finalized. It is advisable to keep the generalized mathematical model, which forms the core of the computer experiment, as insensitive as possible to modifications made to the parameters it uses.

The output parameters displayed to the student are also likely to experience adjustments during the development of a computer experiment. These modifications tend to be either improvements to the display methods or addition of new responses. The latter inevitably involves modifications to the way the mathematical model is implemented.

Operational Characteristics

A major characteristic of interactive CAL programs is that their educational value matters more than their computational accuracy. The qualitative behavior of a system is normally its most significant feature except when accuracy itself plays a critical role in the educational objective (e.g., in the comparison of two or more mathematical models).

An important factor is the speed of service. The terminal response time and time taken to produce results should be short. The former is dependent on the hosting system and its operational load, whereas the latter also depends on the characteristics of the model and its implementation.

A slow terminal response time reduces the immediacy of interaction and might result in student frustration. The time taken by the computer experiment to respond visibly to a user request should not be longer than 2 seconds [3]. This is not an ambitious figure since the ratio between [central processing unit] (CPU) time and elapsed time is small for interactive CAL. Because of time taken by students to observe and decide, on average about one third of the active experiments in a multiuser environment compete for the CPU with a maximum load of about two thirds.

The efficiency of implementation of the calculations is important since it affects the rate at which results are produced. As noted earlier, one of the fundamental criteria in implementing interactive CAL is the speed of service. Paradoxically, during lengthy calculations it is better to sacrifice efficiency in order to give a visual indication of the progress of computation. To sustain student interest and confidence the apparently "dead" terminal should be avoided by producing evidence of activity at periodic intervals. Although this type of output slows calculation, the student is prepared to wait a little longer provided he is certain that the computer experiment is active and he can predict how long he has to wait.

It is good policy to set a maximum limit on the length of time allowed to elapse before visual information is given to the student about the progress of the requested computation. This limit is critical since it affects both the speed of effective service and the student interest. Ideally, the period of apparent inactivity should not be longer than the terminal response time.

Although the experiment and the operating environment must provide a fast service, the student should not be harassed into making hasty decisions. The experiment should be paced so that at critical points the rate of progress can be controlled by the user. The only control the student can have over the computer program is through input—either when a new action is being requested or a new parameter value is being entered. As the decision points correspond with these input requests the student can work at his own pace providing the system does not interfere with impatient reminders such as "WAITING". The observations affecting the decisions are usually made when results are being displayed by the program; one way of al-

lowing time for the student to study the results is by handing over control through a dummy input request like "PRESS RETURN TO CONTINUE". The user can thus determine exactly when the experiment should proceed to the next stage.

Medium of Interaction

The computer terminals used during an experiment affect its educational value as the type of display will be limited by the capability of the device. Apart from the desirability of a high rate of output, the ability to display results in graphical form is of immense advantage in most engineering experiments.

The major disadvantages of electromechanical devices is their slowness and lack of sufficient definition for plotting graphs. The [cathode ray terminals] (CRTs) offer a higher rate of throughput. Alphanumeric displays on [video display unit] devices are inadequate as the definition is scarcely better than the ordinary teletype. Although better definition can be achieved on graphics terminals with about one screen point per millimeter, quite often this proves to be insufficient for interactive CAL experiments in engineering. The graphics display terminal with about five screen points per millimeter provides a fast and flexible medium of output for graphs, explanatory diagrams, tables, and textual information [. . .]. However, information displayed on a CRT device is transient and the student is unable to obtain a permanent record of the results for future reference unless a screen-to-paper copier is available and its use can be afforded.

Possibly, the best way to achieve a balance is to provide a facility for transcribing graphical information to a printing device upon student request. This usually involves the dumping of the coordinates used for the plot on to paper. The printing device can be fast and shared (above 1200 baud) or slow and dedicated. The former is better especially when coupled with a print-spooling system where output is buffered on to a disk and student activity is not held up during the printing.

Program Structure

Interactive CAL programs should provide an environment which promotes a conversational investigation of the system being modeled. Unlike the single-shot execution possible with batch CAL, the program should be flexible and make provision for a larger variety of student influence.

The basic structure of most interactive programs can be seen as a continuous loop with the input parameter modification, calculation, and result output modules forming the nodes [. . .]. This basic structure is typically extended by a variety of options embedded in each of the three modules. For example, an alteration made to a single input parameter should not necessitate the respecification of all other parameters; there might be a number of different output parameters that can be investigated with different calculation methods; the student should be able to choose the mode and medium of the results displayed. Typical interaction facilities provided in an interactive CAL program could be the selection of:

Input parameters to be altered

Display of the current input parameters

A submodel by name

Output parameter(s) to be investigated

Mode and method of calculation (single value or range of values)

The value or range of values to be used in calculations

Output parameter to display

Medium of display (on paper or screen)

Retention of results for future comparative display

Dropping of retained results

Comparative display of results

These facilities are effectively switches within the implementation which activate a relevant segment of code, and can be embodied in a hierarchical structure. [. . .] The program structure can reflect the hierarchical structure of the options provided. This promotes modularity of implementation where the code dealing with each specific facility is written as a subroutine. A modular design aids the testing and debugging of programs and gives flexibility to the implementation by localizing, and therefore to a large extent, aiding future program modifications. [. . .]

Interacting with the Student

[. . .] The student may be presented with a large variety of options to manipulate the model. More flexibility necessitates the introduction of new paths of control and therefore more options. As the number of options available to the student increases, the method of interaction becomes more important. There are normally two alternative approaches to this problem in the context of CAL dealing with the modeling of systems. Upon an invitation from the program either the student could select the desired path by specifying an alphanumeric command string, or a numbered list of options may be presented and the student invited to choose a path by typing in the number that corresponds to it.

The first method avoids the repetitive display of text but it necessitates either the learning of the commands or frequent references to a command dictionary. As the number of available options increases, valuable time will be wasted while the student tries to cope with the command vocabulary rather than the educational material the experiment embodies. A minor problem associated with this approach is that it necessitates familiarity with the keyboard. If the student does not have any previous experience, the speed of progress will be limited by his typing ability and this will lead to frustration. A similar problem arises if the commands are entered in free-form plain language and the program recognizes certain keywords in the input text. Although the learning of commands requires much less effort there is a danger that the student may misjudge the extent of the program's capabilities. The use of this approach in the modeling of systems for CAL rarely justifies the programming effort involved.

The option-list method is less elaborate and offers a good solution to most of these problems. Numbers are easier to type, and at all stages the student is presented with the repertoire of facilities that are relevant at that juncture. [. . .] It is easier to check the validity of student requests and recognize the option chosen. However, this method is feasible only if the medium of display for the option lists is a fast device. The option sets will get repetitively displayed whenever they become effective and on a slow teletype the speed of student progress will be seriously affected. The damage arising from this is potentially more serious than the problems caused by the command-language approach.

Program Reliability

Reliability involves both the credibility of the results and the durability of the program and its integrity throughout the experiment. The former is dependent on the inherent characteristics of the mathematical model and the accuracy of implementation. To have any educational value, a program's credibility has to be established for both the teacher involved and the students. This can be ascertained through trial runs and, if needed, traditional debugging techniques. In order to preserve program integrity, the program must be crashproof.

Program crashes have more serious consequences in an interactive CAL environment where an interrupted experiment causes a block in the learning process. In some cases the experience gained will allow rapid recovery of the precrash status when the experiment restarts; in others most of the preliminary work might have to be repeated. Apart from the inconvenience, this will result in the loss of valuable time and have a negative effect on the student's confidence and interest.

Program crashes, assuming a correct implementation of the model, are caused either by faulty input or [by] abnormal conditions in the host computer system. The former is of more interest as it can be detected within the program.

An implementation is sensitive to erroneous data in two different ways. First, a program crash might occur if there is an input conversion error due to a mistyped line of input. The principal cause of this is the student's inability to fully appreciate the rigid way in which most programming languages analyze their input. A solution is to bypass the standard input facilities available in the implementation language and instead to program an analysis of free-format input. Any illegal characters appearing in the input buffer can then be dealt with, and a gentle error message sent to the user with a request for another try.

The second way in which erroneous data affects program integrity is usually caused by the student's failure to realize the limitations of the mathematical model and its implementation. Unreasonable data might render the model invalid and cause misleading results. Certain parameter values or combinations of values might make a program crash due to an illegal computation. In most cases meaningful ranges of values can be defined for input parameters and the student input restricted accordingly, with error messages for unacceptable values. However, in some cases, checking combinations of values might require an expensive algorithm and it might not be feasible to detect the errors during input. In others, the error condition might become apparent only during the calculations (e.g., convergence problems). The solution to this is the insertion of tests in the calculation modules so that computation can be terminated whenever an illegal operation is imminent. At the expense of computational efficiency, a program crash can be avoided and explanatory error messages given to the student under program control.

Calculation and Display

Normally, in a computer experiment, the student will have to request a series of trial calculations which will eventually lead him to a desired goal and thereby increase his understanding of the system modeled. In most cases a graph of the system's response is essential and the student can be program assisted in three ways.

First, the student can be provided with the minimal facility to observe the response for a spot value. By careful selection of the input values the student can obtain a collection of coordinates to plot a graph of the response.

Second, the program may calculate the requested response over a range of values. This involves the repetition of the same computation, without intermediate student action, for a series of equally spaced spot values lying within the specified range. The student can thus obtain a list of coordinates and plot the graph.

The third possibility is the program generation of a graph of the system response over a specified range.

The manual work involved in the first two approaches encourages the development of an expertise which is essential to any student dealing with graphs. However, this is not a significant contribution toward a better understanding of the important issues in the system under investigation. On the contrary, since the graph obtained at each stage serves to guide the student toward a new computation, excessive manual work during the computer experiment will delay progress. Program-generated plots of the graphs promote learning at the terminal by removing the routine work and facilitating a faster feedback to the student. Freed from the overhead of trial calculations, the student will feel more en-

couraged to learn by experimenting. One should however be wary of promoting mindless manipulation by making graphics too easily available.

Graph plotting can be performed in two ways. If the range of the axes can be correctly predicted prior to the commencement of the calculations, the graph can be advanced each time a new pair of coordinates is obtained. However, inaccurate prediction of the range will result in either the inefficient use of the plotting space or the loss of coordinates that fall outside the range of the axes. An alternative method is to delay the graphical output until all the coordinates are calculated and the range of axes accurately determined. This approach also has some drawbacks. It necessitates more program space to store the coordinates and there is a longer period of inactivity at the terminal during the calculations.

In most cases, despite the feasibility of determining the range of axes, it is advantageous to store the coordinates prior to display. This gives flexibility to the choice of the medium of display (e.g., a listing of the coordinates for future reference) without the need for recalculation. The scaling of the axes could be readjusted according to student requests, thus facilitating a more detailed study of selected portions of the graph; it might be possible to derive an associated output parameter from the stored coordinates.

A compromise method exists for calculations where the range of axes can be confidently predicted. The coordinates can be stored and plotted as soon as they are calculated. The idle terminal time is thus eliminated and at the same time the benefits deriving from stored coordinate values utilized. Even if the range of axes are inaccurately predicted and the graph produced during the calculations is unsatisfactory, the graph can be reconstructed once the full set of coordinates is available.

Retention of Results for Multiple Display

A useful extension to automatic graphical output is the ability to superimpose several graphs to facilitate a comparative study of responses to different submodels. In some cases the discovery of the relative properties of the responses is essential to guide the student in his investigation of the model; in others the student will gain a better understanding of the model by observing its sensitivity to adjustments made to certain parameters.

The multiple display facility is the superimposition of several graphs on the same set of axes. [. . .] Markers can be superimposed on each graph and a key table of markers displayed for identification. There is sometimes a problem of making available detailed data pertaining to each set, especially where there are more than two items in the multiple display. A solution is the program generation of an internal reference number for the identification of each retained graph. Result retention may be achieved by the storing of all the constituent coordinates of a response upon student request. Whenever required, the aggregate range of axes for the multiple plot can be determined, and the selected responses displayed. This approach can sometimes be very expensive with respect to memory requirements. As a consequence there has to be a limit on the number of results that can be simultaneously referenced. A reasonable solution is to allow the student a chance to drop the results which he feels are no longer important, thus freeing storage space for the retention of others.

An alternative method of result retention is the storage of only the properties of the results instead of the actual coordinates. This would include the values of all the input parameters together with the range of axes used in the eventual plot. The coordinates can then be recalculated whenever there is a request for a multiple display. This is obviously going to be time-consuming for lengthy calculations and the saving in core space might not represent an adequate justification. However, as the range of axes can be readily determined prior to the calculations, the graphs can be plotted during coordinate generation and the terminal will not remain idle.

Another alternative is the use of secondary memory for the storage of both the range of axes and the actual coordinates. The aggregate range of axes can be determined and the graphs plotted by using a direct transfer from the file to the plotting device. This minimizes core space requirements at the expense of a small loss in speed.

Concluding Remarks

Some of the factors affecting the educational impact of interactive CAL have been described. Most of the ideas outlined here have evolved over a period of 12 years at the CATU where about forty different computer experiments are currently offered to students in the Faculty of Engineering. [. . .]

Over the years, the CATU laboratory and the techniques used for interactive CAL experiments have developed with a number of design objectives. These were:

Requiring minimal computing ability of the student

Shielding the student from implementation-dependent error messages

Protecting the integrity of the experiment

Providing easy interaction and promoting an investigatory approach

Making best use of the terminal devices available

Providing a fast service

Avoiding long silent periods during computational activity

Providing easy and fast access to all the experiments

Keeping the implementation in its most general form

REFERENCES

1. Smith, P. R., Computers in Engineering Education in the United Kingdom. *Comput. Educ.* 1 (1976).

2. Smith, P. R., A CAL Package in reactor kinetics. *J. Inst. Nuc. Eng.* 17, 147 (1976).

3. Balman, T., and Smith, P. R., Organisation of a computer assisted teaching laboratory. *Proc. DECUS.* London (1977).

11 Advisement and Management Strategies as Design Variables in Computer-Assisted Instruction

Robert D. Tennyson

University of Minnesota

Thomas Buttrey

Eisenhower Senior High School
Hopkins, Minnesota

Abstract

Some studies of computer-assisted instruction have shown that when students control the amount of instruction they receive, they often terminate too early and fail to learn what they should. While sophisticated adaptive systems may eliminate the problem of premature termination of study, they neglect the important goal of learner responsibility.

These researchers were interested in whether giving learners information about their achievement in relation to the criterion during instruction would improve learning in both learner-controlled and program-controlled systems. Success was measured in terms of posttest scores, time on task, and number of instructional examples required during instruction.

Control of the amount and sequence of instructional stimuli has been a recurring problem in the design of computer-assisted learning environments. Designs have ranged from those in which the learner plays a direct role in decision making to more highly sophisticated adaptive systems (Tennyson and Rothen, 1979). The adaptive systems include

Robert D. Tennyson and Thomas Buttrey, "Advisement and Management Strategies as Design Variables in Computer-Assisted Instruction," *Educational Communication and Technology Journal,* 28 (Fall 1980), 169–176. Reprinted by permission of the Association for Educational Communications and Technology.

processes for assessing both the student's skills (for example, general aptitudes, prior achievement, and on-task learning progress) and the characteristics of the learning task (difficulty level, content structure, and conceptual attributes) so that an initial instructional program can be adjusted continuously to meet on-task student learning needs. Instructional research (DiVesta, 1975) and applied projects (Steinberg, 1977) dealing with variables of learner control (using rather large or complex learning tasks) have failed to demonstrate that students can make and carry out decisions related to content elements and personal assessment. Therefore, it appears that program-controlled management systems are necessary for effective computer-assisted instruction.

Given poor student performance with learner-controlled systems consisting of a complex content structure and demanding greater prerequisite knowledge, Tennyson and associates designed (Rothen and Tennyson, 1978) and tested (Park and Tennyson, 1980; Tennyson and Rothen, 1977; Tennyson, Tennyson, and Rothen, 1980) the Minnesota Adaptive Instructional System (MAIS). The MAIS uses a Bayesian statistical method to integrate (a) assignment of a specific treatment based on a premeasure of cognitive ability, (b) an initial amount of instructional support based on a pretest measure of prior achievement, and (c) an adjusted amount of instructional support and sequence based on on-task learning need. Our first purpose in this study was to test the MAIS against a learner-control strategy (one in which the student decides when to terminate instruction and begin the posttest). On the basis of Tennyson and Rothen's (1977) finding that the MAIS management strategy was significantly more effective than a nonadaptive management strategy, we hypothesized that adaptive control would be more effective than learner control in helping students learn concept tasks.

While adaptive control systems do make use of modern computing power (Johansen and Tennyson, in press), they do not take into consideration the educational goal of in-

dividual responsibility for learning and consequent intellectual development. To address this goal, instructional program strategies have attempted to provide students with post hoc advice about possible remedial instruction.[1] We propose, however, that if students are given meaningful information (advisement) about their own learning development while they are performing the task, their own cognitive strategy may further refine the diagnosis and prescription made by an adaptive management system. Thus, advisement as used in this study is a form of information that consists of diagnostic and prescriptive data generated from the MAIS management control system and given to students during the learning process. Operationally, advisement implies several things. First, at the start of their instruction, students are advised of (a) their initial level of knowledge compared with the desired learning criterion (diagnosis) and (b) the amount and sequence of instruction necessary for them to obtain the objective (prescription). Second, students are continuously advised while performing the task of their learning development (updated diagnosis) and the instructional needs (updated prescription) necessary for task mastery.

For the independent variable of advisement, we hypothesized that students would perform better when they received advisement than they would when they were instructed via a conventional computer-assisted instructional program that lacked advisement. We further hypothesized that a learner-control strategy with advisement would not only be as effective in student acquisition of the learning task as the adaptive control strategy (that is, students in both these strategy conditions would surpass the criterion of mastery), but also that it would be more efficient in terms of student on-task learning time. An additional hypothesis was that the interaction of learner control with advisement would be the best treatment (of the four treatment conditions resulting from the two independent variables) in terms of both performance and time on task, whereas the learner-control-without-advisement condition would be the least effective (that is, students would not reach mastery).

Method

Subjects

Participants ($N = 139$) were twelfth grade male and female students from psychology classes at Eisenhower Senior High School in Hopkins, Minnesota. Students were assigned randomly to one of four treatment conditions as they appeared for the experiment. They understood that they would be given credit for participation and that their teacher would grade their posttests. This contingency was included to stimulate an actual classroom-related incentive missing from most learner-control studies. Without such a contingency, as Felixbrod and O'Leary (1974) have shown, students in learner-control situations tend to terminate early and thus learn less. A strong incentive to master the material—in this instance, a course grade—provides a better comparison between a program-control condition, which relies on a relatively captive audience, and a learner-control condition.

Learning Program

Coordinate concepts selected for this study—positive reinforcement, negative reinforcement, positive punishment, and negative punishment—were drawn from the field of psychology[2] and developed by Tennyson, Tennyson, and Rothen (1980). Three subordinate concepts—stimulus, aversive stimulus, and attractive stimulus—were included, in addition to a superordinate concept that dealt with the consequences of behavior resulting from the stimulus. Examples used in the learning program and accompanying tests were written according to the concept-design strategy developed by Merrill and Tennyson (1977). Of eighty-eight examples

in the learning program, forty were used in the instructional lessons (10 per concept), twenty-four in the pretest, and twenty-four in the posttest.

Using Tennyson's (1980) revision of Merrill and Tennyson's (1977) procedures for designing concept-learning lessons, the experimental learning program was developed. First, a printed booklet presented the instructional directions and the concept definitions with one best example per concept. The directions explained that the purpose of the definitions was to help the student understand the critical attributes of each concept, whereas the best examples were to be used during the instructional presentation to compare and contrast with the instructional examples. Second, a computerized instructional program presented the examples in two presentation forms—expository and inquisitory (Tennyson, Chao, and Youngers, in press). In the expository presentation form, one example of each concept was displayed and students were directed to study how each of these examples differed from the best examples. After studying the four expository examples, students received their remaining examples in the inquisitory presentation form. Directions for the inquisitory presentation form instructed students to use the best examples when determining the correct classification of each example. (This procedure helps a student learn to use the prototype in developing the intellectual skills of generalization and discrimination.) After each response, students were informed whether their answer was correct or incorrect. Students in the two advisement groups also received an update on the number of examples still needed for mastery.

To validate the learning program we used a formative evaluation procedure for assessing instructional materials (Tennyson, 1978). Several subject matter experts first reviewed the definitions and instances. Then, after appropriate revisions of the definitions and instances, a one-to-one tryout of each learning program was conducted with six students randomly selected from the sample population. This was followed by simulation tryouts of each treatment condition (six students per treatment). Final refinements on the learning program and computer software were made from this tryout.

Minnesota Adaptive Instructional System

To study the management strategy variable, we used for the adaptive control strategy the computer-based Minnesota Adaptive Instructional System developed by Rothen and Tennyson (1978). This computer-management system determines the number of examples each student receives from three parameter values: achievement level, a mastery criterion (.7), and loss ratio (1.5), defined as the disutilities associated with a false advance compared with a false retain decision. The estimate of the student's ability to learn a concept was characterized in terms of probabilities. From the initial achievement level, which was determined by the pretest score and the other two parameter values, the probability was used to decide the initial number of examples per concept the student needed. This probability figure was adjusted according to the student's on-task performance level; then the prescribed number of examples was modified. Student performance on each concept was calculated separately, with a criterion level set at 1.0 on the initial assessment. That is, if the student answered all six examples of any concept correctly on the pretest or during the initial part of the learning program, he or she received no more examples of that concept unless it was needed for discriminating coordinate concepts. (For a complete review of this response-sensitive procedure, see Tennyson and Park, 1980, or Park and Tennyson, 1980.) If a student failed to achieve total mastery on the initial assessment, the criterion level was adjusted to suggest a prior distribution slightly greater than .5 to the region above the criterion level: $P = (\pi \geq \pi_o / x, n) > .5$, where π_o is the objective's criterion level, π is the student's true achievement level, n is test length, and x is the student's score (Tennyson and Rothen, 1979).

Treatment Programs

The two independent variables of management strategy (adaptive control and learner control) and advisement (with and without) were tested with a pretest–posttest, two-way factorial design that involved four treatment groups. In the adaptive control strategy, the number of instances presented to each student was based on the student's pretask and on-task performance in relationship to the learning objective, and the sequence of instances was determined according to the student's response pattern to the given example. Following the pretest, students in the adaptive control condition were given program directions and informed that they would receive a posttest at the conclusion of the instruction. In the learner-control strategy, the students themselves decided whether to continue receiving examples (and if so, which concept they wanted to see next) or to go to the posttest. Students were informed in the program directions that they had complete control of the amount and sequence of instruction.

For the second independent variable, advisement, the two conditions (with and without advisement) were designed operationally as follows: in the advisement condition for adaptive control, students were informed, following the pretest and after each response, of the number of examples needed to reach mastery (diagnosis and prescription information determined by the MAIS). Program directions for the adaptive control strategy informed students that advisement was determined according to their individual learning development in relation to mastering the concepts; in the learner-control strategy, they were told that it would aid them in deciding the amount and sequence of instruction. The adaptive control condition without advisement did not provide students with information on their learning progress; nor did the learner-control condition without advisement provide students with diagnostic help. Four computer-based instructional treatment programs were developed from these four conditions.

Program 1. Students had control over the amount and sequence of instruction. Advisement was given following the pretest and updated after each response (Group 1: learner control with advisement).

Program 2. Control of the amount and sequence of instruction was determined by the computer-based management program. Students were advised of their learning progress at the completion of the pretest and after each response (Group 2: adaptive control with advisement).

Program 3. Students selected the amount and sequence of instruction but without advisement on their learning needs (Group 3: learner control without advisement).

Program 4. The amount and sequence of instruction were controlled by the computer-based management program and no advisement was given students (Group 4: adaptive control without advisement).

Facilities

The experiment was conducted in a small room in the math–science resource center at Eisenhower Senior High School. Two ADDS 780 cathode ray teletype computer terminals were used for the study. Each terminal, operating at 30 characters per second, was connected on-line by telephone to a Control Data 6400 computer at the University of Minnesota.

Procedure

As students reported for the experiment, each was assigned to a treatment program. The experimenter turned on the terminal and entered each student's treatment program number. After receiving direction on operating the terminal, students were first administered a twenty-four-item pretest. Then they received a print copy of the four

concept definitions and prototype examples from the experimenter and were instructed to refer to these definitions and prototype examples during the learning program. After studying the definitions and examples, students raised their hands to indicate readiness to study the examples in the learning program.

The experimenter entered the appropriate command on the terminal for students to begin the learning program. After a student classified an example in the learning program he or she received feedback on whether the classification was correct or incorrect. When each student finished the program, the experimenter took the definition and best example sheet and entered the appropriate command on the terminal for the posttest to begin. All student entries were single-letter alphanumeric responses to multiple-choice questions. The tests and learning program required no other entries by the student. After the students had finished, the experimenter thanked them and they left the experiment room. Others were then signed on to the terminal.

Results

The data analysis consisted of a multivariate analysis with univariate tests on each dependent variable followed by mean comparison tests (Student–Newman–Keuls). Dependent variables included the correct score on the posttest, learning program time (the measured time period in which students interacted with the learning task, excluding pretest or posttest times), and the number of learning program examples. The tests for homogeneity of regression of within-class and between-class linearity were nonsignificant ($p > .05$).

For the multivariate test, we used as dependent variables posttest score and time on task. The main effect of management strategy was significant, $U(1, \frac{1}{2}, 137) = .24, p < .001$. The test on the second main effect, advisement, was likewise significant, $U(1, \frac{1}{2}, 137)$

= .95, $p < .05$. The interaction test between the two independent variables was nonsignificant ($p > .05$). Following are the univariate test results on each of the dependent variables.

Posttest Correct Score

The analysis of variance on the posttest correct score (Table 1) showed a difference between the two management strategies, $F(1, 135) = 24.07$, $p < .001$. Students in the learner-control condition ($M = 16.9$, 70 percent correct) had a posttest score 4 points lower than students in the adaptive-control condition ($M = 21.1$, 88 percent correct). For the main effect of advisement, the F test was significant, $F(1, 135) = 16.54$, $p < .001$, with the group receiving advisement ($M = 20.8$, 86 percent correct) having scores more than 3 points higher than groups receiving no advisement ($M = 17.3$, 72 percent correct). The Student–Newman–Keuls multiple range test was used to compare posttest correct mean score differences between the four groups. At the .01 level, Group 3 (learner control without advisement) had the lowest posttest score, while the other three groups were equal. All groups achieved mastery except this one.

Criterion for mastery was set at .7 on the posttest. Group 1 (learner control with advisement), Group 2 (adaptive control with advisement), and Group 4 (adaptive control without advisement) achieved mastery at the .82, .90, and .86 levels—12 to 20 percent above criterion. Group 3 did not reach criterion, falling short by 13 percent (.57).

Time on Task

Average time spent on the pretest was 7.6 minutes; time spent on the posttest averaged 9.3 minutes. No significant differences appeared between groups in the pretest and posttest times ($p > .05$). The univariate test on the main effect for management strategy was significant, $F(1, 135) = 89.18$, $p < .001$. Students in the two learner-control groups spent 6 minutes ($M = 10.0$ minutes) less on task than those in the adaptive-control groups ($M = 16.1$ minutes) (Table 2). For the main effect of advisement, the F test likewise was significant, $F(1, 135) = 8.76$, $p < .05$, with the two groups receiving advisement spending 2.3 minutes more on task ($M = 14.3$ minutes) than the groups not receiving advisement ($M = 12.0$ minutes). A comparison of mean time differences for the four groups by the Student–Newman–Keuls multiple range test showed that Group 3 spent significantly less time ($p < .01$) than Group 1. By the same token, Group 1 spent less time ($p < .01$) than Group 2 or Group 4, which spent the same amount of time ($p > .05$).

TABLE 1: Mean Scores on Posttest[a]

Advisement Condition	Management Strategy	
	Learner Control	Adaptive Control
With Advisement	Group 1	Group 2
M	19.9	21.6
SD	3.3	3.2
Without Advisement	Group 3	Group 4
M	13.9	20.6
SD	3.3	3.7

[a] Maximum posttest score = 24.

TABLE 2: Mean Time on Task and Number of Examples

	Management Strategy			
	Learner Control		Adaptive Control	
Advisement Condition	Time (min)	Number of Examples	Time (min)	Number of Examples
With Advisement	Group 1		Group 2	
M	12.5	20.2	16.0	26.7
SD	5.5	9.0	4.4	5.6
Without Advisement	Group 3		Group 4	
M	7.7	10.1	16.2	27.3
SD	6.7	8.7	3.0	4.2

Number of Examples

The difference in learning time is directly related to the number of examples presented in the instruction. The analysis of variance test on number of examples for the management strategy main effect was significant, $F (1, 135) = 168.37, p < .001$, with the learner-control groups using a mean difference of 12 fewer instances ($M = 15.2$) than the adaptive groups ($M = 27.0$). For the main effect of advisement, $F (1, 135) = 35.18, p < .01$, the groups receiving advisement ($M = 23.5$) used an average mean of five more examples than the groups without it ($M = 18.7$). The Student–Newman–Keuls multiple range test showed that Group 3 studied the fewest number of examples ($p < .05$), Group 1 the next least number ($p < .05$), and Groups 2 and 4 ($p > .05$) more than Groups 1 and 3 ($p > .01$). In other words, while students in the learner-control-without-advisement condition used, on the average, only 25 percent of the possible examples, the learner-control-with-advisement condition used 51 percent. This was 17 percent fewer than the two adaptive control conditions (both at 68 percent).

Discussion

Research on learner-control variables has not produced instructional-design variables that are generic. That is, learner control seems to be a useful management format once the correct contingency is identified, but this seems to be successful only in highly limited and well defined occupational areas (Steinberg, 1977). Too often, contingencies associated with school-related learning, such as grades, praise, and rewards, vary in relationship to individual variables, such as sex, age, race, and home environment. This frequently results in variables and conditions too confusing for practical application or theoretical development. One purpose of this study was to introduce a variable to the basic computer-assisted learner-control management strategy unlike that of previous research variables. It dealt with actual on-task learning develop-

ment—advising students of both their learning progress (diagnosis) and their individual learning need (prescription) to help them master the learning objective. Students would thus have meaningful information on which to make judgments about the amount and sequence of instruction.

As operationally defined, the variable of advisement was highly significant in providing students in the learner-control condition with meaningful information with which to make appropriate decisions about acquisition of the coordinate concepts. On the posttest, students in the learner-control-with-advisement condition (Group 1) did as well as students in the two adaptive control conditions (Groups 2 and 4, each over 80 percent correct). The significance of this result is apparent in contrast to performance in the learner-control-without-advisement condition (Group 3), in which students responded to only 58 percent of the posttest items correctly (identical to the pretest). This outcome of the learner-control-without-advisement condition is consistent with previous research (Tennyson, 1980), which has shown that even with a strong contingency such as a grade, students learn little from instruction; furthermore, research has shown that no matter what level of on-task attainment is reached, all students leave instruction at approximately the same time (see Tennyson and Rothen, 1979).

The dependent variable of time is important to consider in the study of learner-control management strategies because students in a learner-control condition consistently leave instruction before mastering the objective (Tennyson, Tennyson, and Rothen, 1980). In contrast to this basic finding, students in the learner-control group that received advisement stayed on task long enough to obtain mastery. In fact, they were on task approximately 39 percent longer than the students in the conventional learner-control condition. It was our thesis that if students in a learner-control strategy were given advisement in the form of adaptive diagnostics and prescriptions, they would master the objective in less time and use less instruction than in a program-controlled adaptive system. The assumption was that the cognitive strategy students used in learning would further refine the adaptive information. The findings support this notion. The two conditions using the adaptive information (adaptive control and learner-adaptive control) had identical posttest-score means, but the learner-control-with-advisement condition showed significant decreases in on-task time (22 percent less) and amount of instruction (25 percent less).

In conclusion, a learner-control condition can be a valuable instructional management system, especially for computer-based instruction, if students receive sufficient information about their learning development—information that continuously shows them what progress they have made toward mastery of the objective and provides meaningful advice on appropriate stimuli necessary to obtain it.

NOTES

1. Bunderson, C. V. *Team production of learner-controlled courseware: A progress report* (ICUE Technical Report No. 1). Provo, Utah: Institute for Computer Uses in Education, May 1973.

2. Tiemann, P. W., Kroeker, L. P., and Markle, S. M. *Teaching verbally-mediated coordinate concepts in an ongoing college course.* Paper presented at the annual meeting of the American Educational Research Association, New York, April 1977.

REFERENCES

DiVesta, F. J. Trait-treatment interactions, cognitive processes, and research on communication media. *AV Communications Review,* 1975, 23, 185–196.

Felixbrod, J. J., and O'Leary, K. D. Self-determination of academic standards by children: Toward freedom from external control. *Journal of Educational Psychology,* 1974, 66, 845–850.

Johansen, K., and Tennyson, R. D. Review of the theory and research on the computer-based Minnesota Adaptive Instructional System. *Educational Psychologist,* in press.

Merrill, M. D., and Tennyson, R. D. *Teaching concepts: An instructional design guide.* Englewood Cliffs, N.J.: Educational Technology, 1977.

Park, O., and Tennyson, R. D. Adaptive design strategies for selecting number and presentation of examples in coordinate concept acquisition. *Journal of Educational Psychology,* 1980, 72, 362–370.

Rothen, W., and Tennyson, R. D. Application of Bayes's theory in designing computer-based adaptive instructional strategies. *Educational Psychologist,* 1978, 12, 317–323.

Steinberg, E. R. Review of student control in computer-assisted instruction. *Journal of Computer-Based Instruction,* 1977, 3, 84–90.

Tennyson, C. L., Tennyson, R. D., and Rothen, W. Content structure and management strategies as design variables in concept acquisition. *Journal of Educational Psychology,* 1980, 72, 499–505.

Tennyson, R. D. Evaluation technology in instructional development. *Journal of Instructional Development,* 1978, 2(1), 19–26.

Tennyson, R. D. Instructional control strategies and content structure as design variables in concept acquisition using computer-based instruction. *Journal of Educational Psychology,* 1980, 72, 525–532.

Tennyson, R. D., Chao, J. N., and Youngers, J. Concept learning effectiveness using prototype and skill development presentation forms. *Journal of Educational Psychology,* in press.

Tennyson, R. D., and Park, O. The teaching of concepts: A review of instructional design research literature. *Review of Educational Research,* 1980, 50, 55–70.

Tennyson, R. D., and Rothen, W. Pretask and on-task adaptive design strategies for selecting number of instances in concept acquisition. *Journal of Educational Psychology,* 1977, 69, 586–592.

Tennyson, R. D., and Rothen, W. Management of computer-based instruction: Design of an adaptive control strategy. *Journal of Computer-Based Instruction,* 1979, 5, 126–134.

12 Computer Applications in Special Education

G. Phillip Cartwright
Pennsylvania State University

Computer-assisted instruction (CAI) theoretically holds substantial promise for the field of special education. Much of what is known about the learning characteristics of mentally handicapped children indicates that CAI should be an extremely useful tool in their instruction. Their needs for systematic presentation of small increments of curriculum materials, for immediate feedback and positive reinforcement, for repetition and "overlearning," and for individualized programs of study make CAI a particularly suitable teaching device for handicapped children (Chiang, 1978).

The quotation above introduces a final report of a study of the use of CAI with elementary–junior high children who are educable mentally retarded, educationally handicapped, language disabled, and oral language handicapped. It raises several important points pertinent to the subject of computer applications in special education. First, the Chiang study was a serious effort to make instructional uses of the computer an integral part of the curriculum of handicapped youngsters in elementary and junior high school. Second, the youngsters for whom the instruction was intended are the mildly handicapped population. By far, most instructional computing applications for the handicapped have been with the mildly handicapped. Finally, the Chiang report litanizes the most popular and obvious arguments for computer-assisted instruction with handicapped children and youth:

1. Systematic presentation of instruction
2. Small increments of instruction
3. Immediate feedback
4. Positive reinforcement
5. Repetition and overlearning
6. Individualized instruction

In Public Law 94-142, the Education for All Handicapped Children Act of 1975, handicapped children are defined as those children evaluated and diagnosed "as being mentally retarded, hard of hearing, deaf, speech impaired, visually handicapped, seriously emotionally disturbed, orthopedically impaired, other health impaired, deaf–blind, multi-handicapped, or as having specific learning disabilities who because of those impairments need special education and related services" (U.S. Office of Education, 1977, p. 42478). The term "special education" is defined in detail by this law, which, among other things, requires that a handicapped child must be educated in the least restrictive environment. Thus, the term "mainstreaming" has arisen to signify that a handicapped child should be educated in the "main stream" of education, in regular classes if possible.

The presence of one or more computers in a conventional class would allow less able youngsters or those with particular problems to receive specialized instruction right in the regular class environment. Children with severe and profound handicaps are educated in more restrictive settings: full-time special classes, special day schools, and institutions. Many youngsters can be served by a combination of settings. With supportive services, for example, a mildly retarded youngster might well be able to spend at least part of a school day with nonretarded youngsters in a regular class. One type of supportive service might be individualized instruction delivered by means of CAI.

General Design Considerations

Principles of Good Instructional Design

The group of youngsters roughly categorized as "handicapped" is a diverse, extremely heterogeneous group—much more heterogeneous than the nonhandicapped group. Learning characteristics of handicapped youngsters are so diverse and the youngsters' needs so variable that radically different procedures must be used depending upon the level of severity and type of handicap. Consider, for the moment, the diverse needs of a profoundly retarded 6-year-old and an 18-year-old gifted, but seriously disturbed youngster. No *one* set of instructional procedures can be applied wholesale. The same is true, of course, for that diverse group of youngsters known as "normal."

In general, efforts are being made in special education to capitalize upon hardware and software advances, and to build quality software based upon sound principles of design. Hannaford and Taber (Hannaford and Taber, 1982; Taber, 1983) outline a series of important design principles and other considerations in planning computer implementation with handicapped youngsters. They point out three areas about which potential developers or purchasers of software must be concerned: educational compatibility, instructional design adequacy, and technical adequacy. With respect to educational compatibility, factors pertinent to the cognitive, affective, and sensory/psychomotor domains are suggested. Cognitive factors include intellectual capacity of the learner, current level of performance, attentional problems, and learning style. Affective considerations include interest level of the child, motivation, feedback, and reinforcement. Sensory/psychomotor problems are not as explicit in the Hannaford and Taber article. Hannaford and

Taber emphasize one point that deals with the affective domain: many handicapped youngsters are said to have "self-concept" problems. Hannaford and Taber point out that the use of sarcastic or mildly pejorative feedback (e.g., "Wrong answer, dummy!") might be even more offensive and counterproductive for handicapped children than for nonhandicapped youngsters.

Under instructional design adequacy, Hannaford and Taber present an overview of important design considerations, most of which are pertinent to handicapped and nonhandicapped children alike. For example, they list the following, among others: assessment of student entry level performance, accuracy and completeness of information, content organization, size and layout of stimulus materials, amount of information presented, reading level, mode of instruction, feedback strategies, and response analysis. Under the general heading of technical adequacy, Hannaford and Taber list such factors as user friendliness, use of full capabilities of the microcomputer system and available peripherals, error trapping, reliability, and freedom from "bugs."

The monograph by Taber (1983) provides a brief overview of many factors which beginners should consider prior to purchasing hardware and software for use with handicapped students. In addition to an introduction to the basics of computers, the monograph includes the following topics: hardware and software considerations and evaluations, media selection, overview of instructional and administrative uses, and elementary programming. Additional references and sources of information are included.

Similar concerns about planning for integrated use of microprocessor technology in special education were presented by Hoffmeister (1983). He suggests that effective use of computers with handicapped children in the schools will necessitate *more* not less professional time. The computer can't stand alone, and much professional time will be required to plan, develop, and implement computer instruction and to integrate it into existing programs.

Isaacson (1983) related the design of instructional software to techniques proven successful with film. He suggested that these six steps be followed:

Statement of a problem

Writing objectives

Creating a storyboard

Writing pseudocode

Manual walkthrough

Coding and documentation

On the other hand, Chaffin, Maxwell, and Thompson (1982) studied successful video arcade games and attempted to capture some of the arcade excitement in their educational programs. These writers systematically observed and interviewed players of arcade video games and spent many hours playing the games themselves. They suggested the following features were important and should be incorporated into education programs when possible.

MOTIVATIONAL   FEATURES   OF   ARCADE
GAMES
Feedback

Obvious improvement with practice

High response rates

Unlimited performance ceilings

Interestingly, they felt that the obvious features of graphics, color, and sound were not as important as the four motivational features. As a result of their studies, the authors developed a series of desirable characteristics of education games based on the motivational features and built games incorporating the characteristics (Chaffin, Maxwell, and Thompson, 1982).

Some Obvious Variations

Two general concerns with special significance for handicapped groups are stimulus and response modalities. Clearly, a youngster who is seriously visually impaired should not be presented with a great deal of reading material. A deaf child will not respond well to the phonics approach to teaching reading. A less trivial case, though, is that of a child with a specific learning disability. A dyslexic youngster may have 20/20 vision yet be unable to acquire information and meaning from the printed word.

The response modality is of significant concern with some handicapped youngsters, usually those with severe physical impairments. Youngsters with high spinal injuries resulting in quadriplegia must be provided with an efficient response mechanism. Instructional materials must be designed to place minimal demands upon the child's response repertoire while still demanding high cognitive response. Similarly, youngsters with serious speech impairments (resulting from traumatic head or spinal injuries, cerebral palsy, deafness, etc.) must be accorded a means for response. In some cases, a computer- or microprocessor-based artificial voice may be necessary.

Input and output considerations aside, cognitive capabilities—both capacity and style—must be considered when developing instructional procedures and materials for handicapped children. Youngsters who are mentally retarded have cognitive capacity problems in the sense that they cannot respond to intellectual demands with the speed or depth of nonretarded youngsters. Learning-disabled (LD) youngsters, on the other hand, have the intellectual capacity but have other variations in learning style which detract from their ability to acquire language, information, or concepts in a manner akin to other nondisabled youngsters. Preparation of instruction for mentally retarded children in many cases may be a pacing problem. For LD youngsters the problem is not so much pacing as it is other concerns such as modality, attention, and style. Learning problems attributable to mental retardation usually are pervasive and affect the entire range of academic instruction. Learning problems resulting from a specific learning disability are, by definition, specific to one or a limited number of academic tasks.

Indirect Applications of Computers in Special Education

Tawney and Cartwright (1981) outlined two broad uses of computers and technology with handicapped individuals: direct and indirect applications. Direct applications of technology are those which are used by the handicapped person and would include electronic guidance devices for the blind, communication aids for persons with speech or hearing problems, computer-based reading systems (e.g., Kurzweil Reading Machine), mobility aids, and CAI. The bulk of the applications described in this review are direct applications, specifically computer-based instructional applications. First, though, we will describe some of the more common indirect uses of computers in special education.

Indirect applications, on the other hand, "are those in which technology is used by others on behalf of handicapped individuals" (Tawney and Cartwright, 1981, p. 11). Limiting the discussion to education-related computer applications, one thinks immediately of the rather common test scoring computer programs, class scheduling, grade reporting, and the like—the kind of activities which are becoming commonplace in many American schools. Wilson (1982) produced a list of special education applications of computers which, when added to the increasingly prevalent types of use at all levels of the schools, provides a nearly exhaustive catalog.

SPECIFIC APPLICATIONS OF COMPUTERS IN SPECIAL EDUCATION

Counts of students screened, assessed, placed, and reviewed

Reimbursement computation according to state and federal formulas

Generalization of standard local, state, and federal reports

Reports of student due process status and compliance with PL 94-142

Child counts cross-referenced by class, teacher, school, and handicap

Reports on student achievement and evaluation status

Detailed records and summaries of diagnostic testing

Personalized mailings to parents regarding individual education programs (IEPs) and review meetings

Lists of incomplete information on student records

Audit trails for program placement and review

Interactive creation of IEP goals and objectives from curriculum files

Generation of quarterly student reports

Recommending appropriate activities for students

Locating learning materials

Describing diagnostic materials

Reminders when notices are due or should be sent out

Maintaining information on health history and special medication

Electronic mail

Interactive access to related services information, e.g., transportation

Financial planning programs for "what if" analysis and budget planning (Wilson, 1982, p. 3)

Hoffmeister (1982), Wieck (1980), and Bennett (1982) write of a variety of applications and provide good overviews of special education uses and caveats. Hoffmeister listed the following categories of software and hardware applications:

Management

Professional development

Specialized pupil services

Testing

CAI

Computer science

Information systems (Hoffmeister, 1982, p. 115)

In addition to raising concerns about reading disabilities of handicapped students who are presented with conventional education programs, and general appropriateness of presentation, fragmentation, and response considerations, Hoffmeister (1982, 1983), touched on an interesting side effect of computer technology. He used the phrase "new life to dead issues" to suggest the possible powerful psychological impact of an official-looking computer printout. "Educators may tend to see computer-generated information as far more valid and objective than warranted by reality" (Hoffmeister, 1982, p. 119).

The general categories of administration, assessment, instruction, related services, and staff development are outlined by Bennett (1982) in a brief article on microcomputer applications in special education. Some variations of the previous applications (Hoffmeister, 1982; Wilson, 1982) are given, with communication aids receiving special attention. Finally, Wieck (1980) reports on the uses of computer-based education with various groups of handicapped children and forecasts an upturn in frequency of usage of computers in special education as costs go down and hardware and software become more user friendly and appropriate.

Examples of Indirect Applications

Computer-Managed Instruction. Probably the best general example of the use of computer-managed instruction (CMI) in special education is in the area of IEP. In this application, a computer (micro or mainframe) is used to assist education personnel in the development of individual education programs for handi-

capped children. PL 94-142 requires that an IEP be prepared for each child identified as having a handicap. To be included in the IEP are:

1. Present education level of child
2. Statement of annual goals and short-term objectives
3. Specific services to be provided
4. Education program to be followed
5. Date services to begin
6. Duration of services
7. Measures to be used to assess child's progress.

The child's parent(s) and the school representatives must agree on the nature and details of the IEP. Shortly after this requirement went into effect, it became apparent that many hours were required of teachers and other school personnel to prepare each IEP. The task was so great that many teachers' unions began to write IEP preparation days into the teacher contracts.

In an effort to cut down on the professional time required, some schools and organizations began to develop computer-based programs to assist teachers in the IEP process. A key feature of these programs was a large inventory of specific behavioral objectives with cross-references. Eliminating the need for each teacher to generate specific annual goals and short-term objectives anew for each child was a large savings. Additional items were furnished and most permitted a great deal of flexibility. Today there are at least a dozen such programs available, some of which go considerably beyond mere data base manipulation and provide for monitoring of programs. (See, for example, Eckert and Crouthamel, 1983; Reith, 1983; Lillie and Edwards, undated.) This latter group of programs utilizes sophisticated recording and data base manipulation techniques to help school officials monitor a given child's progress, sometimes on a weekly, or even daily, basis.

Once an IEP has been written and approved, PL 94-142 and state laws require that considerable information about each handicapped child be readily accessible, especially when local schools must document expenses for excess costs recovery. To ease this burden, state-wide child tracking systems have been developed, as have local district child information management systems. Also, programs for use within a single classroom have been developed. (For example, see Wesson, 1983; Brown, 1982; Ragghianti and Miller, 1982; Rosenberg and Sindelar, 1981; Meuer, 1982; Schiffman, 1982; Hayden, 1982.)

Behavioral Scheduling. Frankel (1979) developed a computer-based method of generating precise instructional schedules for children with learning and behavior problems. His system is aligned closely with instructional goals and has been used with autistic, seriously disturbed, and aphasic children.

Telecommunications. SpecialNet is a telecommunication system targeted for the special education community. It is under development by the National Association of State Directors of Special Education and National Systems Management, Inc., and is supported in part through contracts with the U.S. Department of Education. SpecialNet links hundreds of individuals, most state education agencies, and many college/university special education departments. In addition to the electronic mail service, SpecialNet offers 20 bulletin boards which cover a range of topics of interest to persons working with handicapped youngsters. Some of the current boards are:

Federal

Litigation

Multihandicapped

Request for proposals

Congress

Assistive devices

Early childhood

Television

Policy

Consultant

Opinions

Computer

Education technology

Employment

Vision

Personnel development

Each of the bulletin boards can be accessed by any user. Information available on the bulletin boards changes often, and it is possible to keep up with new policies and practices in the field by using the bulletin board system and following up on the information posted. The "Federal" bulletin board has been useful in alerting professional and advocacy groups to the rapidly changing Washington and congressional scene, and mobilizing these groups for lobbying efforts on behalf of handicapped youngsters. For additional information, see Snodgrass and Campbell (1982).

Direct Uses of the Computer

Prosthetic Applications

A prosthesis is an addition to the body to supply a missing part or to compensate for a defect. The most obvious example of a prosthetic device is a pair of eyeglasses. A high percentage of the population wears glasses to compensate for a deficit in vision. Used broadly, a great many assistive devices of rather common origin and function are used to help handicapped individuals cope with daily living. These devices assist handicapped people in travel, communication, personal grooming and hygiene, and in routine job or home activities. Crutches, canes, amplified telephones, large print books, and similar devices are often used by persons who do not consider themselves disabled as well as by those who have more permanent and pervasive impairments.

A great many assistive devices are available to help disabled individuals function more effectively in two major domains: communication and mobility. Fewer devices are available for use in the intellectual domain. Increasingly, microprocessor technology is being used to enhance prosthetic devices, to make them smaller, and to provide for functions not possible with older technologies.

For the most part, assistive devices for communication and mobility are outside the scope of this reading and will not be covered. For additional information about this important area, the reader might review publications of the Johns Hopkins University Applied Physics Laboratory. Annually, this organization sponsors a conference which covers developments in this area. Their 1980 publication, *Application of Personal Computing to Aid the Handicapped,* is quite informative. *Technology and Handicapped People,* published by the Office of Technology Assessment (1982), is a valuable reference work, too.

Computer-Assisted Instruction

CAI is designed to help students acquire skills, information, or concepts which are *planned in advance.* Since by definition all handicapped children must have IEPs and IEPs must contain specific goals and objectives, the CAI application is a natural one. The application is natural for tutorial as well as for drill and practice. Tutorial CAI is designed to help students acquire *new* skills, information, or concepts. Drill and practice is designed to help students solidify concepts already acquired, or to maintain skills and concepts. The latter application is especially attractive to many special educators. The next section illustrates applications of both these two main uses of CAI.

Much of the software developed for non-handicapped children may be applicable with certain handicapped children. If sensory and response modalities are adequate,

mental level is equivalent to the task, prerequisites are met, and objectives are appropriate, then a given piece of instructional software might be tried with selected handicapped youngsters. In fact, many of the studies reported below used existing software with little or no modification. It is a tribute to the software developers (or perhaps to the tenacity of the researchers) that many success stories can be found.

Mildly Handicapped

Learning disabled (LD), educable mentally retarded (EMR), and socially and emotionally disturbed (SED) individuals often are classified as mildly handicapped. Sensory and response functions usually are adequate and, with the exception of a few very bright youngsters, intellectual functioning falls squarely in the middle of the distribution. Consequently, given the factors listed in the last paragraph of the preceding section, there are no compelling reasons to treat these three groups as radically different when planning instructional programs. Many instructional procedures are appropriate for all, and when very specific objectives are taught, behaviors of the three groups are indistinguishable. Thus, you will see a good deal of overlap among these groups in the literature.

A case in point is the study carried out over a 2-year period by Alice Chiang and her associates at the Cupertino Union School District in California (Chiang, 1978). Two hundred handicapped youngsters in eight schools participated in the study. The handicapped youngsters were classified into four groups:

Educable mentally retarded (EMR); IQ range 50–80

Educationally handicapped minors (EHM); normal intelligence but have behavioral disorders or neurological handicaps

Learning disabled (LD); serious learning problems but not retarded, emotionally disturbed, or sensorially impaired

Severe oral language handicapped (SOLH); similar to LD but with more severe oral communication problems

During the course of the study, teachers in the eight schools created 975 CAI lessons: 581 in reading, 106 in language, and 288 in math. The subject matter to be taught dictated the content, not the category of the handicap. No lessons were written exclusively for a single type of handicap; rather, the lessons were created to be objective driven and applicable across groups.

Children worked on the CAI lessons only about 30 minutes per week. At the end of the second year, the CAI treatment group outscored the control group of 200 children on 18 of 24 comparisons on standardized achievement tests. Covariance analyses revealed significant main treatment effects for math and reading recognition but not for reading comprehension. Further, treatment effects attributable to type of handicap, and interaction of treatment and type of handicap, were minimal.

Since the teachers created the lessons and integrated the lessons into their ongoing programs, it is no surprise that 87 to 94 percent of the teachers felt that the project was quite successful and that the CAI approach was worthwhile and effective (Chiang, 1978).

Other investigators working with LD children tend to report generally positive results; i.e., the technology is accepted by students and staff, as well as academic gains resulting from the computer programs. It is often less clear whether equal or superior gains could be achieved through other instructional procedures.

Elementary math, reading fundamentals, spelling, and certain language arts are used often in this field both in tutorial and drill-and-practice modes. Watkins and Webb (1981) report a study of the efficacy of CAI programs in elementary math for LD students. They found significant increases in academic achievement in math as a result of the project. Howe (1980) reports similar results with reading attack skills. He worked with LD and behaviorally disordered children and studied the development of freer, nondrill computer-based instruction.

Mason and Mason (1983) conducted a longitudinal study of the use of CAI with LD and EMR students. Their project (MASS—Microcomputer Assistance for Special Students) tested the effectiveness of a K–12 microcomputer-based program designed for the special needs of LD and EMR children and youth. Their project also contains an inservice training program to help educators incorporate CAI into ongoing education programs.

Other investigators have concentrated on a single disability group—dyslexic (specific reading disability). For example, Sevcik and Sevcik (1980) and Pollard (1979) report the use of a microcomputer program targeted to teach specific skills to dyslexic youngsters. Hasselbring (1982) and Hasselbring and Crossland (1982) illustrate the effectiveness of using CAI as a remedial technique for teaching spelling to LD children.

Emotionally Disturbed

The argument has been advanced that CAI might be a useful medium for teaching children who have behavior disorders, based on the general agreement that such disturbed youngsters have very serious problems relating to people. The computer can be considered a "neutral" teaching medium with none of the problems inherent in working one on one or in small groups with disturbed youngsters. One successful application of this type is reported by Kleiman (1981). He found that hyperactive children and those with "attention deficits" stayed with computer instruction longer than conventional instruction; they finished half as many math problems using paper and pencil as computer instruction. Similar results with a CAI reading program were reported by Aaron (1975), who studied behaviorally disordered adolescents.

The most extensive use of CAI with autistic children is the work done in conjunction with Seymour Papert's laboratory at the Massachusetts Institute of Technology. Goldenberg (1979) details several applications of the M.I.T. LOGO language with autistic children and with children who have very serious language, intellectual, and/or physical problems. Especially with autistic children, who seem to relate better to objects and machines than to humans, the instructional paradigm proceeds from three-dimensional objects to two-dimensional portrayals of objects to more abstract forms. Initially, the youngster learns to command a three-dimensional "turtle" through remote computer commands. Then, the "turtle" is shown as a two-dimensional representation on a computer screen. Gradually, the student learns to control the "turtle" and to control the system. Skills in mathematics and in reading are enhanced through this instructional procedure but the real strength, say its developers, is the development of problem-solving skills.

Severely Handicapped

The severely handicapped include youngsters who have serious physical disabilities and/or who are severely or profoundly retarded. In almost all cases, children who are profoundly retarded have concomitant physical disabilities. Usually, the physical problems were present at birth. For such youngsters, the shape of instruction is greatly different from the more academic orientation directed to the mildly handicapped. Most educational objectives are in the mobility and personal care domains rather than in the cognitive. Body positioning, reduction or control of self-mutilating behaviors, and basic communication are critical, priority goals. Clearly, customary academic goals are not primary with this group. There are, however, projects which attempt to match the capabilities of computers and technology with the needs of severely handicapped children and youth.

A special issue of the *Journal of Special Education Technology,* edited by Joseph Stowitschek, addresses applications of media technology with the seriously handicapped. (Stowitschek, 1981) Although all the articles do not deal directly with computers, many foretell computer applications or linkages.

Interestingly, most of the reported instructional uses of computers with the severely handicapped deal with very young handicapped or high risk children. The applications are not direct applications per se. Rather they are home-based curricula designed to help parents work with their youngsters. Aeschleman and Tawney (1978) used a small computer and a telecommunications linkup to provide instruction in the home to severely handicapped preschoolers and their parents in rural Kentucky. A similar concept was used by Lutz and Taylor (1981).

Other investigators have used the power and immediate feedback capability of the computer to teach (some might say condition) high risk infants to react systematically to computer-controlled stimuli. The purpose has been to train the babies to exercise control over their immediate environments. Much of this research depends upon the development of sensing devices and interfaces between the computer and the baby crib, toys, etc. (See Behrmann, 1983; Rostron and Lovett, 1981; Brinker and Lewis, 1982.)

Hearing Impaired

Of all the disability areas, educators of the deaf and hearing impaired have been the quickest to embrace new forms of technology. Tracing the emergence of educational applications of technology—film, television, programmed instruction, videodisk, computers, etc.—one almost always finds that such applications were tried, even developed, for use with children or youth with serious hearing problems.

One of the best known large-scale trials of CAI was with deaf students. Fletcher and Suppes (1973) and Fletcher (1976) carried out a study of CAI in language arts and mathematics for approximately 4,000 deaf students in 15 schools for the deaf in five states. The results were uniformly positive, in terms of both academic achievement and economic practicality. A more detailed account of the experiences with CAI of one school for the deaf is found in an article by Arcanin (1979). The California School for the Deaf at Berkeley is described with reference to its extensive use of CAI.

The Arcanin paper appears in a special issue of the *American Annals of the Deaf* devoted to uses of educational media with the deaf. Two years later, *Volta Review,* another leading publication dealing with areas of interest to the deaf community, devoted an issue to the application of technology to the education of hearing-impaired students (Withrow, 1981).

Predictably, a major concern of researchers and educators of the deaf has been the development of language and communication skills. Several projects exemplify activities in this important area of curriculum. Galbraith (1978), and Dugdale and Vogel (1978) report classroom applications of CAI with deaf children. The latter project used the PLATO system because it allowed the investigators to use the following features, all of which were considered to be important in their work with deaf children:

Pictorial displays

Teacher-defined assignments

Variable lesson difficulty

Response analysis

Error trapping

The National Technical Institute for the Deaf (NTID) in Rochester, New York, and Gallaudet College in Washington, D.C., are colleges for deaf students. Both these institutions have spent considerable time and energy developing CAI for their deaf students. The DAVID system—Data Analysis Video Interactive Device—links video instruction and computer-assisted instruction at NTID (Sims, 1979; Cronin, 1979). Available for young children is CARIS (Computer Animated Reading Instruction System). This system, designed for hearing-impaired children, simultaneously prints words on the screen and animates their meanings (CARIS, undated).

A review of other uses of the computer with deaf children can be found in Watson (1979).

Visually Impaired

Educators of the blind have been in the forefront of application of technology on behalf of blind individuals. Much activity in the past decade has focused on two areas: guidance devices and reading devices. As such, the emphasis has been to provide *access* to conventional instructional materials or to adaptations of those materials. Unlike the deaf, who often have learning problems associated with difficulties in acquiring language, the blind usually have no unique language problems. Measured intellectual levels are on a par with an undifferentiated nonhandicapped population. Thus, if adaptations to equipment can be made, visually impaired children may be able to profit from instructional procedures developed for nonhandicapped youngsters.

Farmer (1975) presented a detailed description of several mobility aids and characteristics of acceptable aids. Such a functional analysis is an ideal procedure for a similar analysis necessary to describe characteristics of appropriate teaching aids. Tawney and Cartwright (1981) review certain characteristics and a number of guidance and reading devices available. Computer-based guidance devices or mobility aids for the blind are not commonplace but pilot models are available. For example, the Lasercane looks much like the familiar white cane often used by blind persons but it emits low-powered laser beams to detect obstacles. Different sound patterns are used to indicate the presence of low, medium, or high obstacles. The Mowat Sensor is a small hand-held device which indicates the distance of an obstacle to the device by means of vibrations. The Sonicguide looks much like a pair of heavy horn-rimmed glasses. Sound patterns reflected from nearby obstacles are transmitted to the wearer in the manner of a spectacle-style hearing aid. The VDETS (Voice Data Entry Terminal System) is usable by physically handicapped as well as blind persons. It is a voice-activated system which can be "trained" to recognize its primary user's voice. It can be linked to a computer terminal or microcomputer to give access to a wide variety of computer applications. In addition to the Tawney and Cartwright article, further descriptions of these and other devices for use by the blind can be found in Ashcroft and Bourgeois (1980) and Ruconich (1983).

Access to computer terminals and chemistry laboratory equipment was discussed by Lunney and Morrison (1981). Although their prime interest was not CAI, solving the problems of access to terminals and lab equipment clears the way for development of appropriate computer-based instructional materials for visually impaired youth.

The most exciting advance in computer technology applied to the blind is the Kurzweil Reading Machine (KRM). The KRM is a table-top device which looks like a photocopy machine. (Xerox now distributes the device.) The user places a book or article face down on the glass and presses a few buttons on a small control device. A scanner locates the print and transmits the images of the letters to a built-in microprocessor. The microprocessor consults its internal table of 1,100 linguistic rules and 1,500 exceptions and directs a speech synthesizer to produce words. The result: clearly distinguishable English sentences. This breakthrough gives access to the world's libraries to blind persons. Further, a simple attachment connects the machine to a computer terminal and provides access to text-based CAI programs as well as telecommunication services. Thus, a wide range of CAI programs can now be made available to blind children. (See Weinberg, 1980.)

Physically Impaired

Physical impairment does not automatically result in mental retardation. Most of us have been or will be physically disabled at some time in our lives. Thus, instructional considerations for physically impaired youngsters most often focus on access. The prosthetic value of computers is paramount here. Computer-based systems for mobility and communication are becoming increasingly commonplace in society at large, if not in the schools. Goldenberg (1979) reported the use of the M.I.T. LOGO system with physically handicapped children. (See the section on emotional disturbance above.)

In a special issue of *Exceptional Children,* Foulds (1982) reviewed current applications of microcomputers in programs for physically handicapped children. His research showed that the predominant use of the microcomputer with physically handicapped children is to facilitate communication.

In 1977 Vanderheiden and Grilley published a document which reviews needs of physically handicapped individuals with respect to communication and mobility, and outlined the major types and characteristics of prostheses. A major concern of the monograph was the provision of a means of communication to individuals with such severe speech or physical disabilities that conventional speech is not possible. The authors outlined the three major types of communication aid or device—scanning, encoding, and direct selection. A scanning device or technique provides a mechanical or electronic means of displaying a predetermined set or pattern of symbols, pictures, letters, words, phrases, or commands. As the array is presented to the user at a rate determined by the user, he or she signals by a variety of means (foot switch, head pointer, even grunts or puffs of breath) the intended message.

With control over one or two muscles, a severely physically handicapped person can learn to send a kind of code—thus the encoding type of device. Morse code can be tapped out by tensing a neck muscle rigged with a sensitive switching device. A combination of muscle contractions can be incorporated into a more sophisticated and faster system which is readily understandable by the untrained observer. The proper interface triggers electronic displays of words or letters.

The direct selection procedure allows communication by providing the student with an array of pictures, letters, words, or phrases. The student points to the desired picture or operation. The Apple Computer Lisa uses this approach by controlling the screen cursor by means of a hand-controlled "mouse." Needless to say, all these techniques—direct selection, encoding, and scanning—can be used to help a student communicate with a computer terminal and thus gain additional access to instructional and information systems.

The Vanderheiden and Grilley document has become a "classic" in this relatively young field. It is representative of the considerable interest and attention given to the development of microprocessor-based communication and response devices for the physically handicapped. Since the needs of many physically disabled individuals are in the area of communication, this topic will be pursued in the next section.

Speech Handicapped

There is considerable overlap in the areas of speech impairment and physical impairment when the discussion is focused upon speech production. Many children and adults have serious speech and language problems and the cause of the problems are quite varied: hearing impairment, cerebral palsy, cardiovascular accident, head trauma, to name a few. Sometimes, the speech pathologists determine that conventional speech therapy by itself is insufficient to help an individual achieve greater independence in society. In addition to therapy, a vocal communication aid is recommended to augment the individual's residual communication system. These aids must be readily portable and usable in a variety of social and education situations. There are numerous aids commercially available. One type accepts input from microswitches or keyboards and produces a printed output. Another type accepts the same kind of input but produces synthetic speech output. When these devices are interfaced with a microcomputer or mainframe, CAI or telecommunication services can be made available to individuals with serious physical problems. Rushakoff (1983) has reviewed current linkups and describes applications of

the microcomputer as a speech communication aid.

In other applications of the computer as an instructional system for speech-handicapped children, Wilson and Fox (1982) describe their computer-based program for teaching language to LD and bilingual children. Their computer testing and teaching program is used with children with mental ages as low as 9 months. Fitch (1983) reviewed other applications in the area of communication disorders, although most of these are clinical rather than instructional uses.

Summary

It should be clear that there are a multitude of computer applications in special education. Most of the applications are indirect uses, the computer being used on behalf of, rather than directly by, a handicapped youngster. In general, development of computer-based instructional materials for handicapped children follows the same design principles that should be employed for any group of youngsters. Certain obvious variations must be observed, of course, but solving general instructional design problems will be as useful for special education as for general education.

For purposes of discussion of instructional systems development in this context, three major, overlapping groupings exist. One group, the mildly handicapped, has no input or output problems; their problems lie in the behavioral and intellectual domains. Modifications in rate and level of general instructional programs represents a first cut at adapting materials for them. The second group has physical or sensory problems which prohibit access to conventional materials. The third group has serious mental deficiencies (and may have concomitant physical disabilities) which prevent the use of nearly all currently available computer-based instruction procedures.

Modern technology, including the miniaturization of microprocessors, may bring significant enhancements to education programs for the handicapped. The greatest strides in the immediate future may likely be in improved communication systems and in interface devices. As communication and response systems improve, greater access to all aspects of general education programs will be available for all handicapped children.

REFERENCES

Aaron, R. Computer-managed instruction for behaviorally disordered adolescents. *Reading Improvement,* 1975, 12, 103–107.

Aeschleman, S., and Tawney, J. Interacting: A computer-based telecommunications system for educating severely handicapped preschoolers in their homes. *Educational Technology,* 1978, 18, 30–35.

Arcanin, J. Computer-assisted instruction at the California School for the Deaf—Past, present, and future: An administrator's view. *American Annals of the Deaf,* 1979, 124, 573–577.

Ashcroft, S., and Bourgeois, M. Recent technological developments for the visually impaired: State of the art. *Journal of Special Education Technology,* 1980, 3, 5–10.

Behrmann, M. Critical learning—Multiply handicapped babies get on-line. Fairfax, Va.: George Mason University, 1983.

Bennett, R. E. Applications of microcomputer technology to special education. *Exceptional Children,* 1982, 49, 106–113.

Brinker, R. P., and Lewis, M. Making the world work with microcomputers: A learning prosthesis for handicapped infants. *Exceptional Children,* 1982, 49, 163–170.

Brown, N. P. CAMEO: Computer administered management of educational objectives. *Exceptional Children,* 1982, 49, 151–153.

CARIS—Computer Animated Reading Instruction System. Chicago: Encyclopedia Britannica, undated.

Chaffin, J. D., Maxwell, B., and Thompson, B. ARC-ED Curriculum: The application of video game formats to educational software. *Exceptional Children,* 1982, 49, 173–178.

Chiang, A. *Demonstration of the Use of Computer-assisted Instruction with Handicapped Children.* Arlington, Va.: RMC Research Corp., 1978. (ED 166913)

Cronin, B. The DAVID system: Development of an interactive video system at the National Technical Institute for the Deaf. *American Annals of the Deaf,* 1979, 124, 616–618.

Dugdale, S., and Vogel, P. Computer based instruction for hearing impaired children in the classroom. *American Annals of the Deaf,* 1978, 123, 730–743.

Eckert, J., and Crouthamel, B. Computer generated goal and objective statements—A time saver for teachers. Atlanta: Georgia Learning Resources System, 1983.

Farmer, L. W. Travel in adverse weather using electronic mobility guidance devices. *New Outlook for the Blind,* 1975, 69, 433–439.

Fitch, J. Microcomputers in communication disorders. Mobile: University of South Alabama, 1983.

Fletcher, J. D. Stanford Project on CAI for Hearing Impaired Students. *Journal of Computer Based Instruction,* 1976, 3, 1–12.

Fletcher, J. D., and Suppes, P. CAI in mathematics and language arts for the deaf. Final Report. Palo Alto, Calif.: Stanford University Institute for Mathematical Studies in Social Sciences, 1973.

Foulds, R. A. Applications of microcomputers in the education of the physically disabled child. *Exceptional Children,* 1982, 49, 155–162.

Frankel, F. Individualizing schedules of instruction for school children with learning and behavioral problems. *Psychology in the Schools,* 1979, 16, 270–279.

Galbraith, G. An interactive computer system for teaching language skills to deaf children. *American Annals of the Deaf,* 1978, 123, 706–711.

Goldenberg, E. P. *Special Technology for Special Children.* Baltimore: University Park Press, 1979.

Hannaford, A., and Taber, F. Microcomputer software for the handicapped: Development and evaluation. *Exceptional Children,* 1982, 49, 137–142.

Hasselbring, T., Remediating spelling problems of learning handicapped students through the use of microcomputers. *Educational Technology,* 1982, 22, 31–32.

Hasselbring, T., and Crossland, C. Application of microcomputer technology to spelling assessment of learning disabled students. *Learning Disability Quarterly,* 1982, 5, 80–82.

Hayden, D. A special education management system—SEMS. *Journal of Learning Disability,* 1982, 15, 374–375.

Hoffmeister, A. Microcomputers in perspective. *Exceptional Children,* 1982, 49, 115–121.

Hoffmeister, A. Microcomputers: Rational planning for implementation. Logan: Utah State University, 1983.

Howe, J. Computers: A researcher's view. *Special Education: Forward Trends,* 1980, 7, 17–21.

Isaacson, D. How to design educational microcomputer programs for the exceptional student. Fresno, Calif.: School and Home Courseware, Inc., 1983.

Kleiman, G. Microcomputers and hyperactive children. *Creative Computing,* 1981, 7, 93–94.

Lillie, D. L., and Edwards, J. D. UNISTAR I. Burlington, N.C.: Southern Microsystems, undated.

Lunney, D., and Morrison, R. High technology laboratory aids for visually handicapped chemistry students. *Journal of Chemical Education,* 1981, 58, 228–231.

Lutz, J., and Taylor, P. A computerized home-based curriculum for high-risk preschoolers. *AEDS Journal,* 1981, 15, 1–9.

Mason, M., and Mason, W. B. Longitudinal results of using computer-assisted instruction with LD and EMR students. Palatine, Ill.: Mason Computer Services, 1983.

Meuer, L. T. Special education management system using microcomputers. *Educational Computer,* 1982, 2, pp. 12–13, 44–46, 48.

Office of Technology Assessment. *Technology and Handicapped People.* Congress of the United States, Washington, D.C., 1982.

Pollard, J. Testimony to a microcomputer—Peter can now read. *Recreational Computing,* 1979, 7, 8–12.

Ragghianti, S., and Miller, R. The microcomputer and special education management. *Exceptional Children,* 1982, 49, 131–135.

Reith, H. Using microcomputers to assess, remediate, and monitor individual education programs. Bloomington, Ind.: Center for Innovation in Teaching the Handicapped, 1983.

Rosenberg, M., and Sindelar, P. Computer-assisted data management of instructional programming. *Education Unlimited,* 1981, 86, 37–40.

Rostron, A., and Lovett, S. A new outlook with the computer. *Special Education: Forward Trends,* 1981, 8, 29–31.

Ruconich, S. Enabling blind students to use microcomputers. Nashville: Peabody College, 1983.

Rushakoff, G. E. Microcomputer as an efficient speech-output communication aid. Las Cruces: New Mexico State University, 1983.

Schiffman, G. Personal computers for the learning disabled. *Journal of Learning Disabilities,* 1982, 15, 422–425.

Sevcik, E., and Sevcik, J. PET Reading Program: A learning program for problem readers. *Recreational Computing,* 1980, 8, 25–28.

Sims, D. A pilot experiment in computer-assisted speechreading. *American Annals of the Deaf,* 1979, 124, 618–623.

Snodgrass, G., and Campbell, R. Communication/Information Systems in Special Education. In J. Dominguez and A. Waldstein (Eds.), *Educational Applications of Electric Technology.* Monmouth, Ore.: WESTAR, 1982.

Stowitschek, J. Media technology: Exploring applications and innovations in severely handicapped students. *Journal of Special Education Technology,* 1981, 4, 1–85.

Taber, F. *Microcomputers in Special Education.* Reston, Va.: Council for Exceptional Children, 1983.

Tawney, J., and Cartwright, G. P. Teaching in a technologically oriented society. *Teacher Education and Special Education,* 1981, 4, 3–14.

U.S. Office of Education. Implementation of Part B of the Education of the Handicapped Act. *Federal Register,* Aug. 23, 1977, 42, 42474–42518.

Vanderheiden, G. C., and Grilley, K. *Nonvocal Communication Techniques and Aids for the Severely Handicapped.* Baltimore: University Park Press, 1977.

Watkins, M. W., and Webb, C. Computer-assisted instruction with learning disabled students. *Educational Computer,* 1981, 1, 24–27.

Watson, P. Utilization of the computer with deaf learners. *Educational Technology,* 1979, 18, 47–49.

Weinberg, B. The Kurzweil Machine: Half a miracle. *American Libraries,* 1980, 11, 603–604, 627.

Wesson, C. Data-based programs modification system. Commack, N.Y.: Winnicomac Elementary School, 1983.

Wieck, C. Computer resources: Will educators accept, respect, or neglect in the future? *Education Unlimited,* 1980, 2, 24–27.

Wilson, K. Computer systems for special educators. In J. Dominguez and A. Waldstein (Eds.), *Educational Applications of Electronic Technology.* Albuquerque, N.M.: WESTAR, 1982. 1–21.

Wilson, M. S., and Fox, B. J. Computer-administered bilingual language assessment and intervention. *Exceptional Children,* 1982, 49, 145–149.

Withrow, F. Learning technology and the hearing impaired. *Volta Review,* 1981, 83, 263–358.

13 Some Rules for Good Simulations

Neil C. Rowe

I've just spent an interlude reviewing some commercial simulation programs intended to help in biology teaching. Generally speaking, I wasn't much impressed. Despite the fact they were from several different sources and aimed at different levels of students, they were all pretty poor—hard to use and hard to understand.

Clearly it's hard to write a good simulation, just as it is difficult to design any quality product. This is probably the main reason for the above. But it is also difficult for people without computer backgrounds to evaluate competing products and to discern just why a quality product is preferable. Thus, poor products may continue to sell through ignorance. Toward this end I have made a list of evaluation criteria for simulations, much in the style of rules for good prose writing, since good simulation writing is indeed an art.

This list has another, perhaps even more useful purpose: *it may be used by simulation writers as a checklist of things to be sure to address in writing a good simulation.* These are things it's often easy to forget, especially when students themselves are writing the simulation as a valuable educational project in itself. For this audience I have tried to state the rules as imperatives in rather simple English.

1. Setting Simulation Parameters

1.1 Describe parameters clearly.

This is harder than it sounds, because what's obvious to one person may not be obvious to another. For instance, consider the question "Generation time?" in a population growth simulation. The simulation writer means this is the interval between successive generations of the population, an important parameter in his program. But to the user who doesn't know much about computers (henceforth called the "naive" user), "generation time" could be the time to "generate" a simulation and put it on the screen. Or, it could mean the current time of day, the "time" he's going to be "generating" output.

Even if "generation time" refers to a population, the user has other problems. Does it mean the average time a generation lives? Or maybe it means the dates a particular generation lived, like from 1900 to 1970? Or maybe it is the time to "generate" offspring, which could be different from the time it takes a generation to become reproducing adults. After all, the user who could learn the most from a population simulation would be one who didn't understand the importance of the concept of generation time in the first place.

Ambiguous parameter descriptions can be cured by more explicitness. As, for instance, by asking either "Average time between successive generations of this organism?" or "The average length of time from when an organism is born until it reproduces?"

Neil C. Rowe, "Some Rules for Good Simulations," *Educational Computer Magazine* (November/December 1981), 37–40. Reprinted by permission of *Educational Computer Magazine*.

1.2 Give the units.

When indicating a numeric value, a simulation should give the units of measure: for instance, whether time is in minutes, hours, days, or years. If units can be arbitrary, the simulation should say that too. If units can be arbitrary, but must be consistent with other units (like those of generation time and longevity in a population model), this should be noted as well.

1.3 Give the normal parameter range.

A naive user may not know what a "reasonable" value is for some parameter. This is especially true for complicated or "fudge factor" parameters that are difficult to relate to the real world, as, for instance, an "inhibition factor" of one population that works against the growth of another. The solution is to describe in a few words the range of values the parameter can take (e.g., "10 is normal, 0 is no inhibition, 100 is strong inhibition"). Ranges sometimes depend on other ranges, and this should be noted when it's important.

1.4 Parameters should be significant.

A parameter that doesn't much affect the results of a simulation can be eliminated (although sometimes there can be an educational value in letting users find this out for themselves). Too many knobs on a control panel make things confusing.

1.5 Handle related parameters together.

One way to decrease ambiguity of parameter description (and hence user bother and chance of error) is to ask for similar parameters together. For instance, put parameters of initial conditions first, then those governing routine processes, then those covering special cases or situations. Within each class, mention parameters of size first, then parameters in units of time.

In some cases the simulation is composed of several distinct phenomena, each with its own parameters, and this criterion can be used to group parameters too, either "above" or "below" the groupings mentioned. An example of this is a simulation of several different populations in an ecosystem.

1.6 Handle setting and resetting parameters differently.

Generally a user will want to run a simulation many times, changing parameters slightly each time. Thus, while it may be okay to follow a fixed-format "fill-in-the-blanks" approach the first time around, the user will probably want a "menu selection" format for resetting, since this will let him refer quickly to only the few parameters he wants to change. That means a numbered or lettered list of the parameters (grouped per Rule 1.5), with succinct but clear descriptions of each, followed by a prompt to the user to select the letter or number of the one he wants to change.

2. Questions to the user

2.1 Make it clear you are asking a question.

That is, say "The time between successive generations?" or "Please type in the time between each succeeding generation" rather than "Time between successive generations," which doesn't say what you want to do with "time," and could be misconstrued as an order to "time" something.

2.2 Make yes/no questions easy.

Questions with either a "yes" or a "no" answer arise all the time, so they should be made as easy for the user to answer as possible. For instance, the user shouldn't be required to type in all three letters of "yes" or to have to code "yes" as 1 and "no" as 2 (numbers are a poor way to represent nonnumeric things). One good approach is to arrange things so that "yes" answers always happen more likely than "no" answers, and make "yes" the "default" (see Rule 2.4) so that a carriage return means "yes," the letter "n" means "no."

2.3 Be consistent with menus.

When a user has a menu of options to choose from, it's important that the way of selecting be clear. Don't mix letter codes (as a, b, c, . . .) with number codes (as 1, 2, 3, . . .) in the same simulation. And make sure it's clear to the user what the code is. For in "Give genes of the mother: (1) AA (2) Aa (3) aa", it's not clear if the user should type something like "AA", something like "(1)", or something like "1".

2.4 Use defaults.

Entering values for parameters can be a lot of work for users. Anything you can do so they can type less will be appreciated. Defaults are an example; that is, no response at all to a question about a parameter (i.e., an immediate carriage return) sets the value of the parameter to its most common or most representative value. For instance, 25 years might be a good default generation time for human population studies; "Population A" might be a good default name for a population; and following Rule 2.2., "yes" might be a good default for the question, "Do you want to run this simulation again?"

2.5 Check for user mistakes on input.

User mistakes on parameter values can include a lot of things. It's very important to check for them, however, because one badly mistaken value that slips through can easily ruin the whole simulation, and leave the naive user discouraged and muttering nasty things about "dumb computers."

Some mistakes are easy to catch, like letters interpolated in the middle of numbers, which can be found by type checking. Others can be caught by comparing with a list of permissible values, like the month "September" and the answer "maybe" to a yes/no question. Numeric parameters can be given upper and lower limits, like 0 to 150 for human ages. Other parameters can be checked for consistency within a broad range with other parameter values, as the generation time with the time between successive plotted points on a population graph, so that a user doesn't try to plot for every month a population that reproduces every 100 years.

2.6 Have a "let's start over" response.

Occasionally a user may make mistakes in parameters, and find it easier to start over than to continue. This should be possible via a special key on the keyboard.

2.7 Have a "tell me more" response.

Sometimes parameters are hard to describe in a few words. Or perhaps there are additional facts about a parameter that a user doesn't need to know most of the time. A special key on the keyboard that requests further information is helpful.

2.8 Show previous parameter values when setting new ones.

Generally this means a compact summary of previous parameter values at the top of the screen (or page). If possible, then, this summary display can be modified directly as the user changes parameters, and the user only needs a line or two of space at the bottom of the screen to see what he's typing. This may be hard when there are many parameters, but it should be a goal.

3. Display of Simulation Results

3.1 Show all interesting behavior.

For results displayed as columns of numbers, this just means a sufficient number of digits for each number. For graphs of various sorts it means a sufficient number of distinct locations on the screen or page to distinguish values that deserve to be. For example, if there is an interesting small seasonal variation in an animal's population, this should be displayed clearly. So, if population is indicated by position in an 80-character line, you won't see anything if the population is less than 10 percent of maximum and the seasonal variation is less than 10 percent of that.

3.2 Let users adjust the scale.

Even if phenomena are theoretically visible, you have to pick the right scale factor (or "resolution"). If it's too big, valuable information is lost, but if it's too small, the user is drowned in a sea of mostly useless data. Since best scaling will vary a lot for interesting simulations, it is essential that scalings be user adjustable. This means both values of parameters and the time between successive "snapshots" of them.

3.3 Key the symbols.

Symbols are a useful way to encode information in tables and graphs, but it's very easy to forget what they stand for. Hence a key is necessary for every screen or page of information displayed.

3.4 Use footnotes freely.

Often simulation displays try to cram things into too little space. Good examples are the titles of rows and columns of tables, where designers often believe every character they save means a little more room for the much more valuable data, leading to cryptic, am-

biguous phrases and abbreviations. You can save space without being cryptic by explaining titles with footnotes at the bottom of the screen. Footnotes can be used with any kind of display symbol, too.

3.5 Don't clutter results with unnecessary details.

If screen or page space is tight, only important data should be shown. For instance, eliminate a statistic like total population that is the sum of other data for individual populations, or a statistic that is negligible for the survey period (though have a footnote for it).

3.6 When space is cheap, use it.

On the other hand, when it is not necessary to display a lot, explicit descriptions of parameters or simulation behavior should be encouraged. It can't hurt to be clearer.

3.7 Center data.

This applies mainly to columns of numbers. Centering them makes them easier to read than right or left justifying them (as fixed-format output forces you to do), which often creates large blank columns. Analogously, round numbers, don't truncate them.

3.8 Use logarithmic scales where appropriate.

For many statistics, an equal percentage change amounts to about the same thing, no matter what the original amount was. Examples include population and financial income for a company. This means by definition that a logarithmic scale is better for graphing it.

3.9 Flag off-the-scale conditions.

When a statistic becomes too large for either a graphic or numeric representation, this must be clearly called to the user's attention, since values are now invisible.

4. Simulation Behavior in General

4.1 Have several distinct modes of behavior.

A simulation that always gives the same sort of results isn't very interesting. Such domains should be studied by other methods like mathematics, not by a simulation.

4.2 Distinct modes of behavior shouldn't be hard to get.

A good simulation should convey to the user a sense of its possibilities. If interesting behavior can be evoked only with a narrow range of input parameters, redesign the simulation, preferably; or at least give help by hints or statements of consistent ranges (following Rules 1.3 and 2.5). An example would be a population whose size oscillates periodically for certain starting conditions, while most populations show only exponential growth.

4.3 Make the persistence of user actions clear.

Some simulations allow some kind of user control while they are running. If so, the exact effect of those actions must be clearly stated. For instance, in a population model one must distinguish actions that only affect a single generation from those that persist forever.

4.4 Make real-time features clear.

If a simulation is dependent on exactly what times the user answers questions (i.e., has "real-time" capabilities), the user must be warned carefully. Conversely, if the user can

take his time answering questions, this should be stated.

4.5 Stop the simulation when results are meaningless.

"Meaningless" means different things for different cases. It can mean that all parameters no longer change with time (i.e., equilibrium), or that initial assumptions are no longer satisfied. An example of the first is a stable population of coexisting species. An example of the second is a population that has gotten so small that statistical generalizations no longer apply.

4.6 State the main ideas clearly.

A simulation hasn't much value unless the user understands what it's trying to do and how it's doing it, at least in general terms.

4.7 Note major omissions from the simulation model.

In attempting to simulate a complex real-world situation, not all features can be included. It's important the user be told what is missing. For instance, a population model may assume that matings are statistically random, or that there are no seasonal effects.

4.8 Fairly approximate the simulation domain.

This is just the "consumer product claim" law for simulations: it should do what it's advertised to do. If it's a population simulation, it should show features of real populations and not be just a "toy."

5. Overall Organization

5.1 Avoid Changes of Style.

The more consistent a simulation is, the less likely a user is to be confused. Format consistency can include many things, like the size and grammar of descriptions and parameters, the number and order of questions asked the user under different conditions, or the way different kinds of simulation graphs are presented.

Some examples of inconsistency:

"Give initial size of population one" and "What is the starting population of group 2?"

Initial parameters are defined several to a line, while they must be given one to a line when reset.

The user is asked whether he wants to rerun the simulation after a normal run, but not when it stops due to unusual conditions like overrange.

5.2 Try to Find User Conceptual Errors.

There are two main kinds. The easier to see is the user's apparent unawareness of available options. For instance, if there's a range of a certain parameter that a user hasn't used yet, a range that would lead to demonstration of an interesting new class of simulation behavior, mention this to him. Infer this by keep-

ing a record of what range of values he uses.

The other kind is the user's unawareness of underlying mechanisms in the simulation, like, for instance, the notion that an increase in the population of a predator directly causes a decrease in the population of the prey. Again, one could infer this from patterns in the parameter values he mentions (as when he changes the initial population size of the prey a lot in order to keep it from decreasing, but never seems to succeed), and offer comments.

5.3 Design around an Estimate of Per-person Usage.

If the simulation is a simple one that can be thoroughly explored in a half-hour, it's a whole different situation from when it's complicated. In the first case, formats can be rigorously consistent, with no "shortcut" options available. In the second, users will be expected to run the simulation many times, and they will appreciate all the helpful shortcut options that can be devised (so long as they remain sufficiently clear).

5.4 Design for a Class of Users.

Simulations should be targeted for a particular level of user sophistication, both in the domain they cover and general sophistication of the user. This affects the explicitness of the descriptions and graphics in a simulation.

4 Evaluating Educational Software

As we use the term in this section, "evaluation" means three things: the assessment of the quality of a piece of educational software, the appraisal of the effectiveness of a computer-based program to affect student learning, and the use of the computer's capabilities to assess the progress of a given student through a program of study.

By definition and by its use in education, evaluation invokes value judgments. Is it sufficient, as some have argued, that an educational program be engaging and absorbing? Is the primary criterion the impact of the program on student knowledge? Is learning to learn, rather than knowledge itself, the mark of a quality program?

The readings in this section do not attempt to answer such value questions. Rather, they discuss several perspectives on the process of evaluation. Reeves and Lent offer a view of the different layers of evaluation. Our own paper summarizes some of the issues involved in different kinds of evaluation. These are both overviews of the complex activity that is called "evaluation."

CAI and other variants of computer-based learning have been around for three decades. There have been many attempts to compare the effectiveness of computer-based programs with the outcomes of other curricula. Kulik, Bangert, and Williams report their meta-analysis of CAI and their conclusions about its effectiveness. The studies on which the summary is based were conducted a number of years ago; evaluations of more recently developed programs have yet to be reported. Evaluations of microcomputer programs are rare and not yet available in sufficient quantity to justify discussion.

The capability of computers to accumulate information about students' responses and keep a running tally on student progress makes it possible to integrate testing and student performance in an educational program. Kreitzberg, Stocking, and Swanson describe some of the issues involved in this emerging field of testing and assessment. This reading presents only one example of the complexities and promise of this dimension of evaluation.

Evaluation is a mixture of sophisticated experimental design with values, judgment, and bias of the evaluator and those who commission the evaluative study. It is a field that will continue to arouse interest and controversy. This section should orient the reader to some of the most salient problems and possibilities.

14

Levels of Evaluation for Computer-Based Instruction

Thomas C. Reeves
University of Georgia

Richard M. Lent
University of Maryland

The purpose of this paper is to present the uses and methods of four levels of evaluation which can be conducted during the development and implementation of computer-based instruction (CBI). The overall goal of evaluation during the development and implementation of CBI (or any other program) is to provide decision makers such as sponsors, administrators, developers, programmers, and instructors with timely, accurate information which will contribute to decisions about the improvement, continuance, and/or expansion of the program (Anderson and Ball, 1978). To accomplish the goal of providing a CBI project's sponsors and personnel with information for making decisions, four levels or types of evaluation are recommended: documentation, formative evaluation, assessment of immediate learner effectiveness, and impact evaluation.

Before describing the uses and methods of these four levels of evaluation, it should be noted that a review of the CBI literature reveals that very few CBI projects have employed more than one or two of these levels. For example, Fitzpatrick and Howard (1976), Muston and Wagstaff (1976), and Rubin, Geller, and Hanks (1977) all concentrated their evaluation efforts at the formative level, using the ubiquitous student questionnaire. Fletcher and Suppes (1976), Su and Eman (1975), and Swigger (1976), on the other hand, spent their evaluation dollar in attempts to assess the immediate learner effectiveness of their CBI, utilizing tests and quasi-experimental designs. The authors of this paper will not argue that every CBI project should include all four levels of evaluation, but do maintain that CBI projects would benefit from a wider consideration of the decision-related information needs of their participants and consequent fuller representation of the evaluation levels described below.

Level 1: Documentation

In the simplest sense, documentation involves keeping records of when and where various project activities occur, what the activities cost, and who participates in them. Documentation is important for at least two reasons: administrators must have documentation data to account for the use of project resources, and documentation data are required for the other three levels of evaluation described in this paper.

It is easy for participants in a CBI project to become so involved in the creative and logistical aspects of the project that basic documentation data about the design and development of CBI programs, and who uses them, when, where, for how long, at what rate, and so forth, can be uncollected or lost. To avoid these problems, computer-based data collection and data management systems and simple record-keeping instruments are recommended.

Thomas C. Reeves and Richard M. Lent, "Levels of Evaluation for Computer-Based Instruction," pp. 1–14, with figures and references. This is a paper presented at the annual meeting of the American Educational Research Association, New York, March 20, 1982. Reprinted by permission of the authors.

Documentation of a CBI project's activities is a fundamental part of the evaluation effort regardless of the particular stage that the project is in: from design and development, to production and delivery, and finally to implementation and long-term operation of the instructional system. Economists refer to these stages as a project's "life cycle." It is important for the evaluator to document aspects of each of these stages because each involves its own subset of inputs, processes, and outcomes, which ultimately will add up to the project's overall results. Furthermore, it is only by tracking the pattern of decisions, events, resources, and activities (of both project staff and student users) throughout the project's life that explanations for the nature of the final results can be developed. Some specific aspects of documentation—level evaluation activities appropriate to all states of a project's life—are described here.

Documentation of Project Costs

During all stages of the project it is important to gather data on the type, cost, and rationale for the resources being consumed by the project. A CBI project represents a special investment of resources to develop an approach to an instructional problem. On a short-term basis, the amount of resources expended on a CBI project is not likely to be justified by the nature of the immediate benefits received. Instead, the hope is that the initial research and development investment which a CBI project represents will ultimately be justified by the long-term benefits to be received as the project's products (materials and ideas) are put into use over time. For example, funds spent to develop CBI which teaches the handicapped about career opportunities may seem extravagant in the age of "Reaganomics," but completely

Resource or Cost Categories

Life Cycle Stages	Category 1	Category 2	Category 3	Category $4, \ldots, n$	Total Cost
Design and development					$
Production and delivery					$
Implementation and operation					$
Total Costs:	$	$	$	$	

Key

Life Cycle Stages: Dividing project activities into key periods of resource consumption corresponding to the characteristic nature of the resource requirements of each stage.

   Design and Development Generally a fixed, nonrecurring investment in planning design and development activities.

   Production and Delivery Capital investment in goods and services needed to put plans into action. Generally this means a variable, nonrecurring cost which fluctuates according to scale of implementation and time horizon.

   Implementation and Operation Variable, recurring costs whose size varies with scale and cycles of operation.

Cost Center: A cost center refers to that which is being costed — a project, course, organizational unit, etc. The particular cost centers to be employed in a given study depend on the purpose of the analysis and the concerns of the decision makers.

Resource or Cost Category: While the life cycle and cost center dimensions of the model represent project or program functions, the resource or cost category dimension represents the specific type of resources being consumed. All resources assigned to or consumed by the cost center are organized into categories. The consumption of that resource in its natural units (like hours, number of pieces of hardware) and the dollar value of those units are reported. Typical categories for analyses of instructional technology projects include: personnel salaries and benefits, administrative time, services, hardware, software, and facilities. See Figure 2 for further cost category descriptions relevant to this project.

FIGURE 1: Resource analysis model for a single cost center

justified if an unintended outcome of the project is the discovery of new technologies through which handicapped persons may interact with computers.

It is beyond the intent and scope of this paper to present a thorough delineation of the methods of conducting cost-effectiveness analyses of instructional technology projects. The interested reader is referred to Beilby (1979), Felden and Pearson (1978), and Lent, (1979, 1980). However, it is important to point out that such analyses are impossible if project costs are not documented throughout the life of the project. Figure 1 presents a general model for the analysis of project resources across a project's life cycles. Each cell of the model indicates a particular type of resource likely to be consumed by the project. The amount and value ($) of each resource being consumed must be documented and its properties as a fixed or variable, and recurring or nonrecurring cost of the project, determined. Figure 2 presents one of the fundamental data collection instruments used to obtain the detailed information necessary for useful cost analyses of instructional technology projects. The "activ-

ity log" shown is a form used by each member of the project to log his or her time and to assign it to a major cost center and a specific development, production or operation stage of project activity. Such data are periodically entered into a computer-based management system and will ultimately be used to determine the extent and allocation of personnel resources across the matrix in Figure 1.

Automatic Record Keeping

One of the major strengths of CBI is that the same computers which "deliver" the instruction can also be programmed to collect most of the evaluation data required for project documentation. However, the unobtrusive collection of documentation data must be carefully planned and meticulously incorporated into the instructional programs. To begin, a complete list of the types of documentation data to be collected by the computer must be constructed. This list will be derived from the decision-based information needs of the project participants. Examples of such data include demographic data (names, ID

NAME _____   DATE(S) _____

COST CENTER CODES

| 1 = EXISTING LESSONS | 2 = NEW GENERAL MILITARY LESSONS | 3 = NEW MOS SPECIFIC LESSONS |

ACTIVITY CODES

DEVELOPMENT CYCLE
1.1 Needs/Task Analysis and Hierarchies
1.2 Courseware Development/Programs
1.3 Software Development
1.4 Videodisk Production—Premaster
1.5 Audio Production—Original/Scripts
1.6 Hardware Development
1.7 Evaluation
1.8 Project Administration

PRODUCTION/DELIVERY CYCLE
2.1 Hardware/Software Purchase
2.2 Media Production/Replication
2.3 Distribution and Training

OPERATION CYCLE
3.1 Hardware Maintenance
3.2 Software Maintenance
3.3 Courseware Maintenance
3.4 Instruction
3.5 Program Administration

DATE	HOURS	COST CENTER	ACTIVITY	EXPLANATION

FIGURE 2: Cost categories

numbers, educational status), time-on-system (sign-in/sign-off), student responses (tests, questionnaires), and curricular progress status. Time-on-system is an especially important type of data because it is required for the computation of other data, e.g., student rate of lesson completion, and because time-on-task has been demonstrated to be a powerful explanatory variable in research and evaluation of instructional systems (Rosenshine, 1977). Therefore, a real-time clock mechanism will be a necessary component of the system hardware of most CBI projects.

The inclusion of record-keeping routines in CBI will enable project personnel to obtain accurate answers to decision-oriented questions at any time. For example, timely information about system utilization at different sites should permit project administrators to make better decisions about project site changes. Similarly, rapid turnaround of student response data may allow program developers to make critical adjustments in the instructional programs.

If microcomputers are used in a CBI project, it may be necessary to arrange for the uploading of the micro-collected data to a larger computer for analysis using standardized data analysis programs such as SPSS (Nie, et al., 1975). Such a procedure will also lessen the drain on the micro's memory caused by the data collection and maintenance programs.

It is critical that computer-based data collection be as unobtrusive as possible. This is especially important when the intended users are children or adult learners who may be easily frustrated by tedious questions and responses. The simulation power of computers, especially when integrated with videodisks, can be used to collect data in an interesting and even motivating manner. For example, a CBI project presently under development at the University of Maryland uses an "Adventure"-like simulation to obtain necessary demographic data. Students enter an unusual building and go from floor to floor in a simulated elevator to sign up as members of an elite time-traveling force. During this brief but stimulating simulation, students not only provide the computer with the required demographic data, but they also learn to use the student response components of the microcomputer system, viz., the keyboard and touch-sensitive screen.

Personal Observation

Not all the data for complete and meaningful documentation of a CBI project can be collected by computer-based programs. Human beings must collect and report data concerning external factors which may affect the implementation of CBI such as power failures, equipment breakdowns, and fluctuations in the available student population. Figure 3 is a site manager's incident report form used to record incidents which may have powerful explanatory power in evaluating the outcomes of a particular CBI project. Another important type of documentation data is the eyewitness account of the processes and outcomes of the project. Figure 4 is an anecdotal record form to be used by project participants to record the incidents observed by or reported to them. These "stories" will often make an otherwise cold and impersonal evaluation report an alive and human source of decision-based information.

To summarize, the first level of evaluation, documentation, involves the systematic recording of all the "who," "what," "when," "where," and "for how much" data required for accounting for the use of project resources, making information-based decisions, and/or carrying out higher levels of evaluation. In the process of documentation, the following recommendations should be heeded.

1. Cost analysis is a fundamental part of any project evaluation. A useful cost analysis requires a thorough documentation of all resources consumed by the project through all stages of the project's life. Furthermore, these resources must be further identified as to whether they represent fixed or variable and recurring or nonrecurring expenditures for a project of this type.

Instructions for Site Manager's Incident Report Forms

During the operation of the Computer-Based Instruction Project, you are requested to report any unusual occurrences which may influence this project. Please use the [appropriate form] to record all deviations from normal operating procedures, e.g., equipment breakdowns or major declines in the student population. At the same time, if the problem requires assistance from the CBI office, call the University of Maryland, Heidelberg.

It is important that you record all incidents whether or not you have to call Heidelberg. Please make your explanation of the incident as complete as possible so that the CBI Project personnel will understand the problem. For example, if the system breaks down in the middle of a lesson, please describe exactly what appeared on the screen when the problem occurred. Or if the problem involves a decline in student population, describe the reasons, e.g., maneuvers or PCS.

An example of a complete form is below. These forms will be collected during site visits by project personnel. Thank you for your assistance.

Site Manager's Incident Report Form

DATE: *09 September 1981*   TIME: *10:30 AM*

INCIDENT: *A student was in the middle of lesson 6304 when the computer made a funny noise and "A)" appeared on the screen.*

EXPLANATION: *Called Heidelberg. They said to restart the system from the beginning, without doing the submits then check the student's file using editor.*

ACTION TAKEN: *Did what they suggested and everything's working again.*

FIGURE 3: Incident report form

2. Whenever possible, the computer itself should be used to collect documentation data, especially if it can be done unobtrusively.

3. Human data collection, employing simple forms, is necessary whenever an evaluation is intended to inform its audiences about the personal or qualitative "story" of the development, implementation, or outcomes of a CBI project.

Level 2: Formative Evaluation

Formative evaluation, which is the collection of the opinions, suggestions, and criticisms of project participants, is of critical importance to the revision and improvement of a CBI project. As with the first level of evaluation, the types of formative evaluation activity will differ according to whether the project is in the development or implementation phase. Formative evaluation methods such as expert review and pilot tests are integral parts of the lesson design and development process followed in any CBI project. And yet, as critical as formative evaluation is during the development phase, it cannot be de-emphasized during the implementation phase. Even the most rigorous design and development process cannot yield CBI programs immune to installation and implementation problems.

Sometimes formative evaluation is belit-

Anecdotal Record Form Instructions

As a member of the CBI Project, you will observe incidents or listen to reports of incidents which relate to the development and impact of the project. It is important that this kind of anecdotal information be systematically recorded so that the story of the development and outcomes of this project can be written. Therefore, you are requested to complete one of the [accompanying] Anecdotal Record forms whenever you witness or hear of a significant incident related to the project's progress and accomplishments. An anecdotal record is a verbal account that exhibits these characteristics.

1. Each anecdote should be limited to a single incident.

2. It should contain a factual, noninferential description of the observed or reported incident. (Example: The soldier said "I've never enjoyed learning anything before" instead of "The soldier expressed satisfaction with the learning situation.")

3. It should include a description of the situation in which the incident occurred so that the meaning of the behavior can be understood.

4. It should be written as soon as possible after witnessing or hearing about the incident so that all the important details can be included.

5. It should include a separate section describing your interpretation or feelings about the anecdote. Your personal evaluation is important because your judgments about the project are valued highly.

ANECDOTAL RECORD FORM

DATE _____   PLACE _____

NAME OF OBSERVER _____

Description of the incident:

Interpretation:

FIGURE 4: Anecdotal record form

tled as being not much more than a "smiles test" to find out whether program users like an education or training activity. However, formative evaluation methods such as questionnaires, interviews, observation, and expert review can be used to collect data much more useful than simply the degree of program acceptance. Information about the appropriateness of program objectives, content, instructional methods, sequence, and pace can be collected by formative evaluation methods and used to increase the effectiveness and efficiency of CBI.

Two major approaches to formative evaluation are internal review and operational testing. Internal review is the process of systematically reviewing the content and instructional processes of CBI before it is put into operation. Internal review includes such activities as small-scale pilot tests and expert review. Operational testing refers to the process of collecting information for improving instruction during and after its actual implementation. Operational testing employs such methods as computer-based questionnaires, personal interviews, and observation.

Internal Review

It is true that most CBI is developed using some sort of systematic approach involving needs assessment, specification of goals and objectives, instructional design and production, and program evaluation. Models for developing CBI include many suggestions for formative evaluation. (See, for example, O'Neil, 1979, or Rahmlow, Fratini, and Ghesquiere, 1980.)

Internal review can be relatively informal or highly systematic. An informal review might consist of development staff or content experts addressing questions such as:

a. Is the instructional content accurate? Content experts can be hired to periodically review instructional content, both before and after it is programmed.

b. Are the principles and practices of effective CBI incorporated into lessons?

Figure 5 is a CAI readiness checklist developed by McPherson-Turner (1979) for review of CBI. Such a checklist should be regularly used by instructional developers to review the quality of their products.

c. Does the instruction account for all the planned outcomes? Instructional experts can often detect whether all the intended outcomes for a particular

sequence of CBI are actually addressed during the activity. This may at first seem self-evident, but it is not uncommon for developers of CBI to have objectives (particularly affective ones) for which no instructional activities are designed. For example, CBI can be designed to teach new accounting procedures adequately, but may fail to motivate the learners to implement the changes.

Instructions: The following 25 items represent both instructional design and technical design criteria for a well-developed CAI lesson. As you review your lesson, check for the presence or absence of these attributes. A negative response signals need for a possible modification of the lesson.

Yes	No	
( )	( )	1. Specific skills, knowledge, or abilities required for a learner to interact with the lesson have been specified.
( )	( )	2. The learner knows what is expected of him or her; that is, objectives have been clearly identified.
( )	( )	3. A test is included at the beginning of the lesson for diagnostic purposes.
( )	( )	4. The lesson is structured so that a learner may interact with all or part of the lesson as appropriate for his or her abilities.
( )	( )	5. The lesson presents new information in a context that directly relates what the learner already knows to the new material.
( )	( )	6. The lesson is organized so that the learner acquires basic skills before attempting to demonstrate more advanced skills.
( )	( )	7. A variety of explanations has been presented.
( )	( )	8. Exercises, problems, or questions are provided for the learner to practice the types of skills, attitudes, or knowledge specified by the objectives.
( )	( )	9. The lesson is written in such a way as to provide clues to key concepts (use of asterisks, underlining, etc.).
( )	( )	10. Outlines, summaries, or reviews are provided to help the student organize key ideas.
( )	( )	11. A variety of different questioning formats (multiple choice, matching, true-false, completion) are utilized.
( )	( )	12. Questions elicit responses relevant to the content being presented.

Yes	No	
( )	( )	13. Restatement of important concepts is provided to learners to reinforce learning.
( )	( )	14. When a learner answers incorrectly, feedback is provided to suggest what information appropriate responses should include.
( )	( )	15. Vocabulary appropriate for the learner has been used.
( )	( )	16. A posttest is included to determine learner achievement of stated objectives.
( )	( )	17. The learner knows what to do; any specific procedures for interacting with the computer/terminal have been explained.
( )	( )	18. Opportunities for frequent interaction between learner and computer have been provided.
( )	( )	19. The learner is informed about his or her status (score, how many lessons completed, etc.).
( )	( )	20. The typing skills necessary to make a response have been minimized.
( )	( )	21. Flexibility in accepting learner responses, especially synonyms, has been developed.
( )	( )	22. Opportunities for assistance within the lesson (as HELP, RESTART, and REVIEW) are available.
( )	( )	23. The lesson is not so lengthy as to be tiring.
( )	( )	24. Any supplementary materials necessary for the use of the lesson are provided for the learners.
( )	( )	25. The lesson is different than a textbook, lecture, or programmed instruction book.

FIGURE 5: Computer-assisted instruction (CAI) readiness checklist

d. Is the activity interesting? All too often, CBI takes the form of monotonous sequences of pretests, lessons, and posttests. If the power of the computer to simulate is used adequately, learners can be put into situations in which they want to learn. For example, if you wish to teach functionally illiterate soldiers how to use a military indexing system, you can simulate an unusual and entertaining "manual" about sports, cars, or other interests which soldiers will want to read. They will learn the appropriate reference skills in order to progress further in the simulation.

A more systematic review of CBI would involve a small-scale pilot test with a sample of potential users. Learner performance and reactions as well as observers' evaluations can provide information concerning necessary revisions of the inputs, processes, and effects of CBI. The feedback from users and observers can provide information needed to address questions such as:

a. What knowledge, skills, and attitudes are prerequisite to the CBI?

b. What parts of the CBI work and which don't?

c. What intended outcomes are accomplished?

d. What unintended outcomes are detected?

A primary source for formative information during a pilot test is participant postinstructional performance on measures of the intended outcomes. However, this is true only when the performance measures or tests are carefully constructed and well validated. CBI rarely enjoys the benefits of reliable and valid outcome measures, and other data sources such as student reactions and observer reports must be the basis for program revision.

If, on the other hand, reliable and valid tests of student performance are available, they can provide excellent information, espe-

cially if the links between program objectives, instructional processes, and outcome measures have been carefully explicated. Once again, the power of computers to simulate reality can frequently be used. For example, CBI can be developed to teach [cardiopulmonary resuscitation] using a programmed manikin. If participants in pilot tests of this instruction have difficulty with a particular step as indicated by performance measures involving the dummy, the CBI designed to teach that step can be augmented or revised.

A second source for formative evaluation data during a pilot test is user reaction to the program. During operational testing student reaction is usually collected by computer-based questionnaires, but an individual or group interview is a better method in a small-scale pilot test. These interviews should be open ended and participants should be encouraged to be as critical as possible. Participants in pilot tests can also be asked to record their reactions as they progress through CBI, noting the high and low points and making suggestions for improvement.

A third valuable source of information during a pilot test can be observers who are experts in either the content of the lessons or the processes of CBI. Even a nonexpert observer can be useful, especially in interacting with the learner to point out "leaps" and "gaps" in the lessons or unclear content presentations. As with all the procedures during a pilot test, emphasis during observations should be placed on diagnosing problems and suggesting remedies.

In summary, before an educational activity is actually implemented it should be subjected to internal review procedures including, if possible, small-scale pilot tests with potential users. Unfortunately, few CBI development projects have the budget or timeline to spend large amounts of money and time on these procedures. Realistically, much formative evaluation will be conducted during or after the CBI is actually implemented using the techniques of operational testing.

Operational Testing

Operational testing is the process of collecting data for the improvement of CBI during or after its actual implementation. The major sources of information during operational testing are: (a) measures of participant performance, (b) computer-based questions and personal interviews about user reactions, and (c) observations by designers and other observers. Operational testing is essential because CBI is usually developed to be used in many different settings over a relatively long period of time. As noted earlier, even the more rigorously designed and developed CBI can be improved after it is installed.

In operational testing, user performance is an essential variable for scrutiny if and only if reliable and valid measures of performance are used. More will be explained about the issues of the reliability and validity of computer-based tests in the next section of this paper concerning "Assessment of Immediate Learner Effectiveness." What is important to understand now is that given good measures of the outcomes of CBI, the results will serve as excellent indicators of the relative success or failure of various parts of the computer-based lessons. However, any information collected with poor tests is worse than useless.

If it is true (as it will be argued later) that few examples of CBI have reliable and valid outcomes measures, then participants' reactions to programs will be the major source of information during operational testing. Programmed questionnaires, euphemistically called "smilometers," are the most frequently used method of collecting participant reaction data during and after CBI. One of the advantages of CBI is that brief questionnaires or individual items can be programmed into the lesson whenever required. However, the evaluator must be alert to the obtrusiveness of his or her questions. Figure 6 is an example of some questions included in a sequence of military-related CBI lessons. In addition to indicators of the participants' global reactions to the CBI, specific information about the perceived difficulty of the lessons,

the pace and relevance of the instruction, the reliability of the CBI system, and so forth can be collected. Even more useful information can be gathered with open-ended questions about the best and worst parts of the CBI and specific suggestions for improvement.

The burdensome and time-consuming tasks of processing, analyzing, and reporting such data can be lessened if efforts are made to incorporate data management and analysis programs on the computer. Time invested in setting up such programs before the data are collected will pay off in terms of increasing the timeliness and accuracy of evaluation reports.

Though computer-based questions may be the most frequently used means of collecting participant reaction data, sometimes interviews will yield qualitatively more useful information. Follow-up interviews of CBI users 2 to 6 weeks after completion of a sequence of instruction can be particularly revealing. A program component which may have seemed unnoteworthy during CBI may loom large in the minds of participants after they are in another setting for a time. In addition, in-depth and probing interview questions asked of a few people can often provide better information than the data from a thousand programmed questions.

Another major source of formative evaluation data during operational testing is the observations made by CBI designers and other observers. Figure 7 is an example of a form used by observers to record their observations of students proceeding through CBI designed according to the PLATO system. In addition, CBI can be submitted to systematic review using a package such as MicroSIFT's *Evaluator's Guide for Microcomputer-Based Instructional Packages* (MicroSIFT, 1982).

To summarize, the second level of evaluation, formative evaluation, is the collection of information for the improvement of CBI. Internal review procedures including expert review and small-scale pilot tests are conducted before CBI is actually implemented. Operational testing procedures including computer-based questions, personal interviews, and observations are conducted dur-

Strand 1

1. The introductory lesson made it easy to use the computer.

   YES   NO   NOT SURE

2. The computer is difficult to use.

   YES   NO   NOT SURE

3. I think I can learn a lot with this computer.

   YES   NO   NOT SURE

4. I would rather learn this material in a regular class than with this computer.

   YES   NO   NOT SURE

5. Have you ever learned from a computer before?

   YES   NO   NOT SURE

Strand 2

1. I like using the computer.

   YES   MOST OF   SOME OF   NO
            THE TIME   THE TIME

2. I am learning a lot with this computer.

   YES   NO   NOT SURE

3. I would rather learn this material in a regular class than with this computer.

   YES   NO   NOT SURE

4. The lessons challenge me to do my best work.

   YES   MOST OF   SOME OF   NO
            THE TIME   THE TIME

5. Taking the tests helped me know if I really understood the material.

   YES   MOST OF   SOME OF   NO
            THE TIME   THE TIME

FIGURE 6: Computer-based evaluation questions

6. I would like to take more lessons on the computer.

   YES   NO   NOT SURE

7. The computer was available when I wanted to use it.

   YES   MOST OF   SOME OF   NO
            THE TIME   THE TIME

8. These lessons have encouraged me to improve my basic skills.

   YES   NO   NOT SURE

9. The computer allowed me to work at my own pace.

   YES   MOST OF   SOME OF   NO
            THE TIME   THE TIME

10. I tried to just finish the lessons rather than learn the material.

    YES   MOST OF   SOME OF   NO
             THE TIME   THE TIME

11. The computer always seemed to be breaking down.

    USUALLY   SOMETIMES   NEVER   NOT SURE

12. Someone was available to help me when there were computer failures or other problems.

    USUALLY   SOMETIMES   NEVER   NOT SURE

13. For [me], most of the work in these lessons was:

    VERY   DIFFICULT   ABOUT   TOO
    DIFFICULT   RIGHT   EASY

14. [Should the Army] continue to develop lessons for the computer?

    YES   NO   NOT SURE

15. I can use what I learned from these lessons on the job.

    YES   NO   NOT SURE

ing or after the actual implementation of CBI. As trite as it sounds, formative evaluation is a continuing process. Though it must be done within the limits of real time and money, formative evaluation is an activity which encourages creativity and innovation for improving CBI, and therefore can be extremely rewarding.

Level 3: Assessment of Immediate Learner Effectiveness

A CBI project has many different goals and objectives which may be classified as either immediate or long term. Immediate goals/objectives can be accomplished within the timeframe of the project, whereas long-term goals/objectives may not be accomplished until some time after the completion of a

Module _____

PLATO File Name _____

Name _____

Date

Student User Evaluation Form A

While reviewing the lesson, use this form to write down any problems you may have. Also, indicate any section that is particularly interesting or clearly explains the material. Record the screen number in the first column. You will find the number in the highlighted area in the lower left-hand corner of the screen.

Screen Number	Problem/Comment

FIGURE 7: Observation form

project. An immediate goal of a CBI project might be to teach decision analysis strategies to medical students, while a long-term goal of the same project might be to increase the cost effectiveness of laboratory tests ordered by physicians.

One of the most common methods of evaluating the immediate learner effectiveness of CBI is to include pretests and posttests in the instructional programs themselves. Unfortunately, though these tests are useful as diagnostic and motivational instruments, they cannot be regarded as adequate indicators of the instructional effectiveness of CBI programs. First, such tests are usually too brief to have adequate reliability. Second, the time lapse between the administration of the pretest and the posttest is often so short that students may choose a correct response after simply eliminating an earlier incorrect response. Thus improvement in test performance may result more from remembering the test than from learning the knowledge and skills necessary to pass the test.

Assessment of immediate learner effectiveness should include comprehensive measurement of a CBI program's terminal skill and knowledge objectives in as realistic a setting as possible. Computer simulations offer the best alternatives to traditional testing procedures. Interactive microcomputer/videodisk simulations can be designed which require students to demonstrate a full range of the learning they have achieved.

A military-related CBI project currently under development at the University of Maryland's Center for Instructional Development and Evaluation provides an excellent example of simulation used to evaluate the immediate learner effectiveness of CBI. The program is intended to teach functional literacy skills to enlisted personnel in military contexts. Rather than present students with pretests and posttests to determine their progress through the lessons in the tired, old lockstep manner of most CBI, students sign up as military "time travelers" who are sent backward and forward into unique times and places. Once there, the soldiers are put into situations which require them to employ their functional literacy skills to solve military-related problems. For example, a soldier student may travel back in time to the "Battle of the Bulge" where he or she has to follow directions and interpret maps to deliver an urgent message to General Patton. Another mission involves a journey to a futuristic city where the soldier has to locate and read information in his or her *Soldier's Manual of Common Tasks* to "see, communicate, navigate, shoot, and survive" in an unfamiliar and hostile environment.

A student enters an instructional lesson if and only if his or her performance in the simulation indicates a need for that instruction. In other words, the problems posed by the simulation serve as the pretests to determine the instructional needs of the students and as the posttests to assess whether they've learned the required skills. These strategies not only completely individualize the instruction according to the unique functional literacy needs of each student, they also permit the testing and retesting of the functional literacy skills, thus yielding a meaningful evaluation of the instructional effectiveness of the lessons. During a student's first trip or mission, he or she may require a considerable number of the "lessons," but this number should substantially decrease from journey to journey.

Another advantage of using simulations to evaluate the immediate instructional effectiveness of CBI is that the negative effects of traditional testing are avoided. Many students, especially adult learners, have come to expect failure in a testing situation. Computer simulations, which can "test" just as completely as any multiple-choice or open-ended questions, permit students to display their knowledge and skills without anxiety. In the same functional literacy CBI project described above, students report that the computer gives them a new lease on their educational lives. This kind of fresh start for students with a long history of failure is invaluable.

Of course, there are situations in which traditional tests are warranted. If reliable and valid tests matching the objectives of a particular CBI program are available, there is no reason why they cannot be used for estimating lesson effectiveness. All too often, however, tests do not reflect the actual learning objectives of CBI or they are administered in a manner which invalidates their results.

Whatever types of measures of the immediate instructional effectiveness (simulations, tests, checklists, rating scales) are used, the evaluator should also make some effort to measure the actual implementation of the CBI and relate this information to the outcome data. CBI is usually delivered at a number of different sites under a variety of conditions. The implementation or actual use of a particular CBI program may vary considerably from site to site. The assumption that a student at Site A experiences the same instructional program as a student at Site B should not go untested. Environmental factors such as hardware reliability, physical setting, power fluctuations, computer system load, and so forth can greatly affect the implementation of CBI. Personal factors such as local support by teachers or administrators can have similar impact on the kind of CBI a student actually experiences. A full discussion of the importance of assessing the actual implementation of CBI (versus the planned implementation) and the procedures for relating this information to outcome data cannot be accomplished in this paper. The interested reader is referred to Reeves (1979).

To summarize, assessment of the immediate learner effectiveness of CBI involves measuring the degree to which the short-term learning objectives of CBI have been accomplished. Computer simulations and tests (both of which must meet acceptable standards of reliability and validity) and measures of the actual implementation of CBI are used for this level of evaluation. Obviously, assessing the immediate instructional effectiveness of CBI is a time-consuming and expensive undertaking. If reliable and valid measures of program outcomes and processes are not available, poor measures should not be substituted. It is better to concentrate on other levels of evaluation than to administer unreliable instruments in an effort to evaluate immediate learner effectiveness.

Level 4: Impact Evaluation

It is beyond the scope and means of most CBI projects to evaluate definitively the ultimate impact of the CBI programs. For example, CBI used to teach functional literacy to soldiers will not only influence the lives and job performances of individual soldiers but will also affect the overall performance of their military units. Furthermore, many CBI projects result in advances in the technology and delivery of CBI which may ultimately impact on other CBI projects. Unfortunately, the current state of the art of evaluation does not permit the adequate measurement of these kinds of impact nor their conclusive attribution to a specific project. Still another problem is that the time span of a CBI project often ends before impacts on the participants or the contexts in which they work can be observed.

Nevertheless, some effort must be made to assess the long-term impact of CBI. Two approaches are recommended. First, interviews and anecdotal records can be used to answer questions about the transfer of the knowledge and skills learned through CBI to other environments. These procedures can also be used to collect multiple perspectives on the intended and unintended outcomes of a particular project. Second, a model for relating program inputs and processes to program outcomes can be used in an attempt to explain the costs and effects of a CBI project so that the findings can be used in the development of other CBI projects.

Interview protocols are adequately described in other sources (Benjamin, 1974; Guba and Lincoln, 1981) and anecdotal records are described above (see Figure 4). These qualitative data collection procedures can be used to estimate the impact of a CBI project from the multiple perspectives of all the participants. Developers and site managers can use anecdotal records to record revealing stories of the long-range influence of CBI projects on users. For example, an anecdote from a military CBI project describes the case of a particularly unmotivated soldier who became so involved in using a computer

for instructional purposes that his commanders noted a radical change in work attitude. Interviews conducted 6 weeks to 6 months after participation in CBI can be used to estimate the relevance of knowledge, skills, and attitudes acquired through CBI from the viewpoints of users. In a training situation, interviews can be employed to collect supervisors' opinions of the relevance and transfer of learning through CBI. Though such "soft" data are out of favor in some circles, they can be reported in reliable and meaningful formats so as to affect the decision making of program sponsors and other decision makers.

As noted above, a second approach to impact evaluation involves attempts to explain the effects of a CBI project in terms of a project's inputs and processes. This is not something to be undertaken casually, but it can be very rewarding. Evaluation theorists, practitioners, and users have all recently called for comprehensive evaluations which relate program inputs and processes to program outcomes. Very few projects have successfully implemented this approach to evaluation.

Though it is obvious that the outcomes of most instructional programs (CBI or otherwise) can be explained in terms of the abilities and prior achievements students bring to the program and the instructional activities in which they participate during the programs, many if not most evaluations concentrate solely on measuring program outcomes. A notable exception to outcomes-oriented evaluations is the Instructional Dimensions study conducted by Cooley and Leinhardt (1980). These researchers used a simple model of classroom processes (see Figure 8) to evaluate the effectiveness of several reading and math programs in elementary schools. Their approach not only enabled Cooley and Leinhardt to indicate the relative effectiveness of the various programs they examined, but also allowed them to specify the particular components of the programs which explained their relative effectiveness.

Leinhardt (1980) lists the requirements for this type of evaluation as methods of measuring processes as well as inputs and outcomes, causal models of the influence of

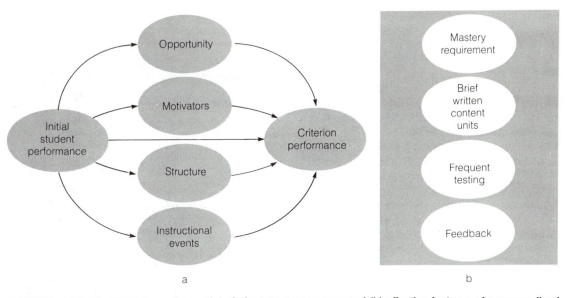

FIGURE 8: (a) Basic dimensions of a model of classroom processes and (b) effective features of a personalized system of instruction

process on outcomes, and techniques for analyzing the data. She points out that the measurement of instructional processes is often very difficult and expensive. Fortunately, CBI, unlike many other instructional treatments, permits the accurate and efficient collection of instructional process data. CBI, because of the data collection ability of the computer itself, provides a unique opportunity to conduct evaluation research which is not only relevant to explaining the effects of a particular CBI program, but also significant for research on CBI in general. Techniques for managing and analyzing such evaluation data are also available. What is missing is a causal model which relates student characteristics and the effective dimensions of CBI to outcomes. The authors are currently constructing a model using the techniques of meta-analysis (Glass, 1976; McGaw and Glass, 1980). When this work is completed, an attempt to validate the model will be made using the data from a large scale military CBI project.

In summary, impact evaluation is the process of assessing the long-term effects of CBI. Despite the difficulties described above,

some efforts to evaluate the long-term impacts of CBI must be made. The sponsors and consumers of CBI should be as [well] informed as possible about the ultimate effects of CBI when they make decisions about continuance, expansion, or selection. Furthermore, resources for CBI will probably always be less than desirable, and the competition for these resources should be based on impact data rather than politics or whimsy.

Conclusion

As noted above, a review of CBI literature reveals that very few CBI projects have employed more than one or two of the four levels of evaluation: documentation, formative evaluation, evaluation of immediate learner effectiveness, and impact evaluation. Partially, this is due to time and budget constraints. In addition, it is suggested that many CBI developers have not considered the full range of evaluation levels applicable in CBI projects. This paper provides CBI project personnel with guidelines and a few sample instruments for the systematic evaluation of the development and implementation of CBI. Figure 9 [. . .] illustrates the various evaluation methods which can be employed at each level of evaluation.

The developers of CBI have a unique opportunity, if not a responsibility, to thoroughly evaluate their efforts. Unlike many other approaches to instruction, CBI uses a teacher which can be programmed to systematically record every response of the student as well as every instructional strategy of the "teacher." Used systematically and creatively, the instructional monitoring power of computers can yield accurate, timely information which can influence the decision making of project participants in ways impossible in many other education and training contexts.

REFERENCES

Anderson, S. B., and Ball, S. *The profession and practice of program evaluation.* San Francisco: Jossey-Bass, 1978.

Beilby, A. "Determining instructional costs through functional cost analysis." *Journal of Instructional Development,* 3(2), 1979.

Benjamin, A. *The helping interview* (2nd ed.). Boston: Houghton Mifflin, 1974.

Cooley, W. W., and Leinhardt, G. "The instructional dimensions study." *Educational Evaluation and Policy Analysis,* 1980, 2(1), 7–25.

Felden, J., and Pearson, P. K. *The cost of learning with computers.* London: Council for Educational Technology, 1978.

Fitzpatrick, M. J., and Howard, J. A. "Field evaluation of a microprocessor-based computer for educational applications" (Abstract). *Journal of Computer-Based Instruction,* 1976, *2,* 103–104.

Fletcher, J. D., and Suppes, P. "The Stanford project on computer-assisted instruction for hearing-impaired students." *Journal of Computer-Based Instruction,* 1976, *3,* 1–12.

Glass, G. V. "Primary, secondary, and meta-analysis of research." *Educational Researcher,* 1976, *5,* 3–8.

Evaluation Area	Test Scores	Questionnaire or Interview Data	Logs, Anecdotal Records	Observation	Ratings	Computer-Managed Records	Expert Review	Previous Research Findings	Cost Data and Cost Performance Models
Cost analysis		✔	✔	✔		✔		✔	✔
Documentation			✔			✔			✔
Formative evaluation	✔	✔	✔	✔		✔	✔		
Instructional effectiveness	✔	✔	✔			✔			
Impact	✔	✔	✔		✔	✔	✔		
Cost effectiveness	✔	✔	✔	✔	✔	✔	✔	✔	✔

FIGURE 9: Evaluation level by matrix method (Adapted from Anderson and Ball, 1978)

Guba, E. G., and Lincoln, Y. S. *Effective evaluation*. San Francisco: Jossey-Bass, 1981.

Leinhardt, G. "Modeling and measuring educational treatment in evaluation." *Review of Educational Research*, 1980, *50*(3), 393–420.

Lent, R. M. "A model for applying cost-effectiveness analysis to decisions involving the use of instructional technology." *Journal of Instructional Development*, 2(5), 1979.

Lent, R. M. "An examination of the methods of cost-effectiveness analysis as applied to instructional technology." (Doctoral dissertation, Syracuse University, 1980.) *Dissertation Abstracts International*, 1980, *41*, 2409-A.

McGaw, B., and Glass, G. V. "Choice of the metric for effect size in meta-analysis." *American Educational Research Journal*, 1980, *17*(3), 325–337.

McPherson-Turner, C. "CAI readiness checklist: Formative author-evaluation of CAI lessons." *Journal of Computer-Based Instruction*, 1979, 6(2), 47–49.

MicroSIFT. *Evaluator's Guide for Microcomputer-Based Instructional Packages*. Portland, Ore.: ICCE, 1982.

Muston, R., and Wagstaff, R. "Introducing the computer into teacher education" (Abstract). *Journal of Computer-Based Instruction*, 1976, 2, 108–109.

Nie, N. H., Hull, C. H., Jenkins, J. G., Steinbrenner, K., and Bent, D. H. *Statistical package for the social studies* (2nd ed.). New York: McGraw-Hill, 1975.

O'Neil, H. F., Jr. (Ed.). *Procedures for instructional systems development*. New York: Academic Press, 1979.

Rahmlow, H. F., Fratini, R. C., and Ghesquiere, J. R. *Plato* (From Instructional Design Library, Vol. 30.) Englewood Cliffs, N.J.: Educational Technology Publications, 1980.

Reeves, T. C. "Evaluating the implementation of an instructional design across settings." (Doctoral dissertation, Syracuse University, 1979.) *Dissertation Abstracts*, 1979, *40.5*, 2616-A (University Microfilms No. 7925615).

Rosenshine, B. V. "Primary grades instruction and student achievement gain." Paper presented at the annual meeting of the American Educational Research Association, New York, 1977.

Rubin, H., Geller, J., and Hanks, J. "Computer simulation as a teaching tool in biology—A case study: The Biological Systems Analysis and Simulation Laboratory of the City University of New York." *Journal of Computer-Based Instruction*, 1977, 3, 91–96.

Su, S.Y.W., and Eman, A. E. "Teaching the principles of software systems on a minicomputer." *Journal of Computer-Based Instruction*, 1975, 1, 73–79.

Swigger, K. M. "Automated Flanders Interactional Analysis." *Journal of Computer-Based Instruction*, 1976, 2, 63–66.

15 Evaluation in Courseware Development

Decker F. Walker
Robert D. Hess

Stanford University

Introduction

It is easy to criticize the quality of educational software. Some established professionals in the field of computer-based education claim that 95 percent of the educational software available for microcomputers is of poor quality. Although this is an extreme view, few openly express satisfaction with the current state of educational software. Yet on what are such judgments based? Certainly not on formal evaluation studies. In fact, some argue that it is impossible to talk sensibly about formally evaluating educational software; to do so would be analogous to trying to identify high quality books or "blackboard courseware."

Nonetheless, judgments will be made about software: informally, as part of a decision to purchase or not to purchase a given program, or in the more formal terms of published review articles. Although it is not easy to define precisely a universal set of criteria for evaluating educational software, the effort to make explicit the basis for our judgments and to provide for them a foundation that can be subjected to discussion, criticism, and possibly even empirical test is an important part of the overall task of improving educational software.

Diverse Audiences, Diverse Criteria

Programmers can improve the quality of their products by recognizing the multifaceted na-ture of the total evaluative process. Evaluation is not a single isolated stage of product development; it is an ongoing, continual confrontation between the features of the program and the assessments of the people who create it, authorize it, buy it, use it, read about it, and hear about it. The fate of the program is passed from hand to hand as different people assess it and make their judgments, often with only partial information, hastily acquired. Each of these audiences brings its own criteria to bear in different ways. A good evaluation illuminates the choices made by all members of the policy-shaping community, as we and our associates in *Toward Reform of Program Evaluation* (Cronbach et al., 1981) termed the parties concerned in an evaluation.

The major audience groups who appraise software include:

Developers

Reviewers

Publishers

Users

Less directly concerned, but sometimes also powerful, audiences include:

Educational and psychological researchers

Educational policy makers (local, state, and federal)

Influential social and political leaders

Media concerned with education

Foundation officials

Corporate leadership of firms in the industry

All these groups have a stake in computer-based education. Anything an evaluation can do to clarify the criteria these groups apply as they make decisions affecting the development of educational software will contribute to the overall improvement of education and to the evolution of an appropriate role for the computer in the education of the future. Even an evaluation intended only for the eyes of the developer would do well to address the concerns of these other audiences whose assessment may determine the fate of the product.

It hardly needs saying that the criteria used by those who assess a piece of courseware are affected by the role the assessors play in the educational process. Sometimes these criteria are implicit in the personal, intuitive judgments they make in the course of their daily affairs. A person who comes in contact with the program in the ordinary business of the day may be attracted or repelled by some subtle feature that the developer may hardly have noticed, but about which this person has a strong opinion. Such offhand responses may ignore other aspects that others consider even more important.

Somewhat more formally, judgments may be based on explicit, stated criteria of educational value. Professional educators are encouraged to develop clear "philosophies of education" that make such criteria explicit. Schools and districts often develop stated criteria that are used in materials selection.

A further step ahead in sophistication consists of criteria based on psychological or instructional principles. These often draw on theories or models of motivation, of cognition, of learning and memory. The body of research and theory available to guide the assessment of software is significant and growing.

The strongest basis one could offer for a program presumably is demonstrated effectiveness in promoting student learning. This implies some sort of formal evaluation of the impact of the program on students.

Evaluation Options for the Developer

Faced with such a multiplicity of types of criteria, let alone the criteria themselves and priorities among them, how should the developer proceed with evaluations? One starting point is that the variety of types of evaluation ought to reflect the variety of roles and criteria. From an array of evaluation options, developers ought to be able to choose those best suited to the particular situations they face. What are some of these options?

Option A: Informal Evaluation by the Developer

Evaluation is built into the activity of courseware development. Whether working alone or in a team, courseware developers are constantly using their own experience and judgment to weigh the pros and cons of thousands of possible features of their working designs. Every decision to use a particular feature is an implicit evaluation of the usefulness of this feature in comparison with other choices.

Everything the developer knows can enter into these judgments about what works and what doesn't, what is an improvement and what is not. Developers make evaluative judgments continually as the work proceeds, and the validity of these judgments reflects the developer's skill and experience. The readings in this volume were selected to help the developer be more explicit and deliberate in making these informal self-evaluations.

These informal evaluation efforts are both necessary and desirable, but they are not sufficient. Developers cannot always accurately predict what will work in practice. The user's perspectives and needs are so diverse that no developer is likely to be able to anticipate all the perspectives groups of users will bring to the courseware being developed. Writers who construct test items are often surprised by the interpretations some test takers give to the most carefully constructed items. Courseware writers have the same problem.

Literal-minded students have been known to answer questions like "Can you find more ways to explain this?" with "YES." On a larger scale, material that is excruciatingly dull for someone who has already learned it may be quite interesting to the student who is encountering it for the first time and experiencing the thrill of mastery.

Informal judgments are a necessary starting point, but they can be improved in several ways. We will consider four further options: reviews using formal criteria, open-ended reviews, field trials, and formal evaluations of student learning.

Option B: Systematic Reviews Using Formal Criteria

All judgments of the merit of anything are based on some criteria, but the criteria are often implicit and unexpressed. People may be entirely unaware of the criteria that underlie their judgments. It can be an arduous discipline to try to state explicitly what one counts as a strong point in favor of a piece of courseware or a weak point against it. It can be infuriating to be pressed to give a reason for your opinion when your preferences are very strong and firm but you cannot easily find a rationale for them. But the stretch toward explicitness, order, and consistency can add clarity and wisdom to unexamined choices and make the effort worthwhile.

A number of organizations and individuals have enumerated points to consider in evaluating educational software designed for use with microcomputers. We have drawn up a list for use in the Interactive Educational Technology program at Stanford (see Table 1). It includes many of the criteria that appear on checklists published by prominent educational organizations, but it is organized to emphasize those we believe have more fundamental educational significance. (A list of some educational organizations that have published criteria for software evaluation is appended to this reading.)

Courseware developers should draw up

TABLE 1: Educational Software Review Criteria

Interactive Educational Technology Program
School of Education
Stanford University

I. Quality of Content and Goals

1. Accuracy
2. Importance
3. Completeness
4. Balance
5. Interest
6. Fairness
7. Appropriateness to user's situation

II. Instructional Quality

1. Provides opportunity to learn
2. Provides aids to learning
3. Motivational quality
4. Instructional flexibility
5. Relation to rest of educational program
6. Social quality of the instructional interaction
7. Quality of testing and assessment
8. Likely impact on students
9. Likely impact on teachers and teaching

III. Technical Quality

1. Reliability
2. Ease of use
3. Quality of display
4. Quality of response handling
5. Quality of program management
6. Quality of documentation
7. Other technical qualities (specify)

their own list of criteria reflecting their own values, but with an eye on what other audiences look for and value in courseware. Programs under development should be reviewed in a formal way by applying such a checklist of criteria early and often. The proposal stage is not too early to subject a plan to formal review both to ensure that it is worthwhile and to determine how it can be strengthened. If a full storyboard or other readily interpretable specification process is used, this can be rated as well. A fully functional version of the courseware should be rated both by developers themselves and by representative users.

Reviews such as these can be made the subject of conferences among developers at various stages of the project. The ratings can help to focus such discussions and to elevate debate above the "Well, I like it" stage toward a more objective, user-oriented perspective.

Although they are useful, formal criteria are not the complete answer to the problem of evaluating courseware. Sometimes genuine, substantial virtues are not touched by the categories of the finest list of criteria. A program can be excellent in ways that the creators of the categories never anticipated. The same is true of weaknesses and shortcomings.

Finally, ratings are themselves judgments that call on the skills, knowledge, and experience of the rater. The criteria are often stated in vague and general terms (e.g., quality, interest, appropriateness) that do not spell out the standards that are to be applied. For these reasons, it is useful to invite others to apply their own judgment and perspectives. Such open-ended reviews by experts offer another perspective and approach in evaluating courseware.

Option C: Open-Ended Reviews

An experienced, perceptive courseware reviewer offers a breadth and depth of perspective that can be applied in an unfettered way to the courseware at hand. Such a reviewer examines dozens, perhaps hundreds of programs each year and develops a keen eye for the strengths and limitations of a variety of different programs.

The easiest and best way to demonstrate how valuable a sensitive, penetrating review by an impartial expert can be is to show one. Leslie Czechowicz's review is an outstanding example of criticism that is balanced, constructive, and helpful to both user and developer.

English Basics Part II
Concepts in Language Arts[*]

Educational Activities, Inc.

Leslie I. Czechowicz

Computer programs are being developed for more curricular areas than ever before. It is encouraging to see the increasing number of programs to support the language arts. Educational Activities, Inc., has developed a set of English programs authored by Dr. Stefan Irving and William Arnold, appropriate for grades 3 through 6. The programs are divided into two areas: Parts of Speech, and Concepts in Language Arts. Parts of Speech includes nouns, pronouns, verbs, adjectives, and adverbs. Concepts in Language Arts includes homonyms, synonyms, antonyms, and contractions. I have examined two of the programs: synonyms and antonyms, and contractions.

While I would be hesitant to recommend the programs I examined, for reasons which follow, I shall try to help the novice software purchaser by providing some guidelines for program selection. With the large number of software producers in the market and the range of quality available, making a choice is a formidable task.

Good classroom programs assume the user is naive. These programs assume that the student knows that the Return key must be pressed to enter an answer. While this is a standard practice, a good program gives the user all of the information necessary for operating the program.

Detailed documentation is a must! The single greatest failing of educational software today is the lack of documentation. While Educational Activities, Inc., has provided a four-page teacher's guide, it is far from adequate. Documentation of programs for classroom use should include information on the content, structure, and intended use of

[*] Leslie I. Czechowicz, "English Basics Part II Concepts in Language Arts: Educational Activities, Inc.," *Journal of Courseware Review*, Vol. 1, No. 1, pp. 75–79. Reprinted by permission of *Journal of Courseware Review*.

the program. A really useful teacher's guide would include all the synonyms, antonyms, and contractions used in the program and the rationale for their inclusion. It would tell the teacher how the programs are structured. What happens if the student answers five questions wrong consecutively? Flowcharts for the instructional design would give this information succinctly. Detailed instructional objectives and mastery levels should be included. It would be helpful to know the reading level of the text in this program and other programs. Good documentation also provides information on integrating the program into the curriculum.

Computer programs should adapt to individual needs by branching in response to the student's answers. The most exciting thing about the computer in the classroom is its ability to vary the materials presented to the student based on the number and type of errors made. Unfortunately, in the two programs tested, the same exercises were presented, whether or not the questions were all answered correctly.

A student should not be able to break the program by "fooling around" with the keyboard. When the student can stop a computer program or cause it to exit to BASIC code, two things happen; the teacher has to attend to an activity that has been designed to be independent, and the game of breaking the program may become more attractive than the activities on the program. I was able to break these programs by pressing the control (CTRL) key and "C" at certain points in the programs. This was actually supposed to take me back to the menu. I was also able to break the synonyms program by typing continuously when I was supposed to be entering an answer. In the contractions program, pressing Return without entering an answer moved the question up several lines on the screen.

Students should be able to escape from programs without completing all the exercises. Good programs permit the user to exit from them at any time. Recognizing this, Educational Activities designates CTRL and "C" be pressed together as the escape mechanism. Actually, one must sometimes also press Return afterward. Unfortunately, this escape does not always work and, as noted before, sometimes breaks the program.

The best escape mechanisms require just the press of one key to take the user back to the menu.

Good programs use good English. The synonym and antonym, and contractions programs scored relatively high in this regard, though I thought the list of synonyms for "many" would have been improved by deleting "gobs" and "a bunch." Unfortunately, slang expressions such as "right on" and "check this out" are incorporated into the program. Since many teachers are fighting valiantly to promote good English usage and broad vocabularies, programs that use slang expressions are going to have reduced appeal for classroom use. Also, programs that use popular slang expressions to sound timely will eventually sound dated.

Students should control the rate at which materials are presented. Every classroom teacher has a wide range of reading speeds among his or her students. When programs have the student press the space bar or some other key when they are finished reading, the program can be used by each student comfortably. The student has this control throughout most of the two programs reviewed.

Menus should be descriptive. A good menu has descriptive titles or includes a very brief description of the program to guide the user in his or her selection. Without any descriptions the user has no information upon which to base his or her choice. The menus for these programs not only lack description but use two numeration systems. [. . .] A Synonyms-1 is not very informative.

Students should get immediate feedback. Students should know immediately whether their answers were right. These programs do give students that information, but they have fallen into the trap of effusive praise. In an effort to reinforce students for correct answers, the programs respond with statements such as "I like that," "right you are," "right on," "super," "very nice," "wonderful," [and] "good for you." A simple "correct" or "no" gives the needed information. Getting the answer right has a value all its own. Excessive praise for a minor accomplishment has the subtle message of surprise at the student's success.

In the first synonym program, when the student enters the number of the correct answer, a reward statement, such as "OK" [. . .] appears and is followed by an answer statement, saying this is the correct answer because it is the best choice. It takes a long time for this statement to appear, and the student already knows that the answer he gave was correct. The program would be improved if this redundant answer statement did not follow correct answers. [. . .]

When a student makes an error, a second chance, prompting, or an explanation would be in order. With the synonyms program, an error results in a "no", then the appearance of a circular sentence. [. . .] The response to an incorrect answer is better in the antonyms program, where information is given to the student. [. . .]

Effective lessons are interesting. This is true regardless of the instructional media. Computer lessons should be interesting because of the content and the graphics. The use of graphics, cartoon characters, colors, etc., makes programs interesting. These Basic English programs do use inverse video and boxing but are not exciting graphically. However, programs with exciting graphics usually have a higher price tag than those without.

Effective lessons reinforce correct responses. There is a strange phenomenon that occurs in some computer lessons and has been avoided in these: the response to a wrong answer is more fun to get than the response to a right answer. For instance, if a wrong answer causes a cartoon character to take a step in walking the plank, students will start purposely answering questions incorrectly to see this little character meet his demise.

The contractions program would be improved if the correct rather than the incorrect answer were highlighted. Since highlighting a word draws the student's attention to it, highlighting a wrong answer increases the likelihood that the student will remember the wrong answer rather than the right one. [. . .]

Teachers need cost-effective programs. With budgets for education more limited than they have been in 20 years, programs must be designed to provide maximum value. If I were looking for a synonym program for my classroom, I would try to find a driver program, that is, a program that has the structure of the lesson but lets the teacher insert the synonyms the students will be studying. Such a program can be used to reinforce vocabulary from any curricular area. By using a driver program and inserting your own synonyms, or database, you have a program customized to the needs of your class.

Many good programs have HELP keys. By pressing the key designated as the HELP key during a lesson, the student can usually elect to see an example of what is being studied, a review of information necessary for successfully completing the lesson, or [the student] can get back to the menu. HELP keys are particularly valuable in programs designed for independent use.

Beware of "page-turning" programs. When considering a program for your classroom, ask yourself if the program really makes use of the computer's capabilities. There are a lot of programs that essentially display text and have the student push a key to see more text. A "page-turning" program has a minimal amount of student interaction with the computer. These are called "page-turning" programs because, basically, the material could have been presented to the student in book form and have been equally effective.

Programs should be sensitive to the developmental level of the user group. Programs for young children should not require a lot of typing, reading, or remembering long sequences of directions. While students are asked to enter some answers by typing in the Basic English program, there were also portions of the programs where the student selected the number of the correct answer and entered the number. The kind of interaction required of the student should be related to the objectives of the program. You may want a program that has the children enter words by typing them if one of your objectives is to have the students learn to spell the words.

Screen displays should be designed for ease of viewing. Text is much easier to read from a screen if that text appears on every other line. Overuse of spacing can be a distraction. The cosmetic aspects of a program should be as vital as the educational design.

In summary, I recommend keeping the following things in mind when shopping for educational programs.

Good classroom programs assume the user is naive.

Detailed documentation is essential!

Computer programs should adapt to individual needs by branching in response to the student's answers.

A student should not be able to break the program by "fooling around" with the keyboard.

Students should be able to escape from programs without completing all the exercises.

Good programs use good English.

Students should control the rate at which materials are presented.

Menus should be descriptive.

Students should get immediate feedback.

Effective lessons are interesting.

Effective lessons reinforce *correct* responses.

Teachers need cost-effective programs.

Many good programs have HELP keys.

Beware of "page-turning" programs.

Programs should be sensitive to the developmental level of the user group.

Screen displays should be designed for ease of viewing.

Developers who can solicit such a review, even though it may cost a couple of hundred dollars, should consider the money well spent. It is only a small fraction of the total cost involved in developing the courseware, and the information it yields can be exceedingly useful.

Option D: Field Trials

Both formal and informal judgments of the most experienced and astute developers and reviewers need to be supplemented with field trials conducted with users like those for whom the courseware is intended. These field trials take different forms as the development proceeds, beginning with asking a friend or a neighbor's child to try out a section of the program and ranging upward in sophistication to a full-scale, well-designed experimental field study.

We see at least four possibilities: (1) a preliminary tryout, using anyone available, for the purpose of discovering whether particular features work as intended; (2) an informal field trial with a small group of users of a draft version of the entire program or of free-standing modules within it, to discover any major flaws in the overall design as well as any remaining particular problems; (3) tryouts with a teacher and a class under real school conditions as part of an ongoing instructional program, for a full feasibility test but without using any measures or instruments other than perhaps teacher-made tests; and (4) a formal field trial with appropriate pre- and posttests. We discuss below types of field study appropriate to various stages of development and to the various questions uppermost in the minds of developers at each stage.

Any program goes through many stages in its development. The earliest working fragments of a program are suitable only for quick, inexpensive, informal trials. They are the software equivalent of breadboarded circuits—working but still very much under development. The first working version of a piece of courseware often has obvious debilitating flaws that must be revised before the piece can be tried out. But as soon as such gross problems are corrected, some sort of field trial is in order. Otherwise time will be wasted on refinements to features that may not survive subsequent revisions. This is no time to polish. The major decision to be made with this first preliminary version is whether to proceed with the development pretty much as planned or to go back to the drawing boards for substantial redesign.

Often all that's needed at this stage is a naive user of any sort—a friend, a co-worker, . . . what is known in the trade as a "convenience sample." Spend an hour looking over the user's shoulder; notice variations in level and type of psychological involvement with the program; notice when and where errors are made and the kinds of error. Ask users to think aloud and listen to what they say; ask questions, interview the users afterward. You may come away with enough revision work to occupy your next few weeks.

A second useful form of field trial is to try the program with a group of users under realistic field conditions. The situation should be arranged to permit you to observe several students of different abilities. For example, if the program is intended for the sixth grade, you might include some fifth grade and some seventh grade students as a check on your grade placement decision. Also, notice the interaction among the students. Does it interfere with the program or enhance it? If students are constantly looking over one another's shoulder and asking for help, your instructions may be unclear. Notice the variation in time taken to complete a part of the program. Is this within a range that will be accepted by students and teachers?

When all the readily visible major problems have been eliminated, a more extensive and systematic field trial becomes practical. In most cases, these trials will not be funded evaluations, but investigations of a very practical form and function, conducted and supported by the developer. A common form of field trial at this stage is to have an experienced computer-using teacher try out the materials in his or her classroom, if that is the setting for which the program is intended. Such potential users will be volunteers, but they should be representative (except for their experience and willingness to volunteer as pioneering users) of the population for whom the product is intended.

Sometimes it is worthwhile to forgo the advantages of an especially experienced or talented user and go directly to field trials with typical users, including teachers and students with little or no experience with computers. Much can be learned from naive users; their pattern of errors is often quite different from that of experienced users who bring so much more with them to the experience.

The helpfulness of these trials depends on the ability of the teachers and students to supply information about how the program works for them. Users are not always experienced or talented at observing themselves and articulating their reactions. But the most valuable benefit from field trials—identification of serious unsuspected problems—does not require subtle instrumentation. Users will usually be quite clear—even emphatic—in their rejection of a defective piece of software, although they differ greatly in their ability to explain why they did not like it.

It is often helpful to supplement observation data at this stage with interviews, rating sheets, and other self-report data from users. Decisions about what data to collect in field trials depend on the questions most urgently in need of answers. Specific questions will arise about each program, and the developer will compile a list of points that should be covered, but there are more general topics that will usually be of interest.

A common concern of obvious importance is the attention-getting and attention-holding power of the courseware being evaluated. The appeal of the program can be gauged by simple observation under circumstances where users will typically be involved with the program. A more stringent test would be to set up a situation where the program competes with some attractive alternative activity. One developer reports getting excellent feedback on motivational characteristics of a program by setting up a booth at a computer fair and watching fairgoers interact with the program. The developers of *Sesame Street* set up a room with a television set showing forthcoming segments of the program and a slide projector showing interesting photographs, and watched children's reactions through a one-way mirror. This kind of strategy could be adapted for use with computer software.

The ease of use of the courseware will probably be a matter of central importance. Both observational techniques and postuse interviewing can be helpful in assessing whether the program is friendly or formidable, whether the documentation is adequate, and so on.

The ease with which users comprehend the material presented is obviously a primary concern, and field trials give useful information on this point. Are users able to read the text, interpret the diagrams, and respond appropriately when prompted? Observations are helpful in assessing comprehension, but some form of testing is a more effective way to pinpoint comprehension problems. Fortunately, it is quite easy to insert questions in the program designed specifically to measure the user's comprehension of previously presented material.

Is the courseware actually used as intended? Surprisingly, users often find original ways to use courseware. They may skip features developers regard as critical to success with the program. They may fill in any sort of nonsense answer to get the program to tell them the correct answer. The response of the program to an error may be so interesting that users intentionally make mistakes. Users may prefer to guess, having discovered that a few guesses will hit the correct response more quickly than figuring out the correct answer. They may become intrigued by features of the program that are essentially irrelevant to its educational objectives. Courseware designed as a supplement may be used as the entire educational program and courseware designed to bear the main burden of instruction may be used as supplementation.

Field trials should be continued long enough for users to pass the stage of novelty. Observations in a test site that has been using the materials for some time, long enough for users to develop their own habits of use, will often yield surprising insights into how the courseware is actually used. Sometimes it can be modified to bring actual use more in line with intended use.

Option E: Formal Evaluations

The next step upward in sophistication is a controlled formal field test of the educational effectiveness of the program, that is, its impact on students' learning. Such studies are not customary in courseware development, but until such assessments are made, questions will continue to be raised about the util-

ity of computer-based educational materials.

Ideally, sites should be randomly selected to represent the user population. The design of the study should control for various possible contaminating factors. For example, some teachers might be asked to teach two classes; in one they use the materials, in the other they use another curriculum. This helps rule out differences among teachers as a source of bias in the evaluation. Formal instruments with known measurement characteristics should be used to assess learning. If observers and interviewers are part of the study, they will be independent of the development team and, if possible, will be kept uninformed about which classrooms are experimental and which are not.

Formal field trials such as this are relatively expensive and require skills of design and analysis that are currently scarce. These studies are usually done by university-based researchers as dissertations or as part of an externally funded research project. A great deal might be done, however, to foster controlled field tests at reasonable cost through cooperation among schools, universities, and corporations.

Achievement can be measured directly with test items embedded within the instructional program. Posttests can also be administered either by computer or in paper-and-pencil form by the developer or by teachers after the user completes the program. Tests of retention can be administered several weeks later to confirm that what has been learned is still accessible. If the content being taught is expected to be used in contexts other than on a computer, tests should be administered in the target setting as well. For example, if your courseware is a simulated chemistry laboratory intended to substitute for the real thing, you would be well advised in your evaluation to see whether students who have learned to design and interpret chemical experiments on the computer can also do so in a real laboratory situation, given suitable orientation to the new environment.

Unless your courseware is designed to be used by a single user working alone with no other supporting material—readings, classes, exams, etc.—what you actually will be evaluating is a complete program in which your courseware is only one ingredient. The obvious way to distinguish the effect of this one ingredient is to compare a class that is otherwise identical, except that it doesn't use your courseware. If your courseware is a major part of the curriculum, this would clearly create an impossible situation. What do the students do who do not use your courseware? If they "do nothing" (obviously impossible—they will find something to do), the comparison is loaded. If they engage in some other activity thought to be educational, the possibility exists that any differences found in results could have been reversed if a different educational activity had been chosen.

This is a tricky problem for which there is no general resolution, but it is often possible to design a sensible alternative treatment that is comparable but does not use your courseware. Results of such a carefully designed study are likely to show relatively small differences simply because it is unlikely that any one aid to learning is going to do startlingly better than a good, sound educational program using other aids. Nevertheless, it is the hope of many developers to design courseware that makes a major difference. If you hold such hopes, you may want to arrange a carefully designed comparison with the best of conventional instruction. A useful guide in coping with the subtleties of designing evaluation studies is Cronbach's *Designing Evaluations* (1982).

You may wish to extend your evaluation beyond assessment of direct student outcomes to some of the subtler, less direct possible impacts that concern thoughtful educators. For example, the question of educational productivity requires careful assessment of the costs as well as the benefits of both conventional and computer-based programs. The question of equity is of pressing concern to many. Does your program work equally well with boys and girls? With academically talented and academically limited users? With poor users from deprived families and users who have all the advantages the society can provide? What impact does your program have on users' lives? Does it make them want to use computers more, or avoid them? Do users leave your program feeling confident of their ability to use computers or intimidated by them? Is their self-esteem enhanced or degraded?

Do people learn new things from working with computers? Do they, for example, learn to think more clearly and precisely as a result of learning to program? Do they learn how to visualize when they use graphic simulations? Do they learn to use systems thinking in their everyday life? When they are armed with the computer as a tool to carry out calculations, do they gain the confidence to tackle problems that would otherwise be difficult or impossible for them?

Questions like these pose the most difficult measurement and design problems because the effects being sought are not directly observable and may be produced by many competing influences in addition to your program. But beliefs about these ultimate impacts of educational programs often determine adoption or rejection of them, and for their importance alone they deserve our best efforts at confirmation.

Formal evaluations may seem impractical, but they often have unexpected benefits. For example, James Kulik (1981) reviewed formal evaluation studies of CAI programs and discovered something that would not have emerged from decades of informal trials. Figure 1 shows the amount of additional achievement that could be attributed to computer-based instruction in mathematics in the dozens of studies he reviewed. The results clearly show that the effect is greater for younger, less experienced students. This intriguing finding is possible only because the studies Kulik reviewed included formal, quantitative measures of achievement.

Is the Marketplace the Final Evaluator?

In one sense, what finally counts is whether the courseware is bought and used. This de-

Computer-based instruction in mathematics

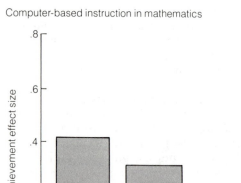

FIGURE 1: Age differences in effect of CAI on performance in math (from Kulik, 1981)

pends on many factors not under the developer's control—quality of the marketing, taste and judgment of the purchaser, availability of funds, how widely the machine for which the courseware is designed is used, size of the potential market, and so on. In all media one can find examples of works eventually regarded as classics and works that heavily influenced other creators that were flops in the marketplace. And many box office hits have gone on to well-deserved oblivion. On the other hand, most classics were also successes in their own time.

A developer can choose to take the market as ultimate indicator of successful courseware or to supplement market success with other criteria, such as reviewers' judgments, respect and regard of other developers, winning of prizes, and satisfaction of personal criteria of good educational practice. But the market is always a consideration, and most developers find themselves urged to make "concessions to the market," i.e., to make revisions they believe to be of questionable educational value because purchasers will set a high value on such revisions.

Although it is definitely unwise for a developer to ignore market preferences, it is not necessary to pander to the market's current tastes. It is possible, though risky, to try to lead and shape consumers' tastes by offering them quality products they may not yet appreciate. Good evaluations can give both developer and consumer confidence that a new or unorthodox product is truly effective.

REFERENCES

Cronbach, L. J., S. A. Ambron, S. M. Dornbusch, R. D. Hess, R. C. Hornik, D. C. Phillips, D. F. Walker, and S. S. Weiner. *Toward Reform of Program Evaluation.* San Francisco: Jossey-Bass, 1981.

Cronbach, Lee J., with the assistance of Karen Shapiro. *Designing Evaluations of Educational and Social Programs.* San Francisco: Jossey-Bass, 1982.

Kulik, James. "Integrating findings from different levels of instruction." Unpublished paper presented at the annual meeting of the American Educational Research Association, Los Angeles, April 1981.

SELECTED SOURCES OF CRITERIA AND GUIDELINES FOR REVIEWING EDUCATIONAL SOFTWARE

Guidelines for Evaluating Computerized Instructional Materials, National Council of Teachers of Mathematics, 1906 Association Drive, Reston, Va., 22091.

K-12 Micromedia Inc., P.O. Box 17, Valley Cottage, N.Y., 10989.

Microcomputer Resource Center, Teachers College, Columbia University, New York, N.Y. 10027.

MicroSIFT News, Northwest Regional Educational Laboratory, 300 S.W. Sixth Ave., Portland, Ore., 97204.

Milliken Publishing Company, 1100 Research Blvd., St. Louis, Mo. 63132.

Minnesota Educational Computer Consortium (MECC), 2520 Broadway Dr., St. Paul, Minn., 55113.

Scholastic Inc., 904 Sylvan Ave., Englewood Cliffs, N.J., 07632.

The Computing Teacher, c/o International Council for Computers in Education, University of Oregon, Eugene, 97403.

The Journal of Courseware Review, c/o Foundation for the Advancement of Computer-aided Instruction, 20863 Stevens Creek Blvd., Building B-2, Suite A-1, Cupertino, Calif., 95014.

Webster/McGraw-Hill, Division, McGraw-Hill Book Company, 1221 Avenue of the Americas, New York, N.Y., 10020.

SELECTED JOURNALS THAT PUBLISH REVIEWS OF EDUCATIONAL SOFTWARE

Classroom Computer News
Box 266
Cambridge, Mass. 02138

Creative Computing
Box 789-M
Morristown, N.J. 07690

Cue Newsletter
c/o Don McKell
Independence High School
1776 Education Park Drive
San Jose, Calif. 95133

Dvorak's Software Review
704 Solano Ave.
Albany, Calif. 94706

Educational Computer
Box 535
Cupertino, Calif. 95015

Educational Technology
140 Sylvan Ave.
Englewood Cliffs, N.J. 07632

Electronic Learning
902 Sylvan Ave.
Englewood Cliffs, N.J. 07632

Journal of Courseware Review
The Foundation for the Advancement of Computer-aided Education (formerly the Apple Foundation)
Box 28426
San Jose, Calif. 95159

MACUL Journal
Michigan Association for Computer Users in Learning
Wayne County ISD
33500 Van Born Rd.
Wayne, Mich. 48184

Mathematics Teacher
National Council of Teachers of Mathematics
1906 Association Drive
Reston, Va. 22091

Microcomputers in Education
Queue
5 Chapel Hill Drive
Fairfield, Conn. 06432

Micro-scope
JEM Research
Discovery Park
University of Victoria
Box 1700
Victoria, B.C. V8W 2Y2 Canada

MicroSIFT
Northwest Regional Educational Laboratory
300 S.W. Sixth Ave.
Portland, Ore. 97204

Peelings II
945 Brook Circle
Las Cruces, N.M. 88001

Personal Computing
50 Essex St.
Rochelle Park, N.J. 07662

Pipeline
Conduit
University of Iowa
Box 388
Iowa City, Iowa 52244

School Microware Reviews
Summer 1981
Dresden Associates
Box 246
Dresden, Maine 04342

Software Review
Microform Review
520 Riverside Ave.
Westport, Conn. 06880

The Computing Teacher
Department of Computer and Information Science
University of Oregon
Eugene, Ore. 97403

16

Effects of Computer-based Teaching on Secondary School Students

James A. Kulik
Robert L. Bangert
George W. Williams

University of Michigan

Programs for computer-based teaching have come a long way in the 20 years since they were first developed. Today's programs come in a variety of sophisticated shapes and sizes, and show few traces of their origins in B. F. Skinner's modest, fill-in-the-blanks teaching machines. The programs tutor and drill students, diagnose learning difficulties, prescribe remedies for problems, keep records of student progress, and present material in print and diagram form. In their own way, they do nearly everything that good teachers do.

Pioneers in the area believed from the start that computer-based instruction [CBI] would bring great benefits to students and teachers (Gerard, 1967). Among the benefits expected for learners were better, more comfortable, and faster learning, since students would learn at their own pace and at their own convenience; opportunities to work with vastly richer materials and more sophisticated problems; personalized tutoring; and automatic measurement of progress. Benefits for teachers were to include less drudgery and repetition, greater ease in updating instructional materials, more accurate appraisal and documentation of student progress, and more time for meaningful contact with learners.

Has CBI produced such benefits? Soon after its introduction, educational researchers started to design evaluation studies to answer this question. In a typical study, a researcher divided a class of students into an experimental and a control group. Students in the experimental group received part of their instruction at computer terminals, whereas those in the control group received their instruction by conventional teaching methods. At the end of the experiment, the researcher compared responses of the two groups on a common examination or on a course evaluation form.

Although these evaluation studies produced potentially valuable information on the effects of computer-based teaching, the message from the studies was not immediately clear. One problem was that each evaluation report was published separately. The total picture was therefore not easy to see. Another more serious problem was that studies were never exact replications of one another. The studies differed in experimental designs, settings, and in the types of computer application they investigated. And worst of all, evaluation results differed from one investigation to another. Findings from different studies were never exactly the same.

Reviews were therefore written to bring the separately published studies together and to find the common threads among their results. The reviews that appeared were of two basic types: box-score reviews and meta-analyses. Box-score reviews usually reported the proportion of studies favorable and unfavorable toward CBI, and often provided narrative comments about the studies as well.

James A. Kulik, Robert L. Bangert, and George W. Williams, "Effects of Computer-based Teaching on Secondary School Students," *Journal of Educational Psychology* (February 1983). Copyright 1983 by the American Psychological Association. Reprinted by permission of the American Psychological Association and James A. Kulik.

Reviewers using Glass's meta-analysis (Glass, McGaw, and Smith, 1981) took a more quantitative approach to their task. Meta-analysts used: (1) objective procedures to locate studies, (2) quantitative or quasi-quantitative techniques to describe study features and outcomes, and (3) statistical methods to summarize overall findings and to explore relationships between study features and outcomes.

Reviewers using box-score and narrative methods usually concluded that computer-based teaching was effective in raising student achievement, especially in elementary schools. Vinsonhaler and Bass's review (1972), for example, reported that results from ten independent studies showed a substantial advantage for computer-augmented instruction. Elementary school children who received computer-supported drill and practice generally showed performance gains of 1 to 8 months over children who received only traditional instruction. Jamison, Suppes, and Wells (1974) also concluded that computer-based teaching when used as a supplement to regular instruction at the elementary level, improved achievement scores, particularly for disadvantaged students. At the secondary and college level, these reviewers concluded, computer-based teaching was at least as effective as traditional instruction, and sometimes resulted in substantial savings in student time. According to Edwards et al. (1975), computer-assisted instruction often produced better results than did conventional teaching on end-of-course examinations, but not on retention examinations. These reviewers also noted that computer-based teaching reduced the time it took students to learn.

Hartley (1977), who was the first to apply meta-analysis to findings on CBI, focused on mathematics education in elementary and secondary schools. She reported that the average effect of CBI in this area was to raise student achievement by .41 standard deviation, or from the 50th percentile to the 66th percentile. Hartley also reported that the effects produced by computer-based teaching were not so large as those produced by pro-

grams of peer and cross-age tutoring, but they were far larger than effects produced by programmed instruction or the use of individual learning packets. Finally, Hartley noted that although correlations between study features and outcomes were not generally high, a few study features significantly affected study outcomes. She pointed out, for example, that elementary students fared better with computer-based teaching than did secondary students.

Burns and Bozeman (1981), like Hartley, used meta-analysis to integrate findings on computer-assisted mathematics instruction in elementary and secondary schools. These reviewers found overall effect sizes of .45 for computer-based tutorial instruction and .34 for drill and practice. They found virtually no evidence of a relationship between experimental design features and study outcomes. Kulik, Kulik, and Cohen (1980) used meta-analysis to reach conclusions about the effectiveness of computer-based college teaching. They found that CBI raised the examination scores of college students by approximately .25 standard deviation. Computer-based teaching also had a moderate effect on the attitudes of students toward instruction and toward the subjects they were studying. Finally, Kulik and his colleagues reported that CBI reduced substantially the amount of time needed for instruction.

Kulik (1981), reviewing evidence from his own quantitative synthesis of findings and from Hartley's (1977), concluded that the effectiveness of computer-based teaching is a function of instructional level, at least in mathematics education. Hartley found that computer-based teaching raised examination scores in mathematics by approximately .4 standard deviation at the elementary level and by approximately .3 standard deviation at the high school level, and Kulik reported that computer-based teaching raised examination scores by only .1 standard deviation in mathematics education at the college level. Kulik suggested that at the lower levels of instruction, learners need the stimulation and guidance provided by a highly reactive teaching medium. At the upper levels of instruction, a highly reactive instructional medium may not only be unnecessary, it may get in the way. College learners apparently profit from working by themselves on problems before receiving individual evaluations and prescriptions for further work.

This article uses meta-analysis to shed further light on the effectiveness of computer-based teaching. Its specific focus is CBI in grades 6 through 12. The article is meant to answer the sorts of questions commonly asked by meta-analysts. How effective is computer-based teaching? Is it especially effective for certain types of outcome or certain types of student? Under which conditions does it appear to be most effective?

Methods

This section describes the procedures used in locating studies, coding study features, and quantifying outcomes of studies. The procedures described here are similar to those used in other meta-analytic studies by Kulik and his associates (e.g., Kulik, Kulik, and Cohen, 1979a,b, 1980).

Sources of Data

The first step in this meta-analysis was to collect a large number of studies that examined effects of CBI on secondary school children.[1] We began the collection process by computer searching three data bases through Lockheed's DIALOG Online Information Service: *ERIC*, a data base on educational materials from the Educational Resources Information Center, consisting of the two files *Research in Education* and *Current Index to Journals in Education; Comprehensive Dissertation Abstracts;* and *Psychological Abstracts.* We developed special sets of key words for the three different data bases. The bibliographies in articles located through the computer searches provided a second source of studies for the meta-analysis.

In all, these bibliographic searches yielded a total of fifty-one studies that met the guidelines for inclusion in our final pool of studies. These guidelines were of three sorts. First, the studies had to take place in actual classrooms in grades 6 through 12. Studies carried out at higher or lower grade levels and studies describing laboratory analogues of classroom teaching did not meet this guideline. Second, studies had to report on measured outcomes in both CBI and control classes. Studies without control groups and studies with anecdotal reports of outcomes failed to meet this criterion. And third, studies had to be free from crippling methodological flaws. Excluded from the pool of usable studies were those in which treatment and control groups differed greatly in aptitude and those in which a criterion test was unfairly "taught" to one of the comparison groups.

In addition, we established guidelines to ensure that each study was counted only once in our analysis. When several papers described the same study, we used the most complete report for the analysis. When the same instructional outcome was measured with several instruments in a single paper, we pooled the results from the instruments to obtain a composite measure. Finally, when a single paper reported findings separately for different school subjects, we pooled results from the various subjects to obtain a composite result. These guidelines kept studies with more detailed analyses (i.e., many test scores and many subgroups) from having a disproportionate influence on overall results.

Characteristics of Studies

The next step in the meta-analysis was to develop variables and categories for describing features of the studies. The first of these variables covered type of computer application, and had five categories: drill and practice, tutoring, computer-managed teaching, simulation, and programming the computer to solve problems. In drill-and-practice studies, brief lessons were administered to the student at a computer terminal as follow-up exercises to a teacher's presentations. In tutoring studies, the computer program provided the presentation as well as the practice. In studies of computer-managed teaching, the computer evaluated student performance, diagnosed weaknesses, and guided students to appropriate instructional resources. In simulation studies, students explored relationships among variables in models simulating aspects of social or physical reality. Finally, in the programming studies, students programmed the computer to solve problems in the fields they were studying.

Two other variables were needed to describe differences in the use of the computer. The first of these variables indicated whether the computer served as a supplement to or substitute for conventional teaching. In studies in which the computer served as a substitute, it replaced teacher presentations, readings, assignments, or some combination of these. In studies where the computer served as a supplement, it did not replace regular course elements, but instead served as an additional resource for students. Another variable indicated the duration of the study. In some studies the computer was used in instruction for a full semester or even longer, whereas in other studies the computer was used for only a single unit, sometimes for as little as a week or two of instruction.

Studies differed not only in their use of the computer but also in other features. To describe these additional features, we defined eleven more variables. Five of these variables covered aspects of the experimental design of the studies: random vs. nonrandom assignment of students to comparison groups, control for teacher effects by using the same teacher for both experimental and control groups, control for historical effects by use of concurrent experimental and control groups, control for scoring bias through use of objective examinations, and control of author bias through use of commercial or standardized examinations. Three other variables described features of the course settings, including class level of students, subject mat-

ter, and average ability level of students. One variable indicated whether course materials were produced commercially or locally. And finally, two variables described publication features of the study: the manner of publication of the study and the year of publication.

Two of the study features initially selected for coding—control for historical effects and control for scoring bias—proved to be of little use because studies showed almost no variation on these features. In almost all studies, experimental and control groups were taught during the same semesters, and objective examinations were used as the criterion of student achievement. Because there was little variation in these features, they could not possibly explain observed variation in study outcomes. These variables were therefore dropped from the analysis at an early point, leaving twelve variables that might explain variation in study outcomes.

Study Outcomes

The fifty-one studies contained findings on effects of CBI in six major areas: final examination performance, performance on retention examinations, attitude toward subject matter taught in the experiment, attitude toward computers, attitude toward instruction, and time to learn. Examination outcomes were based on tests administered to students in both CBI and control classes. Attitudes toward computers, subject matter, and instruction were based on self-report responses to questionnaire items or scales. Student learning times were recorded in minutes.

To quantify outcomes in each of these areas, we used the effect size (*ES*), defined as the difference between the means of two groups divided by the standard deviation of the control group (Glass, McGaw, and Smith, 1981). For studies that reported means and standard deviations for both experimental and control groups, we calculated *ES* from the measurements provided. For less fully reported studies, we calculated *ES* from statistics such as *t* and *F*, using procedures described by Glass, McGaw, and Smith (1981).

To make our study more similar to traditional reviews, we also examined the direction and significance of differences in instructional outcomes in CBI and control classes. On the basis of results, we classified each outcome on the following four-point scale: 1 = difference favored conventional teaching and statistically significant, 2 = difference favored conventional teaching but not statistically significant, 3 = difference favored CBI but not statistically significant, and 4 = difference favored CBI and statistically significant.

In our previous meta-analyses of research on college-level programmed, audiotutorial, and computer-based instruction (Kulik, Kulik, and Cohen, 1979b, 1980; Kulik, Cohen, and Ebeling, 1980), we reported that different measures of effect size agreed remarkably well when applied to the same data set. This also turned out to be the case in the present analysis. For thirty-four of the studies with data on achievement outcomes, for example, we were able to calculate both *ES*s and scores on the four-point scale reflecting direction and significance of observed differences. The correlation between the two indices was .77. Because correlations between indices were generally so high, we were able to write regression equations for "plugging" effect–size measures for cases with some missing data. For example, when a study did not give any indication of within-group variances but did report the direction and significance of the difference between experimental and control means, we were able to use the score on the four-point scale to estimate *ES* with a high degree of accuracy.

Results

This section describes the effects of CBI on student achievement on final examinations and retention examinations; on student attitudes toward subject matter, computers, and instruction; and on amount of time students needed to learn.

Final Examinations

In thirty-nine of the forty-eight studies with results from final examinations, students from the CBI class received the better examination scores; in the nine other studies, students from the conventional class got the better scores. A total of twenty-five of the studies reported a statistically significant difference in results from the teaching approaches. Results of twenty-three of these studies favored CBI, and results of two studies favored conventional instruction. The box-score results therefore strongly favored CBI.

By using the index of effect size *ES,* we were able to describe the influence of CBI with greater precision. The average *ES* in the forty-eight studies was .32; the standard deviation of *ES* was .42; and its standard error was .061. This average *ES* implies that in a typical class, performance of CBI students was raised by .32 standard deviation. To interpret this effect more fully, it is useful to refer to areas of the standard normal curve. Using the guideline, we see that students from CBI classes performed at the 63rd percentile on their examinations, whereas students who received only conventional instruction performed at the 50th percentile on the same examinations. Or put in another way, 63 percent of the students from CBI classes outperformed the average student from the control classes.

Although the effect of CBI was moderate in the typical study, the size of effect varied from study to study (Figure 1). Effects of CBI ranged in size from high positive (e.g., an increase in achievement scores of approximately 1.5 standard deviations in two studies) to moderate negative (e.g., a decrease in achievement of approximately .5 standard deviation in two other studies). It seemed possible that this variation in study outcome might be systematic, and we therefore decided to carry out further analyses to determine whether different types of study were producing different results.

Further analysis of the data, however, did not disclose any strong relationships between study features and final examination scores. Only two of the features listed in Ta-

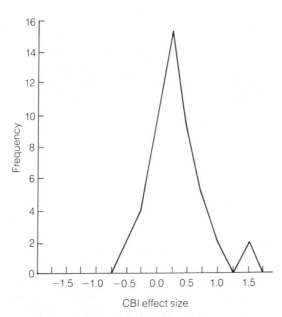

FIGURE 1: Distribution of effect sizes for forty-eight comparative studies of student achievement in computer-based and conventional classes (CBI = computer-based instruction)

TABLE 1: Means and Standard Errors of Achievement Effect Sizes for Different Categories of Studies

Coding Categories	Number of Studies	Effect Size Mean	Effect Size Standard Error
Use of computer			
Managing	11	.33	0.12
Tutoring	11	.36	0.18
Simulation	5	.40	0.33
Programming	8	.20	0.08
Drill and practice	11	.27	0.11
Implementation			
Supplement	14	.21	0.10
Substitute	33	.36	0.08
Random assignment of subjects			
No	26	.34	0.07
Yes	18	.32	0.12
Control for instructor effect			
Different instructor	24	.30	0.08
Same instructor	16	.28	0.10
Control for author bias in test			
Local test	18	.33	0.13
Commercial test	29	.31	0.06
Duration			
4 weeks or less	8	.56	0.26
5-8 weeks	16	.30	0.02
More than 8 weeks	18	.20	0.08
Average ability of students			
Low	11	.45	0.13
Middle	8	.39	0.15
High	4	.13	0.16
Grade level			
6-8	12	.29	0.11
9-12	32	.34	0.08
Subject matter			
Mathematics	27	.24	0.08
Science	11	.31	0.15
Other	10	.50	0.15
Source of publication			
Unpublished	13	.21	0.11
Dissertation	24	.30	0.09
Published	11	.47	0.15
Year of publication			
Before 1970	6	.27	0.08
1970-1974	31	.27	0.08
1975-1979	10	.46	0.16
Production of materials			
Local	34	.33	0.08
Commercial	10	.29	0.14

ble 1 had effects on examination scores that reached borderline levels of statistical significance. These features were year of publication and duration of the study. Effects on final examinations tended to be somewhat higher in more recent studies ($r = .27, p < .10$). Effects were also greater in studies of shorter duration ($r = .29, p < .10$).

Retention Examinations

The five studies with follow-up examinations investigated retention over intervals ranging from 2 to 6 months. In four of the studies, retention examination scores were higher in the CBI class, but none of these four retention effects was large enough to be considered statistically significant. In the remaining study, retention examination scores were significantly higher in the control class. The average *ES* of .17 favored CBI; the standard error of *ES* was .16.

Attitudes Toward Subject Matter

Ten studies reported results on students' attitudes toward the subject matter that they were being taught. In eight of these studies, student attitudes were more positive in classrooms using CBI. Only three of the ten studies, however, reported an effect large enough to be considered statistically reliable. In two of the three studies, the effects favored CBI. The average *ES* was .12, a very small effect; the standard error of *ES* was .094. Because the total number of studies of student attitudes was so small, we did not attempt to compare attitudinal results in different subgroups of studies.

Attitudes Toward Computers

Four studies reported results on student attitudes toward computers. In each of the four studies, student attitudes toward computers were more positive in the CBI class, and in three of the studies, attitudes were significantly more positive among students who used CBI. The average *ES* was .61, and the standard error was .21.

Attitudes Toward Instruction

Another four studies reported on student ratings of the quality of instruction in CBI and conventional classes. In each of the studies, the students from the CBI classes expressed more favorable ratings, but none of the differences between classes was statistically significant. The average *ES* in these studies was .19, with a standard error of .050. This effect is a very small one at best.

Time to Learn

Only two studies contained comparative data on the amount of time students took to learn. In one of the studies (Hughes, 1974) students spent 135 minutes on instruction and study when taught with computers, and 220 minutes when taught in a conventional man-

ner. The 39 percent savings in time was equivalent to an *ES* of .78. In the other study (Lunetta, 1972), students spent 90 minutes on instruction and study when taught with computers, and 745 minutes when taught conventionally. The 88 percent savings in time was obviously great, but we were unable to calculate Glass's *ES* for this effect because Lunetta did not report within-group variances.

Discussion

Our analysis showed that computer-based teaching raised final examination scores by approximately .32 standard deviation, or from the 50th to the 63rd percentile. Computer-based teaching also raised scores on follow-up examinations given several months after the completion of instruction, but these retention effects were not as clear as the immediate effects of computer-based teaching. In addition, students who were taught on computers developed very positive attitudes toward the computer, and also gave favorable ratings to the computer-based courses they were taking. Finally, the computer reduced substantially the amount of time that students needed for learning.

These findings were consistent with predictions from Kulik's (1981) model describing effects of instructional technology on school learning. The model suggested that computer-based teaching would be more effective at the secondary level than it has been at the college level, and this is exactly what we found. Most of the findings from this meta-analysis were also consistent with findings reported in other reviews. Earlier box-score and meta-analytic reviews, for example, also reported moderate-size effects on final examination scores from computer-based teaching, and a number of the reviews (Edwards et al., 1975; Jamison, Suppes, and Well, 1974; Kulik, Kulik, and Cohen, 1980) also stressed the potential importance of the computer in saving instructional time.

A few of our findings, however, introduce a new note into reviews of effectiveness of CBI. Edwards et al. (1975) once suggested, for example, that computer-based teaching has negative effects on retention of learning. We found, on the other hand, that effects on retention measures were basically positive, but not so clear as effects on measures of immediate performance. Our findings on attitudes also came as a small surprise. Other reviewers overlooked attitudinal effects of computer-based teaching. We found that the computer had an important positive effect on student attitudes.

Like other meta-analysts working in this area, we found that features of studies were not strongly related to study outcomes. None of the relationships between study features and outcomes that we investigated, in fact, could be considered clearly statistically significant with the number of studies available to us. Nonetheless, the few small correlations of borderline significance that we found were interesting because they confirmed findings from earlier meta-analyses. Particularly worth noting were the relationships between outcomes and these features: year of publication of studies, manner of publication, and study duration.

First, more recent studies reported stronger effects of computer-based teaching on student achievement. A significant tendency for more recent studies to produce stronger results has been noted several times in the past in meta-analyses on instructional technology. Hartley (1977), for example, noted this tendency in studies of programmed instruction at the elementary and secondary level, and Kulik (1981) noted the same effect in two separate meta-analyses of findings on programmed instruction at the secondary and college levels. It seems unlikely that the stronger effects reported in more recent studies can be attributed to a switch in recent years to better research designs. None of the meta-analyses showed great improvements in research methodology over time, and they all reported little relationship between research design features and study outcomes. It seems

more likely that instructional technology has simply been used more appropriately in recent years.

Second, studies published in journals reported somewhat stronger effects than did dissertation studies. Although the difference was not statistically significant, journal effects were .17 standard deviation higher than dissertations effects. This result is very similar to those from other meta-analyses. Kulik (1981), summarizing findings from three other meta-analyses conducted at the University of Michigan, reported that journal effects in these studies averaged .16 standard deviation higher than dissertation effects, and Smith (1980), summarizing results from twelve University of Colorado meta-analyses, also reported that journal effects averaged .16 standard deviation higher than dissertation effects. It is possible that the quality of studies conducted by graduate students is lower than the quality of studies from more established researchers, and so dissertation research may underestimate the true size of experimental effects. But it is also possible that studies with significant results may more often be accepted for journal publication, and published research may therefore overestimate the true size of effects.

Third, studies that were shorter in duration produced stronger effects than did studies of longer duration. Cohen, Kulik, and Kulik (1982) reported a similar result for programs of cross-age and peer tutoring in elementary and secondary schools: stronger effects from shorter studies. Although the smaller effects reported in longer studies may actually show that experimental effects decrease in potency with extended use—too much of a good thing—it is also possible that shorter studies are better controlled and more likely to estimate true effects.

Hints of other relationships between study features and outcomes appeared in our results. The effects of computer-based teaching seemed especially clear in studies of disadvantaged and low aptitude students, for example, whereas effects appeared to be much smaller in studies of talented students. This is exactly what the review of Jamison, Suppes, and Wells (1974) would lead us to expect. But the relationship was far from statistically significant with the number of studies currently available. The reliability of this and other relationships hinted at in our results must therefore be investigated in further analyses.

ACKNOWLEDGMENTS

This research was supported by the National Science Foundation under Grant No. 79-20742. Any opinions, findings, and conclusions or recommendations expressed in this report are those of the authors and do not necessarily reflect the views of the National Science Foundation.

NOTE

1. A complete list of studies used in the analysis described in this article is available from James A. Kulik, Center for Research on Learning and Teaching, University of Michigan, 109 E. Madison Street, Ann Arbor, Mich. 48109.

REFERENCES

Burns, P. K., and Bozeman, W. C. Computer-assisted instruction and mathematics achievement: Is there a relationship? *Educational Technology,* 1981, *21,* 32–39.

Cohen, P. A., Kulik, J. A., and Kulik, C.-L. C. Educational outcomes of tutoring: A meta-analysis of findings. *American Educational Research Journal,* 1982, *19,* 237–248.

Edwards, J., Norton, S., Taylor, S., Weiss, M, and Dusseldorp, R. How effective is CAI? A review of the research. *Educational Leadership,* 1975, *33,* 147–153.

Gerard, R. W. Computers and education. In R. W. Gerard (Ed.), *Computers and education.* New York: McGraw-Hill, 1967.

Glass, G. V., McGaw, B., and Smith, M. L. *Meta-analysis in social research.* Beverly Hills: Sage Publications, 1981.

Hartley, S. S. Meta-analysis of the effects of individually paced instruction in mathematics. (Doctoral dissertation, University of Colorado, 1977.) *Dissertation Abstracts International,* 1978, *38* (7-A), 4003 (University Microfilms No. 77-29, 926).

Hughes, W. R. A study of the use of computer simulated experiments in the physics classroom. (Doctoral dissertation, Ohio State University, 1973.) *Dissertation Abstracts International,* 1974, *34,* 4910A (University Microfilms No. 74-3205).

Jamison, D., Suppes, P., and Wells, S. The effectiveness of alternative instructional media: A survey. *Review of Educational Research,* 1974, *44,* 1–61.

Kulik, J. A. *Integrating findings from different levels of instruction.* Paper presented to the American Educational Research Association, Los Angeles, April 1981.

Kulik, J. A., Cohen, P. A., and Ebeling, B. J. Effectiveness of programmed instruction in higher education: A meta-analysis of findings. *Educational Evaluation and Policy Analysis,* 1980, *2,* 51–64.

Kulik, J. A., Kulik, C.-L. C., and Cohen, P. A. A meta-analysis of outcome studies of Keller's personalized system of instruction. *American Psychologist,* 1979a, *34,* 307–318.

Kulik, J. A., Kulik, C.-L. C., and Cohen, P. A. Research on audio-tutorial instruction: A meta-analysis of comparative studies. *Research in Higher Education,* 1979b, *11,* 321–341.

Kulik, J. A., Kulik, C.-L. C., and Cohen, P. A. Effectiveness of computer-based college teaching: A meta-analysis of findings. *Review of Educational Research,* 1980, *50,* 525–544.

Lunetta, V. N. The design and evaluation of a series of computer-simulated experiments for use in high school physics. (Doctoral dissertation, University of Connecticut, 1972.) *Dissertation Abstracts International,* 1972, *33,* 2785A (University Microfilm No. 72-32, 153).

Smith, M. L. Publication bias and meta-analysis. *Evaluation in Education: An International Review Series,* 1980, *4*(1), 22–24.

Vinsonhaler, J. F., and Bass, R. K. A summary of ten major studies on CAI drill and practice. *Educational Technology,* 1972, *12,* 29–32.

17 Computerized Adaptive Testing: Principles and Directions

Charles B. Kreitzberg
Martha L. Stocking
Len Swanson

Educational Testing Service

Introduction

Educational and psychological tests are frequently used to formalize judgments about the abilities, competencies, and personalities of individuals. In the early part of this century, most tests were individually administered. Although the outcomes of individually administered tests are subject to some distortion due to examiner effects [1, 2], this disadvantage is balanced by the examiner's ability to clarify ambiguities in items or responses, record response latencies, probe responses of interest and, generally, manipulate the conditions of test administration to obtain maximum information yield. Thus, the individually administered test has the potential to elicit considerable information about the examinee and, because of its high yield, is often employed as a clinical instrument [3]. Unfortunately, individualized administration is too costly and time-consuming a process to be employed in many assessment situations.

The inefficiency of individually administered testing has created a need to adopt less time-consuming and less expensive methods when large numbers of persons are to be tested. The group-administered standardized paper-and-pencil test has become the accepted compromise between the desirability of individual assessment and the need for efficient testing of large numbers of people [4].

The use of a standardized group-administered test, however, poses a number of problems. One is that group-administered tests must, to be of practical value, include a large number of items appropriate for the expected average ability of the group. As a result these tests do not measure with uniform precision throughout the range of ability being tested.

Consider, for example, a test designed to measure verbal ability at the sixth grade level. Most students taking such a test would be expected to perform around the average sixth grade level. If the items were of appropriate difficulty for the average sixth grade level, students at this level would be measured with more precision; students above or below this level would be measured less precisely. It would, of course, be possible to extend the test's range by adding easier and more difficult items, but this procedure would not solve the problem. If the range of difficulty is wide, the easy items are a waste of time for the better examinees. The hard items are worse than a waste of time for the low level examinees. The random errors of measurement arising from their guesses on harder items can seriously impair whatever accuracy of measurement might otherwise result from administering the easier test items [5].

A second problem with conventional group-administered tests is that item characteristics such as difficulty and discriminating power are defined relative to a specific group; comparisons among different populations or among individuals taking different tests is difficult. For example, the difficulty of a particular item on a conventional test is generally calculated as the proportion of correct responses in the group to which it is administered. Thus, an item presented to a high ability group would be characterized as less difficult than the same item administered to a low ability group.

Comparisons between items that differ in discriminating power (i.e., how well an item discriminates between similar levels of ability) can be even more confusing. For example, if two items differ in discrimination, one item may be easier than a second item within a low ability group, and yet appear harder than the second item in a high ability group. This is not a problem if within-group ranking is desired; if, however, it is necessary to compare groups who have taken different tests or to compare different groups who have taken the same test, then item difficulties and item discriminations must be independent of the group taking the test [6]. Classical test theory does not provide a way of determining the difficulty or the discriminating power of an item on any absolute scale, independent of the group taking the test.

The seriousness of these problems with conventional tests depends upon the purpose of the test. If the purpose is to determine whether the testee possesses minimum competency according to some criterion, then the lack of precision at the extremes is not important. Testees with perfect or zero scores would be correctly classified as possessing or not possessing the requisite competency. However, if the purpose of the test is to evaluate a person's level of achievement with some precision, then the problems are more serious.

Adaptive Testing

The more a test contains items appropriate for an individual's ability level, the greater the precision of measurement obtained for that individual. The notion of adaptive testing stems from the desire to adapt or tailor items to the individual ability level of each testee. Ideally, each person would be given a test whose items are of approximately average difficulty given his or her ability level. Unfortunately, to do this would require that the person's ability level be known in advance.

To overcome this circularity, a procedure such as the following may be used.

1. Obtain an initial estimate of the testee's ability level in some convenient way.

2. Use the ability estimate to select an appropriate item from the item pool.

3. Score the item, correct or incorrect, and use this information to revise the estimate of the testee's ability level.

4. If the estimate is sufficiently precise, stop. Otherwise further refine the estimate by returning to Step 2.

Obviously many variations on this procedure are possible, and some have been investigated. The most interesting issues include the strategy which should be used to select items from the pool, the point at which the process should be terminated, and the scoring technique which should be used.

The simplest form of an adaptive test is one in which several "peaked" tests are created, each with overlapping ranges. An examinee who scores in the extreme range of a test is retested with a more appropriate instrument. Such strategies, using classical test theory, have been investigated experimentally.

One such strategy, called the two-stage adaptive test, involves administering a short pretest or "routing test" to all examinees. Based on the results of the routing test, individuals are directed to an appropriate second-stage test whose items are of relatively homogeneous difficulty [4]. Such a peaked test in which all items are of approximately equal difficulty produces its most accurate measurement around one ability level at the expense of less accurate measurement at the extremes [5]. Since the results of the routing test suggest that the individual's level is appropriate for the peaked test, the two-stage strategy should provide fairly accurate measurement.

The two-stage adaptive strategy was tried experimentally by Angoff and Huddleston [8], who concluded that although the use of two narrow-range (peaked) tests was slightly more reliable than a single broad-range test (.89 vs. .85), the increase in validity coefficient for the two-stage procedure would not exceed .02 on the average. One problem with a two-stage adaptive strategy is that errors of measurement would cause some testees to be misclassified by the routing test and therefore routed to an inappropriate second-stage test. Angoff and Huddleston felt that the number of such misclassified students, although small, would be sufficient to cause serious administrative problems and that the advantage of heightened reliability "would not be great enough to warrant changing to the administratively more complex two-level test system" [8]. To overcome these problems, more sophisticated adaptive strategies are required. However, such strategies are not easily developed within the context of classical test theory.

Although it is possible to develop adaptive tests based on classical test theory, there are three issues which are not easily resolved within this theory:

1. *Scoring.* Since different examinees receive different items, the traditional number-right score used by classical test theory is inappropriate. This raises questions regarding the method of scoring the test and the comparison of scores received by different individuals.

2. *Item parameters.* Since appropriate items are selected individually for each examinee, items must be characterized in a way that is independent of the group to which the item is administered. Classical test theory only provides us with group-dependent item characteristics or parameters.

3. *Comparing strategies.* There are many possible strategies for selecting items and scoring responses. Conventional tests are usually evaluated by such measures as reliability and validity. These correlational indices are group dependent and are, therefore, not appropriate for adaptive tests. Adaptive testing requires a reasonable method of comparing different strategies and scoring procedures in order to choose a "best" one which is not dependent upon the group taking the test.

The development of latent trait theory as an alternative to classical test theory provided a structure within which these issues could be addressed.

Latent Trait Theory

Basically, latent trait theory makes the following assumptions.

1. There is an underlying (latent) trait (there may be more than one) that is the sole determinant of examinees' responses to items. This latent trait is frequently referred to as "ability," but other constructs, such as achievement or strength of endorsement, are equally valid.

2. Various mathematical models can be used to describe the relationship between an examinee's ability and his or her responses. The probability of a correct answer for a particular item is generally considered to be a function of the examinee's ability level and the appropriateness of the item for this ability level.

The mathematical development of latent trait theory leads to many important and useful results. Unlike classical test theory, latent trait theory [6] allows the test scores of all examinees to be expressed on a common scale, regardless of the fact that each examinee may have answered different, and even different numbers of items. This metric allows ordering of examinees with respect to the trait to be measured, and quantification of the magnitude of the differences among examinees. Item parameters developed through latent trait theory are independent of the group to which the item is administered. In addition, techniques for comparing item selection strategies and scoring procedures have been developed which involve a consideration of the amount of "information" obtained from a test at various levels of the trait being measured [6], and which are also independent of the group to which the test is administered.

A test item is described by two, or sometimes three, characteristics or parameters. The ability of an item to discriminate among people at different levels of ability is called the item's "discriminating power." The level of ability at which the item discriminates most effectively is termed the item's "difficulty." More elaborate models include a parameter which represents the probability of correctly guessing the answer if the examinee does not know the correct answer. Thus, in latent trait theory, an item is described by its difficulty, discriminating power, and susceptibility to guessing.

Latent trait theory provides several different procedures for estimating item parameters in advance of administration of the test [9] and guarantees that these parameters will be invariant from group to group. Once item parameters have been determined, the estimation of ability from item responses is relatively straightforward. Two asymptotically consistent procedures frequently used are Maximum Likelihood estimators and Bayesian estimators [5]. There are many other procedures which are simpler in form and may be appropriate for some item selection strategies and item pools [10].

Since the classical notions of reliability are insufficient for latent trait theory, item selection strategies and ability estimation procedures are compared through the use of information functions [6]. While the concept of an information function is mathematically precise, its properties have great intuitive appeal.

The information function of a test is inversely proportional to the length of the confidence interval for estimating abilities from scores on that test. This means that the higher the information function, the more precise the estimate of ability. By comparing information functions of tests, we can determine which test yields the greatest amount of precision at different levels of ability.

In addition to its relation to the precision of estimate, the information function of a test is a function of the examinee's ability level. This accords with the intuitive notion that precision of measurement is not the same for all ability levels. We may find, for example, that some tests give more precise estimates at some levels of ability than other tests, and less precise estimates at other levels.

The information function for a conventional test with number-right scoring is proportional to the number of items in the test [6]. This allows any comparison between information functions for a conventional test and a tailored test to be discussed in terms of the number of items that must be added to or deleted from the conventional test to obtain the same amount of information available from a tailored test, at various ability levels. Latent trait theory, then, provides us with powerful psychometric tools with which to construct and compare tailored tests.

Computerized Adaptive Testing

Six steps are involved in applying the concept of adaptive testing to a given testing objective.

1. Select items and test for unidimensionality. (Statistical techniques such as factor analysis are available for determining unidimensionality.)

2. Estimate item parameters.

3. Choose an appropriate item selection strategy.

4. Choose an appropriate scoring procedure.

5. Compute the information function for relevant levels of ability.

6. Compare information functions for alternative strategies.

Generally, the "best" strategy of item selection and scoring would be the one which has the highest information function over the desired trait range.

Administration of the above procedures by hand would be quite burdensome. Fortunately, the computer technology required to administer such a procedure, at a reasonable cost, has now matured to the point where adaptive testing is a practical possibility.

Testing in which the computer is used to individually select items has been variously referred to as adaptive testing [11], programmed testing [12], branching tests [13], response-contingent testing [14], and tailored testing [10]. In this paper, we use the term "computerized adaptive testing," or CAT.

Selected Research

Computerized adaptive testing has been a subject of considerable research over the past few years. Its earliest antecedents are in the work of the Princeton-based Statistical Research Group, which developed sequential analysis and "staircase" testing methods over 30 years ago [14]. The psychometric origins of adaptive testing can be traced back at least 25 years to the work of Hick [15], who described a branching process in which successive items would be chosen in such a way that each would have a 50 percent chance of being correctly answered by the subject, based on his answers to the previous items. The notion of adaptive testing began to be formalized in the 1950s with the work of Krathwohl and Huyser [16], and of Angoff and Huddleston [8]. More recently, Patterson [17], and later Cleary, Linn, Rock, and others advanced programmed testing and established several important results [12, 18, 19].

Although, as noted earlier, it is possible to construct adaptive testing models within the framework of classical test theory [20], the work of Lord [10], coupling latent trait theory to the concept of adaptive testing, provided a psychometric foundation for the field.

At the same time that psychometric developments have provided a theoretical foundation for this work, advances in information technology have allowed the development of cost-effective implementations. In particular, the development of microprocessors and reductions in the cost of on-line (terminal-oriented) systems facilitate the development of computerized adaptive systems.

The convergence of psychometric and technical developments has spurred research and development activities in computerized adaptive testing over the past few years. Among the effects which have been studied are: reliability and validity [21–23], accuracy at extremes [10], ability to reproduce conventional test scores [24], information yield [10], effects of varying step sizes [4, 14], measurement error [14], and number of items presented [4, 14]. McBride [4] provides a good survey of recent research findings.

Several computerized adaptive testing systems have been developed, both to support empirical research and to serve as operational prototypes. The major ones are those at the University of Minnesota [21, 25] and at the U.S. Civil Service Commission [23], although there are a number of others. The Civil Service Commission, which administers tests to 2 million examinees per year, is working toward implementation of an operational computerized adaptive testing system by the end of this decade.

Research in computerized adaptive testing has been of three types: theoretical, simulation, and empirical. Theoretical research has concentrated on the psychometric properties of adaptive tests. Simulation experiments have attempted to project the behavior of adaptive tests based on assumed responses to items or data derived from conventional test administrations. Empirical research has been largely concerned with comparisons to conventional tests; among the comparisons attempted have been: external validity [22, 26], internal consistency reliability [27], test–retest temporal stability [28, 29], and characteristics of score distributions [30]. These comparisons have thus far been inconclusive or unsatisfactory [4].

Psychometric research has, on the other hand, been relatively successful, largely due to the work of Lord [5, 7, 10]. It is now felt that the psychometric obstacles to computerized adaptive testing have been overcome. A U.S. Civil Service Commission study showed costs less than those of paper-and-pencil testing, based on the reduction in number of items administered [31]. While these results must be viewed with some caution, the conclusions and intentions of the Civil Service Commission are suggestive.

The major obstacles remaining to be overcome before computerized adaptive testing becomes widespread now appear to be the following: (1) choice of item selection and scoring strategies for a given testing objective, (2) verification in live testing of the results of theoretical and simulation work, (3) assessment of the operational implications of computerized adaptive testing relative to administrative requirements and effects on testees, and (4) development of suitable operational capabilities. The current pace of research in this field suggests that results in these areas can be expected soon, thus making possible on a large scale the promise and potentials of computerized adaptive testing.

Advantages and Implications of Computerized Adaptive Testing

Much of the research in computerized adaptive testing has been concerned with psychometric aspects of such tests, that is, the measurement properties of group and individual scores on adaptive tests, particularly in comparison with those of conventional paper-and-pencil tests. However, a number of other potential advantages of computerized adaptive testing have also been hypothesized, and some have been explored. These potential advantages include ones related to administrative procedures, affective factors and limitations of the group-administered, multiple-choice mode of testing.

Psychometric Aspects

Perhaps the major advantage of adaptive testing is that, in general, fewer items are required to achieve a specified level of measurement accuracy than are required in a conventional test. Numerous research studies [cf. Reference 10] have confirmed this. The increased efficiency of an adaptive test occurs because the most information is obtained about an examinee if the items administered have a 50 percent probability of being answered correctly (65 percent of the time if guessing is taken into consideration)[4]. Items which are too easy or too hard for a given individual contribute little information about the examinee. Since the purpose of adaptive testing is to choose and administer those items which contribute most to the estimate of an individual's ability level, fewer items are required to achieve the same level of measurement precision. The information function of an adaptive test is higher at any point on the ability scale than that of a conventional unpeaked test, and higher at the extremes than a conventional peaked test. It is also less variable throughout the ability range [5].

Improvements in measurement precision have been established theoretically and verified in simulation studies. The amount of improvement to be expected with a given test depends on the size and characteristics of the item pool. As an example, Urry [23] suggests a roughly 5 to 1 (80 percent) reduction in the number of items required to achieve reliabilities comparable to conventional test scores. These results were obtained in live testing experiments.

As a consequence of its higher and less variable information function throughout the ability range, an adaptive test is particularly superior to a conventional test at the extremes of ability. This situation is depicted in Figure 1. The wider the range of ability being measured, the greater this discrepancy. Since underlying ability is not usually directly measurable, this result cannot be verified empirically; however, it has been demonstrated theoretically [7]. It is a particularly important advantage with respect to testing lower ability students, since in a conventional test the accuracy of such measurements is virtually swamped by random error introduced by guessing.

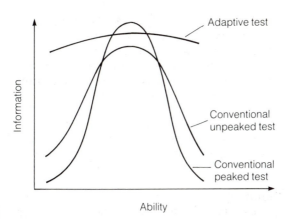

FIGURE 1: Comparison of adaptive and conventional tests

Another consequence of the higher and less variable information function of an adaptive test is that scores better reflect the true distribution of ability in a population. Weiss [32] has demonstrated this in simulation experiments. This is important when group, as well as individual, characteristics are of interest.

The latent trait theory underpinning adaptive testing contributes another important advantage: scores based on latent trait theory are on an interval scale. As McBride [4] points out, scores based on classical test theory are really on only an ordinal scale. Thus the magnitude of differences between scores has a natural meaning in latent trait theory, but not in classical test theory.

There is some evidence to suggest that scores on adaptive tests have greater temporal stability (test–retest reliability). Weiss [21] cites results of live testing experiments that indicate this, and claims that simulation studies show that it holds over the entire ability range.

Finally, computerized adaptive testing may reduce some of the random error in conventional tests due to confounding of power conditions. It has often been noted that, because of administrative requirements, some element of speededness is frequently introduced into group-administered power tests. Weiss [21] cites data showing that speededness differentially affects individuals, thus confounding the predictive qualities of the test. This problem can be virtually eliminated with computerized adaptive testing, since administration of the test is individualized and time limits can be controlled by the examiner.

Administrative Effects

A great deal of attention has been given in both group and individually administered testing to standardization of the testing environment, control of administrator effects, objectivity of scoring, and security of materials. Computerized adaptive testing offers potential advantages over conventional testing in all of these areas.

Urry [33] points out that computerized testing is more standardized because the administrative procedures are programmed and, therefore, more uniform and controlled. This reduces differential effects of the testing environment. In individually administered tests, studies have shown that administrator effects and clerical errors in scoring may seriously compromise test objectivity [21]. For example, factors such as expectancy, knowledge of the testee, degree of rapport, and race have all been shown to influence individual scores. Even in group administrations, the examiner may induce different levels of stress in different individuals [21]. Since computerized testing eliminates the human examiner and precisely controls administration and scoring, these effects should be better controlled, if not eliminated.

Characteristics of the answer sheet and item arrangement have also been shown to affect group scores, as well as differentially affecting individual scores [21]. This compromises the psychometric qualities of the test. In computerized testing these effects are eliminated. They are, however, replaced by a new set of factors relating to the interface between the individual and the testing device. Because of the relative newness of the field, these factors have been largely unexplored. However, computerized testing provides a degree of control impossible in a conventional testing environment. This should make it practical to easily modify the testing environment as new evidence regarding the effects of that environment is uncovered.

Computerized testing should make it easier to safeguard the security of test materials. It has been argued [14] that since test booklets are no longer needed and since different individuals receive different items, the security problem will be diminished. This assumes that adequate procedures to safeguard the integrity and accessibility of the computer have been developed. As computer security systems continue to improve this should be the case.

Computerized testing provides significant advantages in the scheduling of test administrations. Tests can be administered at times and locations convenient to the student. For example, walk-in test centers become possible. Even if test security requires that all administrations be simultaneous, it may be possible to locate terminals at the convenience of the student and virtually eliminate the administrative procedures involved in registration and arrangements for test centers.

Finally, many of the other administrative procedures required for conventional group-administered testing can be reduced or eliminated with computerized testing. The list includes: test booklet and answer sheet printing, storage and distribution, accounting for and return of materials, answer sheet processing, certain aspects of score reporting, and test center management. These administrative procedures are, of course, replaced by others required for computer administration of tests. However, the latter should, once established, be simpler and less costly to carry out on a routine basis.

Affective Factors

Little research has been conducted to date on the affective implications of computerized adaptive testing. Some researchers have hypothesized several advantages of computerized testing in terms of its effects on the testee. Chief among them is that it may increase the student's interest in and motivation for taking the test. Johnson and Mihal [34] report results that showed that blacks perform better on a computerized test, and suggest that motivational and examiner effects might

have been responsible. Weiss [32] found similar effects when feedback on the correctness of a response is provided. These results suggest that the computerized testing environment may in some cases be more motivating or less anxiety producing than the conventional testing environment.

It has also been hypothesized that because items better match the ability level of the testee, adaptive testing may have a positive effect on the attitudes of high and low ability students. Weiss [32] suggests that the high ability student may be bored by a conventional test, with a resulting deterioration in performance. The low ability student may be similarly affected by the frustration and anxiety resulting from attempting items that are overly difficult. In addition, there is evidence that low ability students guess more frequently, thus introducing greater error into the score [21]. Computerized adaptive testing should tend to reduce these negative factors.

Limitations of the Group-Administered, Multiple-Choice Mode of Testing

Computerized adaptive testing potentially offers several other advantages over conventional testing methods. These advantages result from the power and flexibility inherent in computer administration of a test. One advantage is the ability to gather and report additional information about the testing process that cannot readily be gathered in conventional paper-and-pencil testing. For example, Weiss [32] developed a measure he refers to as a "consistency" index on each student. This measure is, roughly, the number of strata or difficulty levels administered to the student. Weiss showed that this measure is generally correlated to the test–retest reliability of the student's score. If this is so, then reporting this measure may provide additional information helpful in evaluating the student's score.

Another example of additional information that can be gathered is response latency—the time is takes a student to answer an item. Green [35] suggests that response latency may be related to guessing. Additional research will be needed to determine the value, if any, of latency information.

Computerized adaptive testing provides an opportunity for greater flexibility in the testing process itself. For example, students can be given feedback on the correctness of their responses. Weiss [32] showed that black students tend to score better and omit fewer items when feedback is provided. Students can also be permitted to retry an item after an incorrect response. This may be useful in analyzing or weighting wrong answers. Finally, information about the testing session, including the student's score(s), can be provided immediately. This may be beneficial to the users of test scores, as well as to the students themselves.

Computerized testing more readily permits alternatives to the multiple-choice item type than does conventional testing. These alternatives might include free or constructed response items, and probabilistic response items (ones in which the student assigns weights or priorities to the choices). While such alternatives can be done with paper and pencil, they are difficult to administer and score. Computerized testing may, therefore, open up new approaches to item design.

Finally, CAT makes possible types of testing that are difficult or impossible to accomplish by conventional means. The assessment of problem-solving skills, in which the student's responses determine the information and questions posed, represents one example. Another is the use of audio and/or pictorial (e.g., moving images) stimuli in the testing process [36]. These represent potentials that are unlikely to be realized without some form of technological support.

Constraints and Operational Requirements

While computerized adaptive testing is generally superior to conventional modes of testing in most situations, its use is subject to a number of very real technical and psychometric constraints. Effective application of CAT techniques in any given testing situation will depend upon the resolution of these constraints and the satisfaction of certain operational requirements.

One of the major potential bars to operational CAT systems is cost. Initial hardware and developmental software costs can be quite high. Because of the relative newness of this field, little real data on costs has been developed. Wood [14] argues that, ignoring hardware requirements, the costs are not likely to be as different from conventional tests as might be thought. McKillip and Urry [31] also regard the cost question as settled in favor of computerized adaptive testing. Moreover, computer costs are clearly decreasing relative to personnel costs. Nevertheless, this issue merits further study and is one that may represent a constraint on the use of CAT, at least initially.

For CAT to be feasible, computer response times must be reasonably fast. An examinee taking a computerized adaptive test must not be required to wait any appreciable amount of time for his answer to be recorded or for the presentation of the next item. In addition, appropriate provisions must be made to handle interruptions due to computer or system failure. These computer capabilities, then, represent important aspects of the operational requirements.

Care must also be exercised in control of the examinee–terminal environment. Examinees should not be required to learn complex tasks associated with the operation of a terminal, and the procedure for responding to items should be made as easy and natural as possible. Instructions and information for the examinee must be kept clear and simple to avoid practice effects. Failures in any of these areas may constrain the effectiveness of a CAT system.

Some explanation to the examinee concerning the test construction technique and scoring procedure will probably be required. Green [37] suggests as an example that two examinees might compare notes, discover that each got about half the items right (although they were different items), but that their scores were widely different. Without some explanation to the examinee, substantial examinee dissatisfaction would result.

Lord [38] points out that a tailored test will probably take longer to administer than a conventional test of the same number of items. This is so because the conventional test contains some items that are too easy, and some items which are too hard, and an examinee can respond relatively quickly to these types of items. There is also evidence that response latency is somewhat greater in a computerized test [39].

In addition to these practical problems, there are a number of more theoretical concerns which may constrain the effectiveness of CAT in a given testing situation. Lord [10] mentions four such concerns.

1. Latent trait theory as it is applied to CAT assumes that only one trait is to be measured. It is not a simple matter to construct items which all measure the same trait.

2. Accurate estimation of the item parameters necessary for tailored testing can be a difficult and expensive process.

3. If there is any doubt concerning the accuracy of the estimation of item parameters, then there will be doubt about the accuracy and fairness of the final estimation of ability.

4. Given an item pool of, say, 500 items, better measurement will often be obtained by selecting the 60 most discriminating items and administering them as a conventional test, rather than by using all 500 items in a tailored test. *This may actually prove to be a fatal objection to any general use of tailored testing.* [Italics due to Lord.]

Wood [14] counters this last argument by suggesting that better strategies for CAT (that is, selecting items on the basis of discriminating power in addition to difficulty) would again make a tailored test superior to the conventional test.

Of great practical importance is the fact that there is no single ''best'' strategy of item selection, and no single ''best'' method of scoring a computerized adaptive test [4, 14, 21]. Rather, strategies and scoring methods tend to be superior for some abilities, and inferior for others. The selection of the most efficient measuring instrument for an examinee requires extensive local knowledge, both about the examinee's ostensible ability and about the items in the item pool. Correct choice of item selection strategies and scoring will be heavily dependent on the careful specification by the measurement specialist of the ability levels to be measured with greatest precision.

None of these contraints on CAT are fatal. They do suggest that additional research on both theoretical and operational matters is imperative.

Areas of Potential Applicability

A discussion of the advantages and constraints of computerized adaptive testing would not be complete without some attempt to identify those types of testing situation or objective where CAT is likely to be most applicable. On the other hand, the range of factors that must be considered is so broad that it is difficult to make categorical statements about the applicability of CAT to any general class of testing. Basically, CAT will be applicable wherever the advantages previously discussed are sufficiently attractive to justify overcoming whatever constraints or obstacles might be present. Generally speaking, such applications appear to fall into three classes: testing situations where a reduction in the number of items required would yield significant benefits, situations where measurement precision over a wide range is needed, or where accuracy at extremes is important, and types of test which cannot be administered by conventional means, or scheduling and administrative problems make conventional modes of testing difficult.

Reduction in Number of Items Required

Since adaptive tests can be made significantly shorter without compromising measurement precision, they will in most cases require less time to administer. This makes CAT useful whenever a high premium is placed on the time or convenience of the test taker. One example might be basic skills or entry-level testing at the adult education or community college level. Students might, at their own convenience, take a battery of tests that would be used for diagnosis and placement. CAT would make it possible to do this without placing an inordinate burden on the student.

Another example is large-scale testing programs in which the amount of time spent on a test represents a real cost to both the user and the testee. The U.S. Civil Service Commission, for example, tests some 2 million individuals per year, so that any reduction in testing time should yield significant cost savings.

Multiple ability or multiple trait batteries also represent a potential area of applicability. CAT permits many subtests to be administered quickly, perhaps even using the results of certain subtests and known correlations between abilities or traits to make immediate decisions on other abilities or traits. Personnel selection and placement might be an area in which computerized multiple-ability batteries might be appropriate.

Precision over a Wide Range

If the testing objective is to measure best at a single point (ability level), then clearly a conventional peaked test, with items chosen to yield maximum information at the desired point, may be superior to any other type of test. However, if the objective is to measure individual differences with high and nearly equal precision at more than one point, and particularly over a broad range, then an adaptive test will generally be superior [4]. This applied to both norm-referenced and criterion-referenced tests, and has been demonstrated repeatedly in simulation studies (although it remains to be corroborated empirically).

An example of a test where precision over a wide range is required might be a test de-

signed to measure some trait at different grade levels. Since all test scores would be on the same scale, direct comparisons between groups at different grade levels could be made. Lord's Broad Range Tailored Test of Verbal Ability [7] is an example of such a test. Another example might be the measurement of heredity of latent traits. Test of this variety require extremely high precision of measurement. The use of an adaptive test yielding a common scale and increased precision makes this possible. Similarly, growth of an individual could be measured with more precision than is now possible by administering the same adaptive test in successive years. The measurement of growth has been a difficult problem in the past because random error frequently swamps real changes.

Computerized adaptive testing would be appropriate for most situations in which accurate measurement of extreme groups (high or low ability students) is important. An example of this might be the classification of mentally retarded individuals. Wood [14] notes that even relatively gross discriminations at the low end of the scale are beyond the capabilities of published individual intelligence tests. An adaptive test with a sufficiently large item pool should be able to resolve this problem. The same might apply to the accurate identification of high ability students, as in scholarship testing.

Special Testing Needs

There are many situations in which testing cannot be done conventionally, or administrative problems make it difficult to administer the test through conventional means. In these situations CAT may represent a solution to special testing needs. Some examples of these special needs might be the following:

Immediate feedback of items or total score is required, possibly in self-assessment or diagnostic testing.

Greater flexibility in the testing process, or the ability to capture additional information (e.g., response latencies) is needed, perhaps for experimental studies.

Security problems are such that it is difficult or impossible to administer secure conventional tests. CAT might provide the solution to item and test security problems.

Alternatives to the multiple-choice item type are required, as for example in tests of problem-solving or patient management skills. Items other than multiple choice are nearly impossible to administer to large groups of people by conventional means.

CAT is clearly applicable to a wide range of testing situations. Ultimately, it is likely to be useful in virtually any situation in which operational capabilities and appropriate procedures can be set up. For this reason CAT may well become the predominant mode of testing within the next decade.

ACKNOWLEDGMENTS

This report describes work that is collaborative in every respect: the order of authorship is alphabetical. The authors wish to express their appreciation to Frederick M. Lord for his helpful advice and suggestions on the paper.

REFERENCES

1. Rosenthal, R. *Experimenter Effects in Behavioral Research,* Appleton-Century-Crofts, New York (1966).

2. Wickes, T. A., Jr. Examiner Influence in a Testing Situation. *J. Consult. Psychol.* 20, 23–26 (1956).

3. Harrison, R., Thematic Apperception Methods. In B.B. Wolman (Ed.), *Handbook of Clinical Psychology,* pp. 562–620, McGraw-Hill, New York (1965).

4. McBride, J. R. *Research on Adaptive Testing. 1973–1976: A Review of the Literature.* University of Minnesota (1976).

5. Lord, F. M. *Some How and Which for Practical Tailored Testing* (Prepublication draft). Educational Testing Service, Princeton, N.J. (1977).

6. Lord, F. M., and Novick, M. R. *Statistical Theories of Mental Test Scores.* Addison–Wesley, Reading, Mass. (1968).

7. Lord, F. M. A Broad-Range Tailored Test of Verbal Ability. *Appl. Psychol. Measur.* 1, 95–100 (1977).

8. Angoff, W. H., and Huddleston, E. M. *The Multi-Level Experiment. A Study of a Two-Stage Test System for the College Board Scholastic Aptitude Test.* Statistical Report 58–21, Educational Testing Service, Princeton, N.J. (1958).

9. Lord, F. M. Estimation of Latent Ability and Item Parameters When There Are Omitted Responses. *Psychometrika* 39, 247–264 (1974).

10. Lord, F. M. Some Test Theory for Tailored Testing. In W. H. Holtzman (Ed.), *Computer-Assisted Instruction. Testing and Guidance,* Chapter 8. Harper & Row, New York (1970).

11. Weiss, D. J., and Betz, N. E. *Ability Measurement: Conventional or Adaptive?* Research Report 73–1, Psychometric Methods Program, Department of Psychology, University of Minnesota (1973).

12. Cleary, T. A., Linn, R. L., and Rock, D. A. An Exploratory Study of Programmed Tests, *Educ. Psychol. Measur.* 28, 345–360 (1968).

13. Bayroff, A. G., and Seeley, L. C. *An Exploratory Study of Branching Tests.* Technical Research Note 188, U.S. Army Behavioral Science Research Laboratory (June 1967).

14. Wood R. Response-Contingent Testing. *Rev. Educ. Res.* 43, 529–544 (1973).

15. Hick, W. E. Information Theory and Intelligence Tests. *Br. J. Psychol. Statist. Sect.* 4, 157–164 (1951).

16. Krathwohl, D. R., and Huyser, R. J. The Sequential Item Test (SIT) (Abstract). *Am. Psychol.* 2, 419 (1956).

17. Patterson, J. J. *An Evaluation of the Sequential Methods of Psychological Testing.* Unpublished doctoral dissertation, Michigan State University (1962).

18. Cleary, T. A., Linn, R. L., and Rock, D. A. Reproduction of Total Test Scores Through the

Use of Sequential Programmed Tests. *J. Educ. Measur.* 5, 183–187 (1968).

19. Linn, R. L., Rock, D. A., and Cleary, T. A. The Development and Evaluation of Several Programmed Testing Methods. *Educ. Psychol. Measur.* 29, 129–146 (1969).

20. Novick, M. R. *Bayesian Methods in Psychological Testing.* Research Bulletin RB-69-31, Educational Testing Service, Princeton, N.J. (1969).

21. Weiss, D. J. *The Stratified Adaptive Computerized Ability Test.* Research Report 73-3, Psychometric Method Program, Department of Psychology, University of Minnesota (1973).

22. Waters, B. *Empirical Investigation of the Stradaptive Testing Model for the Measurement of Human Ability.* Ph.D. Dissertation, Florida State University (1974).

23. Urry, V. W. *Computer-Assisted Testing with Live Examinees: A Rendezvous with Reality.* Personnel Research and Development Center, U.S. Civil Service Commission, Washington, D.C. (1976).

24. Linn, R. L., Rock, D. A., and Cleary, T. A. Sequential Testing for Dichotomous Decision, *Educ. Psychol. Measur.* 32, 85–96 (1972).

25. DeWitt, L. J., and Weiss, D. J. *A Computer Software System for Adaptive Ability Measurement.* Research Report 74-1, Psychometric Methods Program, Department of Psychology, University of Minnesota (January 1974).

26. Olivier, P. *An Evaluation of the Self-Scoring Flexilevel Testing Model.* Unpublished doctoral dissertation. Florida State University (1974).

27. Vale, C. D., and Weiss, D. J. *A Study of Computer-Administered Stradaptive Ability Testing.* Research Report 75-4. Psychometric Methods Program, Department of Psychology, University of Minnesota (1975).

28. Betz, N. E., and Weiss, D. J. *Simulation Studies of Two-Stage Ability Testing.* Research Report 74-4, Psychometric Methods Program, Department of Psychology, University of Minnesota (1974).

29. Larkin, D. C., and Weiss, D. J. *An Empirical Investigation of Computer-Administered Adaptive Ability Testing.* Research Report 74-3, Psychometric Methods Program, Department of Psychology, University of Minnesota (1974).

30. Betz, N. E., and Weiss, D. J. *An Empirical Study of Computer-Administered Two-Stage Ability Testing.* Research Report 73-4, Psychometric Methods Program, Department of Psychology, University of Minnesota (1973).

31. McKillip, R. H., and Urry, V. W. Computer-Assisted Testing: An Orderly Transition from Theory to Practice. *Proceedings of the First Conference on Computerized Adaptive Testing.* Professional Series 75-6, Personnel Research and Development Center. U.S. Civil Service Commission, Washington, D.C. (1975).

32. Weiss, D. J. Adaptive Testing Research at Minnesota: Overview, Recent Results, and Future Directions. *Proceedings of the First Conference on Computerized Adaptive Testing.* Professional Series 75-6, Personnel Research and Development Center, U.S. Civil Service Commission, Washington, D.C. (1975).

33. Urry, V. W. Five Years of Research: Is Computer-Assisted Testing Feasible? *Proceedings of the First Conference on Computerized Adaptive Testing.* Professional Series 75-6, Personnel Research and Development Center, U.S. Civil Service Commission, Washington, D.C. (1975).

34. Johnson, D. F., and Mihal, W. L. Performance of Blacks and Whites in Computerized versus Manual Testing Environments, *Am. Psychol.* 694–699 (August 1973).

35. Green, B. F. Comments on Tailored Testing. In W. H. Holtzmann (Ed.), *Computer-Assisted Instruction, Testing and Guidance,* Chapter 9. Harper & Row, New York (1970).

36. Cory, C. H. Using Computerized Tests to Add New Dimensions to the Measurement of Abilities Which Are Important for On-Job Performance: An Exploratory Study. *Proceedings of the First Conference on Computerized Adaptive Testing.* Professional Series 75-6, Personnel Research and Development Center, U.S. Civil Service Commission, Washington, D.C. (1975).

37. Green, B. F., Jr. Discussion. *Proceedings of the First Conference on Computerized Adaptive Testing.* Professional Series 75-6, Personnel Research and Development Center, U.S. Civil Service Commission, Washington, D.C. (1975).

38. Lord, F. M. Discussion. *Proceedings of the First Conference on Computerized Adaptive Testing.* Professional Series 75–6, Personnel Research and Development Center, U.S. Civil Service Commission, Washington, D.C. (1975).

39. Waters, B. An Empirical Investigation of Weiss' Stradaptive Testing Model. *Proceedings of the First Conference on Computerized Adaptive Testing.* Professional Series 75–6, Personnel Research and Development Center, U.S. Civil Service Commission, Washington, D.C. (1975).

5 Prospects for the Future of Computer-Based Education

The readings in this section deal with two developments from within computer science that are of great potential relevance for the educational software designer. One of these is the matter of programming, programming languages, and authoring systems. The other is intelligent computer-assisted instruction (ICAI), the application of artificial intelligence programming techniques to CAI. These developments have great potential impact on educational computing over the long term.

Learning to use a programming language fluently is a task of some magnitude. Having a more powerful one come along is both an opportunity and a burden. Yet nothing is more fundamental to a programmer's career than the language(s) she or he uses; the programmer's professional future rides on the continued wide use of the language in which he or she writes. In "The Future of Programming" Wasserman and Gutz consider a variety of trends that they believe will have short-, medium-, and long-term effects on programming. Even if you disagree with their conclusions, setting forth your alternatives and your reasons for choosing them will be a challenge and a stimulus to thoughtfulness.

ICAI brings artificial intelligence to computer-based education. Artificial intelligence programming has made possible such feats as computer chess, an elementary form of natural language understanding, and expert systems that diagnose medical problems and prescribe for them, prospect for minerals,

and analyze the chemical composition of complex molecules from their X-ray diffraction patterns. In education, these techniques hold out the promise of expert tutors that can answer student-initiated questions, of programs that can speak and "understand" English, make intelligent and helpful comments on students' writing or mathematics, and diagnose learning difficulties.

The programming techniques and design problems are an order of magnitude more complex in ICAI than in CAI, and the programs cannot now be run on small personal computers. But if memory capacity and speed of personal computers keep increasing at anything approximating their present rate, in a few years schools will be able to afford machines that can run such programs. In the meantime, some of these techniques can be incorporated into ordinary programs to make them accept more varied input, respond more flexibly to students' input, and transfer control among parts of the program more "intelligently." The readings in this section give a basic introduction to a field that is certain to burgeon over the next few years.

In their review, Gable and Page examine the programming techniques of artificial intelligence to determine how a CAI system "could be endowed with approximations to some of the common sense attributes of a human tutor." The questions they deal with include:

What are the identifiable levels of "intelligence" in teaching programs?

How have the techniques of artificial intelligence been applied to teaching programs?

What are the key modules in an intelligent teaching program?

Brown and Burton describe a system for diagnosing the procedural errors that students make in solving problems. Their approach helps not only to point out the errors but also to identify *why* the student made the mistake—that is, the sequence of underlying mental operations that led to the actual error. This paper is in the growing field of program-

ming computers to act as intelligent tutors, diagnosing student errors in a way that helps students understand the bugs in their mental procedures.

Finally, Suppes offers an assessment of ICAI from the perspective of one of the outstanding figures in CAI. He is hopeful, but skeptical. What exactly does the "intelligent" feature of such programs offer a learner? Just how valuable is it, for what sorts of learning, under what circumstances? How do we know it will realize the advantages its advocates claim for it?

18

The Future of Programming

Anthony I. Wasserman

University of California, San Francisco

Steven Gutz*

Digital Equipment Corporation

Introduction

It is well recognized that software is the dominant cost in the development of computer systems. For many systems, software represents 80 percent or more of the total system development cost [6] and there are indications that this figure will continue to grow as hardware costs continue to drop.[1] Computing is a labor-intensive industry, and the number of programmers is proliferating as attempts are made to automate a wider variety of applications. The result is a very sharp increase in money being spent on software, an increase further stimulated by the cost of maintenance and enhancement of existing systems.

This trend cannot continue indefinitely. There is already a serious shortage of skilled programmers and the cost of such a person is expected to surpass $100,000 a year (salary, benefits, overhead) by the mid-1980s. There is clearly a need to gain control over these rising costs and to make programmers more effective.

At the same time, it is necessary to work toward improved software quality. Quality refers not only to reliability and correctness but also to ease of use and maintainability. One key objective is to provide programmers with

*This paper presents the opinion of its authors, which is not necessarily that of Digital Equipment Corporation. Opinions expressed in this paper must not be construed to imply any product commitment on the part of Digital Equipment Corporation.

the process of software production and the quality of the resulting software. An equally important objective is to provide users, many of whom are unfamiliar with the technical details of computer systems, with systems that make the computer a useful tool.

Efforts to attain these objectives must take a variety of forms. Some efforts will be relatively minor, aimed at the short term and at incremental improvements in the software development and evolution process. These efforts will focus primarily upon the development of individual software tools and the reduction of programmer support costs. Other efforts will be less immediate and will aim at changing the nature of programming and providing sophisticated environments for the individual programmer and the software development organization.

We describe some of the work that is needed in order to make programmers more effective and [we] attempt to characterize the changes in the nature of programming that will accompany these envisioned developments. We have arbitrarily divided our view into three sections: (1) the short term, covering the next 5 years, (2) the medium term, from the mid-1980s through the end of the century, (3) the long term, covering the early part of the twenty-first century.

Many of our ideas are, of necessity, speculative. It is not yet possible to provide quantitative data in support of these projections. Nevertheless, we have tried to project some trends based on recent and emerging developments in hardware and software technol-

Anthony I. Wasserman and Steven Gutz, "The Future of Programming," *Communications of the ACM,* 25 (March 1982), 196–206. © 1982 ACM. Reprinted by permission of the Association of Computing Machinery and the authors.

ogy and have pointed to supporting evidence where possible.

In setting the time frame for some of these advances, we have estimated the *mean* point at which we expect the practices and tools to be in use. We recognize that there may be a sizable time span (5–15 years) from the time that the feasibility of an idea is demonstrated to the time that an idea goes into practical application to the time that it is widely accepted and used. Another way to gauge the estimates is by the time at which the average programming organization will adopt the ideas, with the understanding that the "leading edge" organizations will be several years ahead, and the laggards a decade or more behind.[2]

Our purpose, more than that of prognostication, is to identify some goals for research in programming methodology and software engineering, with the intent of encouraging additional work on the key areas that would lead to improved development environments.

The Short Term

Efforts to improve programmer effectiveness over the short term will involve development of software tools, increased use of high level languages, and environmental changes. These changes may each be expected to produce incremental improvements in the productivity of programmers; more importantly, however, they will set the stage for more significant changes over the medium to long term.

Many organizations are presently working to create their own *software development methodology,* a systematic procedure that they can follow from the original concept of a system through its specification, design, development, operation, and evolution [7, 12, 26, 28, 29, 38, 40, 48]. Such a methodology includes technical methods to assist in the critical tasks of problem solving, documentation, hierarchical decomposition, design representation, coding, systematic testing, and software configuration management. Such a methodology also includes management procedures to control the process of development and the deployment of these technical methods. The management and technical aspects of the methodology have a synergistic relationship: the technical methods provide the intermediate results needed for effective managerial control while the management procedures serve to allocate technical resources and to support the development organization.

Software Tools

Another critical aspect of a methodology, however, is an automated development support system (ADSS) in which there is computer-based support for some (not necessarily all) of the tasks carried out as part of the methodology. The ADSS contains a number of automated tools and utilities that can be used by the developer in the course of a project. Among the most common examples of such tools are text editors and compilers; file copying and printing routines are among the most common utilities.

At present, the state of the art of software tools leaves much to be desired. This is not to say that there are no good tools. Indeed, there are a number of sophisticated and effective tools [22, 27, 30] and there are several *programming environments,* notably Unix [21], INTERLISP [36], and Multics [11], that include a substantial number of such tools. Our point is that there are few settings in which the tools actually work effectively in harmony with one another and in support of a software development methodology.

There are two extremely serious problems with most of these tools. First, they fail to support a software development methodology or to capture any data that assist in control of the software development process. A qualitative improvement in tools to provide this critical missing dimension and to augment the power of the tools is needed.

Second, present tools primarily support coding activities and fail to support the software development life cycle in its entirety. There is a need for more tools to assist with software specification, design, and testing, as well as with management of software projects. For example, there are tools that assist with problem specification such as PSL/PSA [35], or detailed design such as a program design language, but they address only a portion of the development process and must be incorporated into methodologies for software development. These points are discussed at greater length in [Reference] 16.

In addition to these primary problems, there are a number of secondary problems with present tools.

1. *Lack of compatibility* Tools are difficult to combine with one another, both at the direct interface level and at the user level; some tools cannot even use the same data or file formats.

2. *Lack of uniformity* The available set of tools differs among different machines, operating systems, and languages, making it difficult for a programmer to move easily from one development environment to another.

3. *Lack of tailorability* Most tools are designed to be used in predetermined ways and cannot easily be customized to support different patterns of use by different developers.

Recently, there has been widespread recognition of these problems, with a resulting effort to develop better software tools [17, 30]. One example of such an effort is the effort by the U.S. Department of Defense to specify needed tool capabilities to support the development of programs written in Ada [1]. Preliminary efforts are under way to develop tools that overcome some of these deficiencies and to gather some evaluative data on the use of tools.

As these tools are developed, it will be necessary to integrate them into *development environments* [3, 17, 39], exemplified by the Ada Program Support Environment framework, intended to provide the developer with a standard, uniform set of tools. Such an environment can represent both a qualitative and quantitative advance over today's state of the art. In order to meet this goal, the tools that are created for this environment will have to possess certain characteristics.

1. *Singularity of purpose* Each tool should carry out one well-defined function or a small number of closely related tasks that perform a single function.

2. *Ease of use* The user must not need elaborate knowledge in order to be able to use a tool.

3. *Levels of use* The casual user of a tool should be able to gain a substantial portion of the benefits of the tool with only a small subset of its available facilities, while the sophisticated user of the same tool may be able to gain additional benefits through the complete set of features.

4. *Consistency with other tools* Each tool should have a standard interface that enables it to be used in conjunction with other tools, and should have a set of usage conventions that conforms to those of other tools in the environment (the Unix "pipe" mechanism is a good example of this consistency).

5. *Adaptability* Tools should be adaptable to specific user requirements and should support different patterns of use by different classes of users; furthermore, tools should contain a meaningful set of defaults that can be altered by the user in order to tailor it to individual preferences and needs.

6. *Local intelligence* Tools should be designed to collect information in a private database concerning profiles of usage of the tool; the data thereby captured could assist in the evolution of that tool and in the development of new tools.

Taken as a whole, the collection of tools must provide support for the software life cycle, providing not only technical support for a specific phase of the life cycle but also management assistance and a mechanism for the transition from one phase of the life cycle to another (both forward and backward!). In this way, information gathered at successive stages of the life cycle can be applied to subsequent stages and properly validated.

Finally, the environment must support not only the individual programmer but also the management of software development. Two kinds of management are essential: configuration management and management of software development personnel. Software configuration management [5] involves keeping track of all the documentation associated with a project along with the emerging product, perhaps in multiple versions.

Information about individual productivity and the amount of effort associated with various parts of a software project organized either by project phase or by module can also be collected. Such information is particularly valuable in gaining a better understanding of the software development process itself, which can lead both to better techniques for estimating the effort required for new projects and to identification and development of improved development environments.

In the short term, these tools will be developed to operate on existing systems, using current terminals and hardware. Over the next 5 years, however, development systems will become increasingly sophisticated and development environments will be created on personal development systems, specifically to support the task of system development [16].

High Level Languages

There is now considerable experience in the use of high level languages for a broad variety of programming tasks including the development of systems software. A number of highly sophisticated systems including operating systems, e.g., Multics and Unix, and telephone switching systems, have been successfully written in high level languages.

Indeed, some computers, e.g., Burroughs B6800, have no visible machine-level language at all.

Programs written in high level languages are less error prone than programs written in machine languages, and programmers are more productive in high level languages [14]. A generally accepted rule of thumb is that the number of lines of code written by a programmer in a day is constant, regardless of the language used. Since a statement in a high level language represents a number of instructions at the machine language level, a programmer may normally complete the programming task more rapidly in a high level language.

This situation holds for those languages that are in widespread use today, e.g., Cobol, PL/I, and Fortran. A principal goal of much of the recent work in programming language design, beginning with Pascal [46] and continuing through Ada [18] and other newer languages [23, 25, 42], has been to provide features that will enhance both the quality of programs and the productivity of programmers still further.

A major shortcoming of the present high level language development environment is that very few of the support tools are integrated with the language itself. In particular, the programmer trying to debug a high level language program often must work with debugging tools that require use of the machine instructions generated by the language compiler. There is a clear need for improved debugging tools tied to the source text of the program.

Indeed, the high level language development setting provides an excellent example of the need for improved tool integration. If a runtime error occurs in a program during its development, the debugging tools should immediately be available to assist the programmer in identifying the source(s) of the error; it should then be possible to invoke the editor to change the program and rerun it, or to exercise the program more thoroughly with an automatically generated set of test data.

The improved productivity to be gained

from high level languages suggests the need to work for still higher level languages, particularly for use in application areas. While we do not expect currently used languages such as Fortran, Cobol, and BLISS to disappear, nor do we expect systems programmers to shift away from procedural programming languages, there is a significant role for very high level languages that are nonprocedural or descriptive in character.

Excellent examples of such languages are the query languages for database management systems, e.g., SQL [9] and Query by Example [50]. Such languages have been designed to provide the nonprogrammer with the ability to formulate queries and thereby receive data from a database. In the past, it was necessary to write ad hoc programs to generate the appropriate reports. Now the end user can specify a request and formulate a query in a nonprocedural language, thereby eliminating the need for a programmer.

Environmental Issues

Many programmers spend relatively little time actually doing programming, i.e., writing, debugging, testing, or documenting code. Much of their time is occupied with mundane chores, meetings, or various breaks and interruptions. Additional time is taken in becoming familiar with new applications or new development environments.

While it is unreasonable to expect a programmer to spend all his time performing programming tasks, it is clear that there is much room for improvement in programmer effectiveness. Some gain can be brought about by the improvement and standardization of tools previously discussed; additional gains can be achieved through environmental changes.

For example, the programmer's physical work environment seems to relate closely to productivity. Such factors as noise level, smoke, terminal type and speed, lighting, and access to library materials and documentation can all affect the programmer, al-

though different programmers will be affected to varying degrees by different factors.

A large portion of programmer overhead is attributable to the time associated with routine chores and clerical tasks. Advances in office automation including word processing systems for documentation, automated mailing systems, and the like, can substantially reduce the time needed for these activities. The software development activity can be integrated with the capabilities of the "electronic office," which offers the developer many features to organize and utilize time more effectively as well as to help facilitate better communication and information sharing among peers and management.

Prototyping of Systems

One of the key problems in analysis and specification of systems is that the eventual users do not have a good idea of what they want the system to do. Without such an idea, they are unable to communicate their needs effectively. Furthermore, they have a difficult time in reviewing a written specification to see whether it will satisfy their needs for functionality, ease of use, and compatibility with their organization. Instead, they approve the written specification and must then wait for a substantial interval of time before they can use the actual system. It is only at that time that they are able to gain experience with the system and to recognize its strengths and weaknesses. The release of such a system into an acceptance test or operational phase is thus typically met with a flurry of requests for changes, many of which require additional analysis and redesign. The result of this process is further delay in the availability of a usable system, along with added software expenses and potential loss of system structure due to the changes.

Instead, it would be far superior to provide development tools that permit the rapid construction and modification of system prototypes [44]. The developer could then present the user with a prototype of the user–program interface, for example, and the user could experiment with the prototype to see if all of the desired functions were available and if the format of the dialogue was comfortable. For programs providing conversational access to databases, for example, an effective prototyping tool can be constructed from a dialogue processor and a database management system.

Several important benefits could be derived from the ability to create prototypes including:

1. More effective user participation in the early project stages.

2. The user could have a temporary version of the system (the prototype) to use while the production version was being built.[3]

3. Development and maintenance costs would be reduced because problem areas and errors could be identified and corrected at a much earlier stage in the software life cycle, reducing the need to redo pieces of the system.

4. It would be possible to experiment with the user interface from a human factors perspective [8, 24, 34, 41] so that the resulting system would be easy to learn and easy to use.

Summary: The Short Term

These changes, which focus upon improved tools and environments, are well within the boundaries of currently available technology and can be achieved within 3 to 5 years. Each of them can have significant beneficial effect upon programming, giving the programmer a greater degree of job satisfaction and making it easier for the programmer to carry out the software development and evolution tasks.

However, none of these changes will have a significant effect upon the nature of programming, and hence the expected improvements will only be incremental. Indeed, the current trends could be expected to continue as more programmers work on the software tools and development environments de-

scribed here. It is only after these tools are developed and in place that some of the more far-reaching changes will begin to take hold and to change the fundamental character of programming.

The Medium Term

More significant changes are foreseen from 1985 until the end of the century. These changes will be evolutionary and can be traced from the present, as well as from assessment of future hardware technology. These changes involve a gradual shift toward greater automation of the development process and the ability to make use of a growing library of program pieces. Some of these changes will be evident in sophisticated organizations within the next few years but it will be a decade or more before these notions have a widespread impact.

These expected changes fall into four major classifications.

1. *Development of certified software components*—A body of rigorously tested and thoroughly documented software modules will be created and available for easy incorporation in new systems.

2. *Personal development systems*—The programming environments developed over the next 5 years will be incorporated into stand-alone development machines that can be interconnected to one another.

3. *Automated code generation from design languages and program schemas*—It will be possible to produce executable programs automatically for certain common classes of systems from a description of the system inputs and associated desired outputs.

4. *Improved programming languages*—There will be much greater use of modern programming languages based on concepts of systematic programming and programming methodology.

As these changes occur, the character of software itself will change as the cost of creating one-of-a-kind systems becomes increasingly expensive.

The Changing Nature of Software

Experience has shown that development of a high-quality software product of any significant size (greater than fifty modules) requires, at a minimum, 5 person-years of effort over 2 years. It thus becomes obvious that very few organizations can afford to purchase custom-built software. The benefits of mass production are apparent, as the development and evolutionary costs can be amortized over a number of customers. Similarly, the development of software tools to be used by a number of different programmers in a number of different organizations is seen to be beneficial since it can provide two kinds of leverage: mass production plus improved developer productivity.

At present, most organizations owning computers have sizable staffs to develop and maintain custom software. However, the growing availability of personal computers, ranging from hobby computers to personal development systems, is rapidly changing that situation. Soon, the majority of computers will be in the hands of people who are not (and do not wish to become) professional software developers. Such people will want to purchase a computer system with a collection of available software that adequately performs a specific set of functions.

As a result, the bulk of software development will shift to address that market, whose characteristics differ from those of the traditional software market. First of all, people who spend no more than a few thousand dollars for a computer system are not going to be willing to spend more than that sum for the software. Hence, the software produced must be inexpensive.

It is clear that the customer cannot expect to acquire custom-built software. Instead, the customer will seek out reliable, economical, easy-to-use software that meets specific needs. From the standpoint of the software vendor, it is not practical to provide ongoing support for these software packages; instead, the developer must provide a high quality package that meets identified needs for a large user community and sell enough copies of the software to make up for the development cost, in much the same way that book publishers operate.

In short, most software will come entirely without support. Software vendors who consistently produce poor software will simply lose out in the marketplace as consumer guides and knowledgeable consumers distinguish the good software from the bad in terms of usability, reliability, documentation, and value received for money spent.

Software vendors may be expected to provide limited warranties for their products in much the same way that vendors of other kinds of product, e.g., toasters, provide warranties. Indeed, one can expect to see occasional product recalls to correct faulty software. Vendors will almost certainly not provide ongoing support for their software, however. Rather, like textbook publishers, they will provide new editions from time to time, and a customer who wants the latest version will have to discard the old version and purchase the new one, with at best a small trade-in allowance.

All this is not to say that the market for custom-built software will disappear, any more than Savile Row is likely to disappear as a source of custom-made suits. There will always be customers who, for various reasons, are willing and able to spend the money for custom development and ongoing support including maintenance and enhancement. As with clothing, though, the market for "off-the-rack" software will soon dominate the industry.

In order to minimize the cost of this body of software, it will be necessary to apply the techniques of mass production, including standardized design techniques and control expenditures for optimization and testing. The desire to reduce production costs involves use of many of the same techniques that are common in other kinds of mass production endeavors, including interchangeability of parts, specialization of personnel and tools, and [design of] work environments to improve productivity.

Software Components

A software system may be seen to consist of a number of components. Typically, the construction of software systems requires that each component be built specifically for each system. There is very little reuse of components from one system to another and few standards for the development of these components. If we are to proceed toward the goal of engineering the creation of software, it is necessary to make more effective use of previously built software [43].

In order to make this possible, we must first identify a large number of frequently required functions in software systems and then develop a corresponding inventory of program components that can easily be modified, reconfigured, and reused. Such an inventory will be roughly analogous to the inventory of prefabricated circuits available from semiconductor manufacturers, and the task of the software implementer will more closely resemble that of the computer designer, who determines the gross system structure and the interconnections between circuits but relies on the prefabricated components for low level operations. Over the past few years, we have seen the development of increasingly larger and more complex hardware components, providing a greater range of components from which to select, with the corresponding potential to restrict low level alternatives severely. A similar trend in the development of software components is needed.

Although some software components already exist, few have been subjected to rigorous testing and evaluation to determine the extent to which they truly constitute basic software building blocks. Careful study will be needed to identify the appropriate components for various application areas. Fur-

thermore, candidate components will need to be studied to determine whether they are, in fact, made up of other candidate components. Gradually, standard functional components must become the major building blocks for future software systems, replacing those that have repeatedly been constructed from low level primitives in the past [4].

The programmer of the future will then work with these standard components, programming in the large [13] with a decreased need for programming in the small. In order to encourage software developers to make use of such components, it will be necessary to provide a great deal of information about the components so that they are accepted and used with confidence.

Accordingly, software components will have to be subjected to rigorous quality control and must be delivered with unambiguous specifications, comprehensible documentation, and data describing its performance characteristics. Of course, the components will also have a warranty; for some classes of components, some kind of formal verification may be appropriate. This component description must be given without resorting to implementation details. It is necessary to devise compact, unambiguous, standard representations of the components and their relevant properties, perhaps in a manner similar to the technical data accompanying a product like a stereo receiver.

Personal Development Systems

As discussed previously, considerable effort will go toward the development of software tools in the short term. In the medium term, these tools will be integrated into a hardware/software development environment that can make it possible for the individual software developer to live and work via a personal machine that provides the maximum possible support for the developer's various activities. In addition to the obvious system development work, the machine can serve as a vehicle for a number of important tasks.

Text processing, including the preparation of system documentation, technical papers and reports, and correspondence, as well as editing or reviewing material typed by others

Information storage and retrieval, including documents associated with various software development projects, telephone directories, mailing lists, and personal databases

Communication, including the sending and receiving of mail throughout both a local network and a larger network involving remote access and conferencing with one or more persons via these networks

Self-management including a long-term diary, short-term (day or week) scheduling, and a "to-do" list, with reminders that can be automatically triggered by a system clock

We may call such a development system a "professional programmer-based system" (PPBS). The typical configuration for a PPBS will provide the programmer with at least the computing power available in a present-day medium scale time-sharing system. The components of this configuration will include.

An intelligent terminal having approximately 1 megabyte of primary memory and the computing power and address space of today's 32-bit minicomputers

Local secondary storage (e.g., a Winchester disk) with upward of 40 megabytes of storage capacity as well as some removable media (e.g., floppy disk)

Graphics capability including multiple character fonts, reverse video, variable intensity, split screen, color, and the ability to display a standard page of text completely on the screen

Networking capability, to connect with other PPBSs in a local network and to geographically dispersed systems

Audio input/output

Within this framework, it should be possible to add additional primary and secondary storage as well as other kinds of peripheral devices, e.g., a print-quality hardcopy device. This configuration not only provides powerful local processing but opens up a broad range of possibilities for user interaction, permitting the use of windows and menus for task selection and sequence control as well as incorporating pictures and eventually voice input. Given the present rate of reduction in hardware costs, it should be possible to produce a PPBS in the price range of $10,000–$20,000 by the late 1980s.

The potential benefits of the PPBS are substantial and not only can make the development organization more productive but also can improve software quality. Among the advantages that the PPBS can provide over the time-sharing approach presently used are improved reliability of hardware, improved hardware performance, private mass storage, and support for nonkeyboard input.

Automation of Programming Tasks

As we gain experience in the design and development of software systems and as we identify a body of software components, certain common program structures and schemas emerge. For example, a command processing program can immediately be decomposed into an input part, a decoding part, and a dispatching part, with each separate command handled by a separate program module. This decomposition is so intuitive that it leads to a very straightforward kind of programming, where one can simply use a standard program schema and insert the appropriate commands and actions. (This particular schema is termed the "transaction model" in Structured Design [49].)

There are already a number of systems that carry out this kind of task:

Parser generators used to construct compilers and other language processing programs [20]

Query languages, as mentioned above, that decompose the nonprocedural request and generate the appropriate operations on the underlying database (which, in turn, uses the access paths for the underlying file system)

Cobol program generation from the input structures, output structures, and operation lists created through use of the Jackson Design Methodology [19]

The class of application for which this type of program generation can be performed will continue to increase so that many of the most common kinds of programs can be produced without having to resort to the level of detail presently required for programming.

Although there will always be boundaries upon acceptable response times and performance, the general issue of performance for some of these applications will be clearly secondary to the ability to express the problem and to obtain the solution without substantial programming effort. Functionality, generality, and correctness will be the predominant considerations.

Modern Programming Languages

The 1970s have seen a vast amount of activity in programming language design based on the recognition that the features of a programming language have a strong effect upon the quality of the resulting software. While it is possible to write a coherent and well-structured program in a "bad" language, and possible to write an incomprehensible and unmaintainable program in a "good" language, it seems clear that there are various languages and language features that encourage good programming practices and others that hinder the use of such practices [47].

Work on the design of a number of languages during the past decade has identified a number of features that seem to be valuable for writing high quality programs, regardless of the intended application area. These features include support for abstraction, particu-

larly abstract objects, support for modularization including separate compilation of modules, support for linear flow of control through powerful language control structures, the use of data types and type checking, and, finally, exception handling to make programs robust against various kinds of exceptional runtime condition, including, but not limited to, user input errors.

Pascal possesses several of these properties and serves as the model for the design of a number of new programming languages, of which Ada seems likely to become the most commonly used. There is preliminary evidence that the programming discipline inherent in the use of Pascal and its descendants has a beneficial effect on software quality and programmer productivity [14]. The widespread use of these new languages and language support systems should have a measurable effect on the programming task.

While it will remain necessary to use presently available languages for the maintenance and enhancement of the large body of software already in existence, newer languages based on these ideas of programming methodology will increasingly be used for new applications.

The use of natural language as a programming language has long intrigued computer scientists, and there have been several projects that have made significant strides toward natural language comprehension by computer [32, 37, 45]. We believe that there will be an increasing number of systems that accept input in a form approximating natural language. Such systems can be particularly useful for the computer-naive user. The potential utility of natural language for database retrieval has been demonstrated [10].

Yet natural language has some important shortcomings when considered as a programming language. First, the volume of input may be much larger than that required for either procedural or nonprocedural query languages. English is relatively compact in this respect, but many other languages require more text to make comparable statements. Second, natural language, particularly English, is inherently ambiguous. In order to overcome this problem, systems must either incorporate a sophisticated interactive procedure to resolve ambiguities or must restrict the input to an artificial subset of natural language or both.

Thus, we believe that people in computer science will continue to write programs in an artificial language for quite some time and that natural language systems are more likely to be used by nonprogrammers as end users of an application program.

Summary: The Medium Term

The medium term advances in programming are based largely on notions presently available as prototypes in research and development settings. The advances in software componentry and in automation of some kinds of programming are largely empirical—experience in developing software systems leads to the identification of commonly used software structures and program modules. These can be made available as separate verified components or can serve as models for programs that can generate a number of programs of a given class.

The PPBS pulls together the advances in software tools with the need for improved development environments and the capabilities of the electronic office. Each programmer can have a PPBS that may be customized to specific personal needs and desires.

These medium-term advances in programming set the stage for more far-reaching advances in the next century, as we develop additional techniques for describing programs in a nonprocedural way and become able to apply the automatic programming notions to broader classes of programs.

The Long Term

There is considerable risk in trying to carry out technology assessment in a field that is changing so rapidly. There is a strong possibility that some kind of revolutionary break-

through will occur and invalidate all the predictions or sharply compress the time scale. Such has certainly been the case with computer hardware. Our projections are based primarily on the foreseeable advances over the short and medium terms and may therefore be regarded as relatively conservative. Furthermore, it is more difficult to be specific about the likely advances. Accordingly, our notion of the long term concentrates on the first few decades of the twenty-first century.

The short- and medium-term advances in programming focused heavily on the development of software tools, the creation of development environments, and the means to make use of experience in software development, while retaining a large measure of the present orientation with procedural programming languages. It seems likely that the longer term advances will change the fundamental nature of programming.

This fundamental change will occur in several ways. First, much of the short-term effort will be placed on developing interfaces that are appropriate for end users, making it feasible for such users to interact directly with the computer for many of their routine needs. Second, programmers will become able to express the desired function of a program in terms of its expected behavior and output(s) without having to specify the precise algorithms involved in performing the processing. Third, many programmers will then move away from concern with the "how" of programming to concentrate more heavily on the "what"; applications programming will then become equivalent to today's task of requirements analysis and specification. In short, both the nature of programming and the nature of programmers will change.

User-Level Programming

Today's query languages for database management systems are the forerunners of a much more sophisticated class of user-level tools that will permit a user to request certain kinds of operation from the computer without any substantial programming knowledge or effort. Tools such as report program generators and database retrieval systems will be equipped with interfaces that facilitate their use by nonprogrammers. Such interfaces, rather than requiring typing, as is the case with today's systems, will permit the user to interact in a variety of different modes including (spoken) natural languages and graphics, as well as typing which will remain a viable alternative in many situations.

This form of user programming will have several major benefits.

> There will be less need for expensive applications programmers to write the programs to carry out these tasks since users will be able to write simple programs.

> Application programmers can be concerned instead with more general facilities, i.e., providing the tools that permit broader kinds of user-level programming.

> Users can request the data and reports they want as needed and as their requirements evolve, thereby eliminating a costly form of maintenance.

This is not to say that the profession of programming will disappear—there will still be a need for systems and applications programmers.[4] It is just that the increased growth in the use of computers will be accompanied by a growth in tools that permit the users to carry out common tasks directly, thereby minimizing the growth in the number of programmers who must be familiar with programming languages and internal software system details.

It should be noted that the software systems to support user-level programming will be extremely sophisticated by today's standards and that the problems of specification, design, and implementation of such systems will require highly skilled professional programmers.

Automatic Programming

The term "automatic programming" has been used for many years to refer to the process by which an executable program may be produced from nonprocedural specifications of the task to be performed. Some limited forms of automatic programming are already available and more will become available in the medium term. Over the longer term, it will be possible for programmers to create running programs by providing a *specification* of program functions and outputs, without having to proceed with a detailed program design or with the production of code.

Two major kinds of specification seem likely to emerge. The first is derived from current work in the area of formal specification languages, in which one is able to describe functions and axioms upon sets of abstract objects, transforming one set of operations and objects into another through successive refinements [15, 31]. These specification languages will be able to use software components that automatically create representations for the abstract objects as well as providing a set of operations. The specification language can be used to generate a program, perhaps in an applicative language, e.g., LISP, that will carry out the desired function.

The second approach to specification applies current research in artificial intelligence. Many decision processes can be expressed by a set of rules, e.g., diagnosis of certain diseases. Work with such systems as MYCIN [33] has shown that it is possible to create a program skeleton that can accept a set of rules as a knowledge base and then produce a set of actions that follows that set of rules. Such a program skeleton has been used to generate a program for an unrelated application in a very short period of time.

Thus, if it is possible to state a set of decision rules for a given problem, it will become a straightforward task to implement those rules in a running program. Eventually, such rule-based systems will be able to accommodate large knowledge bases, maintain integrity constraints on their databases, and verify consistency among their rules. This feature will be particularly important when the knowledge base is modified.

It can be seen that the programmer's problem in such a setting shifts away from the traditional concern with data representation and program structure and toward understanding of the problem itself, a task that is now carried out by analysts who communicate their understanding to programmers through some kind of specification, which is then translated into a design and implementation. In such a setting, optimization can be performed by transforming the automatic solution or by guiding the choices made by the automatic system [2].

The activities of design and implementation require additional people and additional time. Furthermore, the transition between the various phases with their inherently different representations is extremely error prone. Errors in the specification may not be found until the program is tested, and additional errors may be introduced during design and implementation. Hence, the ability to "implement the specification," whether it be in the form of rules or a formal specification language, provides substantial leverage in controlling software costs. Furthermore, as these languages become easier to use and increasingly expressive, it becomes easier to once again customize systems for minor differences in user needs, a capability which is now becoming prohibitively expensive.

The Programmer as Analyst

There is, at present, a difference between the systems programmer and the applications programmer. This distinction is likely to grow stronger in the future as application programmers need to become more aware of the requirements of specific users and specific application areas and less aware of the low level machine details.

We are presently on the verge of a vast explosion of computerized applications as the availability of inexpensive hardware makes the computer an indispensable appliance in people's homes and an essential part of almost every organization. The major roadblock to this path is the low usability of present software. As software tools become more powerful, more programmers will be available to work on applications tasks.

As we have seen, the need will not be for programming skills in the traditional sense but for the ability to communicate with users and to understand the needs of these individuals and their organizations. Thus we may expect future programmers to receive training not only in a computer science-like discipline (essential for systems programmers), but also in an applications area. Such educational programs already exist in areas such as medical computing and management information systems where a large portion of the student's education is aimed at familiarization with the application area—its structure, its information needs, and the roles of various personnel—rather than with the computing aspects of the applications.

This need is reflected in the directions of research in software engineering. Much of the early work was in the area of programming methodology. Much of the recent work has focused on requirements analysis and specification techniques including such activities as modeling organizational structures, functions, and information flows. There is clearly a need for more powerful tools in this area to support the development of sophisticated applications.

Summary: The Long Term

Clearly, the topics mentioned above represent only a small portion of the advances that are likely to occur in the software area over the next 50 years. Other topics that are important include such things as the relationship between software environments and their underlying hardware, with its implications for system portability and the need for system maintenance.

Nonetheless, it can be seen that the nature of programming and programmers is certain to change, and that an increasing share of what we now term programming will be carried out by user–operators, who will have tools at their disposal that permit them to interact naturally with a computer system and specify their requests. It is only when such tools are provided that the exponential growth in the number of programmers and the cost of software can be slowed and that attention may be devoted to making the greatest possible beneficial use of the computer.

Conclusions

Software design and development is the weakest link in the system development process. It has become extraordinarily and prohibitively expensive and remains unpredictable in terms of economically and dependably producing programs that run reliably, correctly, and efficiently.

We have now reached a point where experience in software development combined with advances in hardware technology and research into programming methodology and software engineering can all be brought to bear upon the problem. As a result, we have the opportunity to drastically alter the nature of programming in the foreseeable future.

Over the short term, the benefits are incremental, based largely on the development of improved software tools and their integration into programming environments. Over the medium term, the benefits and changes are more substantial, involving the construction of an inventory of reusable and verifiable software components and the ability to generate programs for certain well-defined classes of problems. These changes then set the stage for more substantial changes over the longer term, turning much of today's programming task into a specification task and providing the users of computer systems with a powerful collection of tools that permit them to carry out their applications without having to rely upon programmers. These changes, in turn, leave programmers free to provide increasingly powerful tools and to work with users to identify their needs and formulate them for the computer.

ACKNOWLEDGMENTS

We gratefully acknowledge the constructive comments of many of our colleagues at the University of California and Digital Equipment Corporation on an earlier draft of this paper. We also appreciate D. D. McCracken's observation concerning the large variation in the adoption of new methods. Computing support for text preparation was provided by National Institutes of Health Grant RR-1081 to the UCSF Computer Graphics Laboratory, Principal Investigator, R. Langridge.

NOTES

1. An important exception to this statement is the area of microprocessor-based systems, where the resulting "embedded" system is replicated thousands of times. In that situation, the total hardware cost may dominate the software costs but the criticality of producing correct and reliable software is even more important than in traditional software systems because of the high cost of modifying the system.

2. Notable recent examples of this phenomenon are the use of structured programming techniques and the use of a modern programming language such as Pascal.

3. In some situations, particularly where efficiency is not important, where the expected lifetime and usage of the system is small, and where development funds are limited, the prototype system alone might suffice.

4. To some extent, the distinction between systems programmers and applications programmers is artificial. For our purposes, though, we may characterize systems programmers as those persons who must be aware of internal details of machine organization.

REFERENCES

1. Advanced Research Projects Agency. Requirements for Ada programming support environments—"STONEMAN." U.S. Department of Defense, Arlington, Va., 1980.

2. Balzer, R. Transformational implementation: An example. *IEEE Transactions on Software Engineering, SE-7,* 1 (January 1981), 3–14.

3. Barstow, D., Shrobe, H., and Sandewall, E.

(Eds.). *Interactive Development Environments.* McGraw-Hill, New York, 1982.

4. Belady, L.A. Evolved software for the '80's. *Computer, 12,* 2 (February 1979), 79–83.

5. Bersoff, E.H., Henderson, V.D., and Siegel, S.G. Software configuration management: A tutorial. *Computer, 12,* 1 (January 1979), 6–14.

6. Boehm, B.W. Software and its impact: A quantitative assessment. *Datamation, 19,* 5 (May 1973), 48–59.

7. Boyd, D.L., and Pizzarello, A. Introduction to the WELLMADE design methodology. *IEEE Transactions on Software Engineering, SE-4,* 4 (July 1978), 276–282.

8. Card, S.K., Moran, T.P., and Newell, A. The keystroke-level model for user performance time with interactive systems. *Commun. ACM, 23,* 7 (July 1980), 396–410.

9. Chamberlin, D.D., et al. SEQUEL2: A unified approach to data definition, manipulation, and control. *IBM J. Res. Devp. 20,* 6 (November 1976), 560–575.

10. Codd, E.F. How about recently? (English dialog with relational data bases using Rendezvous Version 1). In *Databases: Improving Usability and Responsiveness.* B. Shneiderman (Ed.), Academic Press, New York, 1978, pp. 3–28.

11. Corbato, F.J., and Clingen, C.T. A managerial view of the Multics system development. In *Research Directions in Software Technology.* P. Wegner (Ed.). MIT Press, Cambridge, Mass., 1979, pp. 139–158.

12. Davis, C.G., and Vick, C.R. The software development system. *IEEE Transactions on Software Engineering, SE-3,* 1 (January 1977) 69–84.

13. DeRemer, F., and Kron, H. Programming-in-the-large versus programming-in-the-small. *IEEE Transactions on Software Engineering, SE-2,* 2 (June 1976), 80–86.

14. Gannon, J.D., and Horning, J.J. Language design for programming reliability. *IEEE Transactions on Software Engineering, SE-1,* 2 (June 1975), 179–191.

15. Goguen, J., and Tardo, J.J. An introduction of OBJ: A language for writing and testing formal algebraic program specifications. *Proc. Specifications of Reliable Software.* IEEE Computer Society, 1979, 170–189.

16. Gutz, S., Wasserman, A.I., and Spier, M.J. Personal development systems for the professional programmer. *Computer, 14,* 4 (April 1981), 45–52.

17. Hunke, H. (Ed.). *Software Engineering Environments.* North Holland, Amsterdam, 1981.

18. Ichbiah, J.D. (Ed.). *Reference Manual for the Ada Programming Language,* U.S. Department of Defense, Advanced Research Projects Agency, 1980.

19. Jackson, M.A. *Principles of Program Design.* Academic Press, London, 1975.

20. Johnson, S.C., and Lesk, M.E. Language development tools. *Bell Syst. Tech. J., 57,* 6 (July–August 1978), Part 2, 2155–2175.

21. Kernighan, B.W., and Mashey, J.R. The Unix programming environment. *Computer, 14,* 4 (April 1981), 12–24.

22. Kernighan, B.W., and Plauger, P.J. *Software Tools.* Addison-Wesley, Reading, Mass., 1976.

23. Lampson, B.W., et al. Report on the programming language Euclid. *ACM SIGPLAN Notices, 12,* 2 (February 1977), 1–79.

24. Ledgard, H., Singer, A., and Whiteside, J. *Directions in Human Factors for Interactive Systems.* Springer-Verlag, Berlin, 1981. (Lecture Notes in Computer Science, Vol. 103)

25. Liskov, B., et al. *CLU Reference Manual.* Springer-Verlag, Berlin, 1981. (Lecture Notes in Computer Science, Vol. 114)

26. Lundeberg, M., Goldkuhl, G., and Nilsson, A. *Information Systems Development. A Systematic Approach.* Prentice-Hall, Englewood Cliffs, N.J., 1981.

27. Miller, E.F., Jr. (Ed.). *Tutorial: Automated Tools for Software Engineering.* IEEE Computer Society, Los Alamitos, Calif., 1979.

28. Neumann, P.G. Experience with a formal methodology for software development. *Proc. Int. Seminar on Software Engineering Applications,* Capri, 1980.

29. O'Neill, D. The management of software engineering—Part II: Software engineering program. *IBM Syst. J., 19,* 4 (1980), 421–431.

30. Riddle, W.E., and Fairley, R.E. (Eds.). *Software Development Tools.* Springer-Verlag, Heidelberg, 1980.

31. Robinson, L. The HDM Handbook, Vol. 1:

The Foundations of HDM. Project Report 4828, Computer Science Group, SRI International, 1979.

32. Schank, R.C., and Rieger, C.J. Inference and the computer understanding of natural language. *Artif. Intell., 5* (1974), 373–412.

33. Shortliffe, E.H. *Computer-Based Medical Consultations: MYCIN.* American Elsevier, New York, 1976.

34. Smith, H.T., and Green, T.R. (Eds.). *Human Interaction with Computers.* Academic Press, London, 1980.

35. Teichroew, D., and Hershey, E.A., III, PSL/ PSA: A computer-aided technique for structured documentation and analysis of information processing systems. *IEEE Transactions on Software Engineering, SE-3,* 1 (January 1977), 41–48.

36. Teitelman, W., and Masinter, L. The INTERLISP programming environment. *Computer, 14,* 4 (April 1981), 25–33.

37. Walker, D. (Ed.). *Understanding Spoken Language.* Elsevier North-Holland, New York, 1978.

38. Wasserman, A.I. Information system design methodology. *J. Am. Soc. Info. Sci., 31,* 1 (January 1980), 5–24.

39. Wasserman, A.I. (Ed.). *Tutorial: Software Development Environments.* IEEE Computer Society, Los Alamitos, Calif., 1981.

40. Wasserman, A.I. USE: A methodology for the design and development of interactive information systems. In *Formal Models and Practical Tools for Information System Design.*

H.-J. Schneider, (Ed.), North Holland, Amsterdam, 1979, pp. 31–50.

41. Wasserman, A.I. User software engineering and the design of interactive systems. *Proc. 5th Int. Conf. Software Engineering.* San Diego, pp. 387–393.

42. Wasserman, A.I., et al. Revised report on the programming language PLAIN. *ACM SIGPLAN Notices, 16,* 5 (May 1981), 50–80.

43. Wasserman, A.I., and Belady, L.A. Software engineering: The turning point. *Computer, 11, 9* (September 1978), 30–41.

44. Wasserman, A.I., and Shewmake, D.T. Automating the development and evolution of user dialogue in an interactive information system. In *Evolutionary Information Systems.* J. Hawgood and L. Methlie (Eds.), North Holland, Amsterdam, 1981.

45. Winograd, T. *Understanding Natural Language.* Academic Press, New York, 1972.

46. Wirth, N. The programming language Pascal. *Acta Informatica, 1,* 1 (1971), 35–63.

47. Wulf, W.A. Trends in the design and implementation of programming languages. *Computer, 13,* 1 (January 1980), 14–22.

48. Yourdon, E. *Software Development Methodology.* Yourdon, Inc., New York, 1982.

49. Yourdon, E., and Constantine, L.L. *Structured Design.* Prentice-Hall, Englewood Cliffs, N.J., 1979.

50. Zloof, M.M. Query by example. *Proc. AFIPS 1975 NCC, 44,* New York, pp. 431–438.

19

The Use of Artificial Intelligence Techniques in Computer-Assisted Instruction: An Overview

Alice Gable and Carl V. Page

Michigan State University

Introduction

This paper surveys applications of artificial intelligence (AI) techniques in computer-assisted instruction (CAI). The rapidly decreasing cost of computer hardware provides opportunities to design computer-assisted educational systems that are potentially much more cost effective than present commercially available systems. The forthcoming revolution in computers in education is discussed by Zinn (1978) and Banet (1978). But what type of CAI software can use (to advantage) the more extensive and sophisticated hardware that will be generally available? The expanding area of artificial intelligence contains a variety of software techniques for representing and deploying different aspects of knowledge. In the past, such techniques have been expensive but now their cost is becoming almost negligible.

One of the major goals of artificial intelligence research is the development of practical methods for endowing machines with some common sense. Rather than attempting the hopeless task of rigidly defining what AI is or is not, we direct the reader to the fine survey book by Raphael (1976). Some of the methods presented by us as AI may be reminiscent of work in other fields of study. Much of the novelty in AI research is not in the underlying concepts themselves but in the development of practical means to bring general concepts to bear on specific knowledge areas. What was practical in yesterday's large/medium-scale computers on which most AI systems were developed will soon be practical for the inexpensive computers available for the classroom. What can we expect of CAI systems that possess common sense?

The main purpose of this paper is to describe techniques from AI which would allow a CAI system to behave more like an experienced human tutor who possesses common sense. We will discuss various experimental systems which have shown how to implement the major concepts. Some systems, such as at the Stanford BIP project (Barr, Beard, and Atkinson, 1976) and the Bolt Beranek and Newman Inc. group (Burton and Brown, 1976; Brown and Burton *et al.*, 1977; Brown, Rubenstein, and Burton, 1976; Brown, Burton, and Miller *et al.*, 1975; Ash *et al.*, 1977; Brown and Burton, 1974; Collins, Warnock, and Passafiume, 1975; Collins and Grignetti, 1975; Collins, 1976) explore in depth many aspects of the issues which we discuss. Neches (1977) considers several AI techniques in designing a Socratic method tutorial system. The theme of simulating some aspects of a human tutor pervades much work in this area.

Let us list some desirable properties of a human tutor to serve as a reference point in our survey.

1. The tutor causes the problem-solving heuristics of the student to converge to those of the tutor.

Alice Gable and Carl V. Page, "The Use of Artificial Intelligence Techniques in Computer-Assisted Instruction: An Overview," *International Journal of Man–Machine Studies,* 12 (1980), 259–282. Copyright © 1980 Academic Press Inc. (London) Limited. Reprinted by permission of Academic Press Inc. (London) Limited and the authors. Section on theorem proving in CAI on pages 262–264 omitted, appendices omitted, and figures renumbered.

2. The tutor will learn and adopt student solution methods if they are superior.

3. The tutor chooses appropriate examples and problems for the student.

4. When the student needs help, the tutor can recommend solution scheme choices and demonstrate how to apply techniques.

5. The tutor can work arbitrary examples chosen by the student.

6. The tutor is able to adjust to different student backgrounds.

7. The tutor is able to measure the student's progress.

8. The tutor can review previously learned material with the student as the need arises.

9. The tutor will give immediate feedback on errors while allowing the student a free hand in deciding how to solve a problem.

10. After the student solves a problem, the tutor may point out more direct solutions or ones that use recently learned theorems or techniques.

Admittedly this list asks for a lot, since many human tutors do not possess all of these attributes. Polya (1957) points out the important role of knowledge in tutoring, "The first rule of teaching is to know what you are supposed to teach. The second rule of teaching is to know a little more than what you are supposed to teach."

History

After this glimpse at our goals, we briefly examine the evolution of present-day teaching programs. Much of this discussion follows Goldberg (1973).

The lowest level of teaching programs was originated before computers by Pressey (1926). The course material consisted of a sequence of "frames" containing explanatory information and pertinent questions. The mastery of each frame was required before proceeding to the next. At this level, there is no branching and each student must proceed through the same list of questions.

The second level was introduced by Crowder (1962) in the form of his "scrambled textbooks." The student answers a question and on the basis of his or her answer the next question is chosen and retrieved from storage. Here the branching is dependent on the answer to only one question (or possibly a related block of questions). Many second-level teaching systems do not "know" what they teach and branch according to predetermined patterns. Consequently, every statement, question, and branch must be specified by the curriculum writer.

The third level has been called "adaptive." These systems differ from those on the second level only in that their branches are based on a history of responses. This amounts to a model of the student and it is stored for each student between sessions.

The fourth level of systems is called "generative." Generative systems use algorithms to generate problems and answers. This is the stage at which the systems possess the potential to "understand" the material. That is, systems at this stage can possess knowledge which can be deployed for the benefit of the student in far-reaching and unexpected ways.

In the remaining sections various systems which use AI techniques to generate problems and/or answers will be discussed. The techniques are dependent on the types of material being covered by the teaching system. Many early generative programs have been written for mathematics using algorithms to generate problems. These types of algorithm can be exemplified by one that finds coefficients for second degree polynomials by using a random number generator followed by checking to see that certain conditions are met by the generated polynomial, before presenting it to the student.

Theorem Proving

Theorem provers are very logical resources to include in educational systems for mathematics or logic. A theorem prover can be useful both as a proof checker and as a help device when the student is stuck. Programs have previously been written to supply both of these functions. A brief history of these programs and their usefulness is in order. The following history summarizes a similar one in Goldberg (1973). We distinguish between proof checkers and theorem provers.

There are three kinds of proof checkers. The first kind (Abrahams, 1963) can verify mathematical proofs on a step-by-step basis inserting the lines necessary to make the proof rigorous. A second kind, a homework grader, will give feedback only to completed proofs. A student's proof is evaluated and his or her errors are pointed out. The main problem is that there is no immediate feedback, which means that the student may have to rewrite the proof several times before getting it correct. The third kind of proof checker alleviates this problem by examining each proof step as soon as it is entered by the student. Some people object to this kind of immediate feedback because, ultimately, the student is expected to do the proof without feedback.

An interesting example of the third kind of proof checker is the Logic and Algebra Program at Stanford University, a forerunner of a part of Goldberg's system. [. . .] A coded command language was used to represent axioms, theorems, and rules of inference. The student may request any valid command regardless of its relevance to the problem. Hints are available, but since they are prestored, their relevance is open to doubt in many cases. Another technical problem is that there is no means to review the syntax of previously learned commands.

There are two basic types of theorem prover. The first type uses the resolution principle (Robinson, 1965). Resolution has the advantage of being fairly efficient but, unfortunately, the types of step it makes are frequently too alien for human beings to

understand. As a result its proofs are next to useless to a student. Another factor to consider is that it does not illustrate the proof methods used by the students. Furthermore, a technical limitation is that the number of statements it generates frequently expands very rapidly, causing storage space problems.

The second type of theorem prover uses some type of heuristic algorithm to accomplish the theorem proving. An early example is the Logic Theorist (LT) program of Newell, Shaw, and Simon (1956). The program attempts to eliminate differences between a given expression and a goal expression. This elimination is carried out by replacing substructures of the given expression to transform it into the goal expression. LT finds similarities between the structures of logical formulas. The program sometimes works backwards to find the solution. The GPS programs by Newell and Simon (1963) generalized the techniques of LT to wider domains of study.

Quinlan and Hunt (1968) developed the Fortran Deduction System (FDS), a heuristic program that uses rewrite rules. The main disadvantage is that each rewrite can be applied only to the results of the previous rewrite. Like GPS, a look-ahead is used to choose subproblems which are less difficult than the original problem. However, the relative difficulty of different subgoals can be learned rather than fixed as in GPS.

The technology of theorem proving has progressed steadily since the days of LT. Some rather complex proofs in mathematics have been found by recent systems (Bledsoe and Tyson, 1975). In addition, theorem processing programs are integral parts of program correctness verifiers, program synthesizers (Barstow, 1977), and AI systems for controlling robots (Fikes and Nilsson, 1971). [. . .]

Information structured CAI

Carbonell's SCHOLAR program (1970) was designed to teach the geography of South America as a prototype for a knowledge-based system. It was a mixed initiative system (i.e., both the system and the student could ask and answer questions). The data structure used by the program was a Quillian-like semantic network (1968). The system generated its questions from this network.

A semantic network is a set of units composed of properties. Each property has three elements: the property name, the tags used by the program, and the value of the property. The value of the property consists of either a set of properties or a pointer to a unit (see Figure 1). An example of a unit is Argentina, with properties such as country, location, etc. These properties have pointers to other units to avoid duplication of information. There is obviously quite a lot of nesting possible in a semantic network.

The system had two different modes of operation. The entry mode was a mixed-initiative mode in which the computer generally asked questions and the student answered but the student could also ask a few questions to clarify things or relationships. The other mode was the question–answer mode. In this mode the student quizzed the system as he or she desired to gather information. [. . .]

One question that an intelligent observer might ask is how the system decided what information to give when asked [something] like, "Tell me about Peru." The system looks at the unit Peru and lists properties starting at the top of the unit. This method, however, may not always be the best since all the properties can be ordered in terms of interest and this interest may vary from user to user. This problem can be solved by tagging the properties according to desired interest level.

In SCHOLAR there was some attempt to utilize restricted natural language for both input and output. The main restriction that the system placed on the student was in terms of the answers to the questions. Question answers were generally restricted to three types: numbers, atoms, and lists of atoms. The student was allowed a fair amount of freedom in asking questions, though the system would ask for a rephrasing if it did not understand.

For output, SCHOLAR generated questions by means of its semantic network. At the time of generation, a correct answer or set of answers was produced. The restriction on students' answers simplifies the matching technique for deciding the correctness of an answer. But answers are not all equally correct or incorrect. Sometimes questions of rel-

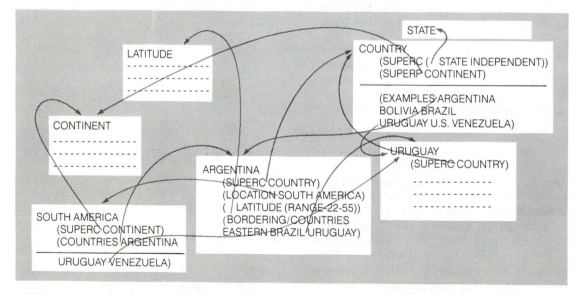

FIGURE 1: A semantic net representation of knowledge of South America (excerpted from Carbonell, 1970)

evancy and completeness enter in. Consequently, for a question requiring a list as an answer, the system points out to the student which elements are correct, which are incorrect, and whether any are missing.

One can identify three types of difficulty preventing the student from getting the correct answer. One of these types involves misconceptions on the part of the student such as misfiled facts, missing information, wrong superordinate, and overgeneralization errors. Another problem type stems from the student's basic learning capabilities such as skill in understanding and following instructions, command of language, and deductive skills. The third type originates in the student's attitudes: his or her interest, initiative, and industriousness. SCHOLAR deals only with the first category of obstacles but an effective system must deal with all three.

Another area of importance is that concerned with the teacher's interactions with the system. These interactions include: preparing the data base, setting conditions of student–computer interaction, collecting results, and supervising the system. Carbonell has suggested the use of the computer to aid the teachers in the first three interactions by using a conversational program to ask them about new units they are entering and the relationships to other units, or by listing the different kinds of ways they can adjust the student–computer interactions. Another role for the teachers could be as a last resort if the computer were unable to answer a question. These facilities are not implemented in this system, though they are definitely labor-saving devices that are important in a practical educational system.

Wexler's program (1970) is a generative, information structured program. It is very much like Carbonell's SCHOLAR program in some respects. The data structure consists of a set of objects grouped into classes forward and backward. A trace is used to collect data objects along a derivational path.

Different kinds of derivational paths can be specified by means of skeletal patterns. The skeletal patterns are rules that determine the search path through the data base. A dynamic search mechanism provides traces with an explanation string which explains the trace to the user. The dynamic search mechanism consists of a sequence of test segments. The test segments step through the net and make tests on selected objects. If the test fails, then backtracking occurs and a new object is selected before proceeding with the trace. The explanation string is a template into which certain words are substituted to explain the particular trace. [...]

We briefly explain the notation, most of which is straightforward. There are three types of output from the system: statements, questions, and interpretations. Each of these has various types of template that can be chosen for it. An example of a question template is:

#Q150 NAME TWO LARGE CITIES IN *P1.@
OK = SP20(V1 = P1, V2 = A1,V4 = A2)

The question pattern starts with a question output to the student ("NAME TWO LARGE CITIES IN"), and ends with the specification of a particular skeletal pattern and its variable assignments. The question is considered correct (denoted @ OK = ...) if the input (A1 and A2) when plugged into the skeletal pattern 20 (SP20) gives a valid trace. If they do not, other traces are initiated to determine the type of misconception on the part of the student. Statement constructs are used to present information, but they are not as flexible as the other two construct types. An example:

#S1 THE CAPITAL OF WISCONSIN IS MADISON.

The third type of construct is the interpretative construct, which is used to explain correct derivational paths to the student. An example:

#I14 (STATE *V1 LINK TO CITY #V3) #V3 IS A CITY IN *V1.

These three types of construct just named are statements in Teacher Programming Language programs. There are three different types of program available. The first is very detailed—the common type in which every question and response and branch is specified in the program. The second is a parameterized program using the constructs in the preceding paragraph, which imposes particular conditions by specifying areas to be questioned and the types of questions to be asked. The system is left the task of deciding which particular questions to ask but the teacher still guides the branching structure of the program. The third type of program is generative. The program is given a list of skeleton patterns and is told how many statements and questions to generate. [. . .] The choice of the questions and the branching are handled by the system. There is obviously quite a lot of choice for the teacher in the amount of control he or she has over the generation of the instructional material.

The system has its own automatic teaching strategy. It will not ask a question until after the statement discussing it [has been] presented and will always have at least one statement between a statement and the question based on it. Missed questions are put on a three-step decay list. Upon first missing a question, a student is given the choice of whether he or she wants help, but missing it again triggers help.

The help that the students receive is in the form of a trace of their response to the question. After each step of the trace an explanation string is printed out and the students are given the chance to say that they see their error by typing "AHA". The students are also presented a valid trace.

The system also has a dialogue mode in which the student can ask for traces of class names and will receive several traces about that class. [. . .]

Simulation: Ordinary and Intelligent

Simulation programs are used a great deal in education, but usually there is no real supervision on the part of the system. The main thing that they offer is an environment in which the student can experiment. The obvious problem with this approach is that the average student may have difficulty thinking of useful experiments to try and may only waste time. These programs can be used in conjunction with a lecture system. One of the authors (A.G.) has worked with two programs like this: JUSSIM, a criminal justice simulation program and CLUG, a land use simulation program. One of the biggest problems these types of program have is with the user entering data. New users often have a great deal of difficulty composing inputs that the computer will accept. Other problems arise from the system accepting input that is inconsistent or just not applicable. This implementation of bad input often causes the program to abort or to generate false information. Simulation programs are particularly vulnerable in this way because, for most of them, there is no way to return to the simulated state before the bad input. This problem can be prevented by storing the internal representation of each state on some external file and then rewinding it to the desired location as has been done in CLUG. Often such programs require a trained operator to input the data correctly to the program and to figure out how to fix errors as the program continues. Most of these types of problem can be solved if a programmer considers the user to be as naive as possible and makes allowances accordingly. A good user-oriented simulation system must be able to recognize bad inputs through error checking and inform the student of acceptable responses.

Having discussed some of the least intelligent simulation programs, let us turn to one that is more intelligent: SOPHIE, developed by Brown and Burton (1974). SOPHIE is an electronic troubleshooting educational monitor. It presents the student with a circuit schematic containing a fault of some specified difficulty. The student then tries to isolate the fault by asking for measurements under any instrument settings. The student then makes a hypothesis about the fault and the system checks its consistency with the measurements the student has made. The student can replace any part in the circuit if he or she can give correct answers about what is wrong with it.

As impressive as these capabilities are, to us, the really interesting feature of SOPHIE is that the student can ask for help and SOPHIE will generate possible hypotheses using the student's measurements. This hypothesis generation is done in two steps. The first step is done by a backward specialist, which examines the output voltages and generates a list of possible hypotheses that explain the measurement. Each such hypothesis is then checked by a forward-working simulation. In some cases the backward specialist generates a fault schema instead of a definite value of some sort. The fault schema with unspecified values cannot be checked using a simulation since there are no numbers to plug in. A nonsimulation program is used in this case to determine ranges of values under the observed conditions. [. . .]

Evaluation of the student's hypothesis begins by appending it to the model. Next, all the student's measurements are repeated on this modified model. The measurements under the hypothetical model are compared to the observed model. There are then four cases.

1. The observed and the hypothetical values agree. The student is correct.

2. The observed value may represent a symptom and the hypothetical value may be normal. The hypothesis does not account for the fault.

3. The observed value may be normal, while the hypothetical value represents a symptom. The hypothesis created symptoms the student did not observe.

4. The observed and hypothetical values may both be symptomatic, but not of the same fault. The value in a working circuit is used to determine whether the other two values differ significantly.

The simulation program itself is built on SPICE, a general purpose circuit simulator.

SPICE accepts a description of an arbitrary circuit and produces exact quantitative results in both working and faulted versions of the circuit. There is a second simulator, which is circuit dependent and incorporates knowledge about the machine that contains the faulted circuits. This simulator is much faster than SPICE and is used for hypothesis generation. A monitor is added to determine what additional parts would fail in a chain reaction from the original fault.

The language input by the user is handled by a top-down, context-free fuzzy parser, which makes its predictions on the basis of semantic rather than syntactic categories. It accepts abbreviations, makes spelling corrections and separates run-on words, and can handle pronoun references by using a context facility added to the parser.

Modeling the Student

Another intelligent system was developed by Koffman and Blount (1975) and Koffman and Perry (1976). They make use of a concept tree and a student model in a generative system to tailor responses to the level of the student. The problems are generated using a probabilistic grammar. A scoring polynomial is used to choose the next concept.

The course structure is in the form of a concept tree—a hierarchical tree in which each node represents a concept. Each node contains a concept number, a concept name, and a list of prerequisite concepts and whether they can be called as a subroutine. Other things contained in each node are the plateau (complexity) of the concept, the name of the problem generator and problem solution routines for that concept, and a list of parameters passed from the problem generator to the solution routine.

The problem generator is a probabilistic grammar consisting of rewrite rules that are dependent on the proficiency of the student. Since probabilistic grammars may be unfamiliar to many readers, we present a sample

G is a probabilistic grammar. G = (S,N,T,R)
S is the start symbol.
N is the nonterminal alphabet [A,*].
T is the terminal alphabet [p,−,q,r,&,v(,)]
R is the set of rewrite rules. [R0,...,R6]

| | | GENERATION PROBABILITY PROFICIENCY LEVEL: | |
		ONE	TWO
R0:	S−−>A	1.00	1.00
R1:	A−−>A=A	.25	.30
R2:	A−−>(−A)	.25	.10
R2:	A−−>p	.25	.20
R3:	A−−>q	.25	.20
R4:	A−−>r	0	.20
R5:	*−−>&	1.00	.50
R6:	*−−>v	0	.50

A sample derivation:

(1)	S
(2)	A
(3)	A*A
(4)	(−A)*A
(5)	(−p)*A
(6)	(−p)*(A*A)
(7)	(−p)*(q*r)
(8)	(−p)*(q&r)
(9)	(−p)V(q&r)

FIGURE 2: Two probabilistic grammars for generating problems for different proficiency levels (simplified from Koffman and Blount, 1975)

derivation in Figure 2 [. . .]. The "probability" at each stage of a generation is the product of the probabilities of the rules which are invoked. For instance in Figure 2, Rule R2 is much more likely to be used at level 1 than at level 2.

The level of proficiency of the student (1 or 2) determines the length and difficulty of the problem generated according to the two columns in the table. After each answer the system checks the student's response and then updates the student's proficiency level. The change in a student's level is dependent on the previous performance of the student. In the case of an incorrect solution, a set of templates is used to explain the problem to the student. The amount of feedback given to the student is dependent on the level of the student. Templates below a certain level of proficiency are not presented to the student. In this manner, the corrections are tailored to the student.

Koffman's student record includes the present level of each concept [. . .], the last level change for each concept, the time and date each concept was last worked, the number of times each concept was last worked in the 0–1 range and in the 1–2 range, the number of times the student rejected each concept, and the number of times each concept was selected by the system and accepted by the student.

The process of concept selection can be handled either by the system or by the student. The student is free to reject any concept selected by the system.

The student record is used in performing concept selections. The actual concept selection is done using a scoring polynomial of the form

$$P = aP1 + bP2 + cP3 + dP4 + eP5 + fP6$$

where a–f are numbers between −1 and 1 and P1 through P6 are parameters. Parameters usually have a range of values such as 1, 0, −1, where 1 means the parameter is strong, 0 means it is neutral and −1 means it is weak.

A list of some parameters considered in his original system were:

P1 This parameter contributes if a student's level in a concept has just dropped.

P2 This parameter favors a concept that has been waiting for the longest to be called.

P3 This parameter favors a new concept.

P4 This parameter favors a concept whose level is changing rapidly.

P5 This parameter favors a concept that is based on more prerequisite concepts than the other available concepts since use of this concept will provide review.

P6 This parameter favors a concept that currently has the lowest level.

The concept selected for presentation to the student is the one for which P is the largest number.

Discussion

It is apparent that the type of structure suitable for a teaching program is dependent on the type of subject material to be taught. For courses in which the material amounts to learning a series of facts and the interrelationships between them, information structured programs are a good idea. The ability of these programs to generate the instructional material from the information network avoids the necessity to type in every question, answer and branching pattern and still allows for a lot of flexibility in the presentation of the course. An advantage of programs like Carbonell's and Wexler's is that these programs need not be changed much in structure in order to cover a different subject area. The major changes would be to define skeletal patterns to describe the new relationships and to produce a new data base. One possible limitation is that the interrelationships might be so complex that it would be hard to represent them in a semantic network or that it would not be a simple matter to describe them with a skeletal pattern. Another possible problem would relate to the size of the data base. If the network became too large, finding the unit with the appropriate name could become a lengthy process. But, for restricted domains, this type of program has the advantage of flexibility.

Simulation programs have been used very fruitfully in education and intelligent simulations seem even more promising. The combination of an instructional program with a simulation program produces this more intelligent approach. SOPHIE is a step above most programs in that it not only can check hypotheses but it can also generate them based on the tests already done by the student. This system operates with an accompanying lecture. More theory presentation would have to be added to the instructional system were it to approach the skills of a human tutor, [. . .].

Koffman uses a student model extensively in his process of concept selection. This process, which is based on using a scoring polynomial, chooses the next concept for the student to work on. The problem generation is done by a probabilistic grammar which produces problems of different levels of difficulty. This limited model of the student adjusts somewhat to conceptual errors but does not deal with basic deficiencies in the background of the student. Perhaps a more ideal system would be smart enough to call in a remedial program when its model of the student shows this to be appropriate. To do so would require a considerable knowledge base on the capabilities of the programs as well as thorough analysis of the student's incorrect responses and perhaps pattern of responses over time. While involving considerable amounts of computation, such analysis could be done off-line while the system is lightly loaded.

Another type of obstacle in the system—student communication—originates in the attitudes of the student. Can the student model include some small part of the student's psychological state in order to conduct more appropriate dialogue? We believe that the PARRY system of Colby (1973) (which simulates a paranoid personality) points to this possibility. PARRY constructs a model of the person using it in order to be ready to insult [him or her] later in some telling way. To do so requires consideration of the intent of the person and the associations between the words in the dialogue and states of PARRY such as "fear" or "anger" (as modeled by the system on a numerical scale). For instance, the input of the word "gun" in a given context causes the system to become more "fearful," perhaps more "angry," and to suspect the intent of the interrogator. In an educational system, one could analyze otherwise unexpected and unrecognized inputs for signs of boredom or anger in order to respond either empathically or in some other appropriate way. The paranoid aspect of PARRY's personality might make it too "human" to be an effective tutor, i.e., it typically becomes "angry" and terminates the session. One need not build in the paranoid aspect of its behavior in an educational system but students might enjoy the possibility of choosing the "personality" of their tutorial system.

Some might prefer a mildly paranoid tutor to escape the monotony of endless mechanical patience.

The use of theorem proving endows Goldberg's program with some of the logical properties of a human tutor. The system's ability to give pertinent aid to the student is based on the connection between the theorem prover and the instructional system. The fact that the heuristics used by the theorem prover are like student methods means that the proofs generated by the theorem prover can be used in helping the student. In addition to individualized responses, the system allows the student a great deal of freedom while working the problem. The use of a binary tree in representing the expression has the advantage that all manipulations made by the system are in terms of replacement of portions of the tree. This approach may not be as reasonable for teaching a subject such as elementary mathematics because the types of manipulation may not correspond to those made by the students. It seems, though, that these types of strategy could be described in terms of the same types of replacement strategy.

A great deal of effort has been spent in developing CAI systems such as PLATO (Bitzer, Sherwood, and Tenczar, 1972). Such systems employ a variety of means of representation of knowledge. An important issue is how, if at all, the additional knowledge structures and techniques of AI might be combined with a conventional existing CAI system to provide a more effective learning environment. Given shortcomings in the educational value of the game "How the West was Won" pointed out by Resnick (1975), a group at Bolt Beranek and Newman (Brown, Burton, et al., 1975) implemented a "tutor" program to provide intelligent comments on the strategies adopted by students. They conclude: "Constructing a tutor who is constantly criticizing is relatively straightforward. The point is to make one that only interrupts when a skilled human tutor would and then generates a succinct remedial comment." Testing on a relatively small sample of students confirmed the designers' belief that their system

makes appropriate comments. Further, nine of ten students felt the tutor "understood" their weaknesses. Given the greater computational power that will be available, combining a strategy tutor of this sort with existing game programs is feasible, thus enriching educational possibilities.

An important area which we shall only touch upon is natural language input and output. Most of these CAI systems have some sort of natural language input/output, but the amount of language recognized is rather limited. The usual techniques are used: filling in templates, finding keywords or their synonyms, and a limited degree of spelling correction.

Besides PARRY, the recent work of Fikes and Hendrix (1977), Sacerdoti (1977), and Schank (1977) suggests that natural language interfaces of considerable power will be available for CAI systems. The improvement in communication between the student and the CAI system which occurs because of improved language capability should not be underestimated. It would seem fair to say that a CAI system without extensive natural language capability is like a tutor who speaks a language foreign to the student.

Returning to our list of desirable characteristics for a tutor, we see that the CAI systems discussed include all but the second property on the list: "The tutor will learn and adopt superior student methods." This is a utopian goal since the student's methods may require concepts and language outside the discipline which is supposedly being taught. To what extent can the system learn or be taught new concepts from the students without being exposed to serious risk of learning invalid methods? The classic works of Samuel (1959, 1967) suggest how difficult is the process of learning, either from an opponent or an expert, in the rigidly defined world of checkers. Thus, a CAI system which is as flexible in learning new methods as an average graduate student does not seem in the offing in the near future.

However, the full utilization of prototype AI techniques would give rise to a "tutor" program possessing many skills of probable educational value. Although quite inflexible in learning during a working session, it could possess many "human" characteristics. Among these characteristics are the abilities to choose appropriate examples, provide help where the student needs it, work arbitrary examples chosen by the students, review previous material, provide immediate feedback, provide alternative solutions, and measure the background and progress of the student. Hopefully, the delegation of these tasks to a machine will free human tutors to focus on other, perhaps more important, aspects of their communication with their students.

REFERENCES

Abrahams, P. (1963). Machine verification of mathematical proof. Doctoral dissertation. Massachusetts Institute of Technology.

Ash, W.B., Bobrow, R.J., Grignetti, M.C., and Hartley, A.K., (1977). Intelligent on-line assistant and tutor system. *BBN Report No. 3607,* January. Bolt Beranek and Newman, Cambridge, Mass.

Banet, B. (1978). Computers and early learning. *Creative Computing,* pp. 90–95, September/October.

Barr, A., Beard, M., and Atkinson, R.C. (1976). The computer as tutorial laboratory: The Stanford BIP Project. *International Journal of Man–Machine Studies, 8,* 567–596.

Barstow, D. (1977). A knowledge-based system for automatic program construction. *Proceedings of the 5th International Conference on Artificial Intelligence,* pp. 382–388.

Bitzer, D.L., Sherwood, B.A., and Tenczar, P. (1972). *CERL Rpt. X–37.* Computer-Based Education Research Laboratory, University of Illinois, Urbana.

Bledsoe, W., and Tyson, M. (1975). The UT interactive theorem prover. *Memorandum ATP–17.* University of Texas at Austin, Mathematics Department, May.

Brown, J.S., and Bobrow, R.J. (1975). Applications of Artificial Intelligence

techniques in maintenance training. In *New Concepts in Maintenance.* Trainers and Performance Aids, TR #NAVTRAEQUIPCEN IH–255, October.

Brown, J.S., and Burton, R.R. (1974). SOPHIE—A pragmatic use of Artificial Intelligence in CAI. *Proceeding of 1974 Annual Conference of ACM.*

Brown, J.S., Burton, R.R., Hausmann, C., Goldstein, I., Huggins, B., and Miller, M. (1977). Aspects of a theory for automated student modelling. *BBN Report No. 3549. ICAI Report No. 4,* May. Bolt Beranek and Newman, Cambridge, Mass.

Brown, J.S., Burton, R., Miller, M., deKleer, J., Purcell, S., Hausmann, C., and Bobrow, R. (1975). Steps toward a theoretical foundation for complex, knowledge-based CAI. *BBN Report No. 3135, ICAI Report No. 2,* August. Bolt Beranek and Newman, Cambridge, Mass.

Brown, J.S., Rubinstein, R., and Burton, R. (1976). Reactive learning environment for computer-assisted electronics instruction. *BBN Report No. 3314, ICAI Report No. 1,* October. Bolt Beranek and Newman, Cambridge, Mass.

Burton, R.R., and Brown, J.S. (1976). A tutoring and student modelling paradigm for gaming environments. *Proceedings for the Symposium on Computer Science and Education,* February.

Carbonell, J.R. (1970). AI in CAI: An Artificial Intelligence approach to Computer-Assisted Instruction. *IEEE Transactions on Man–Machine Systems,* 11(4).

Colby, K.M. (1973). Simulations of belief systems. In Colby, K.M., Schank, R.C., and Freeman, W.H., Eds., *Computer Models of Thought and Language.* San Francisco.

Collins, A. (1976). Processes in acquiring knowledge. In *Schooling and the Acquisition of Knowledge.* Hillsdale, N.J.: Lawrence Erlbaum Associates, January.

Collins, A., and Grignetti, M.C. (1975). Intelligent CAI. *BBN Report No. 3181,* October. Bolt Beranek and Newman, Cambridge, Mass.

Collins, A., Warnock, E.H., and Passafiume, J.J. (1975). Analysis and synthesis of tutorial dialogues. In *The Psychology of Learning and Motivation.* Voeg, New York: Academic Press.

Crowder, J.E. (1962). Intrinsic and extensive programming. In Coulson, J.E., Ed., *Proceedings of Conference on Application of Digital Computers to Instruction.*

Fikes, R.E., and Hendrix, G. (1977). A network-based knowledge representation and its natural deduction system. *Proceedings of the 5th International Joint Conference on Artificial Intelligence,* pp. 235–246.

Fikes, R.E., and Nilsson, N. (1971). STRIPS: A new approach to the application of theorem proving in problem solving. *Artificial Intelligence Journal, 2,* 189–208.

Goldberg, A. (1973). Computer-Assisted Instruction: The application of theorem proving to adaptive response analysis. *Technical Report 203.* Stanford University Institute for Mathematical Studies in the Social Sciences.

Koffman, E.B., and Blount, S.E. (1975). Artificial Intelligence and automatic programming in CAI. *Artificial Intelligence Journal.*

Koffman, E.B., and Perry, J.M. (1976). A model for generative CAI and concept selection. *International Journal of Man–Machine Studies, 8.*

Neches, R. (1977). Intelligent educational dialogue systems. *Report 7701.* Center for Human Information Processors, University of California, San Diego, La Jolla, March 1977.

Newell, A., and Simon, H. (1963). GPS: A program that simulates human thought. In Feigenbaum, E.A., and Feldman, J., Eds., *Computers and Thought.* New York: McGraw-Hill.

Newell, A., Shaw, J.C., and Simon, H. (1956). Empirical explorations with the logic theory machine: A case study in heuristics. In Feigenbaum, E.A., and Feldman, J., Eds., *Computers and Thought.* New York: McGraw-Hill.

Polya, G. (1957). *How to Solve It.* New York: Dover.

Pressey, S. (1926). A simple apparatus which gives tests, and scores and teaches. *School and Society.*

Quillian, M.R. (1968). Semantic memory. In Minsky, Ed., *Semantic Information Processing.* Cambridge, Mass.: MIT Press, pp. 216–270.

Quinlan, J.R., and Hunt, E.A. (1968). A formal deductive system. *Journal of the Association for Computing Machinery, 15,* 625–646.

Raphael, B. (1976). *The Thinking Computer—Mind Inside Matter.* San Francisco: W.H. Freeman.

Resnick, C.A. (1975). Computational models of learners for Computer-Assisted learning. Doctoral dissertation, University of Illinois at Urbana-Champaign.

Robinson, J.A. (1965). A machine-oriented logic based on the resolution principle. *Journal of the Association for Computing Machinery, 12,* 23–41.

Sacerdoti, E. (1977). Language access to distributed data with error recovery. *Proceedings of the 5th International Joint Conference on Artificial Intelligence,* pp. 196–202.

Samuel, A.L. (1967), Some studies in machine learning using the game of checkers. II. Recent progress. *IBM Journal of Research and Development, 6,* 607–617.

Samuel, A.L. (1959). Some studies in machine learning using the game of checkers. In Feigenbaum, E.A., and Feldman, J., Eds., *Computer and Thought.* New York: McGraw-Hill, 1963.

Schank, R.C. (1977). Conceptual dependency and knowledge structures. *Proceedings of the 5th International Joint Conference on Artificial Intelligence,* pp. 988–989.

Wexler, J.D. (1970). Information networks in generative Computer-Assisted Instruction. *IEEE Transactions on Man–Machine Systems, 11*(4), December.

Zinn, K.L. (1978). Personal computers at the University of Michigan and an assessment of potential impact. *Creative Computing.* pp. 84–87, September/October.

20 Diagnostic Models for Procedural Bugs in Basic Mathematical Skills

John Seely Brown
and Richard R. Burton

Xerox Palo Alto Research Center

Abstract

A new diagnostic modeling system for automatically synthesizing a deep-structure model of a student's misconceptions or bugs in his basic mathematical skills provides a mechanism for explaining *why* a student is making a mistake as opposed to simply identifying the mistake. This report is divided into four sections. The first provides examples of the problems that must be handled by a diagnostic model. It then introduces *procedural networks* as a general framework for representing the knowledge underlying a skill. The challenge in designing this representation is to find one that facilitates the discovery of misconceptions or bugs existing in a particular student's encoding of this knowledge. The second section discusses some of the pedagogical issues that have emerged from the use of diagnostic models within an instructional system. This discussion is framed in the context of a computer-based tutoring/gaming system developed to teach students and student teachers how to diagnose bugs strategically as well as how to provide a better understanding of the underlying structure of arithmetic skills. The third section describes our uses of an executable network as a tool for *automatically* diagnosing student behavior, for automatically generating "diagnostic" tests, and for judging the diagnostic quality of a given exam. Included in this section is a discussion of the success of this system in diagnosing 1300 school students from a data base of 20,000 test items. The last section discusses future research directions.

If you can both listen to children and accept their answers not as things to just be judged right or wrong but as pieces of information which may reveal what the child is thinking you will have taken a giant step toward becoming a master teacher rather than merely a disseminator of information.

J. A. Easley, Jr. and R. E. Zwoyer (1975)

Introduction

One of the greatest talents of teachers is their ability to synthesize an accurate "picture," or model, of a student's misconceptions from the meager evidence inherent in his errors. A detailed model of a student's knowledge, including his misconceptions, is a prerequisite to successful remediation. The structure, use, and *inference* of such models for procedural skills in mathematics is the topic of this paper. In particular we shall describe some initial efforts in the development and use of a representational technique called "procedural networks" as the framework for constructing *diagnostic models*—i.e., models that capture a student's common misconceptions or faulty behavior as simple changes to (or mistakes in) a correct model of the underlying knowledge base. By being able to synthesize such deep-structure diagnostic models *automatically,* we can provide both a

John Seely Brown and Richard R. Burton, "Diagnostic Models for Procedural Bugs in Basic Mathematical Skills," *Cognitive Science*, 2 (1978), 155–192. Reprinted by permission of John Seely Brown and Ablex Publishing Corporation.

teacher and an instructional system with not only an identification of *what* mistakes a student is making, but also an explanation of *why* those mistakes are being made. Such a system also has profound implications for testing, since a student need no longer be evaluated solely on the number of errors appearing on his test, but rather on the fundamental misconceptions which he harbors.

This paper consists of four sections. The first provides examples of the problems that must be handled by a diagnostic model. It then introduces procedural networks as a general framework for representing the knowledge underlying a skill. The challenge here is to design a representation that facilitates the discovery of misconceptions or bugs existing in a particular student's encoding of this knowledge. The second section discusses some of the pedagogical issues that have emerged from our use of diagnostic models within an instructional system. This system is a computer-based tutoring game developed to teach both students and student teachers about the strategic diagnosis of bugs. The third section describes our uses of procedural network as a tool for automatically diagnosing student behavior, for automatically generating "diagnostic" tests, and for judging the diagnostic quality of a given exam. Included in this section is a discussion of the success of this system in diagnosing 1300 grade-school students from a data base of 20,000 test items. The last section discusses some future research directions.

1. Diagnostic Models of Basic Skills

The issues addressed in this paper arose from an investigation of the procedural skills necessary to solve high school algebra problems. These skills include not only the generally recognized rules of algebra, but also such normally implicit skills as the reading of formulas, the parsing of expressions, and the determination of which rules to apply next (Brown and Burton, 1975; Brown, Collins, and Harris, 1978; Matz, 1978). For this paper, however, we limit our discussion to exam-

ples encompassing arithmetic skills so that we can concentrate on the critical ideas of diagnosis without the need for a large number of algebraic rules. Limiting our examples to arithmetic also provides a compelling demonstration of the difficulty of the diagnostic task; it clearly demonstrates how much more difficult it is to diagnose what is wrong with a student's method of performing a task—to form a diagnostic model—than it is to perform the task itself. In particular, it is no great challenge to add or subtract two numbers, but, as we shall see, diagnosing misconceptions in these same skills can be quite subtle.

Let us consider diagnosing what is wrong with the arithmetic skills (procedures) of a couple of students. We shall start with a case study in which we examine five "snapshots" of a student's performance doing addition as might be seen on a homework assignment. Before proceeding, look at the following snapshots and try to discover the student's bug.

Sample of the student's work:

41	328	989	66	216
+9	+917	+52	+887	+13
50	1345	1141	1053	229

Once you have discovered the bug, try testing your hypothesis by "simulating" the buggy student so as to predict his results on the following two test problems.

$$446 \qquad 201$$
$$+815 \qquad +399$$

The bug is really quite simple. In computer terms, the student, after determining the carry, forgets to reset the "carry register" to zero and hence the amount carried is accumulated across the columns. For example, in the student's second problem (328 + 917 equals 1345) he proceeds as follows: 8 + 7 = 15 so he writes 5 and carries 1; 2 + 1 = 3 plus the 1 carry is 4; lastly, 3 + 9 = 12 but that 1 carry from the first column is still there—it has not been reset—so adding it in to this column gives 13. If this is the bug, then the answers to the test problems will be

1361 and 700. This bug is not so absurd when one considers that a child might use his fingers to remember the carry and forget to bend back his fingers, or counters, after each carry is added.

A common assumption among teachers is that students do not follow procedures very well and that erratic behavior is the primary cause of a student's inability to perform each step correctly. Our experience has been that students are remarkably competent procedure followers, but that they often follow *the wrong procedures.* One case encountered last year is of special interest. The student proceeded through a good portion of the school year with his teacher thinking that he was exhibiting random behavior in his arithmetic performance. As far as the teacher was concerned there was no systematic explanation for his errors. Here is a sample of his work:

7	9	8	6	8	9	17	19	87
+8	+5	+3	+7	+8	+9	+8	+4	+93
15	14	11	13	16	18	25	23	11

365	679	923	27,493	797
+574	+794	+481	+1,509	+48,632
819	111	114	28,991	48,119

There is a clue to the nature of his bug in the number of ones in his answers. Every time the addition of a column involves a carry, a 1 mysteriously appears in that column; he is simply writing down the carry digit and forgetting about the units digit! One might be misled by 17 + 8, which normally involves a carry yet is added correctly. It would seem that he is able to do simple additions by a completely different procedure—possibly by counting up from the larger number on his fingers.

The manifestation of this student's simple bug carries over to other types of problem which involve addition as a subskill. What answer would he give for the following?

A family has traveled 2975 miles on a tour of the United States. They have 1828 miles to go. How many miles will they have traveled at the end of their tour?

He correctly solved the word problem to obtain the addition problem 2975 + 1875, to which he answered 3191. Since his work was done on a scratch sheet, the teacher saw only the answer which is, of course, wrong. As a result, the teacher assumed that he had trouble with word problems as well as with arithmetic.

When we studied this same student's work in other arithmetic procedures, we discovered a recurrence of the same bug. Here is a sample of his work in multiplication:

68	734	543	758	2764
×46	×37	×206	×296	×53
24	792	141	144	2731

Several bugs are manifested here, the most severe one being that his multiplication algorithm mimics the column behavior of his addition algorithm. But notice that the bug in his addition algorithm is also present in his multiplication procedure. The "determine-unit-and-carry" subprocedure bug shows up in both his multiplication and addition. For example, to do 68 × 46, in the first column he performs 8 × 6, gets 48, and then writes down the "carry," in this case 4, ignoring the units digit. Then, he multiplies 6 × 4 to get 2 for the second column. All along he has a complete and consistent procedure for doing arithmetic. His answers throughout all of his arithmetic work are far from random; in fact, they display near perfection with respect to *his* way of doing it.

A First Approximation to Representing Procedural Skills

For a computer system to be capable of diagnosing aberrant behavior such as the above, the procedural skill being taught must be represented in a form amenable to modeling *incorrect* as well as correct subprocedures of that skill. Furthermore, the representation must allow the intermixing of both the correct and incorrect subskills, so that the model can capture those parts of a skill that are correct as well as those that are wrong. The breakdown of the skill into shared subskills can also account for the recurrence of similar errors in different skills. We introduce the term *diagnostic model* to mean a representation of a student's procedural knowledge or skill that depicts his internalization of a skill as a variant of a correct version of that skill.

In addition to satisfactory representational techniques, the diagnostic modeling task requires that the representation of a particular correct skill make explicit much of the tacit knowledge underlying the skill. In particular, the correct model must contain *all* the knowledge that can possibly be misunderstood by the student or else some student misconceptions will be beyond the diagnostic modeling capabilities of the system. For example, if the model of addition does not include the transcription of the problem, the system would never be able to diagnose a student whose bug is to write 9s that he later misreads as 7s.

The technique we use to represent diagnostic models is a *procedural network.*[1] A procedural network model for a correct skill consists of a collection of procedures with annotations in which the control structure (i.e., calling relationships) between procedures are made explicit by appropriate links. Each procedure node has two main parts: a conceptual part representing the intent of the procedure, and an operational part consisting of methods for carrying out that intent. The methods (also called implementations) are programs that define how the results of other procedures are combined to satisfy the intent of a particular procedure.[2] Any procedure can have more than one implementation, thus providing a way to model *different methods* for performing the same skill. For most skills, the network representation takes the form of a lattice. Figure 1 presents a partial breakdown of a portion of the addition process into a procedural network. Conceptual procedure nodes are enclosed in ellipses. The top procedure in the lattice is addition.[3] Two of the possible algorithms for doing addition are presented as alternative methods under the conceptual node for addition. In Method 1, the standard algorithm, the columns are added from right to left with any carries being written above and included in the column sum of the next column to the left. In Method 2, the columns are added from left to right with any carries being written below the answer in the next column to the left. If any carries occur in the problem, they must be added in a second addition. Notice that these two methods share the common procedures for calculating a column sum and writing a digit in the answer, but differ in the procedure they use when carrying is necessary. One structural aspect of the net-

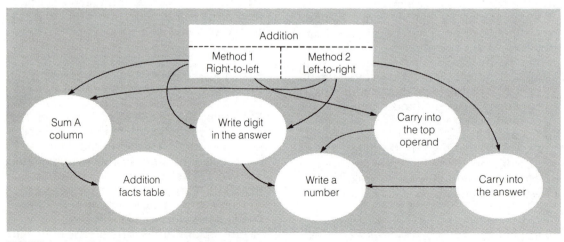

FIGURE 1: A portion of the procedural network for addition

work is to make explicit any subprocedures that can be potentially shared by several higher level procedures.

The decomposition of a complex skill into all its conceptual procedures terminates in some set of primitives that reflect assumed elements of an underlying computational ability. For addition, typical assumed primitives are recognizing a digit, writing a digit, and knowing the concepts of right, left, etc. The complete procedure network explicitly specifies all the subprocedures of a skill and can be evaluated or "executed," thereby simulating the skill for any given set of inputs. By itself, this network merely provides a computational machine that performs the skill and is not of particular import. However, the possible misconceptions in this skill are represented in the network by incorrect implementations associated with subprocedures in its decomposition called "bugs."[4] Each buggy version contains incorrect actions taken in place of the correct ones.[5] An extension to the network evaluator enables the switching in of a *buggy* version of a procedure that allows the network to simulate the behavior of that buggy subskill. This feature provides a computational method for determining the external behavior of the underlying bugs.

Inferring a Diagnostic Model of the Student

The problem of diagnosing a *deep-structure* failure in a student's knowledge of a procedural skill can now be accomplished, at least theoretically, in a straightforward manner. Suppose, as in the examples on pages 270–71, we are provided with several *surface* manifestations of a deep-structure misconception, or bug, in the student's addition procedure. To uncover those possible subprocedures which are at fault, we use the network to simulate the behavior of buggy subprocedures over the set of problems and note those which generate the same behavior as exhibited by the student. To catch a student's misconceptions that involve more than one faulty subprocedure, we must be able to sim-

ulate various combinations of bugs. A student may have a bug in his carrying procedure as well as believing that $8 + 7$ is 17 (a bug in his addition facts table). To model his behavior, *both* buggy versions must be used *together*. A *deep-structure model* of the student's errors is a set of buggy subprocedures that, when invoked, replicates those errors. Each buggy version has associated information such as what the underlying causes of the bug may have been, as well as specific remediations, explanations, interactions, and examples of the bug—all of which may be used by a tutoring system to help correct the student's problem.[6]

Many technical questions are raised by the above brief overview of how to "infer" a diagnostic model. We have deferred a more detailed discussion of these questions until Section 3 in favor of a more general discussion of pedagogical ramifications of the procedural network model of procedural skills. We begin this discussion with a description of the procedural network for a simple skill—subtraction.

A Procedural Network for Subtraction

As an example of the surprising amount of procedural knowledge needed to perform a simple skill, let us consider a more complete network representation of the subtraction of two numbers.[7] Figure 2 shows the links of the procedural network for subtraction that indicate which subprocedures a procedure may use.

The topmost node (SUBTRACT) represents the subtraction of two *n*-digit numbers. It may use the procedures for setting up the problem (SETUP), transforming it if the bottom number is greater than the top (TRANSFORM), and sequencing through each column performing the column subtraction (COLUMN SEQUENCE). The implementation of the column subtraction procedure has to account for cases where borrowing is necessary (BORROW NEEDED) and may call upon many other subprocedures, including taking the borrow from the correct place

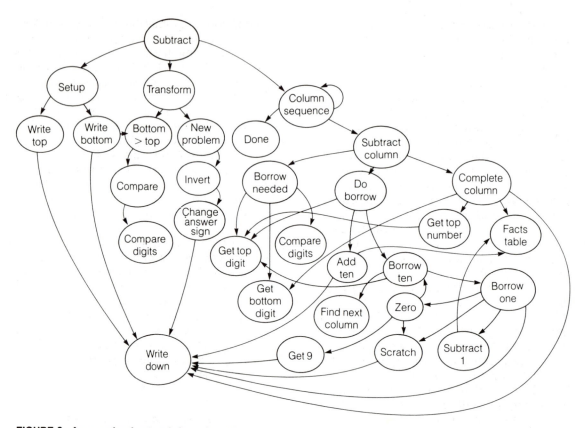

FIGURE 2: A procedural network for subtraction

(DO BORROW), scratching 0 and writing 9 if that place contains a zero (ZERO), and so on. An important subprocedure is the facts table look-up (FACTS TABLE) which allows any of the simple arithmetic facts to be wrong. The facts table subprocedure is called during the addition of 10 to a column digit (ADD 10), during the subtraction of 1 from a column digit in a borrowing operation (SUBTRACT 1), as well as during the subtraction of the bottom from the top digit in a column (COMPLETE COLUMN).

In principle, each of these subprocedures could have many buggy versions associated with it.[8] An example of a common bug is to calculate the column difference by subtracting the smaller digit from the larger regardless of which is on top. In another bug, the SETUP procedure left justifies the top and bottom numbers so that when the student is told to subtract 13 from 185, he gets 55. An interesting aspect of the left-justification bug is that when the student is faced with seemingly impossible problems (185−75) he may be inclined to change the direction in which he subtracts, borrowing from right to left instead of from left to right, or to change his column difference procedure to larger minus smaller, thereby eliminating the need to borrow. Thus, there can exist relationships between bugs such that one bug suggests others. A major challenge in identifying the procedural breakdown or description of a skill is to have the network handle such ramifications and interactions of multiple bugs.

To provide a feeling for the range of "answers" that can come from simple underlying bugs, we have included in Figure 3 "answers" to subtraction problems using some of the bugs in the procedural network for

143
−28
125

The student subtracts the smaller digit in each column from the larger digit regardless of which is on top.

143
−28
125

When the student needs to borrow, he adds 10 to the top digit of the current column without subtracting 1 from the next column to the left.

1300
−522
878

When borrowing from a column whose top digit is 0, the student writes 9 but does not continue borrowing from the column to the left of the 0.

140
−21
121

Whenever the top digit in a column is 0, the student writes the bottom digit in the answer; i.e., $0 - N = N$.

140
−21
120

Whenever the top digit in a column is 0, the student writes 0 in the answer; i.e., $0 - N = 0$.

1300
−522
788

When borrowing from a column where the top digit is 0, the student borrows from the next column to the left correctly but writes 10 instead of 9 in this column.

321
−89
231

When borrowing into a column whose top digit is 1, the student gets 10 instead of 11.

662
−357
205

Once the student needs to borrow from a column, he or she continues to borrow from every column [regardless of whether this is necessary].

662
−357
115

The student always subtracts all borrows from the leftmost digit in the top number.

FIGURE 3: Manifestations of some subtraction bugs

subtraction. Notice that a particular answer to a given problem can have more than one explanation since several distinct bugs can generate the same answer. A special case is that a student may harbor many misconceptions and still get the correct answer to a particular problem!

The Power of Simulating Bugs in the Network

Given a procedural network like the one in Figure 2, it is not always obvious how bugs in any particular subprocedure or set of subprocedures will be manifested on the surface, that is, in the answer. Some of the complicating factors are that a single buggy subprocedure can be used by several higher order procedures in computing an answer or that two bugs can have interactions with each other. These factors are further complicated by the

fact that not all sample problems will manifest all the possible symptoms. If asked to make predictions about the symptoms of a given bug, people often determine the symptoms by considering only the skills or subprocedures used in solving *one* particular sample problem. As a result, they often miss symptoms generated by other procedures that can, in principle, use the given buggy subprocedure but which, because of the characteristics of the particular problem, were not called upon. If a different sample problem had been chosen, it might have caused the particular faulty subprocedure to have been used for a different purpose, thereby generating different symptoms. These observations first led us to consider the value of simulation to systematically verify a conjectured bug.

2. Pedagogical Issues

BUGGY: An Instructional Game for Training Student Teachers (and Others)

As we saw in Section 1, it is often difficult to infer a student's bug from his answers. It was the need for teachers to appreciate this problem and to develop strategies for coping with the possible range of student bugs that led us to construct a game called BUGGY. BUGGY is a computerized game based on the diagnostic interactions of a tutor and a student. The computer plays the part of an errant student whose malady must be identified by the diagnostician (a role played either by an individual or by a team). The diagnostician is presented with an arithmetic homework problem that the "student" has done incorrectly. The "student's" behavior is generated using the procedural network and shows the symptoms of an underlying bug in one of the arithmetic subprocedures. The diagnostician's job is to discover exactly what is the underlying misconception. He does this by providing strategic *test problems* for the "student" to solve. The problems given by the diagnostician are answered by the computer acting as the student using the bugged procedure.

The computer also acts as arbiter in the evaluation of the diagnostician's theory. When the diagnostician indicates that he has discovered the bug, he is asked to describe it. Then, to make certain that he really has found the bug, he is given a five-problem test during which he must answer the problems in the same errant way that the student would. In other words, he must simulate the "student's" bug. When the diagnostician's concept of the bug is sufficiently well formulated that he is able to predict the buggy answer on all five problems, he is considered to have diagnosed the student and he proceeds to a new bug.

We have found it beneficial to allow teachers to team up while playing the diagnostician's role in BUGGY. The interaction between team members encourages verbaliza-

tion of the decision-making processes involved in the game.

The following is a protocol of a team of teachers using BUGGY. The dialogue is interspersed with commentary about the important issues. Those lines typed by the team are marked with a vertical line in the left margin.

Protocol of a Team Using BUGGY

WELCOME TO BUGGY.
I HAVE CHOSEN A BUG. HERE IS AN EXAMPLE OF THE BUG.

$$\begin{array}{r} 17 \\ +5 \\ \hline 13 \end{array}$$

> The system presents an example in which the student does not get the right answer. At present the initial examples are stored in the network linked to the buggy implementation.

NOW YOU CAN GIVE ME PROBLEMS TO DETERMINE THE BUG.

| 18   43
| +6   +79
| ‾‾‾   ‾‾‾
| 15   23

> The team generates problems that are answered by the "student." Notice that the team's test problems are similar to the initial example generated by BUGGY. This is usually a poor diagnostic strategy as it may leave other symptoms of a bug undiscovered.

| Got the bug!

> The team forms an initial hypothesis and tells the system they have discovered the bug. The system now asks the team to describe the bug and then tests them on their understanding. Asking for a description forces the team to verbalize their sometimes fuzzy idea of what the bug is and often makes them realize how ill-defined or vague their idea actually is. In the present system, the descriptions are saved but no attempt is made by the system to understand them.

PLEASE DESCRIBE THE BUG.

| Student adds the number to be carried into the last column worked in.

> This cryptic description is typical of those we have observed. Describing bugs in English is surprisingly difficult. What the team is trying to say is that if a column adds to more than 9, the units digit and the carry digit are added together and the result is written as the answer. For

example, in the first column of the example problem, when 7 and 5 are added, 1 (the carry) and 2 (the units digit) are added to get 3. The same with 8 + 6, 2 + 9, and 3 + 9. (This bug could easily arise if the student were using Method 2 from Figure 1 and mistakenly wrote the carry under the same column.)

The hypothesis does account for the observed behavior. Unfortunately, it is not the student's bug. Notice the possibly humorous, probably disastrous results that would have transpired if the team had stopped at this point and tried to tutor the student on the basis of their initial belief!

HERE ARE SOME PROBLEMS TO TEST YOUR THEORY ABOUT THE BUG. WHAT IS:

```
    21
  +39
|  51
```

To ensure that the team has found the correct bug, the system produces several problems for the team to solve. At present, BUGGY has a heuristic problem generation program that gives a broad range of "different" problems. (For examples in which the bug is very localized, such as requiring a 0 in the top number, a special problem generator can be linked to the bug and will be used instead.) These problems are then filtered to try to get three problems which cause symptoms and two that give correct answers. This simple routine does surprisingly well at producing critical problems. So well, in fact, that a more "intelligent" routine (which determined the set of bugs consistent with the student's data and then selected the test problems which split this set) was discarded as unnecessarily time-consuming. However, this more intelligent technique—based on techniques discussed in Section 3—might be reverted to as our theory of procedural bugs becomes progressively more subtle.

The team's hypothesis is revealed as incorrect by the first of the five test problems. BUGGY presents its answer and then allows the team to enter more problems.

THAT'S NOT THE BUG I HAVE.
USING MY BUG:
el.5l
```
    21
  +39
   15
```

TRY GIVING ME SOME MORE EXAMPLES.

```
|   51      99     68
| +1707    +99    +9
    21      36     23
```

After failing the test, the team gives a greater range of problems, specifically those using bigger numbers.

How is it that 51 + 1707 can add up to 21? By broadening the scope of example problems they are able to reevaluate their initial hypothesis, dismiss it, and develop another one that is complete and consistent with respect to the new errors.

I Got the Bug!

PLEASE DESCRIBE THE BUG YOU THINK I HAVE.

The student is adding all the digits together.

HERE ARE SOME PROBLEMS TO TEST YOUR THEORY ABOUT THE BUG. WHAT IS:

```
    33    1091     8     28     90
  +99     +60    +34    +70     +6
|  24      17     15     17     15
```

This time the team's hypothesis passes the test and they are given the description of the bug stored in the procedural network.

VERY GOOD. MY DESCRIPTION OF THE BUG IS: THE STUDENT ALWAYS SUMS UP ALL THE DIGITS WITH NO REGARD TO COLUMNS.

A variant of this game assigns a cost to each problem the user poses in the process of trying to discover the bug. At the same time, a much higher cost is assigned for claiming to have "discovered" the bug but then failing to pass criterion on the computer-generated test problems. A correctly structured cost algorithm encourages the user to think carefully about the diagnostic value of each problem he creates and not to jump to a conclusion too quickly or too slowly.

Pedagogical Issues for Teachers

One application of BUGGY and the "diagnostic model" view of procedural skills lies in the domain of teacher training. The realization that errors that appear "random" are often the surface manifestations of a systematic underlying bug is a major conceptual breakthrough for many student teachers. All too often, behavior that appears to be random has a simple, intelligent, and complete underlying explanation. By proper diagnosis, remediation for a student can be directed toward his specific weaknesses. The importance of simply admitting that there may exist underlying bugs cannot be overstressed. Without appreciation of this fact, a teacher must view failure on a particular problem as either carelessness or total algorithm failure. In the first case, the predicated remediation is giving more problems, while in the second, it is going over the entire algorithm.[9] When a student's bug (which may manifest itself only occasionally) is not recognized by the teacher, the teacher explains the errant behavior as carelessness, laziness, or worse, thereby often mistakenly lowering his opinions of the student's capabilities.

From the student's viewpoint, the situation is much worse. He is following what he believes to be *the* correct algorithm and, seemingly at random, gets marked *wrong*. This situation can be exacerbated by improper diagnosis. For example, Johnnie subtracts 284 from 437 and gets 253 as an answer. "Of course," says the teacher, "you forgot to subtract 1 from 4 in the hundreds place when you borrowed." Unfortunately Johnnie's algorithm is to subtract the smaller digit in each column from the larger. Johnnie does not have any idea what the teacher is talking about (he never "borrowed"!) and feels that he must be very stupid indeed not to understand. The teacher agrees with this assessment as none of his remediation has had any effect on Johnnie's performance.

BUGGY, in its present form, presents teachers with examples of buggy behavior and provides practice in diagnosing the underlying causes of errors. Using BUGGY, teachers gain experience in forming theories about the relationship between the symptoms of a bug and the underlying bug itself. This experience can be cultivated to make teachers aware that there are methods or strategies that they can use to diagnose bugs properly.

In fact, there are a number of *strategy bugs* that teachers may have in forming hypotheses about a student's misconceptions. That is, the task of diagnosing a student is a procedural skill and as such is susceptible to mislearning by the teachers. A common strategy bug is to jump too quickly to one hypothesis. Prematurely focusing on one hypothesis can cause a teacher to be unaware that there may be other competing hypotheses that are possibly more likely. A common psychological effect of this approach is that the teacher generates problems for the student that confirm his hypothesis! In some cases, teachers may believe their hypotheses so strongly that they will ignore contrary evidence or decide that it is merely random noise. One general diagnostic strategy that avoids this pitfall is the technique of differential diagnosis (Rubin, 1975) in which one always generates at least two hypotheses and then chooses test problems that separate them.

Another common strategy bug is to lock onto only one type of symptom. For example, one student teacher was given the initial example (A), after which he proceeded to generate example problems B and C.

A	B	C
19	23	81
+9	+6	+8
199	236	818

At this point, he concluded that the bug was "writes the bottom digit after the top number." But his hypothesis failed when he was given the first test problem:

$$\begin{array}{r} 8 \\ +12 \\ \hline \end{array}$$

to which he responded 812. The bug is that single digit operands are linked on to the end of the other operand, so that the correct buggy answer is 128. By presenting examples only with a shorter bottom digit, he had obtained what seemed to be confirming evidence of his hypothesis. A general rule which could be employed to avoid this fixation is that whenever an example of incorrect behavior has an asymmetry (length of top and bottom numbers), then try an example with the asymmetry reversed. Using this rule, the teacher would also generate problems with larger top numbers before he reached a conclusion. BUGGY provides an environment in which teachers can experience the ramifications of not employing rules and strategies during diagnosis.[10]

Another important issue concerns the relationship between the language used to describe a student's errors and its effect on what a teacher should do to remediate it. Is the language able to convey to the student what he is doing wrong? Should we expect teachers to be able to use language as the tool for correcting the buggy algorithms of students? Or should we expect teachers only to be able to understand what the bug is and attempt remediation with the student with things like manipulative math tools? The following descriptions of hypotheses given by student teachers, taken from protocols of BUGGY, give a good idea of how difficult it is to express procedural ideas in English. The descriptions in parentheses are BUGGY's pre-stored explanations of the bugs.

"Random errors in carryover." (Carries only when the next column in the top number is blank.)

"If there are fewer digits on the top than on the bottom she adds columns diagonally." (When the top number has fewer digits than the bottom number, the numbers are left justified and then added.)

"Does not like zero in the bottom." (Zero subtracted from any number is zero.)

"Child adds first two numbers correctly. Then when you need to carry in the second set of digits child adds numbers carried to bottom row, then adds third set of digits diagonally, finally carrying over extra digits." (The carry is written in the top number to the left of the column being carried from and is mistaken for another digit in the top number.)

"Sum and carry all columns correctly until get to last column. Then takes furthest left digit in both columns and adds with digit of last carried amount. This is the sum." (When there are an unequal number of digits in the two numbers, the columns that have a blank are filled with the leftmost digit of that number.)

Even when one knows what the bug is in terms of being able to mimic it, how is one going to explain it to the student having problems? Considering the above examples, it is clear that anyone asked to solve a set of problems using these explanations would,

no doubt, have real trouble. One can imagine a student's frustration when the teacher offers an explanation of why he is getting problems marked wrong, and the explanation is as confused and unclear as these are.

For that matter, when the correct procedure is described for the first time, could it, too, be coming across so unclearly!

The problem of adequately describing bugs is further complicated by another surprising fact: fundamentally different bugs can cause identical behavior! In other words, there can be several distinct ways of incorrectly performing a skill that always generate the same "answers." For example, here is a set of problems.

$$
\begin{array}{r} 38 \\ +46 \\ \hline 174 \end{array}
\qquad
\begin{array}{r} 186 \\ +254 \\ \hline 2330 \end{array}
\qquad
\begin{array}{r} 298 \\ +169 \\ \hline 2357 \end{array}
\qquad
\begin{array}{r} 89 \\ +64 \\ \hline 243 \end{array}
$$

One possible bug which accounts for these results is: the columns are added without carries and the leftmost digit in the answer is the total number of carries required in the problem. In this case, the student views the carries as tallies to be counted and added to the left of the answer. But another equally plausible bug also exists; the student places the carry to the left of the next digit in the top number; then, when adding that column, instead of adding the carry to the digit, he mistakes it as a tens column of the top digit—so that when adding 298 and 169, in the second column he adds 19 to 6 instead of 10 to 6. This generates the same symptoms. So even when the teacher is able to describe clearly what he believes is the underlying bug, he may be addressing the wrong one. The student may actually have either one of these bugs.[11]

An Experiment Using BUGGY with Student Teachers

To determine BUGGY's impact on student teachers, we had a group play the game described in the beginning of this section. The goal of the experiment was to explore whether exposure to BUGGY significantly improves the student teacher's ability to detect regular patterns of errors in simple arithmetic problems.[12] The subjects were undergraduate education majors from Lesley College in Cambridge. Their exposure to BUGGY lasted approximately one and a half hours, during which time both addition and subtraction bugs were presented. The effects of their exposure to BUGGY were measured by comparing each subject's performance on the pre- and postexposure debugging test. The detailed analysis and discussion of the experiment is beyond the scope of this paper but has been described in a technical report (Brown et al., 1977). Briefly, though, the results of the experiment showed that exposure to BUGGY significantly improved their ability to detect regular patterns of errors.

We also investigated the qualitative issue of what the student teachers felt they gained from their exposure to BUGGY. To assess their impressions, we convened the entire group after they had finished using BUGGY. At that gathering, we first asked them to write their responses to two questions (discussed below), and then we taped a final group discussion in which we sought their reactions to using BUGGY and their suggestions for its deployment with school-aged students. The following week, their professor, who also participated in the initial experiment, held a second group discussion and reported to us the consensus, which was consistent with what they had written.

[The] Appendix lists some of the written responses to the question "What do you think you learned from this experience?" All twenty-four responded that they came away with something valuable. Many stated that they now appreciated the "complex and logical thought process" that children often use when doing an arithmetic problem incorrectly. "It makes me aware of problems that children have and they sometimes think logically, not carelessly as sometimes teachers think they do." "I never realized the many different ways a child could devise his own system to do a problem." They also stated that they learned better procedures for discovering the underlying bug. "I learned that it is necessary to try many different types of examples to be sure that a child really understands. Different types of difficulties arise with different problems."

We also asked the students "What is your reaction to BUGGY?" Many felt that "BUGGY could be used to sharpen a teacher's awareness of different difficulties with addition and subtraction." They felt that it might be of use in grade school, high school, or with special needs students, or even as a "great experience in beginning to play with computers."

Pedagogical Issues More Specific to Middle School Students

We feel that all the issues discussed above are as important for school-level students as they are for teachers. There is great value in introducing young students to procedural notions. The BUGGY system provides a well-controlled environment for such an introduction, as well as one that can be *easily* integrated into a *standard curriculum*. Also note that for a middle school student to play the diagnostician's role requires his studying the procedural skill per se (i.e., its structure) as opposed to merely performing it. This experience can be especially important as students begin algebra, which is their first exposure to procedure "schema." By presenting procedures as objects of study, BUGGY can thus be used to explore the powerful ideas of hypothesis formation, debugging, debugging strategies, and so on. Of course, such a use requires more than just the BUGGY game.

Another reason for having students develop a language for talking about procedures, processes, bugs, and so forth is that such a language enables them to talk about, and think about, the underlying causes of their own errors. This facility is important in its own right, but it also gives a student the motivation and the apparatus for stepping back and critiquing his own thinking, as well as saying something interesting and useful about his errors. The difficulty in getting a student to test the plausibility of his own answer (such as by estimating it) may be due to the lack of any appropriate introspective skills that the student could use once he knew his answer was wrong.

An important ancillary, nonmathematical benefit of a student's involvement with BUGGY is exposure to the idea of role reversal.[13] To communicate effectively with others, children must learn not only language, but also the use of "social speech"—speech that takes into account the knowledge and perspective of another person (Krauss and Glucksberg, 1977). Piaget uses the term "childhood egocentrism" to describe the child's inability to detach himself from his own point of view and to take into consideration another's perspective. Although Krauss and Glucksberg agree that egocentrism plays a large part in very young children's speech, they believe that even in older children the ability to role-play breaks down when they are faced with a demanding cognitive task. We believe that taking on the viewpoint of the errant student by analyzing another's mistakes can provide valuable practice in role-playing in a demanding situation and can be beneficial to the development of "social speech."

Some Results on Using BUGGY with Seventh and Eighth Graders

To explore the effect of the BUGGY game on seventh and eighth graders and to discover what type of additional instructional material and activities must back up the use of this computer-based system, we placed a terminal running BUGGY in a classroom. The teacher provided a short introduction to the game and the notion of bugs and then the students[14] were free to use the system during the term. During this experience, we noticed the following phenomena. When the students first started trying to discover the underlying bugs in BUGGY, their most common reaction, upon seeing the mistakes of the simulated buggy student, was to exclaim "Wow, how dumb and stupid this kid must be." However, after a week or so of exposure to BUGGY, the students' reactions changed

from believing that the simulated student was dumb to one of appreciating that there was, in fact, a systematic explanation for what this student was doing. They began to see that he (it) had fundamental misconceptions as opposed to being just stupid. This result is particularly exciting, since it paves the way for students to see their own faulty behavior not as being a sign of their stupidity, but as a source of data from which they can understand their own errors.

Unfortunately, we have as yet no data concerning the transferability of this awareness, and whether it will lead to students being more capable and willing to look over their own work for errors.

3. An Automated Diagnostic Modeling System

In this section, we describe a diagnostic system that is based on our arithmetic procedural network, recently completed by Burton. The notion of modeling procedural skills as executable networks and then expressing all potential misconceptions as buggy versions of subprocedures in the network provides a technique for efficiently determining the consequences or symptoms of a given collection of bugs on a set of problems. It therefore has the potential of diagnosing and explaining all the procedurally incorrect answers for any given problem. For example, as we indicated in Section 1, given a procedural network for addition and an addition problem (like 35 + 782), all the buggy subprocedures as well as combinations of buggy subprocedures, can be inserted and then executed in the addition procedure one by one so that all the possible buggy answers to the problem are generated. Those answers can then be compared to a student's work to determine possible explanations of the student's particular misconceptions. In this way, one might use the procedural network to diagnose a student's basic misconceptions over an entire homework assignment or an arithmetic test.

There are, however, several complications

with this simple paradigm for diagnosing a student. One is that the student who has developed a *novel* singleton bug (as opposed to one that arose out of a combination of "primitive" bugs) will not be diagnosed. Another is that students *do* make "random" mistakes (presumably as many while following an *incorrect* procedure as a correct one) that could erroneously lead to the exclusion of his bug or the inclusion of another bug that happened to coincide with his "randomness." Finally, blindly considering all possible combinations of bugs can lead to a combinatorial explosion of possibilities. In what follows, we shall discuss some solutions to these problems.

A Deep-Structure Data Analysis Tool

As a first step in developing techniques for automatically diagnosing a student's errors, we sought a large data base of student answers on some arithmetic test. We started out this way for two reasons. First, an analysis of the student errors not already explained by the existing network can suggest extensions to the network that may have been overlooked. Obviously, if the BUGGY system is going to be useful as a diagnostic tool, its arsenal of bugs must be very extensive! Second, once a "complete" network of bugs has been constructed, analyzing a large data base can provide some evidence of how many student errors are procedural rather than "careless"

errors. Such an analysis also indicates how consistently students apply buggy procedures. Do they use the buggy procedure every time it is appropriate? When they get a correct answer does that contraindicate their use of a buggy procedure, or is it just that the buggy procedure for this problem *does* produce the correct answer? This analysis also reveals which procedural errors occur most often, and in what combinations. Answers to these questions not only influence the design of the diagnostic system (as we will see later) but also have an impact on how that system could be used.

We were fortunate to be able to obtain a large collection of pertinent data[15] already in computer readable form. The data stemmed from an achievement test administered in Nicaragua to fourth, fifth, and sixth graders. There were ten different test versions, each consisting of thirty problems combining both simple and complex addition and subtraction problems. One version of the test is given in Figure 4. The makeup of each test followed a complex procedure discussed by Friend (1976).

Admittedly, these data have the limitation that the particular results derived from them are not necessarily generalizable to American schools. Although the procedures taught for addition and subtraction are similar, the environmental and cultural experiences of the students are quite different. Nevertheless, this data base provides a convenient starting point for this research as well as a general

1 +2	8 −3	7 +9	99 −79	43 +41	353 −342	213 −21	633 −221	521 +502	81 −17
123 13 610 +12	4769 −0	9 91 +6	257 −161	597 +75	6523 −1280	156 873 +311	103 −64	8 54 +9	7315 −6536
505 743 12 +35	1039 −44	77 18 +47	705 −9	917 639 +5	10038 −4319	864 9 4 +3	10060 −98	579 96 833 +43	7001 −94

FIGURE 4: A sample test

idea of the percentage of students making procedural as opposed to "random" errors. In addition, the methods we devised to analyze these data would apply equally well to data collected under other circumstances.

The Process of Organizing the Data

The data base available for this study was large—19,500 problems performed by 1300 students. We limited ourselves to consideration of just the subtraction problems on the test because the addition problems included some in which three or more numbers were to be added—a condition that can produce errors not modeled in the present addition network.

As a first step, we extended the BUGGY system to print out "bug comparison" tables for students as shown in Table 1. These tables summarize how well the student's behavior can be explained or predicted by a simple bug in the network. The format of a table is as follows. The problems with the correct answers appear at the top of each table. The student's answers appear on the next line using the convention that "—" indicates a correct student answer. Each of the remaining lines provides the name of a bug and the answers produced by the assumption that the student had this and only this bug.

For each of these lines a "***" means that the bug predicted the student's incorrect answer. A "*" means that the bug in that row would give the correct answer and also that the student got the correct answer. Thus "*" and "***" indicate places of agreement between the student's behavior and the simulated behavior of the bug. An "!" means that the bug would give the correct answer, but that the student gave an incorrect one.[16] A number which appears in a bug row is the answer that the bug would give when it is different from both the student's answer and the correct answer.[17]

Initially, any bug that explained any of the student's behavior (i.e., generated at least one "***") was included in the table. However, these tables proved to be too large to conveniently read, so a routine was added to delete any bug if there was another bug that accounted for the same set of answers as well as some others.

Analysis of a Bug Comparison Table

When we are determining whether a student has a particular bug, "*" and "***" are confirming evidence that the student has the bug while both "!" and numbers in the bug row are disconfirming evidence. We refer to the results in a bug comparison table as "evi-

TABLE 1: An Initial Bug Comparison Table[a]

8	99	353	633	81	4769	257	6523	103	7315	1039	705	10038	10060	7001
3	79	342	221	17	0	161	1280	64	6536	44	9	4319	98	94
5	20	11	412	64	4769	96	5243	39	779	995	696	5719	9962	6907

Student answers

| — | — | — | — | 98 | — | 418 | — | 169 | 738 | 1095 | 706 | 14319 | 10078 | 7097 |

FORGET/BORROW/OVER/BLANKS

| * | * | * | * | ! | * | ! | * | 139 | ! | *** | *** | 15719 | 10062 | 7007 |

STOPS/BORROW/AT/ZERO

| * | * | * | * | ! | * | ! | * | 49 | ! | *** | *** | 6719 | 10062 | 7017 |

DIFF/0−N=N

| * | * | * | * | ! | * | ! | * | ! | 839 | ! | ! | *** | 9978 | ! |

ADD/INSTEADOF/SUB

| 11 | 178 | 695 | 854 | *** | * | *** | 7803 | 167 | 13851 | 1083 | 714 | 14357 | 10158 | 7095 |

[a] This table presents how well a student's answers are explained by different bugs; "***" and "*" indicate places of agreement. (See text for discussion.)

dence" because there may be several possible explanations for any particular answer to one problem. The student may have made a careless error while following his bugged procedure, therefore leading to a number in that bug row instead of a "***". He may have an unmodeled combination of bugs, only one of which manifested itself and resulted in an "!" in the row of the other bug. Or he may have been following a totally different procedure, or no procedure at all, that just happened to give him the same answer as a bug leading to a "***" in a bug row. The final decision on whether the student is using a buggy subprocedure must be made by considering all the evidence from the test. But how should *conflicting evidence* be weighted and summed?

Let us consider an analysis of the bug comparison table for a particular student, Table 1. Both FORGET/BORROW/OVER/BLANKS and STOPS/BORROW/AT/ZERO produce the same answer in problems 11 (1039 − 44) and 12 (705 − 9)—the errant student answers. But neither has particularly good agreement across the rest of the table. Which, if either, misconception was the student operating under? Our inclination is to believe that neither bug satisfactorily explains the behavior, but how does one decide in general? To answer these questions, we analyzed, by hand, several hundred students' tables like the one in Table 1. During these formative analyses, the tables were examined to ferret out students whose behavior was not captured by any existing bugs. The work of these students was closely scrutinized for any underlying computational pattern. If a pattern could be discerned, the incorrect subprocedure was defined and this new "bug" was added to the network. During this formulation period our list of bugs grew from eighteen to sixty.

Multiple Bugs and Their (Nonobvious) Interactions

Most of the sixty subtraction bugs discovered during this period were primitive, in the sense that each redefined only one subprocedure in the subtraction network. Was it possible that some of the students' behavior was due to multiple bugs that we had failed to notice? To explore this possibility, we programmed the BUGGY diagnostic system to try all *pairs* of bugs. That is, buggy definitions of two subprocedures were systematically inserted and then executed.[18] This process turned up 270 bug combinations whose symptoms were different from any of the primitive bugs and from each other in one test of 15 problems.

In order to illustrate the diagnostic power of this generative technique, consider the example of the student whose work is shown in Table 1. From Table 1, no discernible pattern is evident. The student's work does however admit to a beautifully simple characterization which is the composite of two primitive bugs. Table 2 shows the new bug comparison table that was generated for this student from comparisons using multiple bugs. Notice that the comparison line which

TABLE 2: Multiple Bug Comparison Table

8	99	353	633	81	4769	257	6523	103	7315	1039	705	10038	10060	7001
3	79	342	221	17	0	161	1280	64	6536	44	9	4319	98	94
5	20	11	412	64	4769	96	5243	39	779	995	696	5719	9962	6907

Student answers

| — | — | — | — | 98 | — | 418 | — | 169 | 738 | 1095 | 706 | 14319 | 10078 | 7097 |

DIFF/0−N=N and STOPS/BORROW/AT/ZERO

| * | * | * | * | ! | * | ! | * | *** | 839 | *** | *** | *** | *** | *** |

ADD/INSTEADOF/SUB

| 11 | 178 | 695 | 854 | *** | * | *** | 7803 | 167 | 13851 | 1083 | 714 | 14357 | 10158 | 7095 |

resulted from the combination of the two bugs is substantially different from either of the single bug lines or even from a linear combination of the two comparisons. This is due to the nonobvious interactions of the two bugs, particularly where the intermediate products of one of the bugs enables or disables the other bug. For example, in problem 9 (103 − 64), the "0 − N = N" bug alone will not manifest itself because the borrow from the first column will have changed the 0 in the second column to 9. However, the "stops-borrow-at-zero" bug[19] has the side effect of *not* changing the 0 to 9, and hence enables the "0 − $N = 0$" bug. In general, the interactions between bugs can be arbitrarily complex. This can make a teacher's diagnostic task very difficult.

Judging Diagnostic Credibility

Using the multiple bug comparison tables generated for about one hundred students, we identified which of the students, in our judgment, were making procedural, as opposed to careless or random errors. During this hand-done classification process, we articulated and refined our intuitive use of the evidence from a student's entire test in order to make that decision. Eventually, our understanding and description of the process became precise enough to be computerized so that it could be run on all 1300 students.

Our hand-done study suggested six intuitive groupings of students.

1. Those students who got all the problems correct

2. Those students who erred on any number of problems but whose errors were explained by one bug or one bug pair

3. Those students who clearly exhibited the presence of a bug but also exhibited some behavior that was not explained by the bug

4. Those students who missed only one or two (of fifteen problems) and in a way not consistent with any bug

5. Those students who exhibited some buggy behavior but not consistently

6. Those students whose behavior appeared random relative to the known bugs

Tables 3, 4, and 5 show representative students from Groups 2, 3, and 5. The intuitive justification for these groupings stemmed from the possible tutorial approaches a teacher might take to remediate a student. The classes of students and the possible very general tutorial approaches we saw are:

a. Those students who are correct or very nearly correct and probably just need more practice if anything (Groups 1 and 4)

b. Those students who are exhibiting consistently incorrect behavior and,

TABLE 3: Example of a Student Whose Behavior Is Well Explained by One Bug[a]

8	99	353	633	81	4769	257	6523	103	7315	1039	705	10038	10060	7001
3	79	342	221	17	0	161	1280	64	6536	44	9	4319	98	94
5	20	11	412	64	4769	96	5243	39	779	995	696	5719	9962	6907

Student answers

| − | − | − | − | − | − | − | − | 139 | − | 1995 | 76 | 15719 | 10962 | 7007 |

BORROW/FROM/ZERO

| * | * | * | * | * | * | * | * | *** | * | *** | 796 | *** | *** | *** |

Best guess: BORROW/FROM/ZERO
GROUP=2

[a] The bug, BORROW/FROM/ZERO, is that when borrowing from a column in which the top number is 0, the student writes 9 but does not continue borrowing from the next column to the left.

TABLE 4: Example of a Student Who Exhibits a Consistent Bug but Also Has Other Problems

8	99	353	633	81	4769	257	6523	103	7315	1039	705	10038	10060	7001
3	79	342	221	17	0	161	1280	64	6536	44	9	4319	98	94
5	20	11	412	64	4769	96	5243	39	779	995	696	5719	9962	6907

Student answers

| — | — | — | — | 74 | — | — | — | 9 | 1209 | 95 | 704 | 10019 | 70 | 6007 |

DIFF/0−N=0 and MOVE/OVER/ZERO/BORROW

| * | * | * | * | ! | * | * | * | *** | 809 | *** | 606 | *** | *** | *** |

BORROW/ACROSS/SMALLER/ADDING/TEN/EXCEPT/ZERO and DIFF/0−N=0

| * | * | * | * | ! | * | * | * | *** | 889 | *** | 606 | *** | *** | *** |

SUB/UNITS/SPECIAL and SMALLER/FROM/LARGER&0−N=0

| * | * | * | * | ! | * | 116 | 5363 | ! | *** | 1015 | ! | *** | 10042 | ! |

BORROW/NO/DECREMENT and QUIT/WHEN/BOTTOM/BLANK

| * | * | * | * | *** | 9 | 196 | 5343 | 49 | 1889 | *** | 6 | 6729 | 72 | 17 |

BORROW/NO/DECREMENT

| * | * | * | * | *** | * | 196 | 5343 | 149 | 1889 | 1095 | 706 | 16729 | 10072 | 7017 |

SMALLER/FROM/LARGER

| * | * | * | * | 76 | * | 116 | 5363 | 161 | 1221 | 1015 | *** | 14321 | 10038 | 7093 |

Best guess: DIFF/0−N=0 and MOVE/OVER/ZERO/BORROW

GROUP=3

therefore, whose remediation may profitably be viewed as a process of "debugging" the student's present algorithm (Groups 2 and 3)

c. Those students for whom a thorough reteaching of the entire algorithm appears to be essential (Groups 5 and 6)

We are definitely *not* saying that for all students in Groups 2 and 3 the only or even the best pedagogy is to focus on the student's buggy procedure. Instead, we are trying to identify those students who are consistently making the same mistake and for whom debugging of their procedures *may* be useful.

Classification Algorithm

The algorithm that we eventually converged on for assigning a student to one of the six major categories defined in the preceding

TABLE 5: Example of a Student Who Exhibits Some Buggy Behavior but Not Consistently

8	99	353	633	81	4769	257	6523	103	7315	1039	705	10038	10060	7001
3	79	342	221	17	0	161	1280	64	6536	44	9	431	98	94
5	20	11	412	64	4769	96	5243	39	779	995	696	5719	9962	6907

Student answers

| ! | ! | ! | ! | 70 | ! | 98 | ! | 109 | 839 | 1095 | 706 | 1431 | 10700 | 7001 |

DIFF/0−N=N and STOPS/BORROW/AT/ZERO

| * | * | * | * | ! | * | ! | * | 169 | *** | *** | *** | *** | 10078 | 7097 |

DIFF/0−N=N and FORGET/BORROW/OVER/BLANKS

| * | * | * | * | ! | * | ! | * | 139 | *** | *** | *** | *** | 1078 | 7007 |

DIFF/0−N=0&1−N=1 and STOPS/BORROW/AT/ZERO

| * | * | * | * | 71 | * | ! | * | *** | 809 | *** | *** | 10019 | 10070 | *** |

ZERO/INSTEADOF/BORROW

| * | * | * | * | *** | * | 106 | 5303 | 100 | 1000 | 1005 | 700 | 10020 | 10000 | 7000 |

GROUP=5

section is rather involved, so some readers may prefer to skim the following discussion. If the student erred on at least one problem, each bug was rated according to how well it accounted for this behavior. This rating results in a group number for each bug.[20] The *rating* of each bug depends on the number of answers falling into each of five groups.

a. Those student answers for which the bug predicts the student's incorrect answer (the number of "***"s appearing in the bug's line referred to as N^{***})

b. Those student answers for which the bug predicts the student's correct answer (the number of "*"s—N^*)

c. Those student answers for which the bug predicts the correct answer but which the student answered incorrectly (the number of "!"s—$N!$)

d. Those student answers for which the bug predicts an incorrect answer but which the student answered correctly (Nr)

e. Those student answers for which the bug predicts an incorrect answer different from the student's incorrect answer (Nw)

This analysis gives a symptom vector of five numbers (N^{***}, N^*, $N!$, Nr, Nw).

From the symptom vector, a group number corresponding to the six major categories of student behavior given in the preceding section is calculated for *each bug* using the following procedure.[21]

A bug indicates Group 2 student behavior if it agrees with all the student's answers ($N! + Nr + Nw = 0$) or if it agrees more than 75 percent of the time on problems in which it predicts a wrong answer [$N^{***} \geqslant 3 \times (N! + Nr + Nw)$].

A bug indicates Group 3 behavior if it explains two or more student errors and predicts more correct than incorrect answers ($N^{***} > Nr + Nw + N!/2$). In this formula, those problems in which the bug did not exhibit a symptom are weighted by half—the intuition is that, on these problems, the student may be exhibiting other bugs as well.

A bug is also rated as indicating Group 3

behavior if it is a primitive bug (not multiple) that predicts more than half the student's errors, and predicts erroneous behavior more times than it fails to do so ($N^{***} > N! + Nw$ and $N^{***} > Nr$).

A bug indicates a group 5 behavior if it predicts at least two incorrect answers ($N^{***} \geqslant 2$).

Otherwise a bug is rated Group 6.

The student is assigned the group number of the lowest rated bug. If the lowest rated bug is not Group 2 or 3 and the student has missed only one or two problems, he is put in Group 4. If the student is put in Group 2 or 3, the bug with the lowest group rating (and which accounts for the most symptoms in cases of ties) is chosen as the most likely hypothetical student bug. Examples of this result can be seen in the last line of Tables 3 and 4.

Diagnostic Results for the Nicaraguan Data Base

The above classification procedure was used to analyze the set of test responses for 1325 fourth, fifth, and sixth graders.[22] A summary of the diagnostic classification by grade is given in Table 6. As can be seen, nearly 40 percent of the students exhibited consistently buggy behavior. This figure agrees with a similar result reported by Cox (1975). The similarity across grade level may be due to the fact that addition and subtraction are not presented again after the fourth grade.

Table 7 gives the frequency of the fourteen most common bugs. Most of the difficulties arise while borrowing, especially when a zero is involved. The most common bug was "when borrowing from a column in which the top digit is 0, change the 0 to a 9 but do not continue borrowing from the next column to the left"; it occurred alone or together with other bugs 153 times in the 1325 student tests.

What Does a Test Score Mean?

One of the ramifications of this fully automatic diagnostic technique concerns its ability to

TABLE 6: Totals and Percentages of Student Classifications[a]

Grade	Group														
	1		2		3		4		5		6		Totals	
	No.	(%)	No.	(%)	No.	(%)	No.	(%)	No.	(%)	No.	(%)	No.	(%)
4th	10	2.4	101	20.5	93	18.9	31	6.6	197	39.5	72	14.7	504	100.0
5th	10	3.0	86	22.0	73	18.7	38	10.0	132	33.5	60	15.5	399	100.0
6th	17	4.5	88	21.3	64	15.6	47	11.6	131	31.5	75	18.2	422	100.0
Totals	37	3.2	275	21.2	230	17.8	116	9.2	460	35.2	207	16.1		

[a] Groups 2 and 3 are consistently following an incorrect procedure (see text for further explanation of groups).

score tests based on what a student knows or does not know as opposed to scoring it based *solely* on the number of right and wrong answers on his test. Even with the advances in criterion-referenced testing, it remains true that a test is simply scored by what problems a student gets right or wrong. Because of the embedded nature of most procedural skills, a student can get many problems wrong simply by having one fundamental underlying bug in a primitive subprocedure that he is using to solve different problems on the test. In such a situation, the score that a student gets can bear little relationship to the misconceptions that he actually harbors! A student can receive a low score either because he has many misconceptions, each one of which is more or less the top of the procedural network of skills he is using, or he may possess a few, or even just one misconception that is deep down inside the internal workings of the procedural network and is constantly being used to compute intermediate results used by higher up subprocedures.

Current techniques for correcting tests do not offer easy and reliable methods of separating these two situations. The diagnostic modeling technique discussed above can take the answers that a student gives on a test and, through its modeling system, show not only which questions were answered incorrectly but *why* they were incorrectly answered. It is interesting to note that 107 of the 1325 students tested had a bug in their borrow-from-zero subprocedure and missed

6 out of the 15 problems on the test because of this one underlying bug. The characterization given by BUGGY is a much fairer evaluation than scoring these students 60 percent correct.

A Methodological Tool for Judging the Diagnostic Quality of a Test

The procedural network apparatus also provides a methodological tool for judging the quality or diagnostic capabilities of a given test. This allows one to talk about how well the test can discover and delineate common misconceptions. Given a test, each bug in the network can be used to answer all the problems. The resulting "buggy" responses are then used to partition the bugs: two bugs are put in the same partition if they produce the same answers to all the test problems. "Diagnosticity" of the test can now be defined in terms of the size of the resultant partitions. A diagnostically perfect test has every bug in a partition by itself. Those bugs in the same partition are undifferentiated by the test. Any bugs in the same partition as the correct answers are not tested for at all. Taking the test in Figure 4, this system discovered that a student can have either of two bugs (BORROW/ACROSS/SAME or $N-N = 1$/AFTER /BORROW) and still get 100 percent correct answers.

Such a system could provide professional test designers with a formal tool for establish-

TABLE 7: Bug Frequency Table

The 14 most frequently occurring bugs in a group of 1325 students

57   Students used: BORROW/FROM/ZERO (103 − 45 = 158)
When borrowing from a column whose top digit is 0, the student writes 9, but does not continue borrowing from the column to the left of the 0.

54   Students used: SMALLER/FROM/LARGER (253 − 118 = 145)
The student subtracts the smaller digit in a column from the larger digit regardless of which one is on top.

50   Students used: BORROW/FROM/ZERO and LEFT/TEN/OK (803 − 508 = 395)
The student changes 0 to 9 without further borrowing unless the 0 is part of a 10 in the left part of the top number.

34   Students used: DIFF/0 − $N = N$ and MOVE/OVER/ZERO/BORROW
Whenever the top digit in a column is 0, the student writes the bottom digit in the answer; i.e., $0 − N = N$. When the student needs to borrow from a column whose top digit is 0, he skips that column and borrows from the next one.

14   Students used: DIFF/0 − $N = N$ and STOPS/BORROW/AT/ZERO
Whenever the top digit in a column is 0, the student writes the bottom digit in the answer; i.e., $0 − N = N$. The student borrows from zero incorrectly. He does not subtract 1 from the 0 although he adds 10 correctly to the top digit of the current column.

13   Students used: SMALLER/FROM/LARGER and $0 − N = 0$ (203 − 98 = 205)
The student subtracts the smaller digit in each column from the larger digit regardless of which one is on top. The exception is that when the top digit is 0, a 0 is written as the answer for that column; i.e., $0 − N = 0$.

12   Students used: DIFF/0 − $N = 0$ and MOVE/OVER/ZERO/BORROW
Whenever the top digit in a column is 0, the student writes 0 in the answer; i.e., $0 − N = 0$. When the student needs to borrow from a column whose top digit is 0, he skips that column and borrows from the next one.

11   Students used: BORROW/FROM/ZERO and DIFF/$N − 0 = 0$
When borrowing from a column whose top digit is 0, the student writes 9, but does not continue borrowing from the column to the left of the 0. Whenever the bottom digit in a column is 0, the student writes 0 in the answer; i.e., $N − 0 = 0$.

10   Students used: DIFF/0 − $N = 0$ and $N − 0 = 0$ (302 − 192 = 290)
The student writes 0 in the answer when either the top or the bottom digit is 0.

10   Students used: BORROW/FROM/ZERO and DIFF/0 − $N = N$
When borrowing from a column whose top digit is 0, the student writes 9, but does not continue borrowing from the column to the left of the 0. Whenever the top digit in a column is 0, the student writes the bottom digit in the answer, i.e., $0 − N = N$.

10   Students used: MOVE/OVER/ZERO/BORROW (304 − 75 = 139)
When the student needs to borrow from a column whose top digit is 0, he skips that column and borrows from the next one.

10   Students used: DIFF/$N − 0 = 0$ (403 − 208 = 105)
Whenever the bottom digit in a column is 0, the student writes 0 in the answer; i.e., $N − 0 = 0$.

10   Students used: DIFF/0 − $N = N$ (140 − 21 = 121)
Whenever the top digit in a column is 0, the student writes the bottom digit in the answer; i.e., $0 − N = N$.

9   Students used: DIFF/0 − $N = N$ and LEFT/TEN/OK (908 − 395 = 693)
When there is a 0 on top, the student writes the bottom digit in the answer. The exception is when the 0 is part of 10 in the left columns of the top number.

ing the diagnostic quality of a proposed test. However, our belief is that professional test designers have good intuitions about diagnostic tests. This belief was confirmed by running two standardized national tests through the 330 subtraction bugs: one of the tests left only one bug unexposed in 17 problems while the other left 4 bugs unexposed in 10 problems. The unexposed bugs were rare for they were not even found in the Nicaraguan data. There is a difference, however, between exposing a bug and diagnosing it. *Exposing* a bug amounts to having at least one problem on the test in which the bug is manifested; *diagnosing* a bug requires having test problems which differentiate between it and every other bug.

Using the artificial intelligence paradigm of generate-and-test, it would be straightforward to use BUGGY as a diagnostic test generator. The problem generator must produce "interestingly" different problems. This generation can be done using important features of problems such as the number of times borrowing is necessary, or whether a zero appears in the top number. Sets of generated problems can then be filtered using the procedural network to identify bugs which are not diagnosed. From the bugs left undiagnosed, features can be retrieved which direct the generation of alternative problems to be added to the test. In this way, a highly diagnostic test can be developed. Furthermore, since the answers that would be generated by using the bugs are known, the test could be a multiple-choice test and still maintain its total diagnostic property! Similarly, a real-time adaptive testing system could be created based on these tools.

4. Future Research

This paper has presented some of the problems that must be faced in diagnosing failures in procedural skills, and has described some ideas about the formulation and implementation of diagnostic modeling techniques that address these problems. It has also presented some novel uses of diagnostic models as a gaming/instructional device, as a deep-structure test grader, and as a tool to judge the diagnostic quality of a test or a set of problems. The central idea underlying this research is the use of a *procedural network* as a means of representing diagnostic models. The critical properties of this representa-

tion scheme are its abilities to represent an appropriately structured breakdown of a skill into subskills, to make explicit the control structures underlying a collection of skills, and to make the knowledge encoded this way directly executable. Such a representation enables a particular subskill to be easily modified and then simulated or executed so that the ramifications of the modification can be quickly ascertained. The structure of the network becomes important not only because it allows efficient modification but also because the representation of the modification can be used to contain explanatory or remedial material.[23] In addition, the structure allows certain types of control structure failures to be directly represented in the network and hence articulated—if necessary.

Relationship of Diagnostic Models to Other Kinds of Structural Model

We now turn to a brief look at the past and current work on structural models of students and how they relate to diagnostic models based on procedural networks. Most of the past and current research on this subject has been focused on the intuitively appealing notion that if one has an explicit, well-formulated model of the knowledge base of an expert for a given set of skills or problem domain, then one can model a particular student's knowledge as a simplification of the rules comprising the expert's procedures (Barr, 1974; Brown, 1974; Brown and Burton, 1975; Burton and Brown, 1977; Carbonell and Collins, 1973; Carr and Goldstein, 1977; Collins, Warnock, and Passafiume, 1975). Recently, Goldstein has expanded this concept in his Computer Coach research and has coined the term "overlay model" for capturing how a student's manifested knowledge of skills relates to an expert's knowledge base (Goldstein, 1977).

The work reported in this paper differs in that the basic modeling technique is based on viewing a structural model of the student not as a simplification of the expert's rules but rather as a set of *semantically meaning-*

ful deviations from an expert's knowledge base.[24] Each subskill of the expert is explicitly encoded, along with a set of potential misconceptions of that subskill. The task of inferring a diagnostic model then becomes one of discovering which set of variations or deviations best explains the surface behavior of the student. This view is in concert with, although more structured than, the approach taken by Self (1974) in which he models the student as a set of modified procedures taken from a procedural expert problem solver.

Another closely related approach to modeling a student's knowledge base uses a production rule encoding scheme (Smith and Sleeman, 1977; Young, 1977). However, procedural networks differ both theoretically and computationally from these efforts in that they are designed to make explicit the representation of the control-structure knowledge underlying a macro skill so that it can be efficiently diagnosed and explicitly tutored.

In the remainder of this section, we present our view of the more promising directions for research relating to diagnostic models.

Extensions to the Gaming Environment

In Section 2, we described the BUGGY game, which was designed to introduce the notion of "buggy" behavior and provide practice in diagnosing it. Although this activity was initially designed for training student teachers in diagnosing and articulating procedural bugs, it has also been used as an activity to get kids to introspect on their already known procedures as well as to encounter the concept of bugs and debugging strategies in an easily grasped context.

A limitation of the current gaming environment is that most of what the players learn while using the game they learn or discover on their own. At the moment, BUGGY does no explicit tutoring; it simply provides an environment that challenges their theories and encourages them to articulate their thoughts.[25] The rest of the learning experi-

ence occurs either through the sociology of team learning or from what a person abstracts on his own. The next step in realizing the educational potential of the BUGGY game is to implement an intelligent tutor which can recognize and point out weaknesses (or interesting facets) in a student's debugging strategies.[26] Our experiences indicate that such a tutor would be very helpful for middle school and remedial students who often get caught in unproductive ruts. The tutor could also help focus the student's attention on the structure of the arithmetic procedures themselves. It is worth noting that *some* of the tools for constructing an intelligent tutor for the BUGGY game already exist in the form of the test validation techniques described in the previous section. Nevertheless, these techniques do not provide the right kind of information for explaining to a student *why* the problem he just generated had little or no diagnostic value. We are currently exploring the kind of reasoning required to answer "why."

An intelligent tutor designed specifically to help teachers will profit from a theory of what makes an underlying bug easy or difficult to diagnose. Simple conjectures concerning the depth of the bug from the surface do not seem to work, but more sophisticated measures might. It is hard to see how to predict the degree of difficulty in diagnosing a particular bug without a precise information-processing or cognitive theory of how people actually formulate conjectures about the underlying bug or cause of an error. For example, one such theory is that people walk through their own algorithm, looking for places where a part of the incorrect answer is different from their own and then try to imagine local modifications to their algorithm that could account for the error. Under this theory, one would expect bugs that involve major modification of the procedure, such as changing the direction in which columns are processed, to be difficult to diagnose. Similarly one would expect difficulty if a student's algorithm differs from the diagnostician's. Given an adequate theory, the difficult situations can be watched for and corrected through appropriate tutorial comments during diagnostic training.

Another extension to the BUGGY environment to encourage further exploration of the ideas of hypothesis formation and debugging is the development of a specialized programming language for writing simple arithmetic procedures. Actually having students write procedures provides immediate focus on debugging strategies—a topic usually left until the end in most secondary school programming courses. In this limited environment, it should be possible to construct an intelligent programming assistant as well as a computer-based tutorial helper that can aid a student when he gets stuck. Providing students with a language in which they can write their own procedures also allows use of a game developed in the SOPHIE environment (Brown, Rubinstein, and Burton, 1976), where one student writes a procedure introducing a bug and another student tries to discover it by presenting test problems.

Extensions to the Diagnostic System

Concerning the use of procedural networks as a tool for diagnosing real students, we reiterate that the capabilities of the present system are solely diagnostic: no tutoring is attempted. The issue of what tutorial strategy to use, even when it is known exactly what a student is doing wrong, is still an open question.

One possible strategy is that the "expert" portion of the procedural network could be made *articulate* in the sense of being able to explain and justify the subprocedures it uses. Since the system would know the student's bug, special problems can be chosen and special care can be taken while presenting the steps which illustrate the student's bug. This feature could also be used to allow students to pose their own problems to the system and obtain a running account of the relevant procedures as the "expert" solves the problem. A useful notion for the articulate expert may be to have additional explanation or justification of each symbolic procedure in

the network expressed in terms of a "physical" procedure using manipulative tools such as Dienes's blocks (Dienes and Golding, 1970). In this way, the execution of each *symbolic* procedure could cause its analogous *physical* procedure whose execution could be displayed on a graphics device, thereby letting the student see the numeric or abstract computation unfold in conjunction with a physical model of the computation. This approach directly attacks the problem of getting procedures to take on "meaning" for a student: the acquisition of meaning is, we believe, accomplished by recognizing mappings or relations between the new procedures and existing procedures or experiences.

While we consider the articulation of the expert to have great promise as a corrective tutorial strategy, it is by no means the only possible such strategy. It is possible that with certain bugs (and certain students), a clear description of what is going wrong may be sufficient to allow the student to correct his problem. Or it may be possible to formulate a series of problems (possibly in conjunction with physical models) that enables the student to discover his own error. Or it may be best to abandon his algorithm (rather than trying to debug it) and start over with a different, simpler algorithm to build the student's confidence.

Generalization to Strategic Knowledge

Caution should be exercised in generalizing the procedural network model to other procedural skills. In particular, the aspects of knowledge discussed here are almost totally algorithmic in nature, containing little heuristic or strategic knowledge in selecting or guiding the execution of the primitives (procedures). Many mathematical skills involve an interplay between strategic and algorithmic knowledge. For example, when adding two fractions one does not necessarily compute a common multiple by multiplying together the two denominators. Instead, an examination is made of the relationships between the two denominators such as identity, obvious divisibility of one by the other, relative primeness, and so on. On the basis of such relationships specialized procedures are chosen for adding the given fractions. The rules underlying these decisions can have their own bugs and, therefore, these rules must be modeled within some representation scheme. Although procedural network schemes can represent such decision rules, we believe that other schemes, based perhaps more on annotated production rules (Goldstein and Grimson, 1977), deserve serious consideration. We are currently investigating a hybrid approach for modeling fractions (and their bugs) that involves merging annotated production rules with procedural networks.

Psychological Validity

An important area for exploration concerns the psychological validity of the skill decomposition and buggy variants in the network. That is, how well do the data structures and procedure calls in the network correspond to the structures and skills that we expect people to learn? From the network designer's point of view, the psychological validity can be improved or denigrated by choosing one structural decomposition instead of another. Determining a psychologically "correct" functional breakdown of a skill into its subskills is critical to the behavior of gaming and diagnostic systems using it. If the breakdown of the skill is not correct, common bugs may be difficult to model while those suggested by the model may be judged by people to be "unrealistic." For people playing BUGGY based on a nonvalid network, the relationship between its bugs and the behavior they observe in people will often be obscure. Measuring the "correctness" of a particular network is a problematic issue as there are no clear tests of validity. However, issues such as the ease or "naturalness" of inclusion of newly discovered bugs and the appearance of combinations of bugs within a breakdown can be investigated.

Finally, we have left open the entire issue of a semantic theory of how procedures are *understood* (and learned) by a person and why bugs arise in the first place. The need for a theory of how procedures are learned correctly or incorrectly is important for at least two reasons. First, an interesting theoretical framework that accounts for the entire collection of empirically arrived at bugs will undoubtedly provide insight into how to correct the teaching procedure that produced the bugs in the first place. Second, such a theory would be the next step in a semantically based generative theory of student modeling. As we have stated earlier, bugs have to be hand coded into the network now. One can envision generatively producing bugs by a set of syntactic transformations (additions, deletions, transpositions, etc.) based on some appropriate representation language. While some bugs can be naturally accounted for as "syntactic" bugs, others, such as inappropriate analogy from other operations or incorrect generalization from examples, are best explained outside the representation itself and hence require a "semantic" theory. One of the by-products of the diagnosis of the student data mentioned in the preceding section has been a thorough and precise catalogue of bugs arising in one particular skill, subtraction. This network can now be used to suggest and evaluate theories about the origin of bugs.

Appendix: Student Responses to Buggy

In an experiment described in Section 2, a group of student teachers were exposed to the BUGGY game. This appendix provides a list of responses to the question, "What do you think you learned from this experience?"

I see from this system that you learn from your mistakes. In a certain operation there are so many mistakes that you can make. When you learn what the mistakes are, you learn to do the operation correctly.

That children's errors can be a way of diagnosing the way the child learns material. Also it raises questions about the way a child is tested, both standardized and informally.

A student's errors and/or misunderstanding of a concept may have not been due to carelessness but rather involved a complex and logical thought process.

I learned that it is necessary to try many different types of examples to be sure that a child really understands. Different types of difficulties arise with different problems.

Although it's hard to tell from these pre- and posttests, in the middle is learned a great deal about the complexity of student's errors. I know that young students can get these preconceived notions about how to do things and it's very hard to find a pattern to their errors though it exists and I believe that BUGGY convinced me of [it].

That if you study the errors long enough you can *eventually* come up with a reasonable solution as to why the [error] is occurring.

Through looking carefully at children's math errors it is sometimes possible to discover a pattern to them. This pattern will tell you an area or a concept the child does not understand.

I learned that there could be more to a child's mistakes other than carelessness. Working with children with special needs I have encountered many such problems, yet never stopped to analyze what could be a systematic problem—for this I thank you.

Children do have problems and they are very difficult to spot especially when a number of different operations are used to come to an answer. I've learned to be more aware of how these children reach these "answers" and to help them to correct them; first by knowing how they arrived at the answer.

Although many arithmetic errors may be careless, there may also be a pattern that the kid is locked into. If you pick up on a pattern you can test the child to see if he or she conforms to it and work on it from there.

I found that I have looked closer at the problems, looking for a relationship between the set after working with BUGGY.

How to perceive problems, that don't look too consistent, a little easier.

I learned and was exposed to the many different types of problems children might have. I never realized the many different ways a child could devise to create his own system to do a problem. I am now aware of problems that could arise and I'm sure this will help me [in] my future career as a teacher.

How to more effectively detect "problems" students have with place value.

I have learned several new possible errors students may make in computation. I have also learned somewhat how to diagnose these errors, i.e., what to look for, and how specific errors can be.

I learned about diagnosing math difficulties. It makes me aware of problems that children have, and they sometimes think logically, not carelessly as sometimes teachers think they do.

That there are many problems that you can diagnose about a child by looking at his homework.

If a child has repeatedly made [the] same mistakes, it is more easily identified if the teacher has an opportunity to try and make [the] same mistakes. This method can be solved at least quicker than . . .

Tuned in to picking up malfunctions in simple addition and subtraction which seemed to be realistic problems.

ACKNOWLEDGMENTS

We are especially indebted to Kathy M. Larkin for her extensive assistance on this project and in particular for her contribution in refining the BUGGY activity and in discovering many new arithmetic "bugs."

NOTES

1. This term has been used by Earl Sacerdoti (1977) to describe an interesting modeling technique for a partially ordered sequence of annotated steps in a problem solving "plan" as well as for specifying control information. Our use of procedural nets coincides with his on this latter feature but differs from and is less developed than his with regard to "plans."

2. The language we have used to define these programs is LISP. The particular programming language is unimportant from a theoretical standpoint because an implementation is nonintrospectable. The modeling aspects of the network must occur at the conceptual procedure level. For example, the implementation of the subtraction facts table look-up procedure in the computer is necessarily different from that in the student. However, the conceptual properties of the two implementations can be made to agree to an "appropriate" level of detail. Those aspects which are appropriate for our task—the invoking of other procedures, the values returned, the relevant side effects—are included in the network, while the implementation details that may differ are "swept under the rug" into the program. This distinction between conceptual and implementation details also allows skills to be modeled efficiently at different levels which may be appropriate for different tasks.

3. This simplified representation demonstrates only those features of the procedural network particularly relevant to the diagnostic task. The actual breakdown into subprocedures may be different in a particular network and will be considerably more detailed.

4. The term "bug" is borrowed from computer science where it refers to a mistake in a computer program.

5. A "buggy" implementation does, in general, call other "correct" subprocedures though they may be called at inappropriate times or their results used incorrectly.

6. West (1971) has broken down the diagnostic teaching task into four steps: (1) distinguish between conceptual and careless errors, (2) identify the exact nature of the conceptual error (bug), (3) determine the conceptual basis

(cause) of the bug, and (4) perform the appropriate remediation. The system we describe has been directed toward problems 1 and 2. The buggy implementation nodes in the network provide the proper places to attach information relevant to problems 3 and 4.

7. We have chosen just one of the several subtraction algorithms (the so-called standard algorithm), but the ideas presented here apply equally to others and can handle multiple methods as well.

8. In our current subtraction network, some subprocedures have only one buggy version, while others have as many as fifteen. The average is three or four.

9. In computer programming metaphors, this approach corresponds to the debugging activities of resubmitting the program because the computer must have made a mistake and of throwing the whole program away and starting over from scratch and writing a new program.

10. One job for an "intelligent" tutor for BUGGY is to recognize and point out places where instances of general rules and strategies should be used. This possibility is discussed in Section 4.

11. This possibility leads to an interesting question concerning how one can "prove" that two different bugs entail logically the same surface manifestations.

12. We would like to thank Dr. Mark Spidell of Lesley College for his assistance in this endeavor.

13. This idea is attributable to Tim Barclay, at the Cambridge Friends School, who has been experimenting with various uses of BUGGY with sixth through eighth graders.

14. All the students participating in this activity had already mastered the procedural skills being "bugged." In fact, we have severe reservations about the advisability of younger students using this particular game especially if they have not mastered the correct versions of the skills. However, there are extensions to BUGGY (discussed in Section 4) that make it appropriate for school children in the process of learning the given procedural skills.

15. The data used in this study were made available by the Institute for Mathematical Studies in the Social Sciences at Stanford University. The data were collected in Nicaragua as part of the Nicaragua Radio Mathematics [NRM] Project supported by Contract A10/CM-ta-

C-73-40 from U.S. Agency of International Development. We are grateful to Barbara Searle for allowing us access to the data. See Searle, Friend, and Suppes (1976) for a description of the NRM project.

16. In both the "*" and the "!" cases, the bug has not manifested itself in the answer as an error. For example, if a bug is $0 - N = 0$, it would not show itself in a problem unless there is a 0 in the problem's top number (or 0 is generated during solution by borrowing from a column with a 1).

17. An additional case arises when the student does not answer a problem. Although none of our example tables will include this case, it is marked with a "#"; "#" is also used in a bug row to indicate that the bug could not do the problem. We saw very little evidence of students not doing a problem, possibly because the students were given as much time as they wanted to complete the tests.

18. During this process, bugs which were alternative definitions of the same conceptual procedure, of course, could not be paired. There were also cases where one bug would preclude another. For example, SMALLER/FROM/LARGER precludes any of the bugs in the borrowing procedures as borrowing is never required. In these cases, a bug can prevent other portions of the network from ever being executed and hence "switching in" bugs in the unused portion would be useless as long as the higher bug remained in effect. Rather than an extensive analysis of the potential interactions of bugs, we opted for the simpler solution of comparing the bugs via their symptoms over a fixed set of problems.

19. In the "stops-borrow-at-zero" bug, the student does not know how to borrow from a column which has a 0 in the minuend so he does not do anything to it. He does however add 10 to the column he is processing.

20. In the actual implementation, the bugs are ordered by the number of symptoms accounted for and are rated from the most promising bug until the group number increases.

21. As we have said, the classification scheme was based primarily on empirical studies. There are intuitive justifications (rationalizations) for each of the decisions; however, in the final analysis, this algorithm was used because it classified students in close accordance with our hand-done analysis.

22. An implementation note: The entire data analysis program including the BUGGY subtraction models is written in INTERLISP. The analysis of all 1325 students against the 330 bugs required on the order of 90 minutes of [central processing unit] time on a PDP-KL10.

23. Contrast this with the (admittedly strawman) technique of randomly switching instructions in a machine language program which carries out a skill. Even if a student's behavior could be duplicated, the resulting "model" would be worthless as an explanatory device or as an aid to remediation.

24. Because these deviations are based on both the student's intended goals and the underlying teleology of the subskills, we have no automatic way to generate them (as opposed to what could be done if the deviations were based on the surface syntax of the rules). However, ongoing work by the authors, as well as Miller and Goldstein (1976) and Rich and Schrobe (1976), is directed toward helping to overcome this limitation.

25. As a historical footnote, BUGGY was originally developed to explore the psychological validity of the procedural network model for complex procedural skills. During that investigation we realized the pedagogical potential of even this simple version of BUGGY as an instructional medium.

26. For examples of the types of tutoring, see Brown and Burton (1975, 1977), Carr and Goldstein (1977), and Goldstein (1974).

REFERENCES

Barr, A. A rationale and description of the BASIC instructional program. Psychology and Education Series, Stanford University, Technical Report 228, April 1974.

Brown, J. S. Structural models of a student's knowledge and inferential processes. BBN Proposal No. P74-CSC-10, Bolt Beranek and Newman, Cambridge, Mass., April 1974.

Brown, J. S., and Burton, R. R. Systematic understanding synthesis, analysis, and contingent knowledge in specialized understanding systems. In D. Bobrow and A. Collins (Eds.), *Representation and understanding: Studies in cognitive science.* New York: Academic Press, 1975.

Brown, J. S., and Burton, R. R. A paradigmatic example of an artificially intelligent instructional system. Presented at the First International Conference on Applied General Systems Research: Recent Developments and Trends, Binghamton, N.Y., August 1977.

Brown, J. S., Collins, A., and Harris, G. Artificial intelligence and learning strategies. In H. F. O'Neil (Ed.), *Learning strategies*. New York: Academic Press, 1978.

Brown, J. S., Rubinstein, R., and Burton, R. R. Reactive learning environment for computer assisted electronics instruction. BBN Report No. 3314, A. I. Report No. 1, Bolt Beranek and Newman, Cambridge, Mass., October 1976.

Brown, J. S., Burton, R. R., Hausmann, C., Goldstein, I., Huggins, B., and Miller, M. Aspects of a theory for automated student modeling. BBN Report No. 3549. ICAI Report No. 4. Bolt Beranek and Newman, Cambridge, Mass., May 1977.

Burton, R. R., and Brown, J. S. Semantic grammar: A technique for constructing natural language interfaces to instructional systems. BBN Report No. 3587, ICAI Report No. 5, Bolt Beranek and Newman, Cambridge, Mass., May 1977.

Burton, R. R., and Brown, J. S. A tutoring and student modeling paradigm for gaming environments. In *Proceedings of the Symposium on Computer Science and Education,* Anaheim, Calif., February 1976.

Carbonell, J., and Collins, A. Natural semantics in artificial intelligence. In *Proceedings of the Third International Joint Conference on Artificial Intelligence,* Stanford University, 1973.

Carr, B., and Goldstein, I. Overlays: A theory of modeling for computer aided instruction. Massachusetts Institute of Technology, AI Memo 406, February 1977.

Collins, A., Warnock, E., and Passafiume, J. Analysis and synthesis of tutorial dialogues. In G. H. Bower (Ed.), *The psychology of learning and motivation,* Vol. 9. New York: Academic Press, 1975.

Cox, L. S. Systematic errors in the four vertical algorithms in normal and handicapped populations. *Journal for Research in Mathematics Education,* 1975, 6, 202–220.

Dienes, Z. P., and Golding, E. W. *Learning logic, logical games.* New York: Herder & Herder, 1970.

Easley, J. A., Jr., and Zwoyer, R. E. Teaching by listening—Toward a new day in math classes. *Contemporary Education,* 1975, 47, 19–25.

Friend, J. Description of items to be used in addition/subtraction tests. Internal Memo, Institute for Mathematical Studies in the Social Sciences, Stanford University, 1976.

Goldstein, I. Understanding simple picture programs. Massachusetts Institute of Technology, Artificial Intelligence Laboratory, Technical Report 294, September 1974.

Goldstein, I. The computer as coach: An athletic paradigm for intellectual education. Massachusetts Institute of Technology, AI Memo 389, February 1977.

Goldstein, I., and Grimson, E. Annotated production systems. A model for skill acquisition. *Proceedings of the Seventh International Joint Conference on Artificial Intelligence,* August 1977.

Krauss, R. M., and Glucksberg, S. Social and nonsocial speech. *Scientific American,* 1977, 236, 100–105.

Matz, M. Some issues on building an Articulate Expert for high school algebra. BBN Report, ICAI Report No. 10, Bolt Beranek and Newman, Cambridge, Mass., 1978.

Miller, M., and Goldstein, I. Overview of a linguistic theory of design. Massachusetts Institute of Technology, AI Memo 383, December 1976.

Rich, C., and Schrobe, H. E. Initial report on a LISP programmer's apprentice. Massachusetts Institute of Technology, Artificial Intelligence Laboratory, AI-TR-354, December 1976.

Rubin, A. Hypothesis formation and evaluation in medical diagnosis. Massachusetts Institute of Technology, Artificial Intelligence Laboratory, AI-TR-316, January 1975.

Sacerdoti, E. *A structure for plans and behavior.* Artificial Intelligence Series. New York: Elsevier North-Holland, 1977.

Searle, B., Friend, J., and Suppes, P. *The radio mathematics project: Nicaragua 1974–1975.* Institute for Mathematical Studies in the Social Sciences, Stanford University, 1976.

Self, J. A. Student models in computer-aided instruction. *International Journal of Man–Machine Studies,* 1974, 6, 261–276.

Smith, M. J., and Sleeman, D. H. APRIL: A flexible production rule interpreter. SIGART Newsletter No. 63, June 1977.

West, T. Diagnosing pupil errors: Looking for patterns. *Arithmetic Teacher,* 1971, 64.

Young, R. M. Mixtures of strategies in structurally adaptive production systems: Examples from seriation and subtraction. SIGART Newsletter No. 63, June 1977.

21 Observations About the Application of Artificial Intelligence Research to Education

Patrick Suppes

Stanford University

Modeling the Student

From the beginning of educational theory about instruction there has been a concern to understand what is going on in the student's mind as he learns new concepts and skills. This attitude of many years' standing is well exemplified in the following quotation from John Dewey's famous work, *Democracy and Education* (1916, quotation from 1966 edition).

> We now come to a type of theory which denies the existence of faculties and emphasizes the unique role of subject matter in the development of mental and moral disposition. According to it, education is neither a process of unfolding from within nor is it a training of faculties resident in mind itself. It is rather the formation of mind by setting up certain associations or connections of content by means of a subject matter presented from without (p. 69).

With the powerful opportunities for individualization present in computer-assisted instruction (CAI), there has been an increased concern to model the student in order to have a deep basis for individualization of instruction. Before considering current work, it is important to emphasize that concern with individualization is by no means restricted to computer-assisted instruction. Over the past decade, there has been an intensive effort by leading educational psychologists to identify strong effects of aptitude–treatment interaction. What is meant by this is the attempt to show that by appropriate adaptation of curriculum to the aptitude of a particular student, measurable gains in learning can be obtained. One of the striking features of the recent CAI work reviewed below is the absence of references to this extensive literature on aptitude–treatment interaction. The hope that strong effects can be ob-

Patrick Suppes, "Observations About the Application of Artificial Intelligence Research to Education," is an excerpt from Patrick Suppes, "Current Trends in Computer-Assisted Instruction," in Marshall C. Yovits, Ed., *Advances in Computers, Vol. 18* (New York: Academic Press, 1979), pp. 173–229. Reprinted by permission of Patrick Suppes.

tained from such interaction can be viewed as a recurring romantic theme in education—not necessarily a romantic theme that is incorrect, but one that is romantic all the same because of its implicit hopefulness for obtaining strong learning effects by highly individualized considerations. Unfortunately, the conclusions based upon extensive data analysis, summarized especially in Cronbach and Snow (1977), show how difficult it is in any area to produce such effects. It is fair to conclude at the present time that we do not know how to do it, and from a theoretical standpoint it is not clear how we should proceed.

Keeping these negative empirical results in mind, I turn now to one of the more significant recent research efforts in CAI, namely, the development of what is called intelligent CAI (ICAI), which has as its primary motif the psychological modeling of the student. This work, which is represented in a number of publications, especially ones that are still in technical report form, has been especially contributed to by John Seely Brown, Richard R. Burton, Allan Collins, Ira Goldstein, Guy Groen, Seymour Papert, and a still larger number of collaborators of those whom I have just named. It will not be possible to review all of the publications relevant to this topic, but there is a sufficient consistency of theme emerging that it will be possible in a relatively short space to give a sense, I think, of the main objectives, accomplishments, and weaknesses of the work done thus far.

It is fair to say that the main objective is to design instructional systems that are able to use their accumulated information to act like a good tutor in being able to construct an approximate model of the student. Of course, this concept of constructing a model of the student means a model of the student as a student, not as a person in other respects. Thus, for example, there is little concern for modeling the relation of the student to his peers, his psychological relation to his parents, etc. The models intended are at the present time essentially rather narrowly construed cognitive models of student learning and performance. This restriction is, in my

judgment, a praiseworthy feature. It is quite difficult enough to meet this objective in anything like a reasonably satisfactory fashion. As I have formulated the objective of this work, it should be clear that John Dewey would have felt quite at home with this way of looking at instructional matters. The ICAI movement, however, has a taste for detail and specific developments that go far beyond what Dewey himself was concerned with or was able to produce on his own part or by encouragement of his cohorts in educational theory and philosophy.

Features of ICAI Research

There are a certain number of features or principles of this literature on modeling the student that occur repeatedly and that I have tried to extract and formulate. My formulation, however, is too superficial to do full justice to the subtlety of the surrounding discussion to be found in the various reports by the authors mentioned above. My list consists of seven principles or features.

1. *At a general level the research proposed* (and it is still mainly at the proposal level) *represents an application of information-processing models in psychology,* especially the recent use of production systems first advocated by Allan Newell.

2. *The fundamental psychological assumption is that the student has an internal model of any skill he is using to perform a task. This internal model is responsible primarily for the errors generated, and few of the actual errors that do occur can be regarded as random in character.* This principle corresponds to much of classical psychological theorizing about behavior, but the strong emphasis on the deterministic character of the behavior is unusual after many years of probabilistic models of behavior and of learning in general psychology. The authors are undoubtedly romantic and too optimistic about the correctness of their deterministic views, especially about the possibility of proving their correctness, but the detailed applications have generated a great deal of interest

and it would be a mistake to devalue the efforts because of disagreement about this point.

3. *The analysis of errors made by the student leads to insight into the bugs in the student's model of the procedures he is supposed to be applying.* The explicit emphasis on bugs and their detection has been one of the most important contributions of artificial intelligence to the general theory of cognitive processes. Seymour Papert has emphasized the fundamental character of this idea for years. It has been taken up with great success and in considerable detail by the various authors mentioned above, but especially by Brown et al. (1976, 1977). A particularly interesting application, worked out in great detail, to errors made by students in elementary arithmetic is to be found in Brown and Burton (1978).

4. *The representation of the diagnostic model of the student's behavior can best be done by use of procedural network.* The term *diagnostic model* is used to mean "a representation that depicts the student's internalization of a skill as a variant of a correct version of the skill" (Brown et al., 1977, p. 5). A *procedural network* is defined as a collection of procedures "in which the calling relationships between procedures are made explicit by appropriate links in the network. Each procedure node has two main parts: a conceptual part representing the intent of the procedure, and an operational part consisting of methods for carrying out that intent" (p. 6). It is, of course, clear from this characterization that the notion of a procedural network is not a well-defined mathematical concept but a general concept drawn from ideas that are current in computer programming. The examples of procedural networks to provide diagnostic models of students' algorithms for doing addition and subtraction problems are, when examined in some detail, very close to ideas to be found in the empirical literature on arithmetic that goes back to the 1920s. There is much that is reminiscent of the early work of Edward Thorndike, Guy T. Buswell, C. H. Judd, B. R. Buckingham, and others, and somewhat later

studies that date from the 1940s and 1950s, such as W. A. Brownell (1953), Brownell and Chazal (1958), and Brownell and Moser (1949). These studies are concerned with the effects of practicing constituent parts of a complex arithmetical skill and especially with the comparison of meaningful versus rote learning of subtraction. Unfortunately, this large earlier literature, which from an empirical standpoint is considerably more thorough and sophisticated than the current work on diagnostic models, is not seriously examined or used in this latter work. All the same, there is much that is positive to be said about the approach of Brown and his associates, and if the models can be developed with greater theoretical sophistication and with greater thoroughness of empirical analysis of their strengths and weaknesses, much can be expected in the future.

5. *It is important to make explicit a goal structure for the computer tutor and also a structure of strategies to be used by the tutor.* The concept of goals and subgoals has been one of the most fruitful outcomes of a variety of work, ranging from problem solving to computer programming. Traditional behavioral psychology of 20 years ago did not explicitly introduce the concept of a goal, although of course the concepts of ends and of objectives are classical in the theory of practical reasoning since the time of Aristotle. (The classical source of these matters is the extensive discussion in Aristotle's *Nicomachean Ethics*.) An explicit theory of tutors built around the concept of goal structure has been set forth by Stevens and Collins (1977). Much that is said here is sensible and would be hard to disagree with. The difficulty of the research is that at present it is at a sufficiently general level that it is difficult to evaluate how successful it will be either as a basic theoretical concept or as a powerful approach to implementation of CAI.

6. *A theory of causal and teleological analysis is needed for adequate development of models of the student's procedures.* There is a long history of causal analysis and, more particularly, of teleological analysis that goes back certainly to Aristotle and that has strong

roots in modern philosophy. Immanuel Kant's *Critique of Judgment* presents an elaborate theory of teleology, for example. For many years, however, teleological notions have been in disrepute in psychology and, to a large extent, also in biology. For a certain period, even causal notions were regarded as otiose by philosophers like Bertrand Russell.[1] Fortunately, these mistaken ideas about causality and teleology are now recognized as such and there is a healthy revival of interest in them and in further development of their use. An example of application in the present context is to be found in Stevens et al. (1978), but it is also fair to say that this current literature on ICAI has not carried the constructive literature on causality or teleology to new theoretical ground as yet. There is reason to hope that it will in the future.

7. *There is an essential need for programs that have specialists' knowledge of a given domain; it is not feasible to write universal general programs that will operate successfully across a number of different domains.* The programs referred to in this principle are the programs used by the computer tutor. [. . .] It is unlikely that simple general principles of tutoring will be found that are powerful enough to operate without a great deal of backup from highly particular programs dealing with specialized domains of knowledge. As mentioned, this is a point that is emphasized in some detail by Goldstein and Papert (1977).

In stating these seven features, or principles, I have only tried to catch some of the most general considerations that have dominated the ICAI literature. There are a number of other interesting concepts, for example, Goldstein's concept of an overlay model, which is the intellectual basis of his concept of a computer coach. The overlay model is regarded as a perturbation on the expert's model that produces an accurate model of the student. (See, for example, Carr and Goldstein, 1977.)

The ICAI programs that embody the seven principles or features listed above are as yet still relatively trivial, with one exception, namely, SOPHIE, and it remains to be seen to what extent the high ambitions for the development of individualized tutorial programs will be realized as more complicated subject matters are tackled. From an experimental and conceptual standpoint, however, the examples that have been worked out are of considerable interest and certainly represent examples whose complexity exceeds that of most familiar paradigms in experimental psychology.

Four Examples of ICAI

One attractive example is Carr and Goldstein's (1977; see also Goldstein, 1977) implementation of their concept of a computer approach for the game of Wumpus. They describe the game as follows:

> The Wumpus game was invented by Gregory Yob [1975] and exercises basic knowledge of logic, probability, decision analysis and geometry. Players ranging from children to adults find it enjoyable. The game is a modern day version of Theseus and the Minotaur. The player is initially placed somewhere in a randomly connected warren of caves and told the neighbors of his current location. His goal is to locate the horrid Wumpus and slay it with an arrow. Each move to a neighboring cave yields information regarding that cave's neighbors. The difficulty in choosing a move arises from the existence of dangers in the warren—bats, pits and the Wumpus itself. If the player moves into the Wumpus' [sic] lair, he is eaten. If he walks into a pit, he falls to his death. Bats pick the player up and randomly drop him elsewhere in the warren.
>
> But the player can minimize risk and locate the Wumpus by making the proper logistic and probabilistic inferences from warnings he is given. These warnings are provided whenever the player is in the vicinity of a danger. The Wumpus can be smelled within one or two caves. The squeak of bats can be heard one cave away and the breeze of a pit felt one cave away. The game is won by shooting an arrow into the Wumpus's lair. If the player exhausts his set of five arrows without hitting the creature, the game is lost (p. 5).

The overlay modeling concept of Goldstein was already mentioned above. The simplified rule set of five reasoning skills for analysis of the overlay model of a given student is exemplified in the following five.

L1: (positive evidence rule) A warning in a cave implies that a danger exists in a neighbor.

L2: (negative evidence rule) The absence of a warning implies that no danger exists in any neighbors.

L3: (elimination rule) If a cave has a warning and all but one of its neighbors are known to be safe, then the danger is in the remaining neighbor.

P1: (equal likelihood rule) In the absence of other knowledge, all the neighbors of a cave with a warning are equally likely to contain a danger.

P2: (double evidence rule) Multiple warnings increase the likelihood that a given cave contains a danger.

Overlay models are then characterized in terms of which of these five rules has or has not been mastered. The details of the model are undoubtedly ephemeral at the present time and will not be recapitulated here. The rules just cited do affirm the proposition that the expert programs at the basis of the construction of a computer tutor must be specific to a given domain of knowledge, in this case, knowledge of Wumpus.

A second attractive example is the construction of a computer tutor to help students playing the PLATO game "How the West Was Won," a game constructed to provide drill and practice on elementary arithmetical skills in an enticing game format. This game is played with two opponents, the computer usually being one of them, on a game board consisting of seventy positions with, in standard fashion, various obstacles occurring along the route from the first position to the last position. The object of the game is to get to the last position, represented by a town on the map, which is position 70. On each turn the player gets three spinners to generate random numbers. He can combine the values of the spinners, using any two of the four rational arithmetic operations. The value of the arithmetic expression he generates is the number of spaces he gets to move. He must also, by the way, compute the answer. If he generates a negative number, he moves backward. Along the way there are shortcuts and towns. If a player lands on a shortcut, he advances to the other end of the strip he is on. If he lands on a town, he goes on to the next town. When a player lands on the same place as his opponent, unless he is in a town, his opponent goes back two towns. To win, a player must land exactly on the last town. Both players get the same number of turns, so ties are possible. It is apparent that an optimal strategy for this game is a somewhat complex matter and therefore there is plenty of opportunity for a tutor to improve the actual strategies adopted by students. A relatively elaborate diagnostic model of the sort described above in a general way has been developed for this and is discussed in several publications. The first and most substantial one is Brown et al. (1975b).

A third attractive and at the same time considerably more substantial example, from a pedagogical standpoint, is SOPHIE, which is an operational ICAI system designed to provide tutoring in the domain of electronic troubleshooting (Brown et al., 1975a). As described by Brown et al. (1976), the kernel system called the SOPHIE lab "consists of a large collection of artificial intelligence programs which use a circuit simulator to answer hypothetical questions, evaluate student hypotheses, provide immediate answers to a wider variety of measurement questions, and allow the student to modify a circuit and discover ramifications of his modifications. To enable students to carry on a relatively unrestrained English dialogue with the system, the SOPHIE lab has a flexible and robust natural language front-end" (p. 4). The authors describe several experiments and, in fact, provide one of the few examples in this literature of an attempt at relatively detailed evaluation, although it is scarcely extended or very deep by more general standards of evaluation. One point that the authors stress that is of some interest is that they do not see a conflict between sophisticated ICAI systems and more traditional frame-oriented CAI, for they see the latter offering standard exposition of instructional material and the ICAI system providing sophisticated individual tutoring in what corresponds in the case of SOPHIE to actual troubleshooting exercises.

The learning environment added on top of the SOPHIE lab consists of two main components. One is called the Expert Debugger, which not only can locate faults in a given simulated instrument, but more importantly can articulate exactly the inferences that lead to the location. It can explain its particular top-level troubleshooting strategy, the reason for making a particular measurement, and what follows from the results of the measurement.

The second instructional subsystem added is a troubleshooting game that permits one team to insert an arbitrary fault and requires the other team to locate this fault by making appropriate diagnostic measurements. An interesting requirement for the team that inserts the fault is that it must be able to predict all its consequences, such as other parts blowing out, and also be able to predict the outcomes of any measurement the diagnosing team requests. The preliminary data reported in Brown et al. (1976) show that there is considerable enthusiasm on the part of the students for the kind of environment created by SOPHIE. The number of students with whom the system has yet been tried is still small, and it is not really operational on a large scale, but certainly SOPHIE must be regarded as one of the most promising developments to come out of the ICAI movement.

A fourth and final example to be reviewed here is the development of diagnostic models for procedural bugs in basic mathematical skills by Brown and Burton (1978), referred to earlier. This work especially attempts to implement procedural networks as described in a general way and about which some remarks were made specific to arithmetical skills. Two applications of this work show considerable promise. One is the develop-

ment of an instructional game called BUGGY for training student teachers and others in recognizing how to analyze the nature of student errors. The program simulates student behavior by creating an undebugged procedure, and it is the teacher's problem to diagnose the nature of the underlying misconception. He makes this diagnosis by providing strategic test exercises for the "student" to solve. The computer program also acts as arbiter in the evaluation of the validity of the hypothesis of the teacher. When the teacher thinks he has discovered a bug, he is then asked to describe it, and to make sure that his description has the proper analytical character, he is asked to answer a five-exercise test in the same way that he thinks the "student" would. An experiment with a group of undergraduate education majors using BUGGY as the vehicle for teaching the ability to detect regular patterns of errors indicated significant improvement as a result of this experience. More extensive experimentation would be required to estimate the full significance of the use of BUGGY in comparison with more traditional methods of discussing the nature of student errors, as reflected in the kind of literature going back to the 1920s referred to earlier.

A second application of the diagnostic modeling system for procedural bugs was to a large database collected in Nicaragua as part of the Radio Mathematics Project (Searle et al., 1976). This system was quite successful in diagnosing in a patterned fashion a large number of the errors made by more than 1,300 school students in answering more than 20,000 test items. The program was, in some sense that is difficult to make completely precise, successful in diagnosing a large number of the systematic errors, but what is not clear is what gain was obtained over more traditional methods of analysis of sources of error. For example, the most common bug identified was that when borrowing is required from a column in which the top digit is zero, the student changes the zero to a nine but does not continue borrowing from the next column to the left. This is a classical and well-known source of error of students doing column subtraction problems. The formulation given here does not seem to offer any strong sense of insight beyond the classical discussions of the matter.

A more dubious proposal of the authors is that the characterization of errors given by the program BUGGY is a "much fairer evaluation" than the standard method of scoring errors. The concept of fairness is a complicated and subtle one that has had a great deal of discussion in the theory of tests. The cavalier nature of this judgment is something that is too often present, and it is a negative aspect of the romantic features of the ICAI literature.

Weaknesses of ICAI Work

The four examples I have described, especially the last two, show the potential for ICAI to set a new trend for computer-assisted instruction in the decade ahead. Much has been thought about and something has been accomplished of considerable merit. I have tried to state what I think those merits are. I would like to close by formulating some of the weaknesses present thus far in the ICAI work.

1. The claims for the potential power of ICAI must mainly be regarded as exaggerated in the absence of supporting empirical data of an evaluative sort. The authors of the various reports referred to seem, in the main, to be unaware of the subtle and complicated character of producing new curricula organized in new ways so as to produce substantial evidence of learning gains. After the efforts that have been devoted to such matters thus far, one expects discussions of these matters in the closing decades of the century to be at once skeptical, detailed, and precise.

2. In spite of the interest in student learning, there has been little effort to develop a theory of learning in connection with the work described above. No doubt some of the ideas are intuitively appealing, but it is important to recognize that they are as yet far from being articulated in the form of a systematic theory.

3. There is also missing what might be

termed standard scholarship. The absence of evidence of detailed acquaintanceship or analysis of prior work in the theory of learning is one instance of such lack of scholarship, but the same can be said in general of the thinness of the references to the extensive literature in psychology and education bearing on the topics of central concern to ICAI. Much of the talk of traditional curriculum theory, for example, is closer than might be imagined and has some of the same strengths and weaknesses.

4. The collective effort represented by ICAI is in the tradition of soft analysis characteristic of traditional curriculum theory. The fact that the analysis is soft, not supported by either exactly formulated theory or extensive empirical investigations, does not mean that it is not able to contribute many clever ideas to the current and future trends in CAI. It does mean that a move has got to be made away from the soft analysis to harder theory and more quantitative analysis of data in order to become the kind of applied science it should be.

5. There is running through much of the work on ICAI a problem of identifiability, which is classical in developed sciences such as physics and economics. The workers in this field have commendably turned their attention to underlying structures, especially underlying mental structures, of students learning a new skill or concept, but they have been overly optimistic in much of what they have written thus far about identifying the nature of the structure. I have in fact not seen one really sophisticated discussion of the problems of identifiability that are implicit in the approaches being taken.

6. For researchers interested in modeling the mental structure of students, there is a surprising absence of consideration of powerful nonverbal methods in experimental psychology for making inferences about such structures. I have in mind, first, the importance of latencies or response times as sensitive measures of underlying skill. The relation between such latency measures and the relative difficulty of problems in basic arithmetic has been extensively studied in prior

work of my own (for example, Suppes et al., 1968; Suppes and Morningstar, 1972), but the use of latencies is one of the oldest and most thoroughly understood measures in experimental psychology. The second is the technically more complicated study of eye movements, especially for the kind of theory being advocated in the development of either SOPHIE or BUGGY. The study of eye movements would almost certainly give much additional insight into the undebugged models that students are using for solving problems.

[. . .] I think that none of these weaknesses is irremediable or fatal. The ICAI movement is, from a research standpoint, perhaps the single most salient collective effort in extending the range of CAI in the period under review. The movement has much promise and much can be expected from it in the future.

The Future

It would be foolhardy to make detailed quantitative predictions about CAI usage in the years ahead. The current developments in computers are moving at too fast a pace to permit a forecast to be made of instructional activities that involve computers 10 years from now. However, without attempting a detailed quantitative forecast it is still possible to say some things about the future that are probably correct and that, when not correct, may be interesting because of the kinds of problems they implicitly involve.

1. It is evident that the continued development of more powerful hardware for less dollars will have a decided impact on usage. It is reasonable to anticipate that by 1990 there will be widespread use of CAI in schools and colleges in this country, and a rapidly accelerating pattern of development in other parts of the world, especially in countries like Canada, France, Germany, Great Britain, and Japan. Usage should have increased at least by an order of magnitude by 1990—such an order of magnitude increase in the next 12 years requires a monthly growth rate of some-

thing under 2 percent, which is feasible, even if somewhat optimistic.

2. By the year 2000 it is reasonable to predict a substantial use of home CAI. Advanced delivery systems will still be in the process of being put in place, but it may well be that stand-alone terminals will be widely enough distributed and powerful enough by then to support a variety of educational activities in the home. At this point, the technical problems of getting such instructional instrumentation into the home do not seem as complicated and as difficult as organizing the logistical and bureaucratic effort of course production and accreditation procedures. Extensive research on home instruction in the past 50 years shows clearly enough that one of the central problems is providing clear methods of accreditation for the work done. There is, I think, no reason to believe that this situation will change radically because computers are being used for instruction rather than the simpler means of the past. It will still remain of central importance to the student who is working at home to have well-defined methods of accreditation and a well-defined institutional structure within which to conduct his instructional activities, even though they are centered in the home. There has been a recent increasing movement to offer television courses in community colleges and to reduce drastically the number of times the student is required to come to the campus. There are many reasons to believe that a similar kind of model will be effective in institutionalizing and accrediting home-based instruction of the interactive sort that CAI methods can provide.

3. It is likely that videodisks or similar devices will offer a variety of programming possibilities that are not yet available for CAI. But if videodisk courses are to have anything like the finished-production qualities of educational films or television, the costs will be substantial, and it is not yet clear how those costs can be recovered. To give some idea of the magnitude of the matter, we may take as a very conservative estimate in 1978 dollars that the production of educational films cost

$1,000 per minute. This means that the cost of ten courses, each with 50 hours of instruction, would be approximately $30 million. There is as yet no market to encourage investors to consider seriously investing capital funds in these amounts. No doubt, as good, reliable videodisk systems or their technological equivalents become available, courses will be produced, but there will be a continuing problem about the production of high quality materials because of the high capital costs.

4. Each of the areas of research reviewed [. . .] should have major developments in the next decade. It would indeed be disappointing if by 1990 fairly free natural language processing in limited areas of knowledge were not possible. By then, the critical question may turn out to be how to do it efficiently rather than the question now of how to do it at all. Also, computers that are mainly silent should begin to be noisily talking "creatures" by 1990 and certainly very much so by 2000. It is true that not all uses of computers have a natural place for spoken speech, but many do, and moreover as such speech becomes easily available, it is reasonable to anticipate that auxiliary functions at least will depend upon spoken messages. In any case, the central use of spoken language in instruction is scarcely a debatable issue, and it is conservative to predict that computer-generated speech will be one of the significant CAI efforts in the decade ahead.

The matter of informal mathematical procedures, or rich procedures of a more general sort for mathematics and science instruction, is a narrower and more sharply focused topic than that of either natural language processing or spoken speech, but the implications for teaching of the availability of such procedures are important. By the year 2000, the kind of role that is played by calculators in elementary arithmetical calculations should be played by computers on a very general basis in all kinds of symbolic calculation or in giving the kinds of mathematical proofs now expected of undergraduates in a wide variety of courses. I also predict that the number of people who make use of such

symbolic calculations or mathematical proofs will continue to increase dramatically. One way of making such a prediction dramatic would be to hold that the number of people a hundred years from now who use such procedures will stand in relation to the number now as the number who have taken a course in some kind of symbolic mathematics (algebra or geometry, for example) in the 1970s stand in relation to the number who took such a course in the 1870s. The increase will probably not be this dramatic, but it should be quite impressive all the same, as the penetration of science and technology into all phases of our lives, including our intellectual conception of the world we live in, continues.

It goes without saying that the [. . .] modeling of students will have continued attention, and may, during the next decade, have the most significant rate of change. We should expect by 1990 CAI courses of considerable pedagogical and psychological sophistication. The student should expect penetrating and sophisticated things to be said to him about the character of his work and to be disappointed when the CAI courses with which he is interacting do not have such features.

5. Finally, I come to my last remark about the future, the prediction that as speech-recognition research, which I have not previously mentioned [. . .], begins to make serious progress of the sort that some of the recent work reported indicates may be possible, we should have by the year 2020, or shortly thereafter, CAI courses that have the features that Socrates thought so desirable so long ago. What is said in Plato's dialogue *Phaedrus* about teaching should be true in the twenty-first century, but now the intimate dialogue between student and tutor will be conducted with a sophisticated computer tutor. The computer tutor will be able to talk to the student at great length and will at least be able to accept and to recognize limited responses by the student.

As Phaedrus says in the dialogue named after him, what we should aspire to is "the living word of knowledge which has a soul, and of which the written word is properly no more than an image.''

ACKNOWLEDGMENTS

Research connected with this paper has been supported in part by National Science Foundation Grant No. SED77-09698. I am indebted to Lee Blaine for several useful comments, and to Blaine as well as Robert Laddaga, James McDonald, Arvin Levine, and William Sanders for drawing upon their work in the Institute for Mathematical Studies in the Social Sciences at Stanford.

NOTE

1. Here is one of Russell's more extravagant claims in his famous article on these matters (1913): "The law of causality, I believe, like much that passes muster among philosophers, is a relic of a bygone age, surviving, like the monarchy, only because it is erroneously supposed to do no harm. . . . The principle 'same cause, same effect,' which philosophers imagine to be vital to science, is therefore utterly otiose.''

REFERENCES

Brown, J. S., and Burton, R. R. (1978). Diagnostic models for procedural bugs in basic mathematical skills. *Cognitive Science* 2, 155–192.

Brown, J. S., Burton, R. R., and Bell, A. G. (1975a). SOPHIE: A step toward creating a reactive learning environment. *Int. J. Man-Mach. Stud.,* 7, 675–696.

Brown, J. S., Burton, R., Miller, M., deKleer, J., Purcell, S., Hausmann, C., and Bobrow, R. (1975b). "Steps Toward a Theoretical Foundation for Complex, Knowledge-based CAI'' (BBN Rep. 3135; ICAI Rep. 2). Bolt Beranek and Newman, Cambridge, Mass.

Brown, J. S., Rubinstein, R., and Burton, R. (1976). "Reactive Learning Environment for Computer Assisted Electronics Instruction'' (BBN Rep. 3314; ICAI Rep. 1). Bolt Beranek and Newman, Cambridge, Mass.

Brown, J. S., Burton, R. R., Hausmann, C., Goldstein, I., Huggins, B., and Miller, M. (1977). "Aspects of a Theory for Automated Student Modelling'' (BBN Rep. 3549; ICAI Rep. 4). Bolt Beranek and Newman, Cambridge, Mass.

Brownell, W. A. (1953). Arithmetic readiness as a practical classroom concept. *Elem. School J.* 52, 15–22.

Brownell, W. A., and Chazal, C. B. (1958). Premature drill. In *Research in the Three R's* (C. W. Hunicutt and W. J. Iverson, eds.), pp. 364–366 (2nd ed., 1960). Harper & Row, New York.

Brownell, W. A., and Moser, H. E. (1949). "Meaningful Versus Rote Learning: A Study in Grade III Subtraction'' (Duke University Research in Education TR 8). Duke University Press, Durham, N.C.

Carr, B., and Goldstein, I. P. (1977). "Overlays: A Theory of Modelling for Computer Aided Instruction'' (MIT AI Memo 406: LOGO Memo 40). Artificial Intelligence Laboratory, Massachusetts Institute of Technology, Cambridge.

Dewey, J. (1966). *Democracy and Education.* Free Press, New York.

Cronbach, L. J., and Snow, R. E. (1977). *Aptitudes and Instructional Methods.* Irvington, New York.

Goldstein, I. P. (1977). "The Computer as Coach: An Athletic Paradigm for Intellectual Education'' (MIT AI Memo 389). Artificial Intelligence Laboratory, Massachusetts Institute of Technology, Cambridge.

Goldstein, I. P., and Papert, S. (1977). Artificial intelligence, language, and the study of knowledge. *Cogn. Sci.* 1 (1), 84–123.

Searle, B., Friend, J., and Suppes, P. (1976). "The Radio Mathematics Project: Nicaragua 1974–1975.'' Institute for Mathematical Studies in the Social Sciences, Stanford University, Stanford, Calif.

Stevens, A. L., and Collins, A. (1977). "The Goal Structure of a Socratic Tutor'' (BBN Rep. 3518). Bolt Beranek and Newman, Cambridge, Mass.

Stevens, A. L., Collins, A., and Goldin, S. (1978). "Diagnosing Students' Misconceptions in

Causal Models" (BBN Rep. 3786). Bolt
Beranek and Newman, Cambridge, Mass.

Suppes, P., and Morningstar, M. (1972).
*Computer-assisted Instruction at Stanford.
1966–68: Data, Models, and Evaluation of the
Arithmetic Programs.* Academic Press, New
York.

Suppes, P., Jerman, J., and Brian, D. (1968).
*Computer-assisted Instruction: Stanford's
1965–66 Arithmetic Program.* Academic Press,
New York.

Yob, G. (1975). Hunt the Wumpus. *Creat.
Comput.* September–October, 51–54.